Security in Virtual Worlds, 3D Webs, and Immersive Environments:

Models for Development, Interaction, and Management

Alan Rea
Western Michigan University, USA

INFORMATION SCIENCE REFERENCE

Hershey · New York

Director of Editorial Content:	Kristin Klinger
Director of Book Publications:	Julia Mosemann
Acquisitions Editor:	Lindsay Johnston
Development Editor:	Joel Gamon
Publishing Assistant:	Julia Mosemann, Natalie Pronio
Typesetter:	Natalie Pronio
Production Editor:	Jamie Snavely
Cover Design:	Lisa Tosheff

Published in the United States of America by
Information Science Reference (an imprint of IGI Global)
701 E. Chocolate Avenue
Hershey PA 17033
Tel: 717-533-8845
Fax: 717-533-8661
E-mail: cust@igi-global.com
Web site: http://www.igi-global.com

Library of Congress Cataloging-in-Publication Data

Security in virtual worlds, 3D webs, and immersive environments : models for
development, interaction and management / Alan Rea, editor.
    p. cm.
 Includes bibliographical references and index.
 Summary: "This publication discusses the uses and potential of virtual
technologies and examines secure policy formation and practices that can be
applied specifically to each"--Provided by publisher.
 ISBN 978-1-61520-891-3 (hardcover) -- ISBN 978-1-61520-892-0 (ebook) 1.
Computer networks--Security measures. 2. Web sites--Security measures. 3.
World Wide Web--Security measures. I. Rea, Alan.
 TK5105.59.S442 2011
 005.8--dc22
               2010045520

British Cataloguing in Publication Data
A Cataloguing in Publication record for this book is available from the British Library.

Table of Contents

Detailed Table of Contents

Chapter 1
    Malu Roldan, San Jose State University, USA
    Alan Rea, Western Michigan University, USA

The rapid growth in online usage has resulted in greater concerns about the privacy and security of users. These concerns are no less pertinent in virtual worlds where users often undertake virtual identities
that stretch the boundaries of their real-world identities. These in-world personas may be detrimental
to users' careers and reputations should their in-world activities be linked to their real-world identities
in digital dossiers. This chapter reviews and classifies privacy transgressions in virtual worlds and provides an overview of technological, behavioral and policy solutions to address these transgressions. The
authors conclude with a discussion of the future research and multi-sector collaboration required to integrate disparate, emerging solutions into a federated security infrastructure for the Internet and virtual
worlds. The current state of privacy solutions presents an opportunity for virtual worlds to attract more
mainstream users as part of the ecosystem of organizations providing security services to online users.

Chapter 2
    Yesha Y. Sivan, Metaverse Labs. Ltd. & Shenkar College of Engineering and Design, Israel

This chapter presents the concept of "3D3C Identity" as a linchpin to harnessing the value of virtual
worlds. It is assumed that virtual worlds as a new communication medium is destined to influence our
lives as much as the Internet medium, and even more. To start, virtual worlds are defined as the integration of four factors: a 3D world, Community, Creation and Commerce (aka 3D3C). 3D3C Identity is
defined as the unifying concept encompassing terms like privacy, authentication, trust, rights, tracking,
security, and other associated terms. Specific sample challenges related to 3D3C Identity are presented:
Security of Audience, Anonymity, Virtual Goods, Scams, Adult Content, Enterprise Take, and Virtual
Money. The chapter's conclusion section lists some of the critique on 3D3C Identity. It also covers the

impact of 3D3C Identity under the perspectives of future designers of virtual worlds, present implementers, and infrastructure developers. Lastly some tentative insights about the properties of a systematic framework for 3D3C Identity are presented.

Chapter 3

Vaclav Jirovsky, Czech Technical University, Czech Republic

The new virtual world created by the Internet, with its attendant new technology environment, new actors and new models of societal behavior, has given rise to unexpected and as yet to be described social phenomena. This chapter guides the reader through virtual communities on the Internet, highlighting behavioral anomalies in the community or individual. The main objective of this chapter is to introduce the reader to basic patterns of behavior which may foster illegitimate use of the Internet, including illegal activity, and security incidents. This survey of virtual communities and the threats they create to Internet security, as well as the behavioral change of individuals when exposed to the virtual world, is intended to give the reader a basis for understanding the virtual world's impact on mankind and social reality. Such an understanding could be helpful to discern new Internet threats or to assess expected risks.

Chapter 4

Fariborz Farahmand, Purdue University, USA
Eugene H. Spafford, Purdue University, USA

Virtual worlds have seen tremendous growth in recent years. However, security and privacy risks are major considerations in different forms of commerce and exchange in virtual worlds. The studies of behavioral economics and lessons from markets provide fertile ground in the employment of virtual worlds to demonstrate and examine behaviors. In this chapter, we address user and organizational concerns about security and privacy risks by exploring the relationships among risk, perception of risk, and economic behavior in virtual worlds. To make their interaction more effective, we recommend organizations to understand perceptions of risk in virtual worlds and then implement policies and procedures to enhance trust and reduce risk. Such understanding depends in turn on the multidisciplinary nature of cyber security economics and online behavior.

Chapter 5

The Social Design of 3D Interactive Spaces for Security in Higher Education:
Shalin Hai-Jew, Kansas State University, USA

Immersive spaces offer a unique set of security challenges related to human, data, learning facilitation, and virtual environment risks. Security risks may originate from people, the technology, or a mix of unintended synergistic effects; they may originate from intentional, unintentional, and accidental actions. Understanding the risk environment will be important for those who use persistent, immersive 3D spaces for teaching and learning. Based on the current research and direct experiences in educational immersive spaces, this chapter will first define the security risks and offer real-world examples. Then, it will look at various potential social design interventions. "Social design" refers to protective measures created through awareness-raising among all participants, policy creation and implementation, human facilitation of teaching and learning in immersive spaces, and other efforts to improve and maintain the security for the socio-technical system, the institution of higher education, the learners, the faculty, and the larger cyber-sphere. These social design endeavors, one part of a larger 360 degree security approach, will improve security but never fully attain "perfect security" (a condition of no-risk). This chapter will include an international survey of instructors who teach in 3D immersive spaces to solicit their ideas about security and the social design of protective measures.

Chapter 6

This chapter argues that because in-world social relationships have value and impact on user experience, their security must be addressed by any group entering a virtual environment. Given the constraints imposed by legal structures, the coding of a world's architecture, and social norms and expectations, what options for management of social relationships are practical and effective? A case study of one social group in the virtual world of Second Life® offers a possible model. Elf Circle is a large group that has developed a comprehensive system of social governance—still evolving—to manage social relationships and protect its members. Its policies and procedures, and the reasons for them, are reviewed with the aim of providing some governance strategies that address common issues.

Chapter 7

When simulating three-dimensional environments populated by virtual humanoids, immersion requires the simulation of consistent social behaviors to keep the attention of the users while displaying realistic scenes. However, intelligent virtual actors still lack a kind of collective or social intelligence necessary to reinforce the roles they are playing in the simulated environment (e.g., a waiter, a guide, etc). Decision making for virtual agents has been traditionally modeled under self interested assumptions, which are not suitable for social multi-agent domains. Instead, artificial society models should be introduced to provide virtual actors with socially acceptable decisions, which are needed to cover the user expectations about the roles played in the simulated scenes. This chapter reviews the sociability models oriented to simulate the ability of the agents that are part of an artificial society and, thus, interact among its members. Furthermore, it also includes a full description of a social model for multi-agent systems that allows the actors to evaluate the social impact of their actions, and then to decide how to act in accordance with the simulated society. Finally, the authors show the social outcomes obtained from the simulation of a particular 3D social scenario.

Chapter 8

An important security aspect of Virtual Worlds (in particular Virtual Worlds oriented towards commercial activities) is controlling participants' adherence to the social norms (rules of behavior) and making them follow the acceptable interaction patterns. Rules of behavior in the physical world are usually enforced through a post factum punishment, while in computer-controlled environments we can simply block the actions that are inconsistent with the rules and eliminate rule violations. In order to facilitate enforcing the rules in such automatic manner and allow for frequent rule changes, the rules have to be expressed in a formal way, so that the software can detect both the rules and the actions that can potentially violate them. In this chapter the authors introduce the concept of Virtual Institutions that are Virtual Worlds with normative regulation of interactions. For development of such systems, the authors employ the Virtual Institutions Methodology that separates the development of Normative Virtual Worlds into two independent phases: formal specification of the institutional rules and design of the 3D interaction environment. The methodology is supplied with a set of graphical tools that support the development process on every level, from specification to deployment. The resulting system is capable of enforcing the social norms on the Virtual Worlds' participants and ensuring the validity of their interactions.

Chapter 9

The hype of Second Life is over. But the experience of this truly exciting period lives on in many disciplines and research areas, which are developing emerging technologies in virtual, as well as augmented worlds. And as is the rule with new forming developments, the path is not yet determined and weaves through different stages and platforms, calling for additional prototypes to understand the true impact of virtual worlds, Web 3D, or Augmented Reality. Using broad strokes and looking for a common denominator, most people conclude that it is Web 2.0 with all its (social) functionality and 3D objects as the embodiment of virtual existence. Many publications discuss Web 2.0 features and applications, but most do not focus on the 3D objects in the context of virtual worlds and their implications. In this chapter, the authors examine and observe what (virtual) objects are, as well as which properties should be used for inter-world interoperability. The past technological implementations demonstrate that protecting digital media (i.e. music and video) is an endless endeavor and that no security feature is simultaneously unbreakable and usable. This does not need to be the case for 3D virtual objects because we can learn from the past and achieve a new level of protection in a rising media. In this chapter the authors propose such a solution by putting forth a general 3D object understanding that includes a look at virtual worlds such as Second Life with a feasible concept of object security. They suggest that with a new framework objects can be secured and promote additional growth within, and among, virtual worlds. They propose a Global Object Management System (GOMS) architecture as a potential solution to this challenge.

Chapter 10

Joerg H. Kloss, X3D Consultant and Expert, Germany
Peter Schickel, Bitmanagement Software GmbH, Germany & Web3D Consortium, Germany

This chapter discusses the topic security in standard based virtual worlds with emphasis on X3D as the international ISO/IEC standard for Virtual Worlds. The general security challenges in persistent and economic virtual environments are addressed as well as the importance of standardization and security as the two key success factors for reliable, cost-effective and long-term attractive Virtual World (VW) platforms. Different actual standardization approaches are compared to the established X3D format that follows a clear security standardization path. Based on the Internet standard XML the specific advantages of X3D are emphasized, such as seamless integration into Web applications and deployment of generic XML tools. The generation of encrypted and signed X3D binary files is demonstrated according to the XML Security Recommendation of the W3C consortium. In a practical session the appliance of security approaches to concrete X3D implementation projects is described from the perspective of Bitmanagement, a market leader for interactive Web3D graphics software.

Chapter 11

Vladimir O. Safonov, St. Petersburg University, Russia

This chapter covers the use of aspect-oriented programming (AOP) and Aspect.NET, an AOP toolkit for .NET platform, to implement Web and 3D Web security and privacy. In this chapter the author shows that AOP is quite suitable as a trustworthy software development tool. AOP and Aspect.NET basics are overviewed using simple examples. Principles of applying Aspect.NET for Web and 3D Web security and privacy implementation are also discussed. The chapter presents a library of sample aspects implementing security and privacy for Web programming.

Chapter 12

Krzysztof Walczak, Poznań University of Economics, Poland

This chapter describes a novel approach to building 3D web applications, called Flex-VR, which can be used a basis for implementing security solutions. Two key elements of the approach are described: scene structuralization and content modeling. The scene structuralization enables decomposition of a 3D scene into independent geometrical and behavioral objects, called VR-Beans. Virtual scenes with rich interactivity and behavior can be dynamically created by combining sets of independent VR-Beans. The second element – the content model – is a generalized high-level description of the application content. The model enables efficient manipulation of content elements and dynamic composition of virtual scenes. Flex-VR provides a fine-grained semantically-rich content structure, which can be used as a basis for defining access privileges for users and groups. Five levels of user privileges definition in the Flex-VR approach are described. An application of Flex-VR in the cultural heritage domain is presented that demonstrates how user privileges can be defined at all levels.

There is a need for refining data security and privacy protection in virtual reality systems which are interactive, creative and dynamic, i.e. where at run-time mutually interactive objects can be added or removed in different contexts while their behavior can be modified. In virtual worlds of this kind, operations on particular objects either should or shouldn't be allowed to users playing different roles with respect to inter-object interactions. In the VR-PR method presented in this chapter, where VR-PR stands for "Virtual Reality – Privilege Representation", privileges are represented by pairs, each comprising an object and a meta-operation. Meta-operations are induced automatically from possible object interactions, i.e. generated using automatic analysis of the object method call graphs. Meta-operations reflect the method call scope admitted and are used in the process of creating and modifying privileges, which in turn is controlled by a validation mechanism. Expressive and flexible, privileges based on meta-operations are consistent with a set of objects composing a virtual world, as well as with the interactions between those objects, both interactions and objects permanently evolving. In this chapter it is shown in a series of use cases how the VR-PR approach can be applied to various types of object-oriented virtual worlds. The examples are followed by a broader discussion of the privilege lifecycle in the same virtual environment.

Foreword

Since the beginning of the human race people of all ages have built and played with toys. These early toys were reproductions of reality in the form of model animals, human beings, or accessories used by humans. With the progression of time and technology these toys became more complex and resembled a clearer approximation of reality. For instance in the nineteenth century a model of a mansion was built and presented to Queen Victoria of England. The model is currently on display at Windsor Castle near London. It is amazing: there are printed books in the house library with pages at a scale of about 1cm, crockery of a similar size and a fully functional meat grinder. Building models of real objects is now quite a popular worldwide hobby with model shops selling components for constructing planes, cars, and trains.

During the medieval times in Europe a new type of model emerged: objects that helped adults increase their skills. Examples of such devices are full-scale horse models used to train knights for castle tournaments. With emerging technologies these models have become quite complicated. Many of us have tried--more or less successfully--to ride these mechanical horses installed at amusement parks or bars. In the Unites States, the mechanical bull remains a popular form of simulated riding as well.

Mechanical simulations are not just for amusement. Some models have become indispensable job training components. Perhaps one of the best examples were the *Link Trainers*, also known as the "Blue boxes" or "Pilot Trainers." This series of flight simulators was produced between the early 1930s and early 1950s by Edwin Albert Link, based on technology he pioneered in 1929 at his family's business

Figure 1. Link Trainer (from Wikipedia)

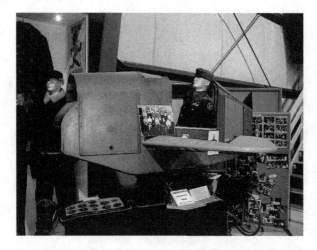

Figure 2. Pong Screen (from Wikipedia)

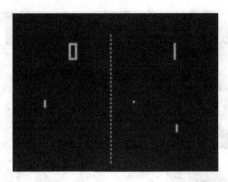

in Binghamton, New York. The simulators were a critical training tool that became famous during World War II, when they were used as a required pilot training aid by almost every combatant nation (Wikipedia, 2010).

The *Link Trainer* was an electro-mechanical device far advanced for its time. However, for a fully electronic model created through the use of digital electronic circuits we needed to wait for over 20 years. In the early 1970s ping pong simulator machines appeared on the market. These were a two-dimensional sports game where competing players controlled in-game paddles by moving their paddle vertically across the side of the screen. Players used the paddles to hit a ball back and forth with the game tracking the score on the top of the screen. The most famous of these games was *Pong*.

When these games appeared in the home, the electronics of the game were attached via a console to an ordinary TV set and paddle movements were controlled by potentiometers on the console or via wires connected to the console (Winter, 2010).

In the 1980s the introduction of PCs led to the development of electronic games. Initially these games were not much more complicated than *Pong*, but there were first attempts to design a flight simulator (Grupping, 2001). In the mid 1980s *Lunar Lander* allowed an operator to simulate man's landing on the surface of the Moon (Bousiges, 2008). The operator could see a simplified instrument panel of a moon-lander and a rudimentary view of the Moon surface on the screen. After a successful landing the screen would show a panorama of the Moon, with the landing craft and a sketchy figure of an astronaut descending the ladder and planting a flag on the Moon's surface.

But raster graphics and line drawings were only the beginning of simulated environments. Lunar landscapes of the past gave way to realistic worlds. As computer graphics, memory, and processing speeds increase, the quality electronic worlds are on a visible permanent and rapid increase. Whether it's the realism of alien worlds that only exist in the developers' minds, or the combat interaction that can sometimes be too realistic, contemporary virtual worlds and environments become alternate realities for many. These games allow the operator to act within a virtual world almost in the same manner as a real person would behave in the physical realm.

This trend has culminated in the emergence of multiple virtual worlds, existing only within the digital realm. *Second Life* is perhaps the most world-wide know application of this type. *Second Life* operators can create people, homes, workplaces, houses, and other objects, as well as interact with the environment and other virtual inhabitants.

These newfound worlds bring about an important challenge: by using their computers to create or to participate in the development of objects in the electronic world, users expose their own system to

Figure 3. Introductory screen of the "Second Life" system

possible attacks launched via these applications or other virtual world inhabitants. Also, by creating objects in that world, they may involuntary embed their own or their workplace's personal information or proprietary data and expose it to attacks and theft because standard security policies and procedures may not readily be applicable in virtual realms.

As a result there is growing interest in the review of privacy issues and security problems related to these new 3D electronic worlds. In this book the authors discuss the uses and potential of virtual technologies and examine secure policy formation and practices that can be applied specifically to each. Moreover, in this book you will find examples of the challenges and successes of organizations and individuals within these virtual offerings. Authors present guidelines, techniques, cases, and methods that explore security in Virtual Worlds, 3D Webs, and Immersive Environments.

REFERENCES

Bousiges, A. (2008). *Lunar Lander*. Retrieved May 16, 2010 from http://www.arcade-history.com/?n=lunar-lander&page=detail&id=1417

Grupping, J. (2001). *Flight Simulator History*. Retrieved May 16, 2010 from http://fshistory.simflight.com/fsh/index.htm

Wikipedia. (2010). *Link Trainer*. Retrieved May 16, 2010 from http://en.wikipedia.org/wiki/Link_Trainer

Winter, D. (2010). *Atari Pong*. Retrieved May 16, 2010 from http://www.pong-story.com/atpong2.htm

Lech J. Janczewski
The University of Auckland, New Zealand

Preface

INTRODUCTION

The virtual realm is upon us. Face to face meetings, sequestered retreats, and international conferences are becoming relics of the past. Instead, the connectivity supplied via a vast interconnected network is providing, among other conveniences, the virtual space to interact on projects via Google documents (Google, 2010), deploy robust software applications via a Web interface, or meet with avatars to produce working prototypes in minutes rather than months.

Yet this new frontier of nearly unlimited connectivity comes with unknown risks and challenges. The corporate world would never conduct its business on a subway or in a sports arena. Similarly, it must be assiduous in protecting sensitive information created and stored in virtual space. For example, can we trust Office Live (Microsoft, 2010) to protect proprietary data? Or should we conduct all business processes using software not installed on local machines? And how can we know avatars are who they say they are?

Moreover, determining how to interact with virtual realms and 3D Web environments can be perilous. Do we adhere to open standards and promote a free exchange of information? Or do we develop proprietary solutions that benefit distinct market segments? Finding a middle ground may avoid a recurrence of the "browser wars" of the mid-90s. Nonetheless, data and resources, whether intellectual property, people or business processes, must be protected from unscrupulous elements in cyberspace.

This book explores the promises and navigates the pitfalls of online interaction. It provides the approaches, discussions, frameworks and insights that will allow organizations and individuals to understand the immersive environments thriving online. We will explore how organizations can safely share and exchange data as well as interact in virtual realms to accomplish goals such as creating commerce or educational opportunities. With careful planning and an understanding of the virtual realm, organizations can guard against unintentional security incidents, as well as malicious user behavior.

WHY THIS BOOK NOW?

The concept of virtuality as represented in the 3D Web, immersive environments, and most recently virtual worlds such as Second Life (Linden Labs, 2010), permeates discussions of business, society, and culture. Undoubtedly we are moving into the next phase of interaction propelled at the same speed or faster than the Web revolution itself (Internet Society, 2010; Leiner, Cerf, Clark, Kahn, Kleinrock, Lynch, Postel, Roberts, & Wolff, 1997).

Although scholarly and popular publications have discussed and studied the usability, features, and functionality of the Web and, by extension, the 3D Web, little has been published on the complexities of creating a secure environment, except to note when attacks have occurred. Discussion is especially warranted when sensitive business data is manipulated via these applications. Risks of using social computing applications for business--or within a business environment--must be examined. Viruses embedded in Facebook (Arrington, 2008; Symons, 2010) are just the beginning of potential compromises. With the influx of interconnected communications comes easier phishing attacks via embedded hyperlinks or VoIP hacks to re-direct communications or intercept sensitive data.

Virtual worlds face security threats as well. Multi-user Virtual Environments (MuVE) are rife not only with technical exploits to glean sensitive data (Sastry, 2007) but also social engineering practices that routinely are used to acquire personal and business information and thus exploit both virtual and physical assets. Instances abound of users offering personal information to a "helpful" virtual citizen who then maliciously creates a profile linked to the real world (Brooke, Paige, Clark, & Stepney, 2004).

Alternatively, organizations once ready to move into public virtual realms, such as Second Life (Linden Labs, 2010), have measured virtual realm risks and have elected to create their own realms for improved security and protection of sensitive business data. IBM has stated that although it realizes the immense potential for virtual collaboration, it has opted to build its own realm for confidentiality and information assurance (Dignan, 2007). This initiative has created OSGrid (2010), an open source alternative to Second Life that allows an organization to create and maintain its own virtual world and to connect (or disconnect) it to others according to organizational policies and risk acceptance.

Although brief, these examples suggest great change and challenges in the digital realm. No longer just a place to check sports scores or weather, the Web is morphing into a realm both beyond, and intertwined, with the physical world. As people and organizations become interconnected, so too does the challenge of educating the Internet populace not only in acceptable interaction with others but also in the risks therein.

Moreover, those planning, deploying, and managing these offerings must be aware of the implications of doing so. Design and policy choices can affect online users at an exponential rate. This book attempts to provide researchers, practitioners, students, and users the knowledge and skills to plan, deploy, manage, and maintain robust and safe virtual realms as well as effectively interact within them.

WHAT TO EXPECT IN THIS BOOK

Our discussion begins with an overview of privacy infractions that can occur in virtual worlds. Roldan and Rea define these transgressions and suggest technological, behavioral and policy solutions. Next Sivan suggests a means to protect and manage one's virtual identity. His "3D3C Identity" enables users to participate in virtual worlds according to their own privacy and security preferences. From these discussions emerges a broader topic: the security risks that virtual environments bring to society. Jirovský examines behavioral anomalies in virtual communities, specifically those that might foster illegitimate uses and attacks.

Moving next to applications within virtual realms, Faramand and Spafford contemplate how organizations can manage and mitigate risk. The authors posit that only after organizations identify their unique risks can they successfully develop policies and implement procedures to reduce risk and enhance trust within virtual realms. Next Hai-Jew identifies how virtual teaching and learning environments have security risks beyond those of brick and mortar classrooms. Using social design principles, Hai-Jew provides guidelines and techniques to mitigate security risks in this socio-technical virtual space.

Discussion of these powerful virtual realms extends next to the shared governance principles within successful Second Life communities. Johnston's detailed case study examines how a large virtual community uses social governance to manage community relationships and protect its members. The author evaluates which governance strategies work within a particular virtual community. Next Grimaldo, Lozano, Barber, and Orduna complement this discussion by examining the social behaviors that can be simulated in virtual realms to enhance the realness and interaction for participants. The authors provide theoretically informed guidelines for creating a sociability model for multi-agent systems.

Shifting to the technical side, the authors focus on security frameworks, objects, and programming challenges within virtual worlds. Bogdanovych and Simoff deploy a virtual worlds methodology to develop frameworks that specify normative institutional rules and design parameters. This formal specification permits the codification and enforcement of social norms and interactions within controlled virtual worlds. Virtual worlds also require safeguards for the objects with which participants need to interact. Reiners, Wriedt and Rea discuss an object-oriented architecture, termed the Global Object Management System (GOMS). This system not only can manage all objects within a virtual world but also allow each object to move among worlds adhering to copyright protections set by the object's owner. Using a multi-layered set of permissions and access controls, the authors' architecture will improve the security and protection of objects, thus encouraging development without relinquishing control of intellectual property.

Like virtual worlds, the World Wide Web also needs increased security measures as it morphs into a 3D-distributed network far too advanced for a standard SSL-encrypted transmission. Turning to the Web, Kloss and Schickel consider how the extensible 3D (X3D) specification may bring secure 3D object exchanges to organizations. X3D is the ISO/IEC standard for virtual world objects, can be implemented using open standards, and enables the use of well-known languages such as XML. Using X3D, the authors present a business case involving Bitmanagement, one of the leaders of interactive Web3D graphics software. In another approach to securing 3D Web transactions, Safonov focuses on aspect-oriented programming (AOP) and Aspect .NET. The author illustrates how his Aspect .NET development framework ensures 3D Web security and privacy and increases trustwhiness in sensitive transactions.

In our final chapters, Walczak explains how the Flex-VR environment allows granular control both of objects and the encompassing content model to create secure, yet malleable, virtual environments. Using VR Beans, developers can create semantically rich content that allows users and groups to have fine access control. Wójtowicz and Cellary extend this concept with their Virtual Reality–Privilege Representation, which allows for fine control of object interactions. Using illustrative cases, the authors demonstrate secure object interaction controlled via a series of meta-operations generated to dynamically create and modify object privileges.

WHERE DO WE GO FROM HERE?

Security research in virtual worlds, the 3D Web, and immersive environments is in its infancy. Yet security is paramount when millions of users interact in persistent virtual realms (Biancuzzi, 2007) such as World of Warcraft (Blizzard Entertainment, 2010). Just as Second Life has its security challenges, so too does the growing population of online gaming communities that reflect a microcosm of the larger economic, social, and cultural strata as well.

One book cannot hope to answer everything within this diverse scholarly discourse. We have written about pedagogy, privacy, virtual object management, and coding secure 3D Web frameworks. Perhaps we have left readers with more questions than answers. But, if you have been challenged to take on these issues, then we have accomplished our goal. Although each author comes from a different discipline, we agree that this burgeoning field demands more critical scholarship and informed application development.

ACKNOWLEDGMENT AND THANKS

Much thanks must go out to my family. Those closest to me realize that my staring at a screen for countless hours can have academic merit. And, lucky for me, life with them is still far more adventurous than virtual reality.

As for those who helped in the creation of this book, I have enjoyed pondering along with you the complexities that the virtual brings into our midst. Our team communicated via discussion lists, Web boards or virtual worlds, so I would not recognize many of them on the street. It's just another irony of our new reality.

Foremost, the authors of these chapters have been my colleagues over the course of this book. Already a few of us are collaborating on new projects as a result of our conversations. It was a pleasure be a part of your latest contributions to this new field of study.

I would be sorely remiss if I did not thank the Editorial Board for its assistance. Its members were always willing to look at "one last thing" from me, whether proposals or polished chapters. They regularly offered input, advice, and encouragement when needed. So thank you Doug, Glenn, Guido, Heinz, Lech, Malu, Mex, Rich, and Torsten.

Finally, I wanted to thank IGI Global for supporting this project. In particular, thanks to my development editor, Joel Gamon, for his patience with a new book editor throughout the process.

REFERENCES

Arrington, Michael. (2008). Elaborate Facebook Worm Virus Spreading. *TechCrunch*. Retrieved August 31, 2008 from http://www.techcrunch.com/2008/08/07/elaborate-facebook-worm-virus-spreading/

Biancuzzi, Federico. (2007). Real Flaws in Virtual Worlds. *SecurityFocus*. Retrieved September 1, 2008 from http://www.securityfocus.com/columnists/461

Blizzard Entertainment. (2010). *World of Warcraft* [Computer Software]. Retrieved from http://worldofwarcraft.com/

Brooke, P. J., Paige, R. F., Clark, J. A., and Stepney, S. (2004). Playing the Game: Cheating, Loopholes, and Virtual Identity. *SIGCAS Comput. Soc. 34*(2), 3.

Dignan, Larry. (2007). IBM Cooks Up Internal Virtual World for Confidentiality, Security. *ZDNet*. Retrieved August 31, 2008 from http://blogs.zdnet.com/BTL/?p=7382

Google. (2010). *Google Docs* [Computer Software]. Retrieved from http://docs.google.com

Internet Society. (2010). Histories of the Internet. Retrieved January 17, 2010 from http://www.isoc.org/internet/history/

Leiner, B. M., Cerf, V. G., Clark, D. D., Kahn, R. E., Kleinrock, L., Lynch, D. C., Postel, J., Roberts, L. G., and Wolff, S. S. (1997). The past and future history of the Internet. *Commun. ACM 40*(2), 102-108.

Linden Labs. (2010). *Second Life* [Computer Software]. Retrieved from http://secondlife.com/

Microsoft. (2010). *Office Live* [Computer Software]. Retrieved from http://www.officelive.com/

OS Grid. (2010). *OSGrid* [Computer Software]. Retrieved from http://www.osgrid.org/elgg/

Sastry, A. (2007). Security in Virtual Worlds: Blurring the Borders. *TechNewsWorld*. Retrieved August 31, 2008 from http://www.technewsworld.com/story/59399.html

Symons, S. (2010). Facebook Employee Interview Reveals Security Issues. *NeoWin*. Retrieved January 17. 2010 from http://www.neowin.net/news/main/10/01/12/facebook-employee-interview-reveals-security-issues

Alan Rea
Western Michigan University, USA

Chapter 1
Individual Privacy and Security in Virtual Worlds

Malu Roldan
San Jose State University, USA

Alan Rea
Western Michigan University, USA

ABSTRACT

The rapid growth in online usage has resulted in greater concerns about the privacy and security of users. These concerns are no less pertinent in virtual worlds where users often undertake virtual identities that stretch the boundaries of their real-world identities. These in-world personas may be detrimental to users' careers and reputations should their in-world activities be linked to their real-world identities in digital dossiers. This chapter reviews and classifies privacy transgressions in virtual worlds and provides an overview of technological, behavioral and policy solutions to address these transgressions. The authors conclude with a discussion of the future research and multi-sector collaboration required to integrate disparate, emerging solutions into a federated security infrastructure for the Internet and virtual worlds. The current state of privacy solutions presents an opportunity for virtual worlds to attract more mainstream users as part of the ecosystem of organizations providing security services to online users.

INTRODUCTION

As with most other prominent platforms on the web, Virtual Worlds have become spaces where users face threats to their security and privacy. Recent high profile breaches underscore the poorly evolved nature of security and privacy technologies for use on the Internet and more specifically the virtual worlds that are hosted on it:

DOI: 10.4018/978-1-61520-891-3.ch001

- In August 2009, a New York trial court granted a model an order that forced Google to reveal the identity of a person who was anonymously destroying her reputation via a blog. The model has reportedly forgiven the blogger but is considering filing suit for defamation (Reputation Whiz, 2009).
- In August 2009, users of top social media services like Twitter, Livejournal and Facebook experienced major service delays and interruptions as attackers sent

millions of junk messages to the services. These messages were sent to discredit and silence a blogger who was providing a controversial account of the territorial war between Russia and the Republic of Georgia. The attack surfaced deficiencies in the security infrastructure of the popular and relative newcomer Twitter service (Wortham & Kramer, 2009).

- Nearly half of all password-stealing Trojan software detected in 2008 targeted massive multiplayer online games like World of Warcraft, Everquest, and Lineage. The goal of such attacks is to steal in-game property and currency for resale on auction sites. A potentially lucrative activity as estimates in 2008 note a total in-game supply of cash and property in Asia at $4 billion! In response Blizzard Entertainment, Inc. (host of World and Warcraft) introduced an authenticator system in 2008 to allow its players to opt-in for stronger authentication protection.

- In September 2006, Linden Lab (the Second Life operator) reported on a data breach estimated to affect data associated with 650,000 accounts. Although Linden labs stated that the suspected hacker was after source code and currency used in Second Life, the breach exposed users' personal data. In response, Linden Lab reset all user passwords, sent email notices of the change to all users, and moved more customer personal information (e.g. passwords, hashed credit card numbers, linden dollar balances) into a secure back-end vault (Lo, 2008)

- A "griefer" disrupted a presentation by one of second life's top entrepreneurs in 2006. Ailin Graef's presentation in CNET's second life theatre by spamming the proceedings with bothersome virtual images (Terdiman, 2006).

These breaches are especially troubling in the Virtual World arena because many users consider these worlds as spaces where they can experiment and stretch definitions of their identities (Yee, n.d.). Hence, many users' in world activities may be construed as exceeding the norms of acceptability in their everyday lives. Breaches could potentially expose these activities and cause damage to users' reputations (among other things) across all arenas where they participate (Lo, 2008). Exacerbating these issues is the fact that Second Life's Terms of Service require users establishing accounts to provide true and accurate information, to ensure that the user is a real person with legitimate, age-appropriate access to Second Life. However, this requirement prevents users from using pseudonyms and other methods for obscuring their real identities and breaking the link between their in world behaviors and their more traditional identities. This requirement facilitates the linkage of potentially non-traditional in world activities to real world identities (Lo, 2008). Second Life also does not allow users to tie multiple identities to a single login profile, thus preventing users from tailoring different avatars to various situations according to criteria such as privacy levels.

Classification of Privacy Violations

For this chapter, we are using the following definitions of privacy and security based on the work of Nath and King (2009)

Privacy transgressions include identity theft, unauthorized secondary use of data, physical and virtual stalking, and attacks, and IP Theft. Security constitutes the protections that an individual and/or organizations puts in place to prevent and remedy such transgressions.

Privacy researchers have proposed several classification schemes. There are several excellent listings of threats in the online space (Hogben, 2007) on which to base a classification scheme

Table 1. Summary of prominent Internet privacy classification schemes

Solove 2006 **Activities that affect privacy**	Rome Memorandum 2008 **Risks for Privacy & Security**	ENISA Position Paper 1 2007 **Principal Threats**	Lee 2009 Lee & Warren 2007 **Security Threat Dimensions**
1. Information Collection 2. Information Processing 3. Information Dissemination 4. Invasions into people's private affairs	1. No oblivion on the Internet 2. The misleading notion of "community" 3. "Free of charge" may in fact not be "for free" 4. Traffic data collection by social network service providers 5. The growing need to refinance services and to make profits may further spur the collection, processing, and use of user data 6. Giving away more personal information than you think you do 7. Misuse of profile data by third parties 8. Wide availability of personal data in user profiles 9. Use of a notoriously insecure infrastructure 10. Existing unsolved security problems of Internet services 11. The introduction of interoperability standards and application programming interfaces	1. Digital dossier aggregation 2. Secondary data collection 3. Face recognition 4. Content-based Image Retrieval 5. Linkability from image metadata 6. Difficulty of complete account deletion 7. Spam 8. Cross-site scripting, viruses, and worms 9. Aggregators 10. Spear phishing using social networking sites and Social network specific phishing 11. Infiltration of networks 12. Profile-squatting and reputation slander through ID theft 13. Stalking 14. Bullying 15. Corporate espionage	1. Privacy and confidentiality 2. Authentication and Identity Theft 3. Intellectual Property Theft 4. Vandalism, Harassment and Stalking 5. Defamation and Disparagement 6. Spam and Cybersquatting 7. Payment and Transaction Integrity 8. Malware and Computer Viruses 9. Frauds and Scams 10. Simulated Virtual Crime

for privacy violations. Four prominent classifications are summarized in Table 1. In most cases we opted to reproduce the language used by the authors in their articles.

The four classifications represent slightly different perspectives on privacy. Solove (2006) identifies high-level categories of activities that affect privacy, aiming to bring greater clarity to the law's definition of privacy, particularly in light of emerging information technologies. The Rome Memorandum (International Working Group on Data Protection in Telecommunications, 2008) focuses on principles, practices, and policies that have eroded and are eroding personal privacy on the Internet. The ENISA Position Paper 1 (Hogben, 2007) is focused on more of the technological bases that enable privacy transgressions. Lee and Warren's work (2009, 2007) focus on security and privacy threats associated with e-commerce.

We have taken the classification schemes from these four sources and consolidated them into a classification system that looks at privacy and security from the point of view of the user. Table 2 cross-references our classification system with the items identified in the four classifications we summarize in Table 1. The numbers refer to the items associated with the classification scheme summarized in each column in Table 1.

We define each item in our classification scheme as follows:

Identity Theft

This is perhaps one of the most widely publicized threats in the online and virtual world platforms. In identity theft, a key identifier of an individual is stolen (e.g. social security number). This identifier is then used to obtain resources that belong to the individual, including credit ratings (e.g. to

Table 2. Classification of privacy and security threats on the internet, cross-referenced with earlier classification schemes. The numbers in each cell refer to the items listed under each classification summary in Table 1.

	Solove	Rome	Enisa	Lee & Warren
Identity Theft	1,2,3,4	2,6,8,9,10	1,2,3,4,5,10,12	1,2,5,6,7,9
Unauthorized secondary use of data	2,3,4	1,2,3,4,5,6,7,8,11	1,2,4,5,6,9,	1,2
Physical and Virtual Stalking and Attacks	4	1,4,9,10,11	3,4,5,7,8,10,11,13,14,15	1,4,5,6,8,9,10
IP Theft	1,2,3	3,9,10	10,15	3

open credit card and other financial accounts), virtual world resources (e.g. in-game property and currency), and real-world assets (e.g. cash in a checking account).

Another form of identity theft involves destroying the reputation of an individual. An example of this is the use of stolen account information to send out spam messages – much like the activity, discussed in the introduction, which caused the Twitter outage in August 2009.

Unauthorized Secondary use of Data

This category of privacy and security violations is rapidly growing as both traditional and social networking companies seek to leverage and monetize the huge stores of user data – both personal information and in world activity data – that they have collected (Hogben, 2007). Although companies may claim and make reasonable efforts to safeguard these data, the prevalence of reported breaches suggests that current measures are inadequate (Privacy Rights Clearinghouse, 2009). Furthermore, these huge stores of data are commonly aggregated into digital dossiers and reports, making it possible to link a user's identity with stored data, even if the data were originally stored and/or collected without user identifiers (Solove 2004; Solove 2006; Krebs, 2009).

These data are vulnerable to theft, government subpoena, and can be purchased from digital dossier aggregators (e.g. Choicepoint, Altegrity) for use in ways that a user was unaware of when he/she provided the data to the virtual world operator. Linden Labs has used its collected data to target billboard advertising in world, much as public dossiers are used for advertising. Another form of secondary data use is mentions of another user's in world activities in a public blog. In this case, a user may participate in virtual world activities that go beyond the norms of his/her everyday life and get inadvertently outed by another participant's blog post about the activity (Lo, 2008).

Solove (2004) proposes that the dangers of secondary data use can be likened to the experience of the protagonist in Kafka's *The Trial*, rather than the more prevalent metaphor of Big Brother in Orwell's *1984*. In the trial, the protagonist is accused of wrongdoing but is never fully apprised of the details of the charge, rather there is a vague, ambiguous notion that somewhere there is a dossier collected on him that somehow justifies the charge. In the same way, companies, governments, target marketers, and information aggregators are consolidating data collected on individuals, now stored across different digital and physical locations, into digital dossiers. Often these data were posted by users themselves and deemed rather innocuous and non-personal as disparate pieces of information. But aggregators are often able to link these data stores to identification data and build a dossier on a user. Decisions about a user's credit, trustworthiness, fitness for a given job and other factors can be based on these dossiers which are bought by decision makers but may be invisible to the user him or herself. The user may therefore be denied a job or credit without ever fully knowing the reasons for this denial.

Physical and Virtual Stalking and Attacks

Virtual Worlds are not immune to the presence of criminal behavior and oftentimes this criminal behavior can spillover into the physical world. It is also possible for other in world participants to view user profiles and obtain real-world personal information that a user, inadvertently or not, includes in his/her public profile (Lo, 2008). There are tools available that allow in world residents to spy on other participants' conversations or online activities. For example, World of Warcraft installed a system, called "The Warden," to detect signs of cheating or abuse. Players then hacked into this system using the Sony BMG rootkit to monitor other players' actions. One of the most common fears of parents about their children's Internet activities is that they may meet an adult online (perhaps posing as a minor) who will then manipulate them to meet in the real world, where the children subsequently become victims of real world crimes.

IP Theft

Theft of intellectual property (IP) is another type of transgression that can happen in the virtual world, particularly to individuals and companies that have a brand or reputation from the real world that they would like to protect or that own the rights to virtual products and properties. In IP Theft, a company or individual's brand is associated with virtual goods that may not be of comparable quality to the real good. The sale of these virtual goods constitutes both a theft of earnings that could have gone to the brand owner, and a theft of the brand's reputation, as the shoddy goods add a negative association to the brand, which could spill over

to the real world (Seidenberg, 2008). IP theft may also be in the form of the theft of virtual goods and currency, such as World of Warcraft gold, Linden Dollars, or virtual goods for purchase and use by in world characters (clothes, furniture, virtual office spaces).

Potential Solutions

These threats should be of great concern to any individual seeking to join a Virtual World. They may also act as deterrent to more people joining Virtual Worlds and thus to the growth of the technology and its entrance into the mainstream. The poor protection of identities and data of Virtual World participants also result in encouraging the growth in the number of breaches and provides more data stores that could be aggregated to become part of the already voluminous digital dossiers that are kept on each and every one of us. In the next part of this chapter we will provide an overview of emerging solutions that are becoming available for individuals seeking to participate in Virtual Worlds in a manner that provides appropriate protections to his/her privacy. As will be seen from the discussion below, many of these solutions are in their early stages and will require multi-sector collaborations to build a system that fully addresses privacy concerns for Internet users, including those participating in virtual worlds.

SOLUTIONS: TECHNOLOGY, BEHAVIORAL AND POLICY

This section discusses three types of solutions: technological, behavioral, and policy. Table 3 links each of the solutions discussed with the four items in our privacy and security threat classification system: identity theft, unauthorized secondary use of data, physical and virtual stalking and attacks, and IP theft. The focus is on solutions that can be implemented by individuals. However, as Table 3 illustrates, much of the work required to establish

Table 3. Solutions addressing the privacy threats in the proposed classification system

Solution	Identity Theft	Unauthorized Secondary Use of Data	Physical & Virtual Stalking, & Attacks	IP Theft
Transparency Tools	T	T	T	
Opacity Tools	T		T	T
Pseudonym Systems	T, P	T		
Authentication Devices	T			T
Strong Password	B			B
Multi-factor Authentication	T, B			T, B
Safe in world behaviors	B	B	B	B
Physical protection of devices and laptops	B	B		B
Informing users of data usage and breaches	P	P		
User Education	P	P	P	P
Context-Sensitive Information and Education provided to users	P	P	P	P
Proactive-Multi-sector development of Commitments to protect human rights	P	P	P	P

Legend: T = Technology Solution, B = Behavioral Solution, P = Policy Solution.

secure and private internet platforms – including those for virtual worlds – has to yet occur in multi-sector conversations to establish appropriate policy and industry practices. There is also a predominance of identity theft technology solutions. This can be expected, as this is the type of solution over which a user has the most control and is a foundational threat that could facilitate the other threats in the classification. Conversely, strong identity protection can have additional benefits for protections against other privacy transgressions, since the other three transgressions are more difficult to achieve when a user's identity is protected and obscured. For example, it is more difficult to steal a user's WoW gold if that user's user name and password is not compromised.

Solutions: Technology

We begin with a review of technology solutions available today to enhance the privacy of Virtual World participants. Technology solutions include privacy devices and tools as well as standards used to build secure infrastructures. These solutions include the set of tools classified under the term Privacy Enhancing Technologies or PET. Fritsch (2007) reviewed the state-of-the-art of these technologies and distinguished between transparency tools and opacity tools, concepts introduced by the Future of Identity in the Information Society project (FIDIS, http://www.fidis. net/). Transparency tools provide insight into the data processing practices of a given Virtual World provider, allowing a user to see what data is being processed how and by whom. Examples of transparency tools are database audit interfaces, audit agents, and log files. Opacity tools, on the other hand, hide a user's identity or its connection to personal data stored and processed by the Virtual World provider. Examples of opacity tools are email and web-surfing anonymizers, as well as pseudonym systems.

Transparency Tools

Fritsch (2007) provided examples of practical implementations of these tools. Transparency Tools include tools that incorporate steganographic technology to detect unlawful use of personal information or intellectual property, and policy management and enforcement tools. Steganographic technologies, such as those provided by Digimarc (digimarc.com), watermark or fingerprint information or digital assets that a user wants to protect. It is then possible to trace where such information or asset is re-used, and if used illegally, address infringements. Digimarc also provides a plug in for Adobe Photoshop that enables users to attach copyright and access restriction information to images (Adobe Corporation, n.d.). Policy management and enforcement tools assist the user with negotiating security terms with a given web service and then ensure that future transactions between the user and the service adhere to these agreements. The World Wide Web consortium's P3P specification (http://www.w3.org/P3P) can be used to structure these negotiations. Policy enforcement tools such as those using the Trusted Computing Specification can then be used to ensure that the P3P agreement is followed. In this specification, the security policy is attached to each data object to which it applies. Only actions allowed by the security policy will be applied to the data object.

Transparency tools also include several services and software packages that are available to help users track and manage their online identities and reputations (Perez, 2008). These tools allow a user to detect material that has been posted about him/her, getting a handle on how one's online reputation is evolving. Since online profiles and mentions generally reflect data that is collected by virtual world providers on a user's in world activities, this is a good way to get an indication of how accurate these profiles are and whether one needs to enact remedies for greater privacy protection and/or correction of inaccurate data.

One of the simplest ways to do this is to set up a custom search using google or technorati (technorati.com), or use one of the web services like Trackur (www.trackur.com), Monitor This (http://alp-uckan.net/free/monitorthis/), Rollyo (http://www.rollyo.com/), and KeoTag (http://www.keotag.com/). These tools allow one to set up keywords (e.g. name, email address, and other relevant identifiers and related words) and focus or expand a search to a given set of search engines, websites, or a specific type of site such as those classified as social networking sites. Most of them are RSS enabled so that users can get periodic updates on a search. The copernic tracker (http://www.copernic.com/) does the same thing but with a local software package – more cost-effective than many of the web services mentioned above.

Naymz (http://www.naymz.com/) is a full service web profile aggregator, reputation metrics, and reputation repair service, allowing one to configure a profile to aggregate information across other online profiles, contact info, endorsements, web activity, tags, etc. Its premium reputation repair service can help one clean up an inaccurate and/or negative online reputation. RapLeaf (http://www.rapleaf.com/) scores online reputations based on information linked to one's email address. The company provides tools for managing one's reputation and online privacy. Lastly, there are companies that provide professional reputation management services that can help with reputation tracking, trend analysis, and reputation repair. These include Umbria (http://www.jdpowerwebintelligence.com/), Advanced Media Productions (http://www.advmediaproductions.com/), biz360, (http://www.biz360.com/) and Visible Technologies (http://www.visibletechnologies.com/), (Perez, 2008).

User-created tools have emerged to help users monitor their privacy in virtual worlds. As of August 2009, there were 634 second life security gadgets available for purchase from XStreet (https://www.xstreetsl.com/modules.php?name=Marketplace&CategoryID=398), a source for Second Life products and linden dollar currency exchange. For example, MystiTool is available for Second Life users. This tool gives a user the ability to detect the position and activities of avatars that are in close proximity of their avatars. A user can use the MystiTool toolkit to reduce eavesdropping on and interference with a user's virtual world activities by other users in close proximity. For example, if a user places the MystiTool user's avatar in a cage, MystiTool will allow the avatar to convert to a "non physical" mode which allows it to walk through the walls of the cage and escape. There are also tools to create private dressing rooms and to listen in on conversations among other users (Lo, 2008).

Opacity Tools

Opacity tools include anonymizers and pseudonym systems. Anonymizers allow a user to send email or surf the web in such a way as to hide his/her identity by coursing the email or web surfing bits through a series of servers that strip the identifying information from the packet stream. A pseudonym system protects a user's identify by providing a separate identity that is only linked to the user at the service that generates the pseudonymous identity. The user can then surf the web, make payments and conduct virtual activities using the pseudonym instead of his/her real world identity. Only relevant information about a user (e.g. is above 18 and has a drivers license) is released to any service in which the user participates. Two implementations of anonymous email protocols are Mixmaster (http://mixmaster.sourceforge.net/) and Mixminion (http://mixminion.net/). Examples of working web-based email anonymizers incor-

porating the MixMaster protocol are Secret 101, GLIC Remailer. Anonymous web surfing can be achieved using the AN.ON protocol (http://anon.inf.tu-dresden.de/index_en.html), the pay service based on it, JonDoNym (https://www.jondos.de/en/), or the Xerobank service (https://xerobank.com/) based on The Onion Routing program.

Pseudonym systems allow users to authenticate their identities in a local and/or trusted site, and then from that point on use a pseudonym – as opposed to their real identities and identifying information – for their online activities. One way of implementing this is by informally creating an account using a pseudonym and false data; however, this goes against some virtual world provider terms and conditions. A more effective way to pseudonymize one's virtual world activity is by using a federated identity infrastructure – also known as cross-domain ID management – that works across organizations and in both the virtual and real worlds.

In the cross-domain approach, users authenticate their identities in their local trusted sites. Security tokens are used across the system to indicate that a user has been authenticated, to provide relevant information on the user, and to identify the level of clearance that the user has to access specific information. Thus, user information is available to all participants only on a "need to know" basis. More importantly, a user's identifying information is decoupled from his/her subsequent online activity. Implementations of this system are still under development and standards are emerging involving groups such as OpenID (http://openid.net), the Oasis standard (http://www.oasis-open.org/committees/tc_home.php?wg_abbrev=security) and the Liberty standard (http://www.projectliberty.org/) (Birch, 2007). These groups have worked to ensure interoperability of their standards through conversations hosted by groups such as the Internet and Identity Workshop (http://www.internetidentityworkshop.com/).

Examples of these systems are starting to emerge in late 2009 with major online providers like Google and Amazon enabling users in a site adhering to the OpenID protocol to login using their Google or Amazon accounts. Google and Amazon then confirm the information that will be sent to the OpenID site, giving the user the opportunity to decide whether access to the site is worth the amount of information about to be shared. This also points to the trust that users have placed on the security practices of Google and Amazon – positioning them as viable user identity certification authorities in the future.

Complementary Tools

Several technologies complement a user's opacity by preventing hackers from using phishing schemes and keylogging software to obtain a user's password. Included in this category of tools are authentication devices such as those used by World of Warcraft (Blizzard Entertainment, n.d.), Paypal and Banks (e.g. Bank of America, Verisign's SafePass). These inexpensive devices add an extra level of security by providing a one-time only six-digit digital code that the user has to enter as part of the login procedure at a site. This ensures that every login includes a unique code that is available only to the holder of the authentication tool at that moment, making it more difficult for hackers to gain entry into an account based on login information that was illegally obtained at another point in time. The random code can be generated using a small token card or device, or sent directly to a user's cell phone. These technologies are usually implemented as part of a two-factor or multi-factor authentication scheme, whereby a user has to authenticate using a combination of several mechanisms – including a one-time unique code, a previously determined sitekey to ensure that the user is entering the information in the correct website, or biometrics.

Solutions: Behavioral

Given the infancy of security and privacy practice in virtual worlds, users need to be especially vigilant in protecting their identities and other personal data generated by their participation in these virtual worlds. Unfortunately, at this point in time, many of the solutions available to users are in early stages of development, difficult for the average user to implement, and a detriment to convenient access to online sites like Virtual Worlds. Furthermore, as Solove's (2004) reference to *The Trial* metaphor suggests, it is very difficult for the average user to determine how his/her information is being aggregated in digital dossiers and how these digital dossiers are impacting some of the most important decisions in his/her life (getting a job, buying a house).

For example, in 2009, Credit Bureau Experian stopped selling FICO credit scores directly to consumers, opting to provide the scores only to lenders. Consumers, hence, do not have a way of previewing their actual credit scores based on data collected by Experian, only an estimate that may be off by many points. This lack of transparency about consequences, along with the inconvenience of implementing security measures at this time, has resulted in a situation where most users consider security measures more trouble than they are worth. Evidence suggests that there needs to be a concentrated push to educate users on the proper protections and behaviors that need to be in place to protect themselves and others that they interact with in online communities (International Working Group on Data Protection in Telecommunications, 2008). This section discusses these behavioral recommendations in terms of password practices, in world behaviors, and physical barriers to data access.

Password Practices

Most common recommendations for security and privacy in any system include provisions for configuring and managing passwords. It is no different in virtual worlds as the password is generally a key part of authenticating a user and connecting him/her to information on his/her identity and other in world data. A stolen password provides a thief unauthorized access to such information as well as the ability to use that information to wreak havoc on the virtual world (e.g. by releasing a Trojan horse) or on the user's reputation (e.g. identity theft), or to steal virtual goods belonging to the user (e.g. WoW gold). Below is a typical list of recommendations for crafting a strong password (United States Computer Emergency Readiness Team, 2009):

- Don't use passwords that are based on personal information that can be easily accessed or guessed.
- Don't use words that can be found in any dictionary of any language.
- Develop a mnemonic for remembering complex passwords.
- Use both lowercase and capital letters.
- Use a combination of letters, numbers, and special characters.
- Use passphrases when you can [a sentence or phrase, longer than a typical 6-8 character password, that is hard to guess]
- Use different passwords on different systems

To assist users in developing strong passwords, several sites have provided password-rating information in the registration pages where users join their service or community. There are also stand-alone sites that will generate strong passwords.

However, because these recommendations are often inconvenient for users, particularly when threats are not obvious or imminent, there is still prevalent use of weak passwords. Several practices are emerging to address this latter issue. For example, some sites will require that users change passwords periodically and check to make sure that users do not use the same passwords consecutively.

Some systems will even check that a new password does not match previous passwords that the user has entered. Sites will also limit the number of times that a user can enter a wrong password, suspending user access for a set period of time or blocking access until the user can provide proof of identity. Sites requiring greater security (e.g. medical and financial sites) will sometimes require that a user enter a code that was mailed to his/her address of record, before access to the account is again granted.

Beyond creating a strong password, users have to protect it. First, by physically controlling access to it – preferably memorizing it and not writing it down (perhaps with the help of a mnemonic), storing any written clues in an inaccessible manner, and not sharing it with others. More importantly, users need to be vigilant so as not to fall prey to ever more creative phishing attacks. These schemes are designed to get a user to divulge important identifying information such as usernames, passwords, and personal information used for additional identification (e.g. mother's maiden name). Users need to take advantage of as many security features provided by a site to protect against phishing. These include multi-factor authentication methods discussed in the previous section. While some of these methods are required (e.g. sitekeys), some are optional and a user should take advantage of as many of these optional methods as possible. Users should always check that any webpage that requires any identifying information at the very least uses SSL and should never send this identifying information via email – especially in response to an email request, no matter how credible the requestor might seem.

In World Behavior

Safe in world behaviors protect not only a user but also other users who interact with him/her. It is possible to be extremely careful and yet have personal and identifying information about oneself disseminated because of a posting by a less careful user. Blogs can reveal in world activities and picture albums can contain photographs of compromising activity. Even simple portraits could be used as identifying information via biometric scanning of facial characteristics and/or mining of the tags that users link to these photographs (International Working Group on Data Protection in Telecommunications, 2008). Mining of these materials can be especially productive – and treacherous for users – when organizations aggregate dossiers across virtual worlds, social networking sites, and other online sites. Linkages among various identities and personae that users take in these various sites (e.g. extreme punk in second life, accountant on Linkedin) may surface information that can be used against an individual in harmful ways (e.g. not being hired for a job). Additionally, users are some of the best safeguards against transgressions and other harmful in world activities. Promptly reporting illegal or harmful behavior by other users helps ensure a pleasant and safe in world environment for all participants (Rosedale, 2008).

The Rome Memorandum of the International Working Group on Data Protection in Telecommunications (2008) provides some extremely useful guidelines for safe behavior in world. These include using pseudonyms in one's profile when possible, changing the settings for information on one's site to restrict both access (e.g. friends only) and indexing by search engines, opting-out of targeted marketing requests, and thinking twice about any data that one publishes on the site considering the implications of secondary access to that information by potential and current employers, clients, and even everyday world friends. The memorandum also stresses awareness of others' privacy suggesting that one check with the other person(s) before publishing anything, including pictures that could reveal their identities. Lastly, they suggest using different identification data on different sites to make it more difficult for data aggregators to link these data with each other to create your digital dossier.

Physical Barriers

One of the weakest links for any security effort is the physical dimension, since users often overlook it. An easily lifted laptop – more than 2 million of them are stolen each year (Lojack, 2009) – can contain a wealth of information on an individual and all other individuals that interact with him/her. To wit, many breaches of organizational data have resulted from the loss or theft of the organization's computers and other storage devices (e.g. hard drives) (Privacy Rights Clearinghouse, 2009). Users need to protect their computers, both desktop and laptop, as well as the growing number of powerful handheld and mobile devices that contain more and more of our personal and identifying information. Aside from password protection and encryption, it is possible to physically lock a computer to a given location as well as store these devices in secure compartments when possible. Services such as Apple's MobileMe, and LoJack allow a user to locate and erase data on a device in the event of theft.

Solutions: Policy

At this point in time, there are many open issues in the area of security and privacy in virtual worlds. Observers have noted that the law has not caught up to many novel situations introduced by such worlds. Key unresolved areas include:

- Enforceability of End User License Agreements (EULA) (Despain & Kumar, 2008)
- Clarifying the definition of privacy in light of new information age technologies and the social networking/virtual worlds era, where the user willingly self-publishes data that may be considered protected and private in other contexts (Solove, 2004)
- The real-world implications of conduct and commerce in virtual worlds (Seidenberg, 2008).

Given these unresolved issues, strengthening privacy and security on the web will require more than just individuals' actions and remedies. Building a federated identity infrastructure will require multi-sector cooperation to establish trusted identity managers as well as the range of sites that will accept these authenticated identity tokens. It will require a wide range of organizations to implement the standards developed by groups like OpenID, Liberty Alliance, and OASIS so that enough users become familiar with the procedures required in federated identity and so that there is a good variety of secure sites that users can choose from to visit with their authenticated identity. Even the establishment of a system that gives a website a "seal of approval" for its security practices is elusive. One study found that sites with the most widely used certification, TRUSTe, are two times as likely to be untrustworthy as uncertified sites (Edelman, 2006).

Regulator Recommendations

The Rome memorandum provides a set of recommendations for both regulators and service providers. At the regulatory level, the memorandum recommends requiring providers to allow pseudonymous identities for users. Currently, a user has to provide his/her true identity and identifying information to virtual world providers, hence increasing the possibility that in world activities become linked to the user's identity. The memorandum also recommends that laws be enacted to provide clear statements of what user's information is to be used for, both primary uses and secondary uses, so that users can decide for themselves which of these uses they will allow. It recommends users be well informed of data breaches and secondary uses of their personal data so that they can guard appropriately against identity theft. Lastly, the memorandum supports the integration of privacy issues into school curricula in order to educate young users of virtual worlds on the dangers and proper protections

required for appropriate privacy and security in these worlds and other online venues.

Service Provider Recommendations

For service providers, the memorandum recommends the provision of transparent, user-friendly information to users about the service provider's policies regarding user data, including how data are stored, what additional uses such data are subject to, which jurisdiction(s) the provider operates in and what the users' rights are regarding their data. An interesting suggestion is to provide context-sensitive information rather than having terms and conditions appear only upon sign-up or system upgrades. Context-sensitive information would deliver appropriate information on privacy policies and implications based on user actions, and go a long way towards educating users on making proper decisions based on their own privacy preferences. Furthermore, the memorandum recommends that this education also include information on how to protect the privacy of other users as they interact and share information with each other in world. The memorandum recommends that service providers allow the use of pseudonyms, as well as set account defaults to the most private and secure levels and provide users with flexibility and control to set privacy levels for different elements in their profiles. Lastly, the memorandum recommends the use of best practice security mechanisms and procedures to ensure the protection of any collected users data as well as minimize unauthorized surveillance of user activities while in world. (International Working Group on Data Protection in Telecommunications, 2008).

Current Initiatives

The issue of online security and privacy is of great concern across many sectors of our global society and many organizations have emerged to grapple with this important issue and provide recommendations and solutions. Already quoted here are the organizations developing standards – Liberty Alliance, OASIS, OpenID, and think tanks such as the International Working Group on Data Protection in Telecommunications, which developed the Rome Memorandum, and the Electronic Privacy Information Center. A newly formed group, The Global Network Initiative, brings together a "multi-stakeholder group of companies, civil society organizations (including human rights and press freedom groups), investors and academics" to "protect and advance freedom of expression and privacy in the [information and communications technologies sector]." They are developing a set of commitments that participants will adhere to in order to ensure the protection of human rights – including privacy and freedom of expression – in virtual platforms and other online worlds. Participating companies already include Google, Microsoft, and Yahoo, and the group has agreed to key guiding principles and implementation guidelines for protecting human rights such as privacy in the conduct of their business, such as how they collect data, and respond to government and third party requests for information on users (Global Network Initiative, 2008).

Service provider practices continue to evolve in response to advocacy by these organizations. Facebook has made several recent changes to its privacy policy, and has asked application developers to respect user privacy settings, in response to recommendations by the Canadian Privacy Commissioner (Electronic Privacy Information Center, 2009). Twitter just released a statement that users own the rights to their tweets (Perez, 2009). The New York trial court order compelling Google to release the name of an anonymous user who was using a blog to destroy a model's reputation is expected to increase service provider demand for security infrastructure and services (Kovar, 2009). The ruling has also impacted users' perceptions of anonymity on the web and possibly making more users think twice about posting with little regard for quality or retaliation.

BUILDING ROBUST VIRTUAL PLATFORMS THAT PROTECT INDIVIDUAL RIGHTS

Based on the review of technology, behavioral and policy solutions provided above, one can conclude that the technologies and practices that can build a secure online system are still in their infancy. It is telling that the top virtual world operators are not listed in the membership rosters of Liberty Alliance, OASIS, OpenID or any of the policy and advocacy groups focused on promoting the establishment of secure practices to protect users' online privacy. Although virtual worlds like Second Life and World of Warcraft have seen phenomenal growth, they are not quite at the level of Facebook, which in September 2009 announced a total user base of 300 million (Stone, 2009). As can be seen from the experience of Facebook, once an online service provider's user base reaches a threshold, it becomes the target of advocates pushing for greater privacy protections. Fortunately, much of the work that Facebook and other top online sites have done to increase security and privacy protections for users can transfer and be applied to virtual worlds.

Increasing Virtual World Participation

Virtual world service providers are able to generate rapid growth and better-than-expected revenues despite the current privacy concerns. However, it is likely that more users would join these worlds if they felt secure that their information would remain private. So instituting privacy mechanisms may not only be a benevolent act on the part of providers, it may also make good business sense, particularly as users become more educated about online privacy threats. Providers also need to develop business models that do not depend on the secondary use of data on their participants. This does not preclude mining of this data to target services and advertisement in world, as long as the provider is clear up front that the data will be used for this and the user opts-in. What this does prevent is the selling and sharing of this data to third parties that the user does not know about and that may have laxer privacy policies that the virtual world provider that has a relationship with the user.

Recommendations for Secure Virtual Worlds

Since, as we mentioned above, the technologies and practices to build a secure online infrastructure are now emerging, our recommendations constitute a call for the implementation and integration of these technologies and practices in virtual worlds, rather than a need for developing entirely new technologies. In line with the recommendations of various advocacy groups, we recommend the following:

- Ideally virtual worlds would be among the early adopters in joining up with the efforts to build a federated identity management infrastructure. Users should be allowed to authenticate with an identity management authority that they trust (e.g. a bank, an online portal, a virtual world provider) and then log into a virtual world and participate pseudonymously. This also means that a virtual world will allow users to establish accounts without requiring them to reveal their personal details. These personal identity details are to be stored only in the trusted identity management authority that authenticates the user and ensures the virtual world provider that the user is indeed a person in the real world, with real world identity credentials, and is of the appropriate age for the in world activities he/she will engage in.
- Bring greater transparency to privacy policies and end user agreements. These should be presented not only upon account

creation but also as context sensitive messages that provide the user with a clearly worded explanation of the implications of a given decision or action they might take while in world. These messages should also include implications for the privacy of individuals that have or are interacting with the user in world. Some of these context sensitive messages could appear at the point when a user logs in – addressing certain unsafe practices, or breaches of the site's terms and conditions that the user may have committed in previous sessions. Granted, this is not a trivial undertaking for any site. But it does create an opportunity for third party services to provide add-ons and services that provide these capabilities to virtual world providers. It will also require the participation of educators, designers and lawyers to make sure that the messages, policies, and agreements are accurate and are presented in a manner that is attractive and meaningful to users.

- Develop an educational campaign to help young users see the full implications of their in world actions and decisions. These should be delivered both in traditional educational settings but also as part of the orientations into the virtual world. The context sensitive message noted above will be useful adjuncts to these campaigns, particularly if both provide integrated messages, and look and feel.
- Greater publicity and transparency regarding virtual world data breaches and the evolution of case law regarding privacy in virtual worlds. At the current time, it is breaches in social networking sites like Facebook, a slightly earlier entrant into the online space, which is getting much of the publicity. The breaches in Second Life, Everquest, and World of Warcraft are not quite the focus of the mainstream press at this time. This may change as these tech-

nologies, particularly Second Life, enter the mainstream. In the meantime, advocacy groups should endeavor to publicize these privacy violations and make them part of the ongoing and evolving societal and legal conversation regarding online privacy, freedom of expression, and security.

FUTURE DIRECTIONS

Currently we are starting to see public implementations of the OpenID standard for federated identity management by major online portal providers (Google, Yahoo, Facebook). The OpenID standard is different from the traditional federated identity systems in that the user can select which providers to trust among the range of sites working in the OpenID ecosystem. Instead of a few trusted sites, OpenID allows the users to authenticate their identities with individually chosen sites. The site could be a portal, a trusted certificate provider (Verisign), or a site that the user trusts because of a long-term relationship with its provider. The user could also select to trust more than one site for authenticating his/her identity. OpenID thus affords the possibility of a market-based determination of trusted authorities that can vouch for a user's identity.

Since users can use a variety of sites on which to authenticate their identities, eventually there will likely be a convergence towards several sites that provide the best combination of trust, privacy, education, and convenience. These sites will emerge as the de facto trusted authorities of the future Internet. It is possible that these trusted authorities will be different from the ones we traditionally deem as such. For example, instead of banks, it may be online retailers and portal providers that can provide users with convenient, good enough, informative security in an accessible manner.

While the implementation of open authentication across sites is starting to become seamless, a lot more needs to be done to make sure that user's data is protected and only relevant information is released to each site participating in the OpenID ecosystem, on a "need to know" basis. To date these protections are still under development in conversations hosted by groups such as the Internet Identity Workshop that have participation from leading online identity standards bodies such as OpenId, Liberty Alliance, and OASIS (Internet Identity Workshop, 2009).

Examples of some of the on-demand educational possibilities are starting to be seen in current implementations of OpenID. For example, when a user selects the Yahoo portal to authenticate his/her identity when signing up for another site, Yahoo checks the privacy policies of the new site. Yahoo then provides the user with a statement listing the information requested by the new site as well as a recommendation about whether or not the user should provide this information to the new site. While these messages are still somewhat cryptic and limited in scope, they are a precursor to the types of on-demand messages that can educate and assist users in making intelligent decisions about the use of their private information. The infrastructure for making these messages possible has been demonstrated as feasible. The next step is to craft these messages to be truly useful for user decision-making. Furthermore, tighter controls over what information is appropriately passed along to each site as well as over how this information is used once collected have to be in place to ensure that the system truly protects user privacy.

Given the state of technology and infrastructure development in this area, there are many potential future research directions to consider, including:

- The Design and Enforcement of User Agreements – How to most effectively present the elements of the agreements – which is the most effective combination of up-front agreements, on-demand notices, conditional notices, etc. What is enforceable in the courts?

- Evolving attitudes towards privacy and security – How do different generations view privacy and security protections and how is it evolving in the era of Web 2.0 and Virtual Worlds where more and more information, previously deemed private, are posted by users themselves with little regard for secondary uses.

- The design and effectiveness of various technological and behavioral solutions – How successful are these solutions in protecting users from the four types of privacy transgressions? Why do some solutions fail and how can they be designed to work more effectively?

- Using transparency both to prevent transgressions as well as address them --How might we design the privacy infrastructure not only to prevent privacy transgressions but also address breaches effectively when they occur?

CONCLUSION

At this juncture we are seeing early versions of components of an integrated internet identity management and education infrastructure of which Virtual Worlds will likely become a major part, particularly as their user numbers rise and their services become more mainstream. These privacy and security offerings are weaker than they could be because they are not integrated and because only a small percentage of sites and users are applying them. We expect that in the coming years, there will be a convergence of market need – as transgressions grow in impact and numbers – and of infrastructure maturity. Virtual World providers can provide leadership in achieving this convergence by using their environments to provide

engaging and educational experiences that train users on safe virtual world practices.

These educational experiences and the application of multi-factor authentication, already in use by WoW, will not only prevent the phishing attacks that are the precursors to IP theft (e.g. of WoW gold) but also position Virtual Worlds to potentially be one of the trusted authorities that users refer to when authenticating themselves on other sites in an OpenID ecosystem. Joining a federated identity infrastructure will also be a way of drawing new users to the Virtual Worlds, particularly if the Virtual World authentication mechanisms are deemed quite engaging, educational, and convenient. This may turn out to be an additional channel for promoting more widespread, mainstream participation in the Virtual Worlds.

Nath and King (2009) found that the trust that users have for an established player (e.g. amazon.com) can transfer to merchants hosted by the established site. Users trust these merchants more than those that only send users to a trusted payment service like PayPal to complete a sales transaction. In the same way, a user may discover a Virtual World provider and build greater trust for it because it is part of a federated identity infrastructure rather than if it was a standalone service. The trust that users have for established portals (Google, Yahoo, Facebook) may transfer to the less known Virtual World, particularly if the Virtual World service provides convenient, educational, and strong privacy protections. Eventually, this trust and the high level protections afforded by the Virtual World provider may result in the user including or even preferring the Virtual World among his/her set of trusted authorities. Hopefully, as mainstream users enter these Virtual Worlds, the privacy protections are to a point where they provide truly strong, transparent, and conveniently applied security procedures that protect even the least tech-savvy mainstream users among us.

REFERENCES

Adobe Corporation. (n.d.). *Adobe photoshop CS4 * adding and viewing digimarc copyright protection.* Retrieved from: http://help.adobe.com/en_US/Photoshop/11.0/WSfd1234e1c4b69f30e-a53e41001031ab64-7728a.html

Birch, D. (2007). *Digital Identity Management.* Surrey, UK: Gower.

Despain, W., & Kumar, M. (2008, May 15). ION: online worlds and real legal disputes. *Gamasutra.* Retrieved from: http://www.gamasutra.com/php-bin/news_index.php?story=18648

Edelman, B. (2006). *Adverse selection in online "trust" certifications.* Working paper retrieved from: http://www.benedelman.org/publications/advsel-trust-draft.pdf

Electronic Privacy Information Center. (2009, August 28). Following Canadian investigation, facebook upgrades privacy. *Epic.org: Social Networking Privacy.* Retrieved from: http://epic.org/privacy/socialnet/default.html

Entertainment, B. (n.d.) *Blizzard Authenticator.* Retrieved from: http://eu.blizzard.com/support/article.xml?locale=en_GB&articleId=28152

Fritsch (2007). *State of the art of privacy-enhancing technology (PET).* Retrieved from: http://publ.nr.no/4589

Global Network Initiative. (2008). *Principles.* Retrieved from: http://www.globalnetworkinitiative.org/principles/index.php

Hogben, G. (2007) *Security issues and recommendations for online social networks.* ENISA Position Paper No. 1. Retrieved from: http://www.enisa.europa.eu/doc/pdf/deliverables/enisa_pp_social_networks.pdf

International Working Group on Data Protection in Telecommunications. (2008). *The rome memorandum.* Retrieved from: http://blog.stefanweiss.net/2008/04/26/rome-memorandum/

Kovar, J. F. (2009, August 20). 'Skanks" case could increase online privacy awareness, security sales. *ChannelWeb.* Retrieved from: http://www.crn.com/security/219400947;jsessionid=ONRGZFL5M1DKVQE1GHPCKHWATMY32JVN

Krebs, B. (2009, July 6). Researchers: social security numbers can be guessed. *The Washington Post.* Retrieved from: http://www.washingtonpost.com/wp-dyn/content/article/2009/07/06/AR2009070602955.html?wprss=rss_business

Lo, J. (2008). *Second life: privacy in virtual worlds.* Retrieved from: http://www.priv.gc.ca/information/pub/sl_080411_e.cfm

Lojack (2009). Lojack for laptops. *Lojack.com.* Retrieved from: http://www.lojack.com/pages/laptop.aspx

Nath, A. K., & King, R. C. (2009). Customers' perceived security: relative effectiveness of trust transference mechanisms. In *AMCIS 2009 Proceedings.* Retrieved from: http://aisel.aisnet.org/amcis2009/766/

Perez, J. C. (2009, September 11). Twitter: your 'tweets' belong to you. *PC World Business Center.* Retrieved from: http://www.pcworld.com/businesscenter/article/171818/twitter_your_tweets_belong_to_you.html

Perez, S. (2008, February 25). How to manage your online reputation. *ReadWriteWeb.* Retrieved from: http://www.readwriteweb.com/archives/how_to_manage_your_online_reputation.php

Privacy Rights Clearinghouse. (2009, September 15). *A chronology of data breaches.* Retrieved from: http://www.privacyrights.org/ar/ChronDataBreaches.htm

Rosedale, P. (2008, April 1). *Prepared statement before the subcommittee on telecommunications and the internet.* Washington, DC: Energy and Commerce Committee of the U.S. House of Representatives. Retrieved from: http://energy-commerce.house.gov/images/stories/Documents/Hearings/PDF/110-ti-hrg.040108.Rosedale-testimony.pdf

Seidenberg, S. (2008, March 1). Virtual knock-offs. *Inside Counsel.* Retrieved from: http://www.insidecounsel.com/Issues/2008/March%202008/Pages/Virtual-Knockoffs.aspx?k=seidenberg

Solove, D. J. (2004). *The digital person: technology and privacy in the information age.* New York: NYU Press.

Solove, D. J. (2006). A taxonomy of privacy. *University of Pennsylvania Law Review, 154*(3), 477–559. Retrieved from http://papers.ssrn.com/sol3/papers.cfm?abstract_id=667622#. doi:10.2307/40041279

Stone, B. (2009, September 15). Facebook says its finances are looking up. *The New York Times Bits Blog.* Retrieved from: http://bits.blogs.nytimes.com/2009/09/15/facebook-says-its-finances-are-looking-up/?dbk

Terdiman, D. (2006, December 20). Newsmaker: virtual magnate shares secrets of success. *CNET News.* Retrieved from: http://news.cnet.com/Virtual-magnate-shares-secrets-of-success/2008-1043_3-6144967.html?tag=item

United States Computer Emergency Readiness Team. (2009, May 21). *Cyber security tip st04-002: choosing and protecting passwords.* Retrieved from: http://www.us-cert.gov/cas/tips/ST04-002.html

Whiz, R. (2009, August 19). Legal impact of the Liskula Cohen court order (the "skank" decision). *Reputation Defender Blog.* Blog entry posted at: http://www.reputationdefenderblog.com/2009/08/19/legal-impact-of-the-liskula-cohen-court-order-the-skank-decision/.

Workshop, I. I. (2009, March 1). *Internet identity workshop 9.* Retrieved from: http://www.internetidentityworkshop.com/

Wortham, J., & Kramer, A. E. (2009, August 7). Professor main target of assault on twitter. *The New York Times.* Retrieved from: http://www.nytimes.com/2009/08/08/technology/internet/08twitter.html?_r=2&hpw

Yee (n.d.). Avatar and identity. *The Daedalus Gateway.* Retrieved from: http://www.nickyee.com/daedalus/gateway_identity.html

ADDITIONAL READING

Alter, A. (2007, August 10). Is this man cheating on his wife? Wall Street Journal. Retrieved from: http://biz.yahoo.com/wallstreet/070810/sb118670164592393622_id.html?v=6

Au, W. J. (2008). *The making of second life: notes from the new world.* New York: HarperCollins Publishers.

Boellstorff, T. (2008). *Coming of age in second life: an anthropologist explores the virtually human.* Princeton, NJ: Princeton University Press.

Bono, S., Caselden, D., Landau, G., and Miller, C. (2009). Reducing the attack surface in massively multiplyer online role-playing games. IEEE security and privacy. 7 (3): 13-19.

Boyd, D. (2008). Facebook's privacy trainwreck: exposure, invasion, and social convergence. Convergence: the international journal of research into new media technologies. 14 (1): 13-20. Retrieved from: http://www.danah.org/papers/FacebookPrivacyTrainwreck.pdf

Claburn, T. (2009, November 6). Google dashboard enhances privacy control. Informationweek. Retrieved from: http://www.informationweek.com/news/internet/google/showArticle.jhtml?articleID=221600693

Eyob, E. (2009). Social implications of data mining. Hershey, PA: Information Science Reference (IGI Global).

Goth, G. (2008). Single sign-on and social networks. IEEE distributed systems online. 9 (12): 1-3.

Johnson, N. F. (2009). Information hiding: steganography & digital watermarking. Retrieved from: http://www.jjtc.com/Steganography/

Kane, S.F. (2009). Virtual judgement: legal implications of online gaming. IEEE security and privacy. 7 (3): 23-28.

Kang, M., & Khashnobish, A. (2009). A peer-to-peer federated authentication system. Proceedings of the 2009 sixth international conference on information technology: new generations. 382-287.

Kantor, P. B., & Lesk, M. E. (2009). *The challenges of seeking security while respecting privacy*. Heidelberg, Germany: Springer Berlin.

Lipton, J. D. (2010). Mapping online privacy. *Northwestern University Law Review, 104*(2). Retrieved from http://papers.ssrn.com/sol3/papers.cfm?abstract_id=1443918.

Lohrmann, D. J. (2008). *Virtual integrity: faithfully navigating the brave new web*. Grand Rapids, MI: Brazos Press.

Mandal, S., & Lim, E. (2009). Second life: limits of creativity or cyber threat? Proceedings of the 2009 sixth international conference on information technology: new generations. 498-503.

Meadows, M. S. (2008). *I Avatar: The culture and consequences of having a second life*. Berkeley, CA: New Riders Press.

Mitterhofer, S., Kruegel, C., Kirda, E., and Platzer, C. (2009). Server-side bot detection in massively multiplayer online games. 7 (3): 29-36.

Recordon, D., & Reed, D. (2006). OpenID 2.0: a platform for user-centric identity management. Proceedings of the second ACM workshop on digital identity management. 2: 11-16

Solove, D. J. (2007). *The future of reputation: gossip, rumor, and privacy on the Internet*. New Haven, CT: Yale University Press.

Solove, D. J. (2008). *Understanding privacy*. Boston, MA: Harvard University Press.

Steel, E. (2009, November 19). Protecting offline privacy: policy makers' concerns spread beyond the internet. Wall Street Journal. Retrieved from: http://online.wsj.com/article/SB100142405274870453390457454340032069323 2.html?mod=WSJ_hpp_sections_tech

Turkle, S. (1997). *Life on the screen: identity in the age of the internet*. New York: Simon & Schuster.

Tutton, M. (2009, November 9). Going to the virtual office in second life. cnn.com Retrieved from: http://www.cnn.com/2009/BUSINESS/11/05/second.life.virtual.collaboration/

Watanabe, R., & Tanaka, T. (2009). Federated authentication mechanism using cellular phone-collaboration with opened. Proceedings of the 2009 sixth international conference on information technology: new generations. 435-442.

Xiaozhao, D., & Jianhai, R. (2009). Users' privacy in the second life library. Proceedings of the 2009 sixth international conference on information technology: new generations. 337-340.

Chapter 2
3D3C Identity:
Towards a Systematic Framework

Yesha Y. Sivan
Metaverse Labs. Ltd. & Tel Aviv-Yaffo Academic College, Israel

ABSTRACT

This chapter presents the concept of "3D3C Identity" as a linchpin to harnessing the value of virtual worlds. It is assumed that virtual worlds as a new communication medium is destined to influence our lives as much as the Internet medium, and even more. To start, virtual worlds are defined as the integration of four factors: a 3D world, Community, Creation and Commerce (aka 3D3C). 3D3C Identity is defined as the unifying concept encompassing terms like privacy, authentication, trust, rights, tracking, security, and other associated terms. Specific sample challenges related to 3D3C Identity are presented: Security of Audience, Anonymity, Virtual Goods, Scams, Adult Content, Enterprise Take, and Virtual Money. The conclusion section lists some of the critique on 3D3C Identity. It also covers the impact of 3D3C Identity under the perspectives of future designers of virtual worlds, present implementers, and infrastructure developers. Lastly some tentative insights about the properties of a systematic framework for 3D3C Identity are presented.

You have to be able to risk your identity for a bigger future than the present you are living. -- Fernando Flores (Brainyquote, 2009).

INTRODUCTION

A Call for 3D3C Identity

Virtual worlds are an emerging medium that is constantly creeping into our lives. Following the success of such gaming worlds as World of Warcraft, The Sims and others, terms like 3D, avatars, chat and real money are rising. For individuals, new forms of interactive entertainment, mostly social, are also pushing virtual worlds. For the enterprise, the drive to save travel costs and the need to gain new customers and retain current ones push this trend even further (Murugensan, 2008).

The promise of Identity is simpler: better, safer, adaptable, and cheaper services for customers and users, as well as for suppliers and manufacturers. I

DOI: 10.4018/978-1-61520-891-3.ch002

want to share my own excitement over the societal value of well-governed identity.

I maintain that Real Virtual Worlds will, eventually, offer a paradigm shift. What we see now with Second Life, World of Warcraft, Club Penguin and more then 100 other worlds, is just the beginning. In comparison to the Internet age, we are at the "Gopher" stage (Gopher was a pre-browser method to view hyperlinked data).

This budding arena of Real Virtual Worlds has its roots in two fields: Virtual Reality (Burda & Coiffet, 2003) including Augmented Reality (Bimber & Raskar, 2005) and Gaming worlds (Bartle, 2004; Alexander, 2003; Alexander, 2005; Taylor, 2006). Other related fields, also affecting virtual worlds, range from economy (for example, of virtual goods), sociology (nature of communities) and law (copyrights and ownership), to biology (new brain based human-computer interfaces), computer science (performance, reliability and scalability) and mathematics (algorithms for 3D rendering and animation).

I use the adjective "real" to distinguish between virtual worlds and gaming worlds. "Real" implies a potential reaching further than imagined today. While today's virtual worlds are clearly used mostly for fun and games – Real Virtual Worlds have the capacity to alter our lives. (Note: for the sake of brevity, I will use Virtual Worlds or simply Worlds).

In the following section, I will briefly present 3D3C virtual worlds as a necessarily needed background. Then, using concrete examples, I shall share some of the challenges that call for a systemic approach to 3D3C Identity. My goal is to expose and highlight some of the challenges for 3D3C Identity and, hopefully to drive people to action. I do not claim to present a complete or even a balanced approach to 3D3C Identity. However, I do claim – emphatically – that we need to think about identity and build it into the next set of virtual worlds standards. Future virtual worlds, when they arrive, and current real worlds that are based on current Internet and IT technologies, will benefit from such a systemic approach to identity.

A Formal Definition of 3D3C Virtual Worlds

I define Real Virtual Worlds as an aggregate of four factors: (Sivan, 2008a)

1. **A 3D World: A three dimensional representation, that is viewable from various perspectives, it is active, and reactive.** In a virtual world, users see objects like avatars, houses, and cars. The world has land, a sky, a sun (maybe more than one), wind, gravity, water, and fire. Avatars move around freely, and the user can examine the world from different points of view. Further, the world is active (moving objects), and reactive (objects can act in a similar way to the physical world).

2. **Community: Set of tools that facilitate communities to operate (including groups, sub groups, permissions, leadership, friends, etc).** Virtual worlds allow users (via their avatars) to meet, chat, shop, watch performances, hang out with friends, team up to fight bad guys, go clubbing... in other words, to interact in countless ways. Within "community," I include related concepts such as groups, permissions, rights, and roles.

3. **Creation: Set of tools that allow users to create in-world, or by importing content. Creation includes actions such as arranging, creating, re-purposing, and performing. Creation refers to both objects and services.** Second Life's (SL - a leading virtual world) greatest technological achievement was giving users the capability to develop their own objects in world interactively. Users can simply move preconstructed objects from one place to another (say, to furnish a home or set up a nightclub), or they may assemble an object (e.g., a house)

from basic components, such as walls and ceilings, and then "paint" them with various textures. SL's programming language, Linden Script Language, even allows users to program behavioral attributes for their objects, so that fish can swim in schools, golf balls can arc through the air, guns can shoot, and people can dance.

4. **Commerce: The ability to connect with real money including: payment, transfer of money from one object/player to another, and facility to transfer money between the virtual world to the real world.** As an example, SL's maker, Linden Lab, has created the Linden Dollar (L$), which has a defined exchange rate with the US dollar (one US$ fluctuates around L$260). This currency is the base for the economics of SL. You can exchange L$ to US$ immediately and at any time at the Linden Dollar Exchange. For instance, if you earn L$2,600 from tips, you could exchange them for about US$10, which would be immediately transferred to your real PayPal or bank account. Going the other way, if you need L$5,200 for a new car, you could immediately buy them for about US$20.

Ultimately, Real Virtual Worlds arise from the **integration** of **3D**, **Community**, **Creation** and **Commerce**. SL reveals the emergence of this integration (and thus I, like others, use this world as the primary example of virtual worlds). In SL you will find prices for objects, permissions (i.e., an object may be restricted from being sold), and ownerships. Commerce is embedded into the world. For example, let us assume that we enjoy Beth's singing (Beth is a real world singer that performs from time to time in SL) and wish to tip her. We point to her and transfer money by clicking a button. If Beth wants to buy a new blouse, she goes to a shop, points to the blouse of her choice and buys it for L$2,000. The blouse is as a unique object in this world, and Beth will not

be able to copy it. The shopkeeper will receive L$500 for the blouse, and the blouse manufacturer will receive L$1,500 (in accordance with a previously defined business agreement between them). At the end of the month, the shopkeeper will pay rent to the landowners, also based on a predetermined agreement.

SL is not the only virtual world with a thriving "real" economy. The Entropia Universe also has a cash-based economy (with a fixed rate of 10 "PED" to one US$), and its maker, MindArk PE AB, has even received preliminary approval for an actual banking license by the Swedish Finance Supervisory. This would allow its users to conduct real-world banking transactions from within the Entropia Universe (Thompson, 2009).

This integration of a 3D world, organized and managed communities, immediate creation capabilities of objects and services and a virtual commerce which actually becomes real – is the basic allure of SL in particular and of Real Virtual Worlds in general

Identity is the Key

The security, privacy, and personalization issues raised by virtual worlds revolve around one key factor: identity. Over the last few years, it has been my good fortune to initiate and participate in several efforts to develop standards for 3D3C virtual worlds (Sivan, 2008b). Repeatedly during these efforts, words like privacy, authentication, trust, rights, tracking, security, and other related ideas came up as a necessary core to virtual worlds. For the sake of brevity, my colleagues and I chose "identity" as the term to designate these concepts.

Both individual and enterprise use of virtual worlds raise many identity issues. Nevertheless, while individual users, who use virtual worlds mostly for entertainment, may ignore lack of identity for a while, real organizations and virtual emerging businesses may not (due, in part, to various regulatory issues.) Thus, a good start in defining 3D3C Identity is to look at it from the point of view of enterprise IT.

Initial enterprise uses of virtual worlds include collaboration (internally and externally), product design and feedback, marketing of products, participation in virtual shows and exhibitions, and — with growing intensity — general experimentation. However, while virtual worlds present new business opportunities, they also pose new IT threats:

- For faster access, virtual worlds use different ports and protocols than Web sites and thus present firewall issues.
- Some worlds allow code to run in them, which raises the risks of malicious code.
- When customers "chat" with an enterprise rep, they may reveal private information. Who stores this information, and how?
- Some worlds allow video to be broadcast inside the world. Cameras left on can transmit to the outside world.
- Your brand and corporate image can spread virtually. Who will protect it?

As we began surveying these identity-related terms, we looked at the current state of IT in general and the Internet industry in particular. For example, the work of Chellappa & Sin that contrast privacy and personalization (2002) or the Internet Society's (2008) *Trust and the Future of the Internet* report (2008) defined trust as a combination of reliability, security, privacy, and liberty, while the Center for Democracy & Technology (2007) outlined several privacy principles for identity in the digital age (2007).

There is good news and bad news. First, the good news: a lot of research, work, analyses, ideas, and even standards regarding identity are being developed, and even used. Now the bad news: in most cases, we are still struggling with competing nonstandard systems in this field. Or, to put it bluntly, as users we still have too many passwords, our data is lost from time to time, and

we are besieged with spam (although this has diminished lately, thanks to smart social antispam managers like the ones Google mail employs). The current combined IT and Internet system lacks a comprehensive system of identity.

In the remainder of the chapter, I will discuss some of the challenges that call for a systemic approach to 3D3C Identity. My goal is to expose some of the problems we face with respect to identity and, I hope, to drive people to action.

3D3C IDENTITY CHALLENGES IN VIRTUAL WORLDS

Security of Audience

One of the common things you do in virtual worlds is talk with other avatars. Talking ranges from the simple and textual to the visual and vocal. Textual talk include instant messages (IMs), much like the ones we are familiar with in services like Yahoo Messenger, ICQ, Microsoft Messenger, and many others. You could also use chat, which is an extension of IM. With chat, many avatars can gather around the fire, in a classroom, or in a meeting room and talk together about their favorite topic. Some virtual worlds also add voice, allowing several avatars to sit in a meeting room and talk to each other in both text and voice. With some advance setup, video could be added too.

These meetings are touted as the next collaborative environment. Note that in SL, after you rent a US$5/month parcel of land, such conversations are free to as many as 40 avatars — in theory, anyhow. In practice, more than 25 avatars often stall the system. Still, having audio conferences with projections of 2D and 3D models for such a low cost seems valuable.

The problem is that such meetings are far from secure. Today, if an avatar wants to sneak in and listen to a discussion (text or voice) – he, or she can simply do so. Let us assume that the authentication is solved and each avatar has an authenticated person behind it. Nevertheless, it is possible to view public chats with relative ease (even if they take place in a closed meeting room); to listen to public voice chats; and to peek behind walls (you can act as a peeping Tom). The physical space gives you an illusion of privacy, which is often not the case. Only with a relatively complex setup could you block other users from your meeting place — and in most cases, you would need a larger landmass to do so (and it would cost you around US$300/month).

Even if you block the interlopers from accessing the area (called "red tape" in SL lingo), other avatars can still hear or see. This is a classic case where the links between permissions, authentication, and services were not built into the system. A better design (or perhaps simply paying attention to identity) would build a solution into the communication stack of the platform. I believe the design team of Wonderland, Sun's supported open virtual world, proposed to solve this by linking chat and voice protocols directly to identity.

Anonymity

One of the key drivers of virtual worlds today — and I emphasize *today* — is the ability to act anonymously. Since most worlds are currently used for entertainment, such worlds really act as extensions of games. In fact, until recently, SL's makers glorified anonymity with statements like "life beyond reality, where imagination knows no bounds... tempt fate without inhibition and court danger without fear."

However, at times we need to cross into reality. In May 2008, federal prosecutors in Los Angeles charged a Missouri mother with fraudulently creating a MySpace account and using it to "cyber-bully" a 13-year-old girl who later committed suicide. The girl, Megan Meier, hanged herself in her upstairs bedroom two years ago, shortly after being jilted by an Internet suitor she thought was a 16-year-old boy. The case caused a furor in the US when it was alleged that the "boy" was

actually Lori Drew, the mother of one of Megan's former friends. As this case shows, virtual worlds can be painfully real (Glover, 2008). As more of these worlds become part of our lives, we need to educate ourselves about the darker sides of anonymity. Real virtual worlds are not a fictions game — they are another part of life, entailing all the good and the bad.

Another angle to the matter involves actual work, training, support, and medical treatment in virtual worlds. All have legal ramifications that call for identity. Teaching a course in SL, taking a test, and doing a joint project mean course credit and grades. Treating someone with Parkinson's or a stroke in the virtual world calls for insurance billing and medical records, which, in turn, means that personal information under federal HIPAA regulations are added.

Another side of anonymity is money laundering. Say you gained US$100 illegally. You distribute it to 10 avatars. These avatars buy a virtual car from you for US$10 each. You consequently report an income of $100. It is that simple. You can even script the entire process and use programmable avatars to save you time.

We must also remember that some countries are not as free as others are. If we kill anonymity, we kill the very limited freedom people in such countries may have. Virtual worlds affect the real world, and the real world affects virtual worlds. The famous case of Google altering search results to satisfy Chinese authorities is an example (Martin, 2006). The challenge is in determining how to preserve the value of anonymity while preventing its perils.

Virtual Goods

The gaming industry has had virtual goods for ages — all those swords, potions, ships, and houses you gain in the game and store in your inventory. Then we were able to put money into the game and buy even more goods, yet the flow of money was always from the real world into the virtual

Figure 1. A sample Pirate Ship © Copyright 2009. Dera Carter. (Used with Permission)

worlds. With the advent of SL and later worlds like IMVU (a 3D chat world with real-money virtual goods) and Entropia (Fantasy world with real money), we can now take money out. Let us say Dera creates a pirate ship (see Figure 1). He puts it up for sale. Jane likes it. She charges her credit card US$1 and she gets about L$260. She transfers the money by selecting "buy" on the ship. The money is transferred to Dera. After Dera requests to withdraw the money, it is transferred to his bank account in a matter of days.

Today in SL, each object has an owner and a creator. The creator selects a few parameters for each object: Copy (allow owner to create copies), Transfer (allow owner to transfer ownership), Modify (allow owner to change the object). In fact, the story is more complex, as each object may contain several other objects that could have their own parameters. For example, a modifiable object may include a scripted object that is not modifiable.

I distinctly remember one of my students submitting an amazing motorcycle as a final project. This was a masterpiece — so much so that I suspected it was copied. Because SL stores both the creator of the objects (which can never change) and the owner of the object (which changes when you sell or give the object away), my teaching assistant and I were able to look at the creator field and discover that the student was indeed the creator. But a few weeks later, we reflected further — could we *really* be sure he created the motorcycle? He could have given his password to another user. He could have used SL to add one more object (which he had indeed created) to an existing motorcycle, and then linked it again to "stamp" his name into the creator field. Now we were entering the field of copyright and ownership.

Rights (and more specifically, copyrights) of virtual goods are a hot topic. Hackers have circumvented SL's internal clients to make illegal copies of objects and textures. One virtual goods merchant, Stroker Serpentine (Kevin Alderman in real life), decided to act and sued a thief (Leatherwood) who was appropriating his objects. Here is what Stroker says in one blog post in March 2008 capture by Heslop (2008):

When Leatherwood was first confronted and served a cease and desist, he made it very clear that he was not going to stop because he felt that his anonymity would protect him. It was also painfully apparent that Linden Lab's [makers and managers of SL] activities would not halt his activities. Given the fact that he cherry picked our most popular and profitable product, we had to make a decision. Ignore it or address it legally.

Leatherwood made mention in a well-publicized interview that he would never be found. He tried to throw us off his trail by giving false accounts. When he was confronted with the cease and desist in real life, he denied knowing anything about the matter. However, his real life friends were willing to testify to the contrary, since he had run to their home and used their IP addresses to continue his activities when the story broke. They were [angry].

This issue came to light by the various IP addresses he had used to connect to SL. These friends were also willing to testify that Leatherwood carried a notebook of dozens of credit card numbers with him everywhere and used them to make online purchases.

When Leatherwood refused to answer the claims against him, we were faced with the decision to mount a full case in federal court. A case that included transaction histories, both real life and SL eyewitnesses (many SL residents who were willing to testify in person btw [by the way]). The statement of the Private Investigator would also have been included, where in one conversation he denied being Catteneo [his SL identity] and retracted it in another. Leatherwood's computer would have been impounded by the FBI and a subsequent examination would have been done by a forensic examiner.

This case, which was settled in a US District Court, involved two important issues: (1) protecting the rights of owners of virtual goods, and (2) making Linden Lab lift the anonymity shield (Silvestrini, 2008).

Protecting rights becomes even a bigger issue when we think about moving the pirate ship Jane purchased from Dera from one world to another: Can Jane store the ship in her local machine or on another machine? How can this be done while not allowing multiple copies of the same ship? To protect the creator's rights, can we store a user "token" in the ship (with expiration)? Can we demand "always-on" operation to enforce digital rights management? Is this another parameter creators should/could/need to worry about?

Let us extend the realm of virtual goods to the area of multilayered marketing. In my opinion, one of the potential key features of future virtual worlds is allowing people to resell derivatives of virtual goods. In fact, IMVU has a structure for that. For example, you can buy mesh for a dress, then color it and resell it. The revenues from the sale will be split between you and the manufacturer of the mesh.

Finally, dealing with virtual money is a new challenge to the enterprise. Imagine doing a purchase order for virtual land (are we in the real estate business?), renting models as salespersons (should HR be involved in this?), or buying skin (why do you need to pay for a skin?). Clearly virtual world commerce will raise a host of issues for the enterprise to consider. Virtual goods propel identity into a new domain that mixes anonymity, rights, ownership, and freedom to move objects from one place to another.

Scams

A scam is defined as obtaining value (usually money) by means of deception. The internet created an entire new area for scammers. Virtual Worlds, allow even more frauds. SL avatar Prad Prathivil (2009) has demonstrated how a classic scam can work in virtual worlds:

[10:39] Imas Cammer: Hey baby! How was your day today?

[10:40] Gull Libel: It was tiring, sweetie... but I'm glad to be home and on Second Life with you:)

[10:40] Gull Libel: And how are you, sweets?

[10:41] Imas Cammer: Hmmm... I have an RL problem.:(

[10:42] Gull Libel: Oh, what's up?

[10:42] Imas Cammer: You remember how I told you a few months back that my father died a few years ago, and that my mom still lives in Nigeria?

[10:43] Gull Libel: I remember, baby. You've had it rough:(

[10:44] Imas Cammer: Yeah:(Well, you remember when you told me how it's good for people to help people less fortunate than themselves?

[10:45] Gull Libel: I remember baby... and I'd do anything to help you:)

[10:46] Imas Cammer::)

[10:46] Imas Cammer: When my dad left the bank he ran, he left quite a lot of money in a bank account in Nigeria, but my mom says she can't touch it unless she gets some help... we'd be happy to share some of it with you if you can....

In SL, instead of some suspect e-mail landing straight in your junk folder, the scam presents itself in the form of an avatar. Someone has put work into making the avatar look pretty, and she starts up a relationship with a potential victim, grooming him over several weeks or months until a trust develops between them. The intensity of the interaction in virtual worlds enables users to build their reputations. One truly sees the person, her house, and her actions. One is temped to trust.

In addition, the scammers are not always after your money. Sometimes, information is just as valuable to them:

[07:21] Imas Cammer: I really feel a strong connection with you, baby — I'd love to call you sometime. What's your phone number?
[21:32] Imas Cammer: Your Second Life name is nice, but I was wondering today what's your real name, baby?
[16:01] Imas Cammer: I found something beautiful in a store today, and I'd love to send it you for your birthday, baby! What's your address?

For starters, people tend to be nice in virtual worlds, and often they encourage real-life courtesy. Imagine a bank teller getting some personal information from an avatar that is being escorted by another avatar — his or her friend. That is one potential leak. Alternatively, consider an avatar that keeps her bag in the office — a bag that was given as a present by a friend. This bag could be a listener that hears everything being said in the virtual office.

Adult Content

Linden, the makers of Second Life, has created two separate worlds: the adult grid (over 18) and the teen grid (under 18), two separate systems with only minimal connectivity. In essence, an adult must go through a rigorous examination to be allowed entry into the teen grid (this include age verification and background check from Ascertain, 2009). Even then, that person is not allowed to roam around in the teen grid. These rules and their like, while designed to protect children, complicate the life of teachers, even to the extent that educators often do not bother to go in. Other problems include moving items from the adult grid to the teen grid and preventing children and their parents from doing things together.

The reason for this adult/grid separation is, of course, the problem of adult content. Without going into definitions of what adult content actually is, I would like to describe a mechanism that seems to work and solve this predicament. In essence, this mechanism combines features from IMVU, SL, and others. The proposed mechanism is based on a combination of an "adult" flag for items, objects, and services and an "adult pass" for avatars that use these items.

As seen in the Table 1, any object, place, avatar or entity may be defined as "adult" by setting the adult flag to on. Once an item is defined as "adult," it has two modes of operation, depending on whether or not the avatar that wants to use it has an "adult pass."

By deploying the adult flag for objects and the adult pass for users, IMVU has essentially resolved the adult/teen grid issue. Technically, they do not manage two different grids. By the way, getting an adult pass costs money and depends on a valid credit card (which includes age information). Therefore, when you get your pass you automatically expose your identity. Note: in March 2009, Linden initiated a new policy regarding adult content that has some similarities with the above mechanism (Linden, 2009).

Table 1. Exhibit--Solving the adult / teen kid dilemma with the adult pass scheme

(Sample Object) What I see if:	I have the adult pass	I do not have adult the pass
Adult outfit	I see it, and the content behind it	I see standard green shirt and pants
Place with adult content	I can enter the place	I am automatically diverted to somewhere else.
Object has an adult picture (texture)	I see the picture	I do not see the original picture – instead, I see neutral scenery, such as a forest.
Avatar's web Page has adult content	I can see the about page of the avatar	I see a sign: "entry for adults only."
Adult item in the store	I see it	I do not see it.
Item in Search	I see it	I do not see it or I see a note about an adult object)
Group is for adults only	I see it and can be accepted to it.	I can not be accepted, nor see the group.

The Enterprise Take

Virtual worlds are gradually entering the enterprise scene. They serve as a place for collaborating inside the enterprise or with outside suppliers and customers, a place to try out new designs, a place to market goods and services, and even a place to sell them. Banks can start to offer services, hospitals can start to treat people, and firms may present their products and allow users to try them.

We are in the initial phase of virtual worlds, and the following identity-related issues require attention *now*, because they may have regulatory, technical, and/or legal ramifications:

- **Networks:** Currently, worlds like SL call for nonstandard network ports. Often, SL will not work behind firewalls. Some people overcome this block with tools that allow limited Web-based access to SL for presence and messages.
- **Code:** Advanced virtual worlds allow code to run, which also means viruses, bots, and other hazards.
- **Group identity:** Is the fact that you are a member of a group considered private or not? Can other members of the group know about your membership? What about people who are not in the group or people that left or were kicked out? Since many firms

start to manage virtual groups, personal information needs to be managed.

- **Tracking:** Imagine you have a virtual bank with a virtual semi-human/semi-automatic teller. It is in contact with a well-authenticated client avatar. Now you need to be able to get instructions from this avatar. She may chat in these instructions, she may send you an IM message, and she may voice these instructions. The teller avatar (or avatars) will need to store and track these instructions.
- **'Doing business:** Even more issues emerge when it comes to business relations in virtual worlds. Identity is necessary when it comes to common business requirements such as contract enforcement, insufficient tax documentation, copyright/IP prosecution and defense, and nondisclosure (Theslrevolution, 2009).

Now that we have presented several virtual worlds with 3D3C Identity challenges, we can turn to a discussion about this term. Whereas the previous challenges of Security of Audience, Anonymity, Virtual Goods, Scams, and the Enterprise Take were concrete and specific, the next section takes a more reflective approach to the term 3D3C Identity.

Virtual Money

While many consider the Linden Dollar as real money, Linden Lab's Terms of Service tell a somewhat different story:

[snap]

1.4 Second Life "currency" is a limited license right available for purchase or free distribution at Linden Lab's discretion, and is not redeemable for monetary value from Linden Lab.

You acknowledge that the Service presently includes a component of in-world fictional currency ("Currency" or "Linden Dollars" or "L$"), which constitutes a limited license right to use a feature of our product when, as, and if allowed by Linden Lab. Linden Lab may charge fees for the right to use Linden Dollars, or may distribute Linden Dollars without charge, in its sole discretion. Regardless of terminology used, Linden Dollars represent a limited license right governed solely under the terms of this Agreement, and are not redeemable for any sum of money or monetary value from Linden Lab at any time. **You agree that Linden Lab has the absolute right to manage, regulate, control, modify and/or eliminate such Currency as it sees fit in its sole discretion, in any general or specific case, and that Linden Lab will have no liability to you based on its exercise of such right.** *[emphasis added]*

[snap]

So far, Linden has treated the Linden Dollar as exchangeable currency, and I see no indication that it will not continue to do so. Nevertheless, *caveat emptor!* Money is an essential feature of Real Virtual Worlds: would you agree for your bank to give you such terms of service?

TOWARDS A SYSTEMATIC APPROACH TO 3D3C IDENTITY

I hope that the previous examples generated some insights into old topics, and perhaps some leads to new topics. In this final section, I call for a systematic framework for 3D3C Identity. I shall start with a demonstrative example that shows how identity can save lives. Then, I shall cover some of the criticisms against the general 3D3C definition and, specifically, 3D3C Identity. Following that, I shall cover the potential impact of 3D3C Identity form players dealing with the present, the future, and with infrastructure. Lastly, I shall list a few initial insights regarding such a framework.

Identity that Saves Lives

Let me share one more example with you, this time from the real world, to drive home the importance of Identity. In some cases, we as users want service providers to use actionable personal data. Christian Renaud (2009) listed one of the best examples:

You can imagine my surprise when I just received an automated telephone call from CostCo, a big-box retailer in the United States, alerting me that the Clif bars that I purchased 'between June and December' were possibly an infection vector in the recent Salmonella Typhimurium Outbreak. (FDA, 2009) (Figure 2)

They were able to determine this based on the fact that each SKU (part number) is tracked through sale, and tied to a particular CostCo member identification number. Since they have my telephone number from the CostCo application, they were able to call me and notify me to trash the Clif bars else risk the wrath of Salmonella.

In fact, there were over 400 products affected by this outbreak. Wouldn't it be beneficial to get phone calls or email messages warning us? Such a system may prevent illness and reduce costs (many users will simply throw away all peanut butter related products). When data is collected and related to our identity service, providers such as CostCo and the manufactures of the Clif Bars can offer us better services that meet our needs and styles.

Critique

Earlier versions of the general 3D3C framework and the specific 3D3C Identity in particular, raised several questions and concerns. Let me summarize them for the benefit of future works.

- **Premature Market: It is too early to think about such things** – the thrust of this claim is that virtual worlds are still very early in their development cycle and early standardization work may stifle innovation. My own take is that it is never too early to think about the future. Different parts of the industry should focus on various short-, mid-, and long-term issues. I do concur, however, with the general notion that early standardization may hamper innovation. On the other hand, belated standards may kill markets.

- **Lack of Novelty: We have seen these 3D3C factors already**. What is new about that? We have seen real money in some other worlds. Creation may be done with standard tools like Blender, and community is clearly present with Facebook, Twitter and the like. My answer is simple: while each of the factors exists in its own right, the integration of the factors into one system is new. For me, such 3D3C integration, which we did not achieve in the Internet, is the key to the immense value of virtual worlds.

- **Missing Factor: 3D3C definition misses the real world**. Since much of the value of virtual worlds stems from connecting the virtual and the real world in terms of sensors and actuators, the core, the very definition, should also hint at the real world. I agree. As my writing states (with the term "real virtual worlds"), I am a great believer in virtual-real connections. Indeed, "Realness" is a strong factor that may extend the 3D3C framework – perhaps into R3D3C notation. This could be done in some future work.

- **Wrong Term: Identity is not the right term**. The essence of this claim is that the

Figure 2. Exhibit--Killer Peanut Bars that were recalled with the aid of Identity © Copyright 2009. Christian Renaud. (Used with Permission)

term "identity" itself is too limited or conversely too general. I would agree with any other term provided it is clear that we are talking about the amalgam of all the previously related issues like privacy, security, permissions, etc. Any ideas?

- **Too interdependent: We need to attack each issue independently**. The sheer complexity and interdependence of 3D3C Identity do present a conceptual and engineering challenge. Practical, time-to-market and other engineering concerns, *do* call for slicing the problem into specific parts, dealing individually with each issue: one subsystem for authentication, another subsystem for tracking, and a third subsystem for rights, etc. This factoring approach into subsystems is often needed to unpack a complex issue. Yet, as we have seen with SL, there are benefits to a coherent systematic approach. In SL, the concepts of groups, authentication, and rights are well integrated. While not complete, such a coherent system does demonstrate the possibility and value of a systemic approach.

- **Missing Issue: What about this or that issue**. As the nature of 3D3C Identity reveals itself, additional issues are needed to be included in the discussion. I agree with this notion. These new issues should be examined, and their relative impact on 3D3C Identity should be assessed. Nevertheless, we cannot wait for *all* the issues to be dealt with. My suggested credo: it is better to have an adequate standard at the right time than to wait for the perfect standard that is too late.

Impact

The nascent nature of the field of Real Virtual Worlds has different impacts on actors in the field. Each actor, be it a world developer, a virtual merchant, a researcher, or a user should examine his actions according to his goals. Each should consider the impact of 3D3C Identity on his current and future actions.

For presentation purposes, let me summarize the potential impact viewed through future, present, and infrastructure, as defined here:

- "Future" means long term (4-5 years and more into the future). Future actors often choose to delve into issues and describe, analyze, and synthesize very specific angles of 3D3C Identity.
- "Present" means now. The immediate present impact of identity in the way we use virtual worlds for users, content creators, worlds managers and the like.
- "Infrastructure" is about the intermediate period between theory and practice. It is for people who have to build the systems and subsystems of virtual worlds. Such infrastructure actors need to balance practical considerations of here and now against future theoretical insights and concerns. Infrastructure teams include the R&D teams of Linden Labs (makers of SL), IMVU, and Oracle/SUN Wonderland, as well as related technology teams that deal with specific issues like Collada, OpenSim, and the latest Google Led O3D (these are just examples of teams that deal with infrastructure.)

Future. My initial review of relevant theoretical works that may relate to 3D3C Identity reveals many resources, including related issues such as authentication, permissions, and privacy, to name a few. What is missing is a systemic approach–, which may be difficult to attain due to the multidisciplinary nature of 3D3C Identity. One potential direction toward a systemic approach could be the connecting of just two concepts; i.e., theoretical research on groups with virtual goods permissions, or level of adultness (how do you mark adult content in virtual worlds?).

Present. Practitioners also face identity issues today. Many of the earlier challenges portray immediate, here and now, issues for individuals and organization. After just few hours in virtual worlds, one meets issues of anonymity, trust, and copyright ("why can't I give this car to my friend?"). Practical actors in virtual worlds could adopt a dual approach of learning and common sense. On the learning side, users should have a deep grasp of current aspects of identity in their virtual worlds (for example, in SL this would mean understanding groups, object permissions, island permissions, etc.). On the common sense side, especially when projects become bigger and more complex, an "identity" attitude should be adopted, asking questions like: with whom do I do business in virtual worlds, who owns the rights for the land or creations, to whom do I give "free" copies of creations, and how do I protect my rights, and respect the rights of others?

Infrastructure. Lastly, infrastructure teams should pay special attention to identity issues. While sometimes difficult and less glitzy, identity issues should get higher priority with infrastructure teams (as a new 3D shadow model, or some other visual effect is more visible than an in-depth identity angle). One often sees bugs (things that where not fixed) or small additions (new features) in identity related issues. SL is rife with examples of things that do not work according to design when it comes to groups and object permissions. Here are some technical identity related examples:

- Why can I only have 25 groups?
- Why I cannot create an object in some places, but I can move objects into those places.
- Why "scripts" can be locked as sub-objects and "textures" cannot.
- Why can I have only one partner?
- Why "reply to IM that arrived in email" is limited to just a few days?

These technical examples demonstrate local specific places where identity should and could call for infrastructure work. I admit that these issues are presented from the users' point of view, not accounting for the various interdependencies within them. For example, having more than 25 groups, may call for changes to the simulator that may affect performance – as a car owned by one group travels from one area to another. Such interdependencies are the core of the infrastructure challenge for 3D3C Identity.

Tentative Insights about 3D3C Identity

My research on Virtual Worlds standards is cyclical in nature, and it is done via real and virtual discussions with colleagues. So, with your permission, I will shift from "I" to "we" to denote that.

We review the state of the art in terms of existing technology, standards, and research; we propose a framework; then we go back to the community to seek feedback to improve the framework. Armed with the framework and the feedback, we again look for updated inputs, develop an improved version to the framework, and again seek feedback. Each cycle takes about a year. Currently we plan to publish the first version (under MPEG-V) in early 2011 (official deadline is October 2010).

Here are some of the initial insights about 3D3C Identity, presented here to gain feedback:

- **Real Identity**: The real identity of an avatar is key to the future value of virtual worlds. I see current anonymity as an interim phase that stems from the current popular use of virtual worlds. This does not negate having anonymous avatars, as they are quite valuable for certain things. It is not merely a technological issue; it also has to do with the patterns of actions of many of the current players/actors in virtual world.
- **Real Money**: To enhance trust in virtual worlds (and to prevent Ponzi / Madoff

schemes) the realness of money must be managed. This is also due to money laundering, crossing national borders and the like. However, the need for an exchange (as the one SL has) is not essential. Fixed rate may be simpler.

- **Real Tracking**: the central storage of processes and actions could, and should, have value. Coupled with the right privacy considerations, such a tracking system would enhance trust, and save on the local need to track and store transactions.
- **Real Permissions**: much of the value of virtual worlds will arise from virtual goods. Creators should be able to trust the system, allow for derivatives, expiration, and so on. This issue includes both marking the creator's intention (a legal/social challenge) and protecting it (a technical challenge).
- **Real Market**: to fully harness the potential of virtual worlds we should have a market for each of the various parts of the system. We want to have an ecosystem of suppliers that can replace each other and innovate at specific points of the value chain. This is true regarding the Internet, where we have various ISPs, browsers, web sites, web site technologies (Flash, HTML, XML, JAVA) etc. However, the issues of Identity should be built into the inherent fabric of the ecosystem. We should strive to have issues like authentication, personal inventory, and friends lists transportable from one provider to another, and have them work within different worlds.
- **Identity as a critical component**: in the network of related concepts and systems of virtual worlds, Identity is clearly a hub. It relates critically to virtual goods, performance, trust and other issues.
- **Identity is less linked with 3Dness**: we have yet to find the connection between the 3Dness of real virtual worlds and identity.

Apparently, the identity framework could very well be done for Internet worlds.

- **Identity and real countries**: one of the most difficult challenges of 3D3C identity is connecting virtual identity with real identity. This problem rises from competing values of various cultures – a clash of deep assumptions about the role and rights of state vs. individuals. As we strive to build a global system, we will have to adapt (for practical reasons) to local demands (much like the example of Google search and the China market).

These insights are work in progress. We still have to explicate their phrasing, internal relations, and relations to other virtual worlds concepts (like 3D rendering or object creation). Furthermore, there is a lot of work to be done as these identity insights moves from theory, via infrastructure, to practice. They will probably change as they go into deployable real systems. Usage by real users is a major challenge. As one examines these issues, one gets a renewed appreciation to the works of Linden Lab with SL, Blizzard with World of Warcraft, and IMVU Inc. with IMVU.

CONCLUSION

As we think about virtual worlds and their future uses, it becomes ever clearer that we need a systemic approach to identity. This is hard work and a moving target. However, such an approach *is* possible — large-scale systems like the Internet, credit cards and the GSM system for mobile phones have proved that. A systematic approach to identity will also facilitate many new products and services, as innovators will be able to focus on innovation, and "outsource" the complex issue of identity. Enormous social and monetary value will be created for both users and service providers.

ACKNOWLEDGMENT

Some of this work was conducted as part of the Metaverse1 project. An earlier version of this work for the Enterprise market was published in the Cutter Journal (Sivan, 2009). A version of this work for submitted for oral presentation at the SLAction conference. I would like to thank the members of the Metaverse1 European team and IETF MMOX group. Their thinking helped shape this paper.

REFERENCES

Alexander, R. (2003). *Massively multiplayer game development*. Hingham, MA: Charles River Media, Inc.

Alexander, R. (2005). *Massively multiplayer game development 2*. Hingham, MA: Charles River Media, Inc.

Ascertain (2009). Retrieved from https://www.ascertainsi.com/secondlife/bgConsent.asp. (Accessed 29-May-2009 14:58).

Bartle, A. (2004). *Designing Virtual Worlds*. Berkeley, CA: New Riders Publishing.

Bimber, O., & Raskar, R. (2005). *Spatial augmented reality: Merging real and virtual worlds*. Wellesley, MA: A K Peters.

Brainyquote (2009). Retrieved from http://www.brainyquote.com/quotes/quotes/f/fernandof1285659.html (Accessed 27-Feb-2009 12:58).

Burdea, G., & Coiffet, P. (2003). *Virtual reality technology*. Hoboken, NJ: John Wiley & Sons.

Center for Democracy & Technology (CDT). (2007). *Privacy principles for identity in the digital age (draft for comment, version 1.2)*. http://www.cdt.org/security/20070327idprinciples.pdf.

Chellappa, R., & Sin, R. (2002). Personalization versus privacy: New exchange relationships on the Web. http://www.zibs.com/techreports/Personalization%20versus%20Privacy.pdf. (Accessed 30-May-2009 10:45).

Food and Drug Administration (U.S.). (2009). Retrieved from http://www.fda.gov/oc/opacom/hottopics/salmonellatyph.html. (Accessed 29-May-2009 14:55).

Glover, S. (2008). Alleged myspace 'cyber-bully' indicted in teen's suicide. *Los Angeles Times*, 16 May 2008 (http://www.latimes.com/news/local/la-me-myspace16-2008may16,0,3642392.story).

Heslop, H. (2008). Stroker serpentine wins moral victory. *SLNN.com*, 25 March 2008. (The article is no longer available at the original URL, but it can be viewed in Google's cache at http://74.125.77.132/search?q=cache:LtEIrPPlM38J:www.slnn.com/article/serpentine-wins-moral-victory/).

Linden Lab. (2009). *Upcoming changes for adult content*. https://blogs.secondlife.com/community/community/blog/2009/03/12/upcoming-changes-for-adult-content. (Accessed 20-May-2009 10:53).

Linden Lab. (2009). Terms of Service. (http://secondlife.com/corporate/tos.php). (Accessed 05-Dec-2009 09:49). Actual quote taken from an earlier version 15-Sep-2008.

Martin, K. (2006). *Google inc., in china* (Case BRI-1004). Business Roundtable Institute for Corporate Ethics, 2006 (http://www.darden.virginia.edu/corporate-ethics/pdf/BRI-1004.pdf).

Murugensan, S. (Ed.). (2008). Finding the real world value in virtual. *Cutter IT Journal for Information Technology Management, 21* (9).

Prathivi, P. (2009). The 419. *The SL Revolution*, 3 February 2009 (http://theslrevolution.wordpress.com/2009/02/03/the-419/). (Accessed 29-May-2009 14:58).

Renaud, C. (2009, January). http://www.christian-renaud.com/weblog/2009/01/the-upside-of-the-lack-of-privacy.html. (Accessed 29-May-2009 14:55).

Silvestrini, E. (2008). Virtual sex toy suit settled. *Tampa Tribune*, 21 March 2008 (http://www2.tbo.com/content/2008/mar/21/virtual-sex-toy-suit-settled).

Sivan, Y. (2008a). 3D3C real virtual worlds defined: The immense potential of merging 3D, community, creation, and commerce. *Journal of Virtual Worlds Research*, *1*(1).

Sivan, Y. (2008b). "The birth of MPEG-V (MPEG for virtual worlds)." *Metaverse1*, 16 February 2008 (http://www.metaverse1.org/2008/02/birth-of-mpeg-v-mpeg-for-virtual-worlds.html).

Sivan, Y. (2009). Identity 3D3C: Controlling the security and privacy challenges in virtual worlds. *Cutter IT Journal for Information Technology Management, 22* (4).

Taylor, T. (2006). *Play between worlds: Exploring online game culture*. Cambridge, MA: MIT Press.

The Internet Society (ISOC). (2008). *Trust and the future of the internet*. (http://www.isoc.org/isoc/mission/initiative/docs/trust-report-2008.pdf).

Theslrevolution, author unknown (2009). The importance of identity when doing business in virtual worlds. *The SL Revolution*, 4 February 2009 (http://theslrevolution.wordpress.com/2009/02/04/identity-in-virtual-worlds). (Accessed 29-May-2009 15:10).

Thompson, M. (2009). Real banking coming to virtual worlds. *Ars Technica*, 20 March 2009 (http://arstechnica.com/gaming/news/2009/03/real-banking-coming-to-virtual-worlds.ars).

ADDITIONAL READING

Sivan, Y. (2009). http://www.dryesha.com/ (Accessed 29-December-2009 17:00).

Chapter 3
Society in a Virtual World

Vaclav Jirovsky
Czech Technical University, Czech Republic

ABSTRACT

The new virtual world created by the Internet, with its attendant new technology environment, new actors and new models of societal behavior, has given rise to unexpected and as yet to be described social phenomena. This chapter guides the reader through virtual communities on the Internet, highlighting behavioral anomalies in the community or individual. The main objective of this chapter is to introduce the reader to basic patterns of behavior which may foster illegitimate use of the Internet, including illegal activity, and security incidents. This survey of virtual communities and the threats they create to Internet security, as well as the behavioral change of individuals when exposed to the virtual world, is intended to give the reader a basis for understanding the virtual world's impact on mankind and social reality. Such an understanding could be helpful to discern new Internet threats or to assess expected risks.

INTRODUCTION

The evolution of the human society is characterized by persistent interaction of individuals and communities, which continuously moves the evolution of the mankind forward. Historically, these interactions existed in the physically sensed and observed world. The actors involved in interaction were real persons or groups of persons. Moreover, these interactions were observed and experienced in the physical environment, ie. in the real world. The playing of children on the street was part of growing up and education, improving their sense of the world and creating necessary perceptual apparatus. Individual communication was usually accompanied by some physical perception. The listener sensed not only the speech of a counterparty but also its movement, body position or facial expression. Interpersonal communication was thus comprised of two balanced components – verbal and non-verbal communication or so called "body language".

With improvement of verbal communication skills and development of new means of

DOI: 10.4018/978-1-61520-891-3.ch003

human expression, non-verbal communication was becoming increasingly concealed and the first instances of mankind's existence in the virtual world emerged. For example, book printing gave access to written messages for ever-broader masses. Book stories shifted readers into an imagined world, letting them to share the lives of fictional or historical characters with their own imagination. This one-way communication allows transferal of information only from writer to reader and lack of interaction leaves a vacuum in normal communication involving speech. Nevertheless the individual, separated from society, could spent a pleasant moments in the circle of his imaginary heroes, not communicating with surrounding society.

Birth of the Virtual World

In this historical context, the most significant change in communication was brought by computers and communication media, chiefly the Internet. Interactivity, impossible with virtual book characters, became the cornerstone of computer communication. The main attributes of the new virtual world are a total absence of non-verbal perception, the possibility to create immortal virtual individuals, simplicity of going across communities and the suppressed need for compromises, all of which can seem more attractive and enjoyable than real world. The virtual world[1] also fosters new dimensions of social life with all its attributes – political, social, emotional, religious, etc. Even major characteristics of existing society have been transferred into the virtual world - life in the virtual world formulates its own rules which often go out of natural order, where human society lives for centuries. Also, the new form of virtual existence brings new or modified risks and new or modified forms of human behavior, to which we either have to adapt or we have to find a means to oppose.

The decentralized nature of the virtual world, without any formally centralized "governing"

authority, seems to impart a highly democratic quality to this world. However, while appearing democratic, the virtual world is more akin to widespread anarchy which, if not limited by technological rules, may in fact annihilate the virtual world or make it unusable. The functionality of the virtual world is ensured by mutual agreement among administrators, who adapt their manners to the majority. We can say that virtual world is "driven" by its users and their general sense of morality and ethics. Anyone who abides by the major rules of the virtual world can enter virtual world; the virtual world is open. The openness of the virtual world provides an environment for an incredibly vast amount of information resident within the virtual world. Anyone can present any information without further redaction or censoring. Anyone can contact other users of the virtual world or "virtual persons" or can create relationships with others due to the freedom to use or misuse the virtual world. Unfortunately this freedom leads to the existence of an "information scrap yard" where anything can be found, but assigning a meaning to information found becomes a crucial problem. The initial problem of the real world – to find appropriate information - has evolved to a more sophisticated and complex process of culling searched information from large amounts of data, weighing up the information found and evaluating the probability of accuracy and meaning of the information found.

Several features of the virtual world, arising from the characteristics mentioned above, facilitate illegal activities in the virtual world. The most important one is a non-transparent environment due to the technological complexity of the system. This technological "shadow" gives a sham sense of safety to the criminal, since the crime scene knows him only by his virtual identity.

The potential for existence of a virtual personality in the virtual world, anywhere and anytime, is a stimulus for creation of different virtual groups and virtual communities. By communication, presentation of personalities in the virtual space and coordination of their activities, we can view formation of different subcultures. At the same time, having more than one subculture in the unique virtual space, there are conditions for subcultures to encounter, quarrel and combat each other. Such combats are either retroactively exposed or mirrored in the real world, with all the consequences of the virtual events.

VIRTUAL POPULATION

The development of global communication technologies creates new space for individual activities and new dimensions in the socialization of mankind. The experiences of the individual, obtained during his stay in the virtual world, influence his psychic, social behavior, his practice and evaluation of society's values. New feelings of the individual when connected to the network, accessing the virtual world, are often compared to his feelings known from the real world – e.g. browsing web pages can be compared to the feelings of traveler exploring a new country (Suler, 1997).

The influence of technology and of the virtual world's effects on mankind are manifestly evident. The population and organization of the virtual world results from projection of the real population into virtual identities, by using specific languages and means of communication, bereft of nonverbal expression or perception. This suppresses the social effects of the communication while increasing the feeling of safety of being in virtual space. As a consequence, we can observe noticeable changes in human psyche and health when his stay in the virtual world is long enough. New types of experience, obtained in the virtual world and being part of virtual communities or subcultures, lead to a clash of virtual and real personality (Jirovsky, 2008). Modern sociology and psychology is dealing with this new "dual" social status of the individual, as well as with mental and physical defects arising from virtual life.

The decentralized nature of virtual world produces the forms of organization of individuals into groups. Virtual communities or subcultures are organized around topics rather than within national boundaries. Groups are created around a few commonly accepted languages; expansion of English in the virtual world is noticeable, as the most users of virtual world are using it. Statistic of top ten Internet languages[2] is shown in the Figure 1.

The existence of virtual groups on the Internet has been the subject of psychological and sociological studies, but the focus has been usually on how reality is reflected in the virtual world (e.g. Douglas, 2007) or on the characterization of virtual groups according to technology usage (e.g. Brandon & Hollingshead, 2007). Other social science studies have examined the effects of Internet usage on the formation and maintenance of personal relationships, group memberships and social identity, mainly as psychological aspect of user's well-being (e.g. Bargh & McKenna, 2004). The effectiveness and dynamic of virtual community work has also been studied (e.g. Walther, Boos & Jonas, 2002). The various studies dealing with network addiction are described in (Young, 1997), but without specific correlation to the threats created by virtual communities or individuals.

Virtual Individuals

Looking at mankind in general, we surprisingly find that most individuals do not need to fulfill their ambitions in the real world. They are quite satisfied with only a virtual resemblance of the fulfillment of ambition (Jirovsky, 2008). As such, the difference between virtual and real experience becomes reflected in virtual and real behavior. For example, to release aggression against an enemy, it is sufficient in many cases to just destroy the symbol of the enemy. Similarly, many individuals could satisfy their ambitions just through symbolic resemblance. While symbolic experience

Figure 1. Percentage of languages used at Internet

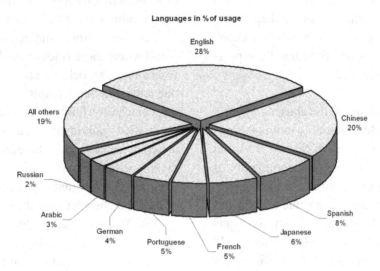

Languages in % of usage

cannot offer a full experience of reality, it does minimize risks for the individual. The individual cannot be physically hurt in the virtual world. The individual can express himself in different roles within communities, changing age or gender when carrying out one's own image[3] of his personality (Hučín, 2000).

The immortality of the individual in virtual world is a specific quality with surprising projection into reality. The addictive person intensively being in the virtual world anchors its perception of its own immortality in such a way that it is transferred to the real world and suppresses the instinct for self-preservation. Hypothetically, the behavior of the respective individual could become more aggressive or violent in the view of his own perceived immortality (Ko et al. - 2009).

While humans cannot in fact use their natural habits in the virtual space, their perceptions are not adapted to the virtual world yet and so are continuously sustaining improper notions of ethics, morality and law in the virtual world. The perception of identity, quite different in real life, leads to the virtualization of the individual and of society in the virtual world. We can introduce simple taxonomy to the population of virtual world by defining following types of users

- Regular users of the virtual world, who are not exhibiting any addiction to the Internet. Typical example of such a user is a traveling salesman reporting on his duties via company web application from hotels. He must do it, but when he finishes, he closes the lid of his notebook and forgets about the Internet;
- "Happy users", who explore features of the virtual world and then use online activities as a tool to enhance their lives in real world. They use e-mail, social networks, Internet shopping and banking etc. quite often, but they do not exhibit an addiction to the Internet;
- Users with addiction to the virtual world, who are entirely captivated by the virtual world and exhibit dependency ("netholism", "netmania") with an invisibly ongoing separation of real and virtual life (see next section);
- Developers: professionals who are continually contributing to the technology's progress while retaining resilient personalities - they accept the virtual world as a part of their profession ;

- Abusers, who are misusing the virtual world for criminal and other illegitimate activities and their main reason for entering the virtual world is to use their presence for malicious acts.

This last group of users, the abusers, forms a growing virtual world community moving criminal activities from the real world to the virtual world. The reason is not only the complexity of systems with many vulnerabilities and abundant targets, but also the increasing value of information as regular social and economic activities gets transferred more and more into the virtual world infrastructure, and because of the difficulty of investigation of digital crime[4].

Addiction to the Virtual World

While in the USA dependency on the virtual world and Internet erotica is a common media topic, the European media are pointing out such symptoms much less often. Research in Germany found every twentieth Internet user dependent on the Internet; in Sweden[5] it is about 40,000 users and in Austria approximately 30,000 users[6]. We can generally expect about 0.6% of users are addicted to the virtual life[7], and this number is sharply increasing.

It is a reality that the virtual world and the Internet have a great impact on human psychology. Seeking of virtual communication and relationships is often a response to low satisfaction in the real world. Troubled personal relationships in the real world lead to frustration and preference for virtual relationships, where one seems to find more understanding and a higher enrichment of life. The virtual world becomes for the addicted person so attractive after while that he would be willing to sacrifice his own real life, reducing it to basic physiological needs. The core symptoms of a pathological inclination to the virtual world, particularly on the Internet, are continuous thought of being on the net, and decreased level

of self-control when being in the virtual world, e.g. inability to suspend Internet sessions.

The escape from cruel reality into the virtual world where there is less need for compromises, where one can behave arbitrarily according to one's wishes, can result in disintegration of the personality (Jirovsky, 2008). Unhappy and unsatisfied individuals, yearning for a simple, understandable world, where they can realize their dreams, discover opportunities in the welcoming environment of virtual world, however at the price of the total absorption of their personalities.

The Websense company (Websense, 2007) found that 25% of employees who are working on the Internet exhibit symptoms of Internet addiction. Moreover, the dependency is supported by compulsive use of computer applications while working. While in the past the salesman had to spend most of his time communicating with his customers either directly face-to-face or over the phone, current company information systems force human to interact by e-mail and with databases. While this increases company productivity the work process is depersonalized and reduced to communication with computer via keyboard and display. Steeped in such an environment it is not surprising that employees search for personal entertainment in the same way – with their computers via the Internet.

The average US office employee spends in total whole one working day per week on Internet activities unrelated to his task, e.g. browsing non-relevant web pages, doing personal e-mail or chatting. The most frequent of these non-task-related activities are online shopping, reading of news and magazines, web erotica and pornography and gambling. Interestingly, over 70% of visits to erotic server pages happen between 9 a.m. and 5 p.m. and more than 60% of Internet shopping is done from company computers. The load of chat servers tracks the worktime day-parts, with a steep rise observed shortly after start of morning business hours, and lasting until approximately 9 p.m., when the load of chat servers slowly decreases.

Net addiction is arguably one of the most risky security threats. The addictive individual believes more in the information and relationships gained in the virtual space than in real life. The communication in virtual space expresses high levels of virtual exhibitionism, and the addictive person in a virtual environment tends to release more information than he would do in real life. Following misuse of revealed information collected from different sources of activity, an addictive individual can cause damage to his employer, partner or even to the state.

Addictive persons feel that their own personal exhibitionism in the virtual environment as something very natural and normal. Social networks and social webs are examples of such exhibitionism We noticed a case when several ministers of the Czech government exhibited themselves on the Facebook website, releasing a lot of information about themselves using nickname[8] (Kottasová & Kubita, 2008). Later, when they have interviewed by journalists about such an activity, they defended themselves as very advanced persons using Facebook as a modern communication medium. On other hand, it should be noted that social networks and social websites are very effective public relations tools for voting campaigns or influencing public opinion for various purposes.

Netholism and Netmania

Dependency on life in the virtual world was originally noted by Ivan Goldberg at PsyCom.Net (Goldberg, 1995). The Internet Addiction Disorder (IAD), or Internet overuse has been defined as pathological computer use that interferes with daily life. Clinical psychologist Kimberly Young, supports the existence of the phenomenon in her paper (Young, 1996), but there is as yet no full agreement among psychiatrists if IAD is formally a mental disease or not. The diagnosis of IAD has many supporters and critics. Research among ninety-four Swiss psychiatrists shows that only twenty of them had rejected the concept of Inter-

net addiction and its importance, not considering it a real clinical problem and consequently not considering the existence of a specific treatment (Thorens, 2009). One of the best-known critics is Welsh researcher Jonathan Bishop, who rejects IAD diagnosis by stating that Internet addiction is impossible. "The Internet is an environment,...You can't be addicted to the environment..." (Goldin, 2006). According to his studies, the problem lies in the Internet user's priorities and can be solved by encouraging them to pursue offline goals.

We can, in fact, see an increasing incidence of events caused by Internet addiction mainly in Asian countries where Internet cafés are frequently used and mental or physical effects are publicly displayed. In the United States and Europe games and virtual sex are accessed from the home, so any attempt to measure the phenomenon is obscured by shame and denial (Block, 2007). Interesting research results have been published in South Korea (Ahn, 2007) where a series of 10 cardiopulmonary-related deaths in Internet cafés and a game-related murder had been reported.

To be diagnosed as having Internet Addiction Disorder, a person must meet certain criteria rated by the American Psychiatric Association. If any of three or more of following criteria are present at any time during a twelve month period, then the person is having substantial addiction to the Internet. These criteria are (Ferris, 1997):

1. The need to spend increasing amounts of time on the Internet to achieve satisfaction and/or with significantly diminished effect with continued use of the same amount of time on the Internet.

2. Two or more withdrawal symptoms developing within days to one month after reduction of Internet use or cessation of Internet use, and these must cause distress or impair social, personal or occupational functioning. These symptoms include psychomotor agitation (i.e. trembling, tremors; anxiety etc.), having fantasies or dreams about the Internet and/or

voluntary or involuntary typing movements of the fingers.

3. Use of the Internet is engaged in to relieve or avoid withdrawal symptoms.

4. The Internet is often accessed more frequently, or for longer periods of time than was intended.

5. A significant amount of time is spent in activities related to Internet use (e.g., Internet books, trying out new World Wide Web browsers, researching Internet vendors, etc.).

6. Important social, occupational, or recreational activities are given up or reduced because of Internet use.

7. The individual risks the loss of a significant relationship, job, educational or career opportunity because of excessive use of the Internet.

Other characteristics have also been identified recently, but the classifications listed above clearly describe the main symptoms of the addiction to the virtual world. The most advanced stage of IAD is usually referred to as "netholism" or "netmania".

In all cases mentioned above one must distinguish between psychological and physical dependency. In the first case, the individual craves the feeling brought by his stay in the virtual world. While this dependency is primarily psychological, it can develop into physical dependency accompanied by physically perceived symptoms as neuralgic pain or stomach ulcer (Jirovsky, 2007).

The graph in the Figure 2 shows the relationship between the dependent and non-dependent population according to the most popular Internet applications (Jirovsky, 2007). While such entertainment applications as chatting or MUD[9] are most popular among the dependent part of the population, information exchange tools exhibit more popularity among the non-dependent part[10]. Some other literature (Lin & Tsai - 1999) exhibits similar results. The studies show average total time of 19 hours per week for Internet dependent individuals, but some studies define Internet de-

pendency starting at 8.5 hours per week. While it is significantly less than the average time spent by teens watching TV, which is around 3 hours per day (Jirovska, 2009), Internet addiction symptoms start earlier, probably because of the interactivity of media. In (Jirovsky, 2007) the case of woman who spent 114 hours per week in the Internet chatting room was described. When talking to the woman, she complain about family problems, low self-esteem and conflicts at work. She seeks attention in the virtual world where she feels more successful, satisfied and happy.

The terminal stage of Internet addiction is often called "Jekyll-Hyde syndrome"[11] (Jirovsky – 2004), when individual's personality disintegrates by living in both worlds, virtual and real, without ability to separate them. Gradual transition from real to virtual world accompanied by resignation from the real surrounding world is a visible symptom of Jekyll-Hyde syndrome. Total addiction to the Internet relationships, loss of ability to suffer and resist the cruelty of real world is often accompanied by suicide attempts. In the farewell letter of a youngster who committed suicide as a result of terminal stage Internet addiction (Jirovsky, 2007) he writes "The Internet is a catalyzer. It is not creating your state of mind but it is amplifying it. If you are happy, you are having more happiness on the Internet. E-mail from a loved person flutters your heart more than electric shock. If you are down-hearted, you feel a much heavier load, much more helplessness, much more envy. But not everyone can withstand it..."

Virtual Communities

Virtual communities recognized in the virtual world are global, a society of virtual individuals without boundaries, linked by similar ideas, religion, political opinion, experiences, interest etc. The behavior of communities which create threats in cyberspace, is often politically or religiously motivated. We can find also business-oriented

Figure 2. The popularity of Internet applications for dependent and independent individual

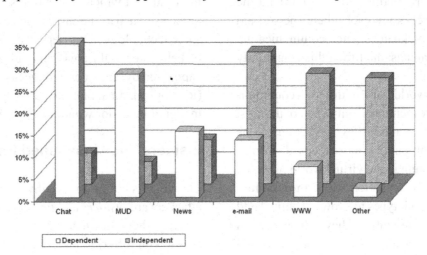

communities on the Internet – virtual corporations in the virtual world targeting market segments and created by its users freely or "on contract" basis.

The most well-Internet community is a hackers' community. Hackers' communities were the first communities on the Internet. Hackers use their own language, have their own cultures and kind of humor, and set of moral rules formulated in their manifesto. The Mentor, a well-known hacker, wrote in his personal manifesto shortly after his arrest: "Yes, I am a criminal. My crime is that of curiosity. My crime is that of judging people by what they say and think, not what they look like. My crime is that of outsmarting you, something that you will never forgive me for. I am a hacker, and this is my manifesto. You may stop this individual, but you can't stop us all... after all, we're all alike." (Mentor, 1986).

Besides hackers' communities known to exist only on the Internet, the chatters' and Internet gambler's communities would be the second largest one. The Internet addiction in this case is not as strong and helps to form some kind of social group based on sharing of common communication media and experiences. In the chatter's community, virtual persons could also be known as physical persons and they could meet at parties commonly organized by the whole group.

We can see very often communities using chat rooms within close territorial proximity e.g. in one city, so the potential for enrichment of social life is obvious.

The gamblers are a community without illegal motivation. They are more addictive to gaming than to the Internet, and exhibit a high level of social contacts. It has to be pointed out that the Internet just represents their tool to access the game and this type of gambling should not be confused with Internet addiction. If they meet personally they usually spend most of their time playing the game or talking about the game. The addicted players exhibit restlessness when not on the Internet, redirecting messages on the status of the game to their cellular phones. Sudden changes in their behavior can be observed as reactions to the messages received, even if they are in real world community, which often observes such a sudden change in behavior with surprise.

The most known virtual community exhibiting features of criminal behavior is the warez scene which manufactures and publishes pirated software and other pirated intellectual property materials (movies, music records etc.). While there is a kind of sporting competition of warez teams within the community, the major activities are criminal. The warez scene is very well organized and members are recruited from all around the world. They rarely know each other in person and they use their nicknames when communicating over covert channels; the life of this community is purely virtual.

The virtual world is full of different communities and we have mentioned only a few of the most important ones. In the following section can be found other communities, more focused on combating and fighting in the virtual world or which exhibit features of cyberterrorism. In the future we can expect both types to grow – criminal and non-criminal communities. They will have much more impact on the day-to-day life of society and the individual. This means for political parties, social organizations and other entities sensitive to public opinion, they should pay much more attention to the Internet, and to Internet communities particularly concentrated around some important topics and to public opinion distributed by means of the Internet.

ATTACKERS AND ATTACKS IN VIRTUAL WORLD

Besides communities enjoying the freedom of the virtual world, whether legally or non-legally, there are real attackers misuses this freedom by remodeling it into a dangerous battlefield. Security in the virtual world, from the point of the user, is reminiscent of security in the middle ages, where castles and towers are surrounded by impressive walls and moats with the surrounding forest teeming with bandits threatening your defenses. The modern analogy to castles would be our banking systems, military computing centers etc., surrounded by the virtual world represented by the publicly accessed network of the Internet.

One should distinguish between two basic models of attacker behavior according to their motivation. The first model represents individually-motivated attackers, who are pursuing some personal goal, such as revenge, which is directed

to the subject which had caused some perceived harm[12], or such as the satisfaction of overcoming some technological barrier[13]. The second model of behavior would cover individuals or groups captivated by some common ideas or movement (ideological, financial etc.) and typical of this model of behavior would be the cyberterrorist.

Insiders and Unsatisfied Employees

The most visible groups of individually-motivated attackers are *insiders* and *unsatisfied employees*. Both of them fulfill the first model described above with differing motivation. While insiders are more externally motivated by gaining some advantage or benefits[14] when they carry out their task, the motivation of unsatisfied employees is more introverted, originating from a sense of personal harm. Nevertheless, very often both motivations are involved. As studies show (e.g. Carnegie-Mellon, 2005), most insiders were also unsatisfied employees and approximately 60% of them left[15] the company a short time before the attack had been initiated. Most such attackers had been in a technical position in the company (programmers, administrators, IT specialist etc.) and only 4% of them were females.

Aside from regular crime, such as stealing computers or CD's with company proprietary data or misuse of company computers for ulterior purposes), non-legal activities of employees can be categorized as follows

- Illegal use of company IT resources (e.g. web site or FTP site). This is the most dangerous misuse of the employer technology because materials ported under the company IP address are in overwhelming majority of cases illegal or at least not "company approved";
- Illegal access to company proprietary data which are outside the employee's security perimeter. In this category is also data which is accessible to the employee for

fulfilling his tasks, but which is handled outside the frame set up by security policy;

• Deletion of data or software in company computer systems. In this case it is necessary to distinguish intentionality, negligence or circumstance.

Most of the threats originating with unsatisfied employees or motivated insiders could be restricted by well-designed company security policies and regular staff training. Performing drills of artificially contrived situations, to test staff decision-making within the frame of company security policy, are useful to keep security policy alive.

Cyber-Crime

The definition of cybercrime is usually understood as any crime committed on the Internet using the computer as either a tool or as a target, (e.g. Aghatise, 2006). But the definition is more difficult from a legal point of view of law, which must use stricter criteria for the qualitative and quantitative characteristics of criminal acts. In this sense, cybercrime would be any behavior of an individual or entity which leads to the lowering of some quantitative or qualitative level of the information society (Grivna & Polcak, 2008), for example deliberate reduction of throughput to an e-shop website or infringement of personal integrity, property rights etc.

All cybercrimes involve both a computer and the person behind it as an attacker or victim. The "Convention on Cyber Crime" (EC, 2001) signed in Budapest by September 23, 2001 recognizes two main categories of cybercrime, according to the target. In the first case the computer is considered as the tool rather than the target. These crimes involve less technical expertise as the damage done manifests itself in the real world and human weaknesses are generally exploited. When the computer itself is a target of criminal act, the major focus is on the content of the

computer system. These crimes require technical knowledge on the attacker's part and are relatively new, having been in existence for only as long as computer technology. The unprepared society in general has difficulty combating these crimes, even though there are numerous crimes of this nature committed daily.

New aspects of cybercrime take into consideration:

• New virtual crime scene,
• New forms of old deviant behavior e.g. theft of CD with important data but also entirely new criminal acts as cracking, hacking etc.,
• New methods of criminal act investigation and new rules for jurisdiction and penalties.

All these new types of criminal act in the virtual world are very closely bound to the population of the virtual world and it is important to understand the new ways of behavior of virtual individuals and virtual communities with respect to their potential to make damage. Very specific behavior can be recognized in organized crime carried out in the virtual environment, where the principle of the crime remains traditional. A good example would be the warez scene, which commits infringement of copyright law or "Natashas" networks - the transnational shadow market of trafficking in women (Hughes, 2001).

Case Study: The Warez Scene

The warez scene is a well-established structure of organized crime which, by using the tools and resources of the virtual environment, brings a new dimension to the old crime of copyright infringement. The *leader* of the warez team makes all important decisions, including recruitment of new members. The *supplier* provides the team with products for new release[16]. The technically most advanced member of the team is a *cracker*, who removes security features of the product while a less advanced team member, the *ripper*, modifies the product to the team's standard release. Last but not least in the team is a *carder*, with the task of getting credit card numbers, software registration numbers and other important information for the team, and the *tester*, who exhaustedly tests the product due for release (Jirovsky, 2007).

The warez scene is a rather self-contained community and difficult to penetrate - new members are recruited by advertising in an .nfo file contained in every release. It should be pointed out, that the warez scene, even it is part of an organized crime community, is in principle a non-profit community. Members of warez teams are volunteers not making any profit from their activities. The most rigorous taboo of the warez scene is to burn CD copies of its releases and selling them, or sell or rent accounts gained on other sites to someone else.

Publishing copies of artworks, software and other intellectual properties on the Internet is a nightmare for copyright protection agencies. Many battles between the warez scene and these agencies have been waged leading to many court cases, but the fight against the warez scene is a never ending story. Until the copyright owners and their agents will use repression tools to protect their content instead of market tools, this combat will be an inseparable part of the virtual life and the warez scene will not leave the virtual world.

Cyberterorrism

Cyber-terrorism, a phenomenon of 21st century, is the product of interaction between classical terrorism, netwars and society's dependence on information technology and communication infrastructure. A basic motivation of terrorists, to attract media attention to propagate their ideology, is well-served by Internet. This network spanning the world with connections to local infrastructures affords plenty of opportunities to the cyberterrorist. Indeed, many terrorist groups familiarize themselves with the Internet and the virtual world of the Internet to disseminate their propaganda, recruit new members and for inter-group communication.

Since Internet technology can be difficult to attack, terrorist groups hire hacker groups for a specific tasks like attacking enemy servers or to post ideological defacement on compromised computers around the world. The hacker groups hired call themselves Hackers for Hire – H4H, and take on tasks based on regular business relations with a purchase order and invoice. Some terrorist organizations have their own specialized units to developing and deploy infoware[17]. These specialized units are groups of highly skilled persons, usually operating only in the virtual world, using electronic means of communication and supporting classical terrorist attacks with accompanying attacks in the virtual world (Jirovsky, 2007a). Attacks carried out by these special units are of high quality and it can be difficult to differentiate an H4H attack from an attack by a military Information Operation Unit[18]. Such attacks usually have a specific strategy and do not last for a long time[19].

Although groups formed in the virtual world of the Internet predominate, there are also individuals taking part in different cyberterrorist activities. A first type of cluster of such individuals is formed by persons with ideological sympathies with political, religious, nationalistic or other movement. By taking part in an activity against the same enemy, they express sympathy for a particular movement. They usually work separately and their attacks are not too sophisticated. The latent threat remains in the potential for coalition amongst these individuals but the probability is very low.

A second type of cluster is created by so called "thrill seekers". These are individuals attracted by either real conflict or conflict in the virtual world. They are not led by any ideology, religion or any kind of the philosophical background. The major driver of thrill seekers is exhibitionism. A good example of such thrill seekers is the China – U.S.A. cyberwar in 2001. On other hand, there is an ideological part to the story, since the Chinese attackers were clearly supported by the Chinese authorities.

Terrorist Utilization of IT

A direct attack on a datacenter or a part of critical infrastructure is the most common means to utilize force against IT. The efficiency of such an attack conducted by traditional means - well trained units with ammunition - is dependent on the displacement of the target or of critical infrastructure and its significance. In fact, direct attacks on computing facilities are rare and attacks are more focused on using psychological operation or targeted at critical infrastructure.

The most common psychological attacks are semantic attacks against web sites, especially defacement. In this case the attacker replaces contents of the page(s) on the targeted site with content publicizing his own ideology. Such defacement has two important effects on the enemy:

- Web pages used by the enemy for propaganda and visited by enemy supporters are suddenly changed to display quite different information,
- The weakness of the enemy's technology is demonstrated, thus damaging trust in the enemy's technological abilities.

Semantic attacks, especially defacements, are often used for so-called *perception management*. Such an attack continually changes small pieces of information on the targeted web page leaving the original look of the page and majority of the text untouched. The part of the page targeted by the attack usually holds some important information, e.g. the price of goods in an e-shop. In this case, the attacker is a mercenary of a competitor who slightly increases the price of selected goods while the competitor keeps the price of the same goods the same or lower. As a result, the turnover of the affected e-shop drops without apparent reason while the competititor increases market share. Such perception management attacks on web pages are often used in more important cases, like elections, public opinion research, ideological battles, etc. (Jirovsky, 2007).

Attacks targeted at critical infrastructure are, in most cases, easily conducted variants of Denial of Service (DoS) or Denial of Access (DoA), which rely on primitive methods of overloading the targeted server or capacity of telecommunication channels used by targeted server. Although the basic approach is quite simple, its implementation can be sophisticated and dangerous. An example of DoS is the cyberattack against Estonia, conducted in the spring of 2007. The attack blocked websites and paralyzed the country's entire Internet infrastructure. At the peak of the crisis, bank cards and mobile-phone networks were temporarily frozen[20].

A more complex attack, Distributed Denial of Service (DDoS), uses systems compromised by attackers using a variety of methods such as Trojan malware. The collection of compromised systems is then used by an attacker to simultaneously flood the bandwidth or resources of a targeted system, usually one or more web servers. Synchronization of the attack could be done by triggering on the date and time or via a hidden channel to zombie agents in the compromised computer[21]. The coordination of a DDoS attack is complicated and time-consuming to commandeer the volume of other computers, but the efficiency of such an attack is devastating and defense is very difficult. The outage caused by a coordinated DDoS attack on Yahoo routers in its main California data centers in February 2000 cost Yahoo millions of dollars[22]. While such an attack usually does not lead to fatal consequences, the operational degradation of servers and financial loss can be enormous.

Misuse of the Virtual World

The virtual world with all its features can be easily used and misused. The real-world political activities, conflicts and military battles of hatred-inspired religious groups are mirrored by virtual battles. Beyond use of the virtual world for communication among terrorists and criminals, the virtual world offers a battlefield for various political movements. Around 50% of hacker group attacks are politically motivated, mostly in the service of political movements, revolutionary ideas, religious terrorism or fundamentalism.

Cyber-terrorism also includes instances of personal or psychotic terrorism, undertaken by a mentally ill attacker to feel satisfaction.. Examples of such personal terrorism in the virtual world are cyberstalking or cyberbullying. In cyberstalking the attacker harasses a victim relying upon the anonymity in virtual world[23]. Cyber-stalking messages differ from ordinary spam in targeting a specific victim with often threatening messages. Cyber-bullying uses the same methods but is targeted against minors.

Indirect Cyber-Terrorism

Indirect cyberterrorism is IT-related terrorism but not directly affecting existing infrastructure. It is significantly bound to the evolution of information age, informatics and telecommunication, misusing the perception of freedom in virtual world. The model for indirect cyberterrorism is based on commonplace skills and value-judgments on the quality of information presented in the virtual world's many channels for information dissemination and exchange. We can observe two major impacts on the real world – on the media and on democratic institutions and mechanisms of society.

Media Terrorism and Hacktivism

The model for media terrorism introduces methods of psychological war and media manipulation into the virtual world. The public is in fact more sensitive to Internet-based news than from traditional media. This phenomenon is particularly apparent in the post-communist countries, where such traditional media as TV, newspapers or radio, are still perceived as government or political party

related[24]. As such, the virtual media's impact on the real world is more intensive than should be expected. Explanations and views of anything, the "truth" about something, become immediately more "clear" and more "truthful" when published via virtual world media. In the virtual world, virtual media, virtual encyclopedias and virtual scientific conclusions quickly become authoritative references without any further judgment.

We can cite two examples of virtual media misuse where cyberterrorist influence is apparent. The first one deal with virtual world newspapers and by using perception management completely new media can be created by taking most of their content from regular and serious sources. Key parts of articles could be slightly modified with the objective of influencing common views of some specific issue. This way public opinion can be easily manipulated, if the virtual medium has built enough reputation among targeted social groups[25].

The misuse of Internet media can be very effective in formal political, advertising, or public relations campaigns creating the impression of being spontaneous. The goal of such a campaign is usually to disguise the efforts of a political or commercial entity as an independent public reaction to a specific entity[26]. Also social web sites can be misused to create and organize revolt against a specific person (political leader, celebrity etc.) by masquerading as a virtual group, but represented by one real person only. Then, based on the impression that mass numbers of enthusiasts advocate some specific cause, specific hostile acts could be initiated even involving physical confrontation[27]. Hactivism[28] and eco-terrorism[29] often use tools of the virtual world to promote their objectives creating the illusion of mass support. They practice the promotion of their agendas by hacking, especially defacing or disabling websites.

The second example is "cybertronic", which is misuse of people's subliminal perception when observing an innocent scene on their monitor. The threat is hidden inside an animated picture, a banner, for example. There is no need for visible animation - the threat is created from a sequence of static pictures where just one of these holds a covert message unrecognizable by the conscious mind[30]. Live-motion animation changes content in fractions of seconds, so hidden information is not consciously noticed. Nevertheless the information is recognized by subliminal perception, affecting the subconscious mind and negatively or positively influencing subsequent thought, behavior, attitudes or beliefs. The practice of subliminal advertising has been banned by media regulators around the world, but in the virtual world it still exists (Taber, 2004).

Processing Terrorism and IT Governance

Processing terrorism and IT governance are not primarily part of the virtual world, but since they use its tools and environment, it is worth mentioning here. The first one, processing terrorism, is based on overloading the processing systems of public institutions – courts, government agencies, etc. When using computing power, the Internet and other means of the virtual world, an institution can be easily overloaded by presenting, for example, legal petitions, requests for decisions on non-existing or useless matters, etc. Moreover, e-mails, not spam, but regular e-mails can persistently be sent to public agencies soliciting responses. Such devices are often used by eco-terrorists, like filing lawsuits against "illegal" construction, or against some official decision about some artificially construed ecological problem. When such terrorists are paid off and they achieve desired publicity, the problem disappears.

IT governance exploits the shadow power of IT and refers to a subset discipline of Corporate Governance on information technology, systems and their performance. The opportunity for abuse derives from board-level executives delegating all key technical decisions to the company's IT professionals. The "black box" nature of IT inhibits IT

managers from independently making and being held solely accountable for poor decisions. So exaggeration of the value of IT skews decision-making, resulting in over-reliance an computer processing (calculation) even when real world evidence contradicts it.

The Virtual Battlefield

The virtual world is not only a domain for virtual personalities and communities but it also allows interaction of the virtual population by providing a virtual battlefield. Cyber-crime, cyberterrorism and other illegal activities became an inseparable part of the virtual life. These activities are global, exploiting the virtuality of the attacker, the intangibility of assets and the distorted perception of ethics and morality in the virtual world.

Cyber-terrorism, cybercrime and other conflicts in the virtual world use the same or similar tools – infoware. Contrary to classical symmetric military strategies, infoware and other weapons used on the virtual battlefield lead to asymmetrical strategy. In the first case, when threats are symmetrical, each party should use a comparable amount of finance and other means to oppose the other party. In asymmetrical combat, the assets of parties significantly differ. A single hacker with a simple personal computer, enough technical knowledge and time, can cause failures of critical infrastructure with subsequent loss of tens millions dollars.

Information warfare can be classified into two basic categories – offensive infoware and intelligence infoware. While offensive hardware typically involves weapon systems[31] aimed at targets within a limited territory, offensive software has a global impact[32]. The infoware software comprises among other things:

- Viruses, worms and logic bombs, implementing malicious functionalities into attacked computers,

- Trojan horses used for implementation of offensive software into compromised computer and providing covert communication with a coordinator of a subsequent distributed attack,
- Psychological infoware used to implement a covert channel to an enemy system and to utilize such a channel to alter enemy systems, perception management manipulation etc.
- Methods for diverting communications via telecom link to intercept this communication with the objective of changing transmitted information ("man in the middle" attack), etc.

Intelligence infoware is aimed at obtaining hidden information from enemy communications and computing systems or to support other means of psychological operations. Best-known examples of this are such global interception systems as US Echelon or Russian FAPSI, used for global eavesdropping of all electronic communications.

The virtual battlefield created by real attackers has become part of our daily life. Cyber-wars are ongoing in the virtual world without even being noticed by public. The weapons are information and processing tools used to gain information superiority to be used for economic or political control.

THE VIRTUAL WORLD AND WEB ATTACKS

According to Netcraft Web Server Survey there is roughly 185 million web servers hosting an estimated 60 billion web pages. A web page is the most visible part of the Internet. But publicly accessed and widely distributed web pages are the easiest target to attack.

Any web page can be attacked or could even be a source of attack. Any attack on the web can have real world impact - chaos, deceit, extortion, identity theft, monetary loss etc. An attack can even cause physical pain or have political impact. Virtual attacks can be classified by common signatures to be taken into account for institutional or government security policy. The classification itself is debatable and a common taxonomy is difficult. For our purpose, some examples based on the typology of the Web Application Security Consortium (WASC) are given below[33].

Impact on the Real World

Close interaction between the virtual world and the real world brings the impact of events in virtual world into our daily life. In the following paragraphs we look at \some of the most common examples of such impacts which had been caused by or have a close relationship to the Internet. The effects of malicious software, spam, spam links, downtime caused by overloading services and other tools are not mentioned below, so it is important to bear in mind that the attacks mentioned below are not only types.

Panic and Chaos

Panic and chaos can be disseminated by means of the virtual world and has an immediate impact on the real world. A rumor propagated via several Internet channels mixed in with elements truth could end up provoking panic, irrational behavior and physical damage or lost lives.

The English edition of the Russian news agency Novosti (Novosti, 2008) reports spreading a rumor about a nuclear accident near St. Petersburg. Hackers attacked Russian nuclear power websites and brought down almost all sites providing access to the Automatic Radiation Environment Control System (ASKRO) which allows users to check radiation background in the region. To spread false rumors of a nuclear accident, the attackers posted on several Internet forums reports of radioactive emissions from the Leningrad Nuclear Power Plant and of a planned evacuation of local residents. Meanwhile, e-mails confirming the rumor were distributed to e-mail addresses in the region.

According to a spokesman for Rosatom, the state nuclear corporation, the cyberattacks on ASKRO servers had been planned and coincided with the release of the reports and e-mails. In 2007, after similar false reports of an accident at the Volgodonsk nuclear plant, several dozen people, believing they could have been affected by radiation, consumed large amounts of iodine and fell ill with iodine poisoning.

Deceit

Deceit is a core feature of many virtual world crimes. Substantial amounts of people get duped or trapped by scams from social engineering via bogus e-mails to perception management, etc.[34]. in a virtual world infested with forged wikipedia pages, misleading hoaxes etc.

John Abell, journalist of Wired magazine, in his story from January 22, 2009 describes hackers counterfeiting his story on Steve Jobs' health[35] (Abell, 2009). The hoaxer creates a cursorily valid-looking page containing an image under a genuine Wired logo banner. The story about Jobs suffering a cardiac arrest was neither his nor true. Actual impact on the real world was disinformation causing possible damage to Apple shares.

Extortion and Racketeering

The threat of physical, social or financial damage and its avoidance by pay-off to a racketeer is one of the oldest crimes. The same model in the virtual world is often used. The story which follows is not exceptional. Celebrities' MySpace pages are regular targets for hackers looking to increase their notoriety or expose private photos and messages.

American rapper Soulja Boy has been targeted by cybervandals who defaced his MySpace profile and published his e-mail and YouTube passwords on the Internet (SMH, 2008). The hackers contacted Soulja Boy and demanded over US$2500 in order to regain control over his account. When he refused, his MySpace page was wiped out and replaced with obscene messages declaring his homosexuality and vilifying messages to fans. The case ended when Soulja Boy's agent contacted MySpace and demanded the account be returned.

Identity Theft

About ten million Americans are victims of identity theft each year. While many of the victims, about 45%, find out about the identity theft within three months, close to 20% of victims take four years or longer before discovering they are victims of identity theft. Over two hundred billion dollars a year is lost by businesses worldwide due to identity theft[36]. The following story (Cadwallader, 2007) is just one of many.

Six suspects in central Ohioans were under investigation for hacking into a government web site and stealing social security numbers to create false credit accounts. Police got suspicious when someone was randomly feeding social security numbers into site, which contained personal information on thousands of people. Once a number was hit on, the name, address, age and other information could be used to obtain credit cards and open bank accounts. According to detectives evidence on more than 270 victims has been turned over to federal authorities, but more people nationwide might have been victimized by the security lapse on that web site.

Financial Loss

Financial loss or loss of sales is a direct or indirect result of every computer hack. Methods of hacks could be different and not necessarily in direct connection with the system hacked. The hijacking via DNS spoofing is a very common method and when the nation's largest e-bill payment system was hijacked, then the monetary loss could be enormous. Brian Krebs of the Washington Post published the story (Krebs, 2008).

Atlanta based CheckFree company controls roughly 70 percent of the U.S. online bill pay market and more than 24 million people use their services. Hackers, using a spoofed DNS site, managed to redirect the customer login page to a Web site in Ukraine for several hours. There is evidence that at least 5,000 people were redirected to the Ukrainian site during the four and half hours of the attack. CheckFree.com was not the only site that the attackers hijacked and redirected to the Ukrainian server. At least 70 other domains pointing to the same Ukrainian address were found during that same time period.

Physical Pain

Computer attacks generally do not directly harm the computer user or do not inflict physical pain on their victims. Rare attacks of such kind are apparently motivated by malice rather than money. Robertson in USA Today (Robertson, 2008) has described a hacker attack who bombarded the Epilepsy Foundation's Web site with hundreds of pictures and links to pages with rapidly flashing images. As is well-known, people with photosensitive epilepsy can get seizures when they're exposed to flickering images - such seizures have been observed with video games and cartoons and in rare cases can be caused by low speed scanning of TV.

The attack used a security hole in the foundation's publishing software that made it possible to quickly upload numerous posts and overwhelm the site's support forums. Within the hacker's posts were small flashing pictures and links to pages that exploded with kaleidoscopic images pulsating with different colors. The breach triggered severe migraines and near-seizure reactions in several site visitors who viewed the images.

Defacement

Defacement, one of the most visible types of attacks, has many forms of implementation and usage. The simplest method of defacement is redirection to another server with the intended content. Defacement is often used by art groups to present their artistic work on compromised servers. Political defacement is used mostly as an ideological tool by political, religious and other movements (Figure 3).

Computer arts known also as computer graffiti is often spread by defacement of innocent servers. Robert Lemos (Lemos, 2001) describes activity of a hacker group, known as PoizonB0x, which put its online graffiti on 12 sites within a week[37]. Sometimes the hacking graffiti has a highly professional colorful look, even including animated graffiti.

Defacement is often used as a tool for political conflict, either by direct defacement of a politi-

Figure 3. Graffiti used by hacker group Silver Lord for hacking in 2005 (black&white copy)

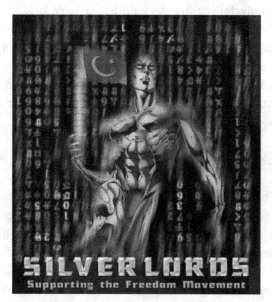

cal adversary's server or by diverting incoming requests to other web pages administered by the hacker. In one such attack recent attack during the last U.S. election campaign, hackers exploited a simple coding vulnerability in Barack Obama's website to redirect visitors to his community blogs section to Hillary Rodham Clinton's official campaign site.

Why Webs

Webs and the www structure are the most visible part of the virtual world. If the user is searching for some information, than it searches web pages – so web pages are most natural way of spreading information. Information presented on web pages are the essential part of the virtual world being accessed by the Internet's large population of users. As has been shown, web pages are misused in many different ways and because of their simple accessibility can be used as a media to create threats or as a tool of attack.

Persons addictive to the Internet are the most vulnerable to web misuse, because their access to the virtual world is via web technologies. As we have seen, the addictive person living in his enjoyable virtual environment tends to believe information presented in virtual world much more than real information from real environment. Moreover, being overloaded by information from the virtual world, the ability to accept further information from the surrounding real world is decreased and unconsciously suppressed. This makes the addictive person, whose opinions are created and modified by information obtained via web pages, most vulnerable to threats and a danger to the security of the environment.

FUTURE RESEARCH DIRECTION

The aforesaid survey suggests several research questions. As we peer into the future, there is much work to do. As a partial list of future directions we should suggest:

- Examine the role of technology in behavioral changes. Combine technological observation of behavior with human judgment. Would there be a tendency for humans to rely overly upon the technology over time?

- Identify the optimal set of condition for prevention of internet addiction and its influence on security in virtual world.

- In psychology and psychiatry we should focus on study of methods of early diagnosis and treatment of netholism and netmania as well as their prevention.

- In sociology, the evolution of virtual communities, their background and influence of virtual communities on daily real life would be the subject of further studies.

- A sharp development of cyber crime and cyber terrorism is expected in coming future, so methods to identify, investigate and fight these illegal activities should be the center of interest of future studies.

- As a matter of fact, the only way for public cyber security is continual education of users. To identify optimal interaction style between cyber security, educational institutions and the public would be a key point for future research in the area of security in virtual world.

We have pointed out some of the most important future direction of research, but the reader can easily identify many other issues for scientific attention.

CONCLUSION

We have covered a substantial part of the sociological and psychological aspects of human behavior in the virtual world of Internet in the context of their impact on security. The virtual individual, and virtual communities formed by such virtual individuals, have created a new virtual world with its own rules which often diverge from the normal order of society over the centuries. The influence of the Internet goes beyond normal bounds by fostering dependency - addiction to the Internet. We have posited that such dependent behavior, Internet Addiction Disorder, is a mental disease.

We have described the basic behavior, goals and ambitions of virtual communities, which are created on the Internet for different reasons. As security threats we have highlighted the formation of virtual communities whose main tendency is to misuse the virtual world for illegal goals. A prime example of this is misuse of the Internet for perception manipulation to subvert public opinion. In this particular case we have noted that Internet addictively creates vulnerable targets for communities or individuals using the virtual world for illegal purposes. Cybercrime, cyberterrorism and the Internet as virtual battlefield have each been analyzed with respect to the sociological and psychological background of the attacker. As a broadly accessed and easily understandable medium, we have described examples of attacks using web pages.

Based on the view of the Internet presented here as part of the virtual world, we should conclude that new forms of virtual existence foster new or modified risks and new or modified forms of human behavior. The broad acceptance, global impact and common awareness of the Internet has brought new ways of attacking counterparties in society, to which we either have to adapt or we have to find a means to oppose. Unfortunately, society's increasing dependence on technology, especially on the Internet, accompanied by addiction to the virtual world, escalates the impact on security. We must therefore incorporate these factors into our new security policies, defense strategies and political assessments, as well as in our daily life.

REFERENCES

Abell, J. C. (2009). Wired.com Image Viewer Hacked to Create Phony Steve Jobs Health Story. *Wired Magazine*. Retrieved from January 22, 2009, Retrieved February 20, 2009 from http://www.wired.com/epicenter/2009/01/wiredcom-imagev/

Aghatise, E. J. (2006). Cybercrime definition. *Computer Crime Research Center*. Retrieved January 20, 2009, from http://www.crime-research.org/articles/joseph06/

Ahn, D. H. (2007). Korean policy on treatment and rehabilitation for adolescents' Internet addiction. In 2007 *International Symposium on the Counseling and Treatment of Youth Internet Addiction*, (pp. 49), Seoul, Korea, National Youth Commission

Bargh, J. A., & McKenna, K. Y. M. (2004). The Internet and Social Life. *Annual Review of Psychology*, 55(February), 573–590. doi:10.1146/annurev.psych.55.090902.141922

Block, J. J. (2007). Pathological computer use in the USA. In *International Symposium on the Counseling and Treatment of Youth Internet Addiction*, (pp. 433), Seoul, Korea, National Youth Commission.

Brandon, P. D., & Hollingshead, A. B. (2007). Characterizing online groups. In Joinson, A. N., McKenna, K. Y. N., Postmes, T., & Reips, U. D. (Eds.), *Oxford Handbook of Internet Psychology* (pp. 105–119). Oxford, UK: Oxford University Press.

Cadwallader, B. (2007). Feds take over municipal court Web-hacking probe. *The Columbus Dispatch*, December 22. Retrieved October 26, 2008 from http://www.dispatch.com/live/content/local_news/stories/2007/12/20/clerkh.html

Carnegie-Mellon. (2005). *Insider Threat Study: Computer System Sabotage in Critical Infrastructure Sectors*. Pittsburgh, PA: Software Engineering Institute, Carnegie Mellon University.

Douglas, K. M. (2007). Psychology, discrimination and hate groups online. In Joinson, A. N., McKenna, K. Y. N., Postmes, T., & Reips, U. D. (Eds.), *Oxford Handbook of Internet Psychology* (pp. 155–163). Oxford, UK: Oxford University Press, Oxford.

EC. (2001). The Convention on Cyber Crime. *Council of Europe - Treaty Office CETS No. 185.* Retrieved April 12, 2006 from http://conventions. coe.int/Treaty/en/Treaties/Html/185.htm

Ferris, J. R. (1997). *Internet Addiction Disorder: Causes, Symptoms and Consequences,* Retrieved September 26, 2001, http://www.files.chem. vt.edu/chem-dept/dessy/honors/papers/ferris. html

Goldberg, I. (1995). *Internet Addiction Disorder (IAD) at PsyCom.Net.* Retrieved January 7, 2001 from http://web.urz.uni-heidelberg.de/Netzdienste/anleitung/wwwtips/8/addict.html

Goldin, R. (2006). Hyping Internet Addiction. *Stats Articles.* Retrived August 17, 2009, from http://stats.org/stories/2006/hype_web_addiction_nov16_06.htm

Grivna, T., & Polcak, R. (2008). *Kyberkriminalita a pravo (Cybercrime and Law).* Prague, Czech Republic: Auditorium.

Hu, J. (2000). Outage a deliberate attack, Yahoo says. *CNET News,* February 7, 2000. Retrieved August 5, 2005 from http://news.cnet.com/2100-1023-236594.html

Hučín, J. (2000). Droga jménem Internet. *Chip CZ, 7/2000,* 7–9.

Hughes, D. M. (2001). The "Natasha" Trade: Transnational Sex Trafficking. *National Institute of Justice Journal January.* Retrieved February 22, 2009 from http://www.ncjrs.gov/pdffiles1/jr000246c.pdf

Jirovska, A. (2009). *Negativni vlivy televize na rozvoj ditete.* Unpublished master thesis, Faculty of Pedagogy, Charles University, Prague, Czech Republic.

Jirovsky, V. (2004). *Kybernalita. Presented at regular student lectures at Faculty of Mathematics and Physics.* Prague: Charles University.

Jirovsky, V. (2007). *Kybernalita – kybernetická kriminalita.* Prague: Grada Publishing.

Jirovsky, V. (2007a). *Virtual communities and cyber terrorism,* Paper presented at Security and Protection of Information Conference, Brno 2007, Czech Republic

Jirovsky, V. (2008). *Kyberprostor.* Paper presented at the meeting of the state attorneys and judges on problem of cyber criminality, Kromeriz, Czech Republic

Ko, C., Yen, J., Liu, S., Huang, C., & Yen, C. (2009). *The Associations Between Aggressive Behaviors and Internet Addiction and Online Activities* in Adolescents. *The Journal of Adolescent Health, 44*(6), 598–605. doi:10.1016/j.jadohealth.2008.11.011

Kottasová, I., & Kubita, J. (2008). Čestí politici vnikli na Facebook. Zatím dva. *Hospodarske noviny,* May 12, 2008. Retrieved September 7, 2008 from http://hn.ihned.cz/2-24682660-500000_d-e4

Krebs, B. (2008). Hackers Hijacked Large E-Bill Payment Site. *The Washington Post,* December 3, 2008. Retrieved January 10, 2009 from http://voices.washingtonpost.com/ securityfix/2008/12/hackers_hijacked_large_e-bill.html

Lemos, R. (2001). Security sites hit by graffiti gang. *ZDNet.com,* June 14, 2001. Retrieved May 17, 2005 from http://news.zdnet.co.uk/security/0,1000000189,2088969,00.htm

Lin, S. S. J., & Tsai, C. C. (1999). *Internet Addiction among High Schoolers in Taiwan*. Paper presented at the Annual Meeting of the American Psychological Association, Boston August 20-24, 1999. Retrieved July 16, 2008 from http://www.eric.ed.gov/ERICDocs/data/ ericdocs2sql/content_storage_01/0000019b/80/29/c4/92.pdf

Mentor. (1986). *The Conscience of a Hacker, 1*(7), Phile 3, Phrack Inc. January 8, 1986.

Novosti. (2008). Russian nuclear power websites attacked amid accident rumor. *RIA Novosti*, May 23, 2008, Retrieved February 10, 2009 from http://en.rian.ru/russia/20080523/ 108202288.html

Poulsen, K. (2007). Cyberwar' and Estonia's Panic Attack. *Wired Magazine*, August 22, 2007. Retrieved November 2, 2007 from http://www.wired.com/threatlevel/2007/08/cyber-war-and-e/

Robertson, J. (2008). Hackers' posts on epilepsy forum cause migraines, seizures. *USA Today*, May 7, 2008. Retrieved September 25, 2008 from http://www.usatoday.com/tech/products/2008-05-07-1007914798_x.htm

Security. (2009). *The Web Application Security Consortium (WASC)*. Retrieved anytime from http://www.webappsec.org/

SMH. (2008). Soulja Boy at war over MySpace hack attack. *stuff.co.nzNews*. Retrieved November 2, 2008 from http://www.stuff.co.nz/technology/609208

Suler, J. (1997). *The Psychology of Cyberspace Homepage* [On-line book]. Retrieved November 12, 2001, from http://www.rider.edu/users/suler/psycyber/psycyber.html

Taber, J. (2004). Liberal justice can be painful. *The Globe and Mail*, Tuesday, June 15, (pp. A6).

Tang, R. (2001). China-U.S. cyber war escalates. *CNN.COM*. Retrieved June 2, 2005 from http://archives.cnn.com/2001/WORLD/asiapcf/east/04/27/china.hackers/index.html

Thorens, G., Khazaal, Y., & Billieux, J., Linden van der M. & Zullino D. (2009). Swiss Psychiatrists' Beliefs and Attitudes About Internet Addiction. *The Psychiatric Quarterly, 80*(2), 117–123. doi:10.1007/s11126-009-9098-2

Tryfonas, T. (2008, April). *IT governance and the role of the information security professional*. Paper presented at Centre for Security, Communications and Network Research University of Plymouth. Retrieved July 7, 2009 from http://www.cisnr.org/presentations/16-04-2008-TheodoreTryfonas.pdf

Walther, J. B., Boos, M., & Jonas, K. J. (2002). Misattribution and attributional redirection in distributed virtual groups. In *Proceedings of the 35th Annual Hawaii International Conference on System Sciences, 2002, IEEE Conference Proceedings*. Washington, DC: IEEE Press.

Websense. (2007). *Information Protection and Control: Targeting the Insider Threat* [White paper]. Retrieved September 9, 2008, from www.bitpipe.com

Young, K. (1996, August). *Internet Addiction: The Emergence of a New Clinical Disorder*. Paper presented at the 104th annual meeting of the American Psychological Association, Toronto, Canada, August 15, 1996

Young, K. S. (1997) *What Makes the Internet Addictive: Potential Explanation for Pathological Internet Use*. Paper presented at the 105th annual conference of the American Psychological Association, August 15, 1997, Chicago, IL

ADDITIONAL READING

The reader interested in virtual communities and Internet psychology should find further information e.g. in following sources:

Careaga, A. (2002). *Hooked on the Net – How to Say "Goodnight" When the Party Never Ends*. Grand Rapids, USA: Kregel Publication.

Ruggiero K.J., Resnick H.S. et all (2006) *Internet-based intervention for mental health and substance use problems in the aftermath of mass violence and disasters: a pilot feasibility study* in Behavior Therapy. 2006; 37(2):190-205

Schell, B. H. (2006). *The Internet and Society: A Reference Handbook*. Oxford, UK: ABC-CLIO.

Spinello, R., & Tavani, H. (2001). *Readings in CyberEthics*. Boston: Jones and Bartlett.

The reader interested in cybercrime and cyberterrorism should find further information in Book Series Lecture Notes in Computer Science published by Springer Berlin in March 2006 with focus on Category Web and Text Mining for Terrorism Informatics. The publication is numbered as Volume 3917/2006 "Book Intelligence and Security Informatics" and marked by ISBN 978-3-540-33361-6. The following sources would also be useful:

Loader, B., & Douglas, T. (2000). *Cybercrime: Security and Surveillance in the Information Age*. New York: Routledge.

Westby, J. (2003). *International Guide to Combating Cybercrime*. Chicago: ABA.

ENDNOTES

[1] The virtual world is sometimes called "cyberspace." The term "cyberspace" was coined by William Gibson in his novel "Burning Chrome" in 1982. We can also use the expression "virtual environment."

[2] The statistic is estimated for pattern of approx. 1.6×10^9 users by the middle of year 2009, original numbers from www.internetworldstats.com.

[3] Chat rooms would be a good example of such behavior.

[4] As a matter of fact, according to police experience, less than 20% of attackers are apprehended, after preliminary hearing only another 20% percent goes to trial and only half of them are found guilty and sentenced.

[5] Sweden has one of the largest penetrations of Internet usage, about 75% of the population.

[6] Statistical research based on numbers from the year 2006 (source www.mafo.at – Austrian Internet Monitor).

[7] This is about one-third higher than addiction on heroin.

[8] A false sense of anonymity and intimacy led them to the conclusion when using a nickname, that no one would know who they are.

[9] MUD – Multi-User Dungeons – types of Internet communication tools similar to the game Dungeons & Dragons. The virtual person in the MUD has his own, manner of conducting combat, choice of weapons, etc.

[10] By "chat" we mean chat room communication only.

[11] According to the novell of Robert L. Stevenson „Strange Case of Dr. Jekyll and Mr. Hyde".

[12] A good example of this model of behavior is an unsatisfied employee who is seeking revenge against his employer who caused him some harm – e.g. he feels not appreciated enough for his work.

[13] Another good example could be hacker satisfaction when he breaks into a well-defended system.

[14] E.g. they could get financial award when they allow access to computer system to the agent of competition.

[15] In 48% they had been released from employment, 38% had resigned and 7% have been sent to compulsory vacations of unidentified length.

[16] The "release" is a final product of the warez team, and teams compete to be the first to publish an error-free product.

[17] The term infoware is used for specialized software for attacking enemy infrastructure.

[18] The military units for information war are specialized units created more less in every well-organized military structure. Their importance arose after the Second World War and especially during the Cold War.

[19] Duration of single attack, not a series of attacks focused on one target.

[20] The cyberattacks came at time when Estonia was embroiled in a dispute with Russia over the removal of a Soviet-era war memorial from the center of Tallinn. Moscow denied any involvement in the attacks, but Estonian officials were convinced of Russia's involvement in the plot.

[21] The hidden channel method is more dangerous for the attacker.

[22] This Distributed Denial of Service attack overwhelmed the Web hosting company's routers beginning at around 10:20 a.m. PST, and apparently ending shortly after 1 p.m. PST at February 7, 2000.

[23] For example, e-mail, instant messaging or messages posted to a Web site or a discussion group.

[24] The most probable explanation of this phenomenon is the sense of freedom in the virtual world, where anyone can say anything without any further censorship.

[25] The Snopes, also known as the Urban Legends Reference Pages, are good example of such misuse – see www.snopes.com.

[26] The term "astroturfing" for such a method of media manipulation had been coined by former US Senator Lloyd Bentsen.

[27] In 2009, the "egg protest" in the Czech Republic was started using Facebook as a medium, where the physical movement of a group had been started and organized by two high school students. As a result, the leader of the social democratic party was repeatedly attacked by "egg throwers" at public meetings.

[28] Hacktivism – the nonviolent use of illegal or legally ambiguous tools of the virtual world in pursuit of political ends. The term was coined by the hackers group "Cult of the Dead Cow".

[29] Movement intended to hinder activities that are marked as damaging to the environment by ecology activists.

[30] Also static pictures are used with messages hidden in a suitably formatted pattern.

[31] For example, an EMG pulse bomb - when the explosive is fired, the coil inside the bomb generates high energy electromagnetic pulse capable of disrupting all electronic devices in range of few hundred meters.

[32] This is one of the reasons why usage of infoware by the Army of United States is under the control and decision of the President, similarly to nuclear weapons.

[33] A more detailed taxonomy and database of attacks cab be found in (Security, 2009).

[34] For example, the efficiency of phishing mails is estimated at a level of 5%.

[35] Steven P. Jobs (born February 24, 1955) is an American businessman, co-founder and CEO of Apple Inc.

[36] See http://www.spamlaws.com/id-theft-statistics.html for the most up to date numbers.

[37] In April 2001, PoizonB0x carry out mass graffiti attack of Chinese sites, getting up almost 300 defacements over two months.

Chapter 4
Understanding Risk and Risk–Taking Behavior in Virtual Worlds

Fariborz Farahmand
Purdue University, USA

Eugene H. Spafford
Purdue University, USA

ABSTRACT

Virtual worlds have seen tremendous growth in recent years. However, security and privacy risks are major considerations in different forms of commerce and exchange in virtual worlds. The studies of behavioral economics and lessons from markets provide fertile ground in the employment of virtual worlds to demonstrate and examine behaviors. In this chapter, we address user and organizational concerns about security and privacy risks by exploring the relationships among risk, perception of risk, and economic behavior in virtual worlds. To make their interaction more effective, we recommend organizations to understand perceptions of risk in virtual worlds and then implement policies and procedures to enhance trust and reduce risk. Such understanding depends in turn on the multidisciplinary nature of cyber security economics and online behavior.

INTRODUCTION

The rich domains of *virtual worlds* provide new environments, new economies and new institutions. Gartner (2009) has predicted that by the end of 2011 80% of active internet users would have a second life in a virtual world and that major enterprises will find value in participating in these venues. These numbers indicate that human interaction with the virtual is expected to approach some of the extremes seen in popular science fiction works such as True Names (Vinge 1981) and Halting State (Stross 2007).

However, activities in virtual worlds, as in any other online environment, can be associated with risks and uncertainties. Gartner Group lists information technology risks, identity and access management concerns, loss of confidentiality, brand and reputation damage, and productivity reduction as issues facing corporations in dealing with virtual worlds (Gartner 2007). The European Network and Information Security Agency

DOI: 10.4018/978-1-61520-891-3.ch004

(ENISA) and Arakji and Lang (2007) list 14 and 7 (respectively) categories of risks associated with virtual worlds. But, how can users and corporations evaluate these risks and the effectiveness of corresponding mitigation mechanisms? What actually motivates people to risk time and actual money in virtual worlds? Finding answers to these questions is essential for managing risks in virtual worlds. This chapter presents a basic overview of perceptions of risk in virtual worlds by different stakeholders and how they may respond to these risks. In particular, we explore some of the factors that may influence the risk evaluations that corporations may make when deciding involvement in virtual worlds. We also explain companies that are planning to operate in the virtual worlds need to understand the roles of trust and risk and should monitor user perceptions in order to understand their relation to risk aversion and risk management.

DEFINING RISK

For us to understand the human behavior in virtual worlds, an explicit and accepted definition of risk is essential; however, the definition of risk is inherently controversial. When planning some course of action, people tend to evaluate issues of cost and benefit against the possibility of losses and adverse consequences. Those potential losses and adverse consequences are known as *risk*. Knight (1921) made his famous distinction between risk and uncertainty by explaining that risk is ordinarily used in a loose way to refer to any sort of uncertainty viewed from the standpoint of an unfavorable contingency, and uncertainty similarly with reference to favorable outcomes. Understanding and measuring risk enables people to choose prudent courses of action and make appropriate investments in protection and mitigation.

In classical decision theory, risk is most commonly conceived as reflecting variation in the distribution of possible outcomes, their likelihoods, and their subjective values (March and Shapira,

1987). Risk is measured either by nonlinearities in the revealed utility for money or by the variance of the probability distribution of possible gains and losses associated with a particular alternative (Pratt 1964, Arrow 1965) --i.e., distorted valuation or irregular risk perception by individuals. Fischhoff et al. (1984) argues that values regarding the relative importance of different possible adverse consequences for a particular decision can change with the changes in the decision maker, the technologies considered, or the decision problem. Fischoff and his co-authors developed a framework showing how these value issues can be systemically addressed while considering the sources of controversy in defining risk.

PRIVACY RISKS

Virtual worlds are commonly perceived as being completely separate from the real lives of their users and therefore immune to the privacy risks posed by other emerging platforms such as social networks (ENISA 2008). However, representing a user as an avatar—the computer representation of the user—is not that different from any other form of online persona – users are free to present as accurate or inaccurate a picture as they choose. This may expose virtual world users to many kinds of privacy risks, (e.g., identity disclosure). Certain characteristics of the avatar owner can be guessed with reasonable accuracy based on statistical analysis. For example, a survey of the 2001 fantasy game Everquest, with 889 users, showed that only 2.5% of female users and 15.7% of male users had played characters of the opposite gender. Thus, using these figures, if an avatar in this game is male, his owner is very likely to be male (84.3% of males and 2.5% of females will play a male character, and male gamers generally vastly outnumber females) (Yee 2001).

According to ENISA (2008) many service providers implement extensive mining features within their gaming environment to detect anomalous and harmful game-play. In-game advertising increasingly uses avatar behavior to infer the characteristics of the avatar owner for advertising purposes.

RELATING SECURITY AND PRIVACY

Questions of who has what rights to information about individuals for what purposes in virtual worlds become more important as we move toward an environment in which it is technically possible to know just about anything about anyone. Deciding how we are to design privacy considerations in technology for the future includes philosophical, legal, and practical dimensions. There is a considerable overlap between issues related to access to resources and issues related to appropriate use of information. Data base security and privacy experts see the former as being primarily in the domain of security (access control), and the latter as being primarily in the domain of privacy protections (Karat et al. 2009).

Security in virtual worlds may refer to many aspects of protecting a system from unauthorized use (e.g., authentication of users). For this chapter, we will limit our treatment of security to the concepts associated with how well a system protects access to information it contains. The concept of privacy goes beyond security to examine how well the use of information conforms to the explicit or implicit assumptions regarding that use that are associated with the personal information. There is an important distinction that we recognize when discussing privacy from a virtual world view: From an end user perspective, privacy can be considered as *preventing storage* of personal information, or it can be viewed as *ensuring appropriate use* of personal information (Karat et al. 2009). For the purposes of this chapter, a simple but useful definition of privacy is: "The ability of virtual world users to control the terms under which their personal information is acquired and used." Virtual world users expect a given activity

in which they participate to be conducted fairly and address their privacy concerns. By ensuring this fairness and respecting privacy, companies give their customers the confidence to disclose personal information—and to allow that information subsequently to be used to create consumer profiles for business use.

In summary, security involves technology to ensure that information is appropriately protected. Security is a required building block for privacy to be protected. Privacy involves mechanisms to support compliance with some basic principles and other explicitly-stated policies. Basic principles suggest that users should be informed about information collection, told in advance what will be done with their information, and given a reasonable opportunity to approve such usage of their information. A related concept, **trust**, is seen as increasing when it is perceived that both security and privacy are appropriately supported.

ROLE OF PERCEPTION IN RISK TAKING BEHAVIOR IN VIRTUAL WORLDS

The role of perception of information security risks has been studied by several researchers. Moores and Dhillon (2003) explain that with each new case of online fraud, the perception by consumers will continue to be that Internet thieves lurk in the shadows of cyberspace, widening the trust gap and constraining the legitimate commerce being carried out online. Kim and Prabhakar (2000) argue that trust in the electronic channel and perceived risks of e-commerce are the major determinants of adoption behavior. Adams (2000) conducted a study of privacy concerns in an audio/video captured environment. Results showed that user perception of privacy was shaped by the perceived identity of the information *receiver*, the perceived *usage* of the information, the subjective *sensitivity* of the disclosed information, and the *context* in which the information was disclosed.

Fischoff and his colleagues (1978) investigated perceptions of technology risks, and particularly ways to determine when a product is acceptably safe. Their nine dimensions of perception of risk translate easily to consideration of perception of risk in different scenarios. For example, here we adapt these nine dimensions to define *risk perception* of virtual world users:

1. Does the user voluntarily get involved in the virtual world (voluntariness)?
2. To what extent is the risk of consequence from the virtual world user's action (to him/her) immediate (immediacy of effect)?
3. To what extent are the risks known (precisely) by the virtual world user who is exposed to those risks (knowledge about risk)?
4. To what extent are the risks precisely known and quantified (knowledge to science)?
5. To what extent can the virtual world user, by personal skill or diligence, avoid the consequences to him/her while engaging in the untoward activity (control over risk)?
6. Does the risk affect the virtual world user over time or is it a risk that affects a larger number of people (virtual or real) at once (chronic-catastrophic)?
7. Are these risks new to the virtual world user or is there some prior experience/conditioning (newness)?
8. Is this a risk that the virtual world user has rationalized and can think about reasonably calmly (common-dread)?
9. When is the risk from the activity realized in the form of consequences to the user (severity of consequences)?

It has been shown that unknown risk and dread risk can be used to account for about 80 percent of the results generated by using all nine variables that were originally introduced by Fischoff and his colleagues (e.g., Johnson and Tversky 1984; Slovic 1987). We have revised the Fischhoff and Slovic model of risk perceptions — introducing

ordinal scales to the identified characteristics of risk perceptions, and incorporating the dynamics of perception by including the important and neglected time element. Here, we present a simplified version of this model applied to virtual worlds. For more information about this model see Farahmand et al. (2008).

Applying Risk Perception Model in Virtual Worlds

We formulated a model based on the psychometric model of risk perception developed by Fischoff, Slovic and others, in which characteristics of a risk are correlated with its acceptance. We then modified that model to condense Fischoff's nine variables of risk by considering *understanding* (familiarity and experience) and *consequences* (scope, duration, and impact) to the stakeholder as the two principal characteristics of information security and privacy risks as shown in Figure 1.

For the first dimension of the model, addressing consequences of the breach, we can posit scenarios to explore the fear virtual world users have of the potential effects of the risk of information security losses.

If we explore the fear virtual world users have of the potential effects to them of the risks of perpetrating IT misuse, we can model the *consequences* of the breach to them. To model this, we

Figure 1. Characteristics of perceptions of information security and privacy risks

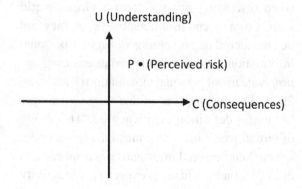

consider three main questions: (1) How serious are effects perceived by the virtual world users? (2) How immediate are effects on virtual world users? and (3) How much do virtual world users fear the effects? Analyzing these questions enables us to assign a simple metric to this dimension of the model. We define five levels of *consequence*:

- **Level 1:** Effects are trivial, temporary and commonplace
- **Level 2:** Effects are potentiality serious but treatable/recoverable
- **Level 3:** Effects are serious, long term but considered normal
- **Level 4:** Effects are serious, ongoing and raise deep concerns
- **Level 5:** Effects are catastrophic, ongoing and highly feared

The level definitions ("trivial," "serious," etc.) are based on those published by the National Institute of Standards and Technology (see Stonebumer et al. 2002). Level 5 and level 1 represent the highest and lowest level of consequences to stakeholders, respectively.

For the second dimension, *understanding*, we can explore the factors motivating virtual world users to consider certain risks while dismissing others. These questions are intended to identify affective factors that influence users' cognitive understanding of cause and effect. This resolves into two main questions: (1) who (among the virtual world users group) understand the hazard? (2) What do virtual world users know?

Our framework for categorizing *understanding* is based on the work of Bloom and Krathwhol (1956). In this, our interest is in understanding risk causes and effects using the cognitive domain, and what adds to virtual world users' motivation to increase understanding using the affective domain. We obtain the following six-level metric for the *understanding* dimension of our model by answering these questions:

- **Level 1: Evaluation:** Can the virtual world user make judgments about the value of ideas or materials?
- **Level 2: Synthesis:** Can the virtual world user build a structure or pattern from diverse elements?
- **Level 3: Analysis:** How virtual world users distinguish between facts and inferences.
- **Level 4: Application:** How virtual world users use a concept in a new situation or unprompted use of an abstraction.
- **Level 5: Comprehension:** Can the virtual world users understand the problem, for e.g. state a problem in his/her own words?
- **Level 6: Knowledge:** Can the virtual world user recall data or information?

Level 6 and level 1 represent the lowest and the highest level of understanding, respectively.

The perceived risk in our model is a function of *consequence* and *understanding*. An approximate perceived risk *score* may be constructed from the consequence metric and the inverse of the understanding metric. The perceived risk score therefore increases whenever the consequences are more severe for stakeholders, and decreases as the stakeholder gains deeper understanding of the nature and limits of the risk. Some cases may not match this model exactly but this score is nonetheless a good match for many case studies and the experiences of the experts interviewed in our validation study.

Example: Stealing identity for credit card fraud of a virtual world user. Imagine the identity of a virtual world user has been stolen during purchasing an island in Second Life—using credit card. As the first incident occurs, virtual world user's understanding is low at first—levels 5 and 4 of "U" dimension. Understanding increases with time, and reaches a maximum—Levels 2 and1. Thereafter, there is little increase for subsequent incidents. Typically, there may be a sudden increase in consequences—from level 2 to level 4 of *"C" Dimension—which may either grow or decrease with time, depending on the kind of fraud perpetrated. Privacy loss may increase with time as the victim is required to expose more details to recover, but eventually the loss subsides to a steady-state of lasting privacy loss.*

ATTITUDES TOWARD RISK

What are the users' perspectives on risk and risk-taking in virtual worlds? These authors argue many findings by previous researchers in the field of decision sciences can be applied to understand the behavior of the virtual world users. According to the traditional principles of finance, to achieve higher potential returns one must incur higher risks. In the light of utility analysis, traditional theories of decision-making identify three types of attitudes towards risk in virtual worlds (Kirkwood 1997):

1. **Risk averse:** A corporation in a virtual world will "sell" an uncertain alternative for less than its expected value to avoid risk of an undesirable outcome.
2. **Risk seeker:** A corporation in a virtual world will "sell" alternatives only for more than their expected values.
3. **Risk neutral:** A corporation in a virtual world will "sell" alternatives for exactly their expected values.

They also define risk tolerance for a particular decision maker by having that person specify the certainty equivalent for a particularly simple alternative, and use this certainty equivalent to determine risk tolerance. Certainty equivalent is the amount of money that is equivalent in a decision maker's mind to a given situation that involves uncertainty. However, empirical investigation by several researchers has questioned this kind of classification and assignment of decision makers

to certain risk attitudes and relationships between risk and return (e.g., March and Shapira 1987).

QUANTIFYING THE COST OF SECURITY INCIDENTS IN THE VIRTUAL WORLDS

Before quantifying the damage that can be caused by an incident, virtual world users should know the values of assets of the user or corporations that are exposed to the threat. However, the definition of assets in virtual space in both legal and social terms is still unclear.

Kane (2009) argues if the online currency and goods that gamers trade have a real-world value, it may seem reasonable that the courts and government will eventually step in to protect and regulate these digital assets. He explains the taxability of virtual goods in the US and abroad will depend on several factors, such as whether the courts will allow users ownership of items they obtain or create. However, in some countries such as Australia and China virtual goods are subjects to taxation. Although in US there is still no law about the virtual properties, but a literate review identifies some lawsuits filed by the virtual world stakeholders. For example, Marc Bragg v. Linden Research, Inc.—filed against Second Life creator Linden Labs over a virtual-property deal gone bad (Bragg 2006)--that is perhaps first one in this type of lawsuits.

According to ENSIA's survey (2008) what are perceived as typical assets by virtual world users—in order of importance—are: credit in virtual currency, objects difficult to obtain, virtual real-state, level attained by avatar, skill, avatar, powers, and reputation of in-world character. These are however, no different from many other kinds of so-called "intangible" assets (as defined in accounting terminology).

Evaluating damage to intangible assets is controversial and often extremely difficult. We suggest qualitative and quantitative approaches for these kinds of evaluations. The quantitative approach assumes that it is possible to associate a level of risk with each hazard identified, and is intended to calculate the value of likely damage should the risk become reality. One common method of doing this is the production of an Annual Loss Expectancy (ALE) figure that is calculated for each threat by establishing two factors:

1. The probability of occurrence of the threat during a specified time period (e.g., annual)
2. The amount of loss that would be incurred if the threat occurred

These quantities are multiplied to obtain the estimated ALE, which is then compared with the costs of suitable control measures. The philosophy here is that, if the cost of a control measure is less than the calculated ALE, then implementing the control measure would be a cost-effective solution, otherwise alternative solutions should be considered. Furthermore, this method can be used to prioritize investments in solutions by addressing the threats with greatest ALE, first.

ALE is one of the best known risk measures among information security professionals. Gordon and Loeb (2006) argue that ALE can assist decision making on information security investments. However, they acknowledge some the shortcomings of this approach. Here we adapt their methodology in the case of investment on security in virtual worlds. Consider the following scenario:

Suppose company X is considering operation in virtual worlds and would like to know how much to invest on information security. Let us say there are n possible breaches that could occur in any one year in virtual world to the company X, and let index $i=1, 2, \ldots, n$ correspond to each possible breach. Let us use the following notations:

I_A: A proposed information security incident investment (e.g., on purchasing some security technology),

I_{no}: "no investment" (considered to be status quo),

$P_i (I_A)$: Possibility of breach I occurring in a year given an information and information security investment of I_A,

$L_i (I_A)$: The annual dollar loss that the company X would suffer if the ith breach were to occur when the firm made the company X made the I_A investment. Then, the ALE would be:

$$ALE(I_A) = \sum_{i=1}^{n} L_i(I_A)P_i(I_A)$$

Thus, loss equals the sum of potential breaches times their dollar loss. This method has some pitfalls such as: does not consider the intangible damages (such damages to the reputation, etc.); it focuses; on expected losses and ignores other relevant characteristics of risk; only looks at the benefit side security investments and does not compare them with costs of security improvements at company X. Although the ALE does not incorporate the costs of virtual security activities, it can be used for determining the invest in information security in virtual worlds. The managers of company X can first compare the benefit of the investment (over the status quo) with the cost of the investment. Using the above notations, the annual benefit of information security investment would be: ALE (I_{no}) – ALE (I_A). To compare the benefits with cost of investment on a comparable basis, the managers of company X can either express the costs of the investment as an annual cost or find the present value of the benefits.

Qualitative vs. Quantitative Approaches

The qualitative approach assesses risks on the basis of a capability to identify threats and vulnerabilities correctly. Unlike the quantitative approach, precise values are not sought and risks are expressed in terms of descriptive variables such as *high*, *medium*, or *low*; the rationale being that the consequences of some types of loss, such as corruption or modification of data, cannot be expressed in terms of monetary value or discrete events. Risks are grouped and evaluated using these descriptions, with mitigations applied based on (in part) effectiveness of responses and available resources.

However, both qualitative and quantitative risk analysis have pros and cons. For example quantitative risk analysis supporters explain that the results of a quantitative risk analysis approach are substantially based on independent objective processes and metrics and they can be expressed in a management-specific language (e.g., monetary value, percentages, probabilities). However, opponents argue that calculations can be complex (assigning costs to security risks and benefits of countermeasures is difficult) and it requires considerable preliminary work. Qualitative risk analysis proponents believe that in their approach the calculations are simple, it is not necessary to quantify threat frequency, and many non-technical issues are easily accounted for. The opponents of the qualitative approach argue that this method is subjective in nature and the results depend heavily on the quality of the risk management expertise available (For more information see Farahmand et al. (2005).

When we examine virtual worlds we are faced with a huge list of unknowns that complicate both quantitative and qualitative risk measurement. We have little in the way of long term measurements, instrumentation, valuation, and knowledge of consequences. Many virtual environments are not based on close correspondence with the real world—for instance, they may include time travel or use of magic spells—and thus experience and models from the real world (and other virtual worlds) may not be useful in risk measurement and estimation.

Acceptable Level of Security Risks

In addition to understanding the risks to individuals, companies may seek a presence in virtual environments. Some may do this to augment their real world presence, while others may be seeking some financial gain from their virtual operations. The bases for risk calculations by companies are similar to that of individuals, although perhaps applied more carefully. In particular, companies may be more calculating in how they determine acceptable risks.

Risk Appetite

Risk appetite is fundamentally a human quality. It is about how much risk a user is willing to accept, manage, and optimize by using a virtual world. A corporation's risk appetite is the risk appetite of the people to whom the consequences of operating in virtual worlds are ultimately transferred. For a corporation, these include executives, managers, shareholders, and all other stakeholders (McCarty & Flynn 2004).

Risk appetite can be expressed in qualitative or quantitative terms. COSO (2004) provides illustrative questions management might ask when considering risk appetite—these can be applied to the corporations which are considering operating virtual worlds, as well as individuals:

- Is the entity prepared to accept more risk than it currently is accepting in the real world and, if so, what return level would be required?
- What level of capital or earnings is the company willing to put at risk given a particular confidence level —e.g., will management accept 50% of its capital at risk of loss with 95% confidence in this amount— and how does this level compare to the risk in the real world?
- How does the company's risk appetite compare with that of peers which operate in the real world?

Risk Tolerance

Risk tolerances are the acceptable levels of variation relative to achievement of objectives. In setting risk tolerances, management considers the relative importance of the related objectives, and aligns risk tolerance with risk appetite (COSO 2004 and COBIT 2008). Howard (1988) suggests certain guidelines for determining a corporation's risk tolerance in terms of total sales, net income, or equity. According to Howard, reasonable values of risk tolerance appear to be 6.4% of total sales, 1.24 times net income, or 15.7% of equity. These figures are based on observations that Howard has made in the course of consulting with various companies. Corporations operating in virtual worlds may consider these numbers as rough estimates for their risk tolerance if they can be applied in some fashion to those new worlds. More research may refine these figures. Different industries may have different ratios for determining reasonable risk tolerance (Clemen & Reilly 2001), as well as differences for varying forms of operational "reality." As experience is gained with both regulatory and legal issues there is likely to be some change in overall risk evaluation.

APPROACHES FOR ACCEPTABLE-RISK DECISIONS

Corporations operating in virtual worlds, when choosing an approach in measuring acceptable risk, may consider families of approaches defined by Fishhoff and his colleagues (1981):

1. **Professional Judgment:** Reliance on the wisdom of the best available technical experts.
2. **Bootstrapping:** Using history as a guide for setting safety standards.
3. **Formal analysis:** Decomposing complex problems into simpler ones and then

combining the results into an over-all recommendation.

The choice among the approaches would depend upon the relative importance one attached to evaluation criteria such as comprehensiveness, logically sound, practicality, open to evaluation, politically acceptable, compatible with institution, conductive to learning, on which one approach can score well (for e.g., practicality in professional judgment and comprehensiveness in formal analysis). The capabilities of the different approaches and the importance of the different evaluation criteria for specific problems may lead to different choices of the most suitable approach. For example, professional judgment may have advantages for some routine decisions and formal analysis may provide more insight into decisions about the fate of technologies.

MOTIVATIONS IN VIRTUAL WORLDS

What motivates users to purchase virtual goods with real money, to spend time in a virtual world, and to interact with other virtual users or games? A literature review identifies several studies about the trade of virtual items for real money (e.g., Guo & barnes 2007; Manninen & Kujanpää, 2007; Starodoumov, 2005). Bessière et al. (2009) identifies motivation as one of the central challenges for the adoption of virtual worlds, and argues the likelihood of trying out a new technology is affected by factors such as self-efficacy, previous experience with similar technologies, favorable impressions, the value that the technology is presumed to have, and curiosity. Bostan (2009) studies the behavior virtual game players based on their psychogenic needs such as materialism, power, affiliation, achievement, information, and sensual needs.

One possible explanation for people's motivation to use a virtual world is the interplay between the perceived benefit and perceived risk.

Findings from our previous research indicate that perceived benefit lowers the perceived risk of electronic activities — when one stands to gain a great deal from a certain activity one is likely to underestimate the risks involved in the activity (Farahmand & Spafford, 2009). Represent by avatars, people can fulfill dreams that are impossible in the real world. The joy of fulfilling these dreams may outweigh the perceived associated risk of activities in virtual worlds.

An explanation for the inverse relationship between perceived risk and benefit by users could be that perceived benefits — compared to perceived risks—are simply more "evaluable": largely they are conceptualized unidimensionally, and are psychologically represented in terms of a convenient and numerical scale (MacGregor et al., 1999).

An implication of the inverse relationship between perceived benefit and risk for corporations is that it might be possible to change perceptions of users towards virtual worlds by changing their perceptions toward risk. It may be more effective for corporations to focus on increasing users' appreciation of virtual worlds, rather than attempting to argue that they are safe.

CONCLUSION

Risk definition and mitigation in virtual worlds is not simple. It depends on issues of risk appetite, market conditions, knowledge of past risks, and a number of other complex factors. Despite this complexity, it is possible to understand risk causes and controls sufficiently well so as to apply cost-effective controls. Perhaps more importantly, we have indicated that similar risks even to similar companies may be evaluated as leading to very different losses and concerns. As such, there are unlikely to be any uniform evaluations and responses available until the field has matured more fully.

Corporations should consider user perceptions of risk when establishing trust with the virtual world users. To address this need, users' perceptions should be aligned with organizational policies. Efforts should be made to develop a standardized approach to trust and risk across different domains to reduce the burden on consumers who seek to better understand and compare policies and practices across these organizations. This standardized approach will also aid organizations that engage in contractual sharing of consumer information, making it easier to assess risks across organizations and to monitor practices for compliance with contracts, policies and law.

Corporations that understand the roles of trust and risk should monitor user perceptions in order to understand their relation to risk aversion and risk management. Virtual world managers can incorporate Bloom's psychometric paradigm, using psychophysical scaling and multivariate analysis techniques to produce quantitative representations, called cognitive maps, of risk attitudes and perceptions. And they can simplify their risk characterization by distilling down the nine characteristics (e.g., immediacy of effect, newness, control, etc.) hypothesized by various authors to influence judgments of perceived and acceptable risk to two dimensions: dread and unknown risk.

We recommend corporations—in choosing policies for users in virtual world—to realize that stakeholder perceptions of uncertainties, risks, and benefits have major impact on the acceptability of the proposals. Therefore, perceptions should enter into the evaluation of incentives, and probabilities of final outcomes.

FUTURE DIRECTIONS

Traditional methods of engineering risk analysis and expected utility decisions, despite all their differences, share a common core: Both rely on the assumption of complete rationality. However, the results of studies by decision science researchers in the past four decades contrast with the outcomes of these traditional methods, which stem from the work of Daniel Bernoulli and Thomas Bayes in the seventeenth century. Not all decisions are completely rational.

Future research in understanding user behavior in virtual worlds will benefit from considering the inverse relationship between perceived risk and benefit, and using decision theories that are able to reflect role of behavioral biases in framing decision of stakeholders. Among those theories, researchers may use prospect theory developed by Amos Tversky and Daniel Kahneman--who won the Nobel Prize in Economics for its development. Prospect theory distinguishes two phases in choice processes: framing and valuation (Tversky & Kahneman, 1979). In the framing phase, the stakeholder constructs a representation of acts, contingencies, and outcomes that are relevant to the decision. In the valuation phase, the stakeholder assesses the value of each prospect and chooses accordingly.

REFERENCES

Adams, A. (2000). Multimedia information changes the whole privacy ballgame. In *Proc. of Computers, Freedom & Privacy '00*, (pp. 25-32).

Arakji, R. Y., & Lang, K. R. (2007). The Virtual Cathedral and the Virtual Bazaar. *The Data Base for Advances in Information Systems, 38*(4), 33–39.

Arrow, K. J. (1965). *Aspects of the Theory of Risk Bearing*. Helsinki: Yijo Jahnssonis Saatio.

Bessière, K., Ellis, J., & Kellogg, W. A. (2009). Acquiring a Professional "Second Life: Problems and Prospects for the Use of Virtual Worlds in Business. In *Proc. of ACM Conference on Human Factors in Computing Systems CHI*, (pp. 2883-2898).

Bloom, B. S., & Krathwohl, D. R. (1956). Taxonomy of educational objectives: The Classification of Educational Goals,by a Committee of College and University Examiners. In *Handbook 1: Cognitive domain*. New York: Longmans.

Bostan, B. (2009). Player Motivations: A Psychological Perspective. *ACM Computers in Entertainment, 7*(2), 22, 1-25.

Bragg, M. (2006). *Marc Bragg v. 1. Linden Research, Inc., case no. 06-4925*. US District Court for the Eastern District of Pennsylvania.

Clemen, R. T., & Reilly, T. (2001). *Making Hard Decisions*. MA: Duxbury.

COBIT. (2008). *Control Objectives for Information and related Technology, Information Systems Audit and Control Association*. ISACA.

COSO. (2004). *Enterprise Risk Management-Integrated Framework*. The Committee of Sponsoring organizations of the Treadway Commission.

ENISA. (2008). Retrieved from http://www.finextra.com/finextradownloads/newsdocs/enisa_pp_security_privacy_virtualworlds.pdf

Farahmand, F., Atallah, M., & Konsynski, B. (2008). Incentives and Perceptions of Information Security Risks. In *Proceedings of the Twenty Ninth International Conference on Information Systems (ICIS)*.

Farahmand, F., Navathe, S. B., Sharp, G. P., & Enslow, P. H. (2005). A Management Perspective on Risk of Security Threats to Information Systems. *Journal of Information Technology Management, 6*, 203–225. doi:10.1007/s10799-005-5880-5

Farahmand, F., & Spafford, E. H. (2009). Insider Behavior: An Analysis of Decision under Risk. In *First International Workshop on Managing Insider Security Threats, International Federation for Information Processing (IFIP) International Conference on Trust Management*, Purdue University.

Fischhoff, B., Lichtenstein, S., Slovic, P., Derby, S. L., & Keeney, R. L. (1981). *Acceptable Risk*. Cambridge, UK: Cambridge University Press.

Fischoff, B. (1978). How Safe Is Safe Enough? A Psychometric Study of Attitudes Towards Technological Risks and Benefits? *Policy Sciences, 9*(2), 127–152. doi:10.1007/BF00143739

Gartner (2007). Retrieved from http://www. businessweek.com/globalbiz/content/aug2007/ gb2007089_070863.htm?chan=globalbiz_ europe+index+page_top+stories

Gartner. (2007) Retrived from http://www.gartner. com/it/page.jsp?id=511370

Gartner. (2009). Retrieved from http://www. gartner.com/it/page.jsp?id=503861

Gordon, L. A., & Loeb, M. P. (2006). *Managing Cyber-Security Resources, A Cost-Benefit Analysis*. New York: McGraw-Hill.

Guo, Y., & Barnes, S. (2007). Why people Buy Virtual items in Virtual Worlds with Real Money. *The Data Base for Advances in Information Systems, 38*(4), 69–76.

Howard, R. A. (1988). Decision Analysis: Practice and promise. *Management Science, 34*, 679–695. doi:10.1287/mnsc.34.6.679

Johnson, E. J., & Tversky, A. (1984). Representations of Perceptions of Risk. *Journal of Experimental Psychology, 113*, 55–70.

Kane, S. F. (2009). Virtual Judgment: Legal Implications of Online Gaming. *IEEE Security and Privacy, 7*(3), 23–28. doi:10.1109/MSP.2009.81

Karat, J. (2009). A Policy Framework for Security and Privacy Management. *IBM Journal of Research and Development, 53*(2). doi:10.1147/ JRD.2009.5429046

Kim, K., & Prabhakar, P. (2000). Initial Trust, Perceived Risk, and the Adoption of the Internet Banking. *International Conference on Information Systems*, (pp.537-543).

Kirkwood, C. W. (1997). *Strategic Decision Making*. MA: Duxbury.

Knight, F. H. (1921) *Risk, Uncertainty and Profit*. Gloucester, UK: Dodo press.

MacGregor, D. G., Slovic, P., Berry, M., & Evensky, H. R. (1999). Perception of Financial Risk: a survey study of advisors and planners. *Journal of Financial Planning, 12*(8), 68–86.

Manninen, T., & Kujanpää, T. (2007). The Value of Virtual Assets – The Role of Game Characters in MMOGs. *International Journal of Business Science and Applied Management, 2*(1), 21–33.

March, J. G., & Shapira, Z. (1987). Managerial Perspectives on Risk and Risk Taking. *Management Science, 33*(11), 1404–1418. doi:10.1287/ mnsc.33.11.1404

McCarthy, M. P., & Flynn, T. P. (2004). *Risk from the CEO and Broad Perspective*. McGraw Hill.

Moores, T. T., & Dhillon, G. (2003). Do Privacy Seals in E-Commerce Really Work? *Communications of the ACM, 46*(12), 265–271. doi:10.1145/953460.953510

Pratt, G. W. (1964). Risk Aversion in the Small and in the Large. *Econometrica, 32*, 122–136. doi:10.2307/1913738

Slovic, P. (1987). Perceptions of Risk. *Science, 236*, 280–285. doi:10.1126/science.3563507

Starodoumov, A. (2005). Real Money Trade Model in Virtual Economies. *Social Science Research Network*, Retrieved June, 2007, from http://papers. ssrn.com/sol3/papers.cfm?abstract_id=958286

Stonebruner, G., Gougen, A., & Feringa, A. (2002). *Risk Management Guide for Information Technology Systems*, NIST SP800-30.

Stross, C. (2007). *Halting State*. New York: Ace Books.

Tversky, A., & Kahneman, D. (1979). Prospect Theory: An Analysis of Decisions under Risk. *Econometrica, 47*(2), 263–291. doi:10.2307/1914185

Vinge, V. (1998). True Names. Retrieved from http://www.facstaff.bucknell.edu/rickard/TRUENAMES.pdf

Wong, K., & Watt, S. (1990). *Managing Information Security: Management Guide*. New York: Elsevier Advanced Technology.

Yee, N. (2001) *Everquest survey.* Retrieved from http://www.nickyee.com/eqt/report.html

ADDITIONAL READING

Castronova, E. (2005). *Synthetic Worlds: The Business and Culture of Online Games*. University of Chicago Press.

Franceschi, K., Lee, R. M., Zanakis, S. H., & Hinds, D. (2009). Engaging Group E-Learning in Virtual Worlds. *Journal of Management Information Systems, 26*(1), 73–100. doi:10.2753/MIS0742-1222260104

MacInnes, I. (2006). Property Rights, Legal Issues, and Business Models in Virtual World Communities. *Electronic Commerce Research, 6*, 39–56. doi:10.1007/s10660-006-5987-8

Chapter 5

The Social Design of 3D Interactive Spaces for Security in Higher Education:
A Preliminary View

Shalin Hai-Jew
Kansas State University, USA

ABSTRACT

Immersive spaces offer a unique set of security challenges related to human, data, learning facilitation, and virtual environment risks. Security risks may originate from people, the technology, or a mix of unintended synergistic effects; they may originate from intentional, unintentional, and accidental actions. Understanding the risk environment will be important for those who use persistent, immersive 3D spaces for teaching and learning. Based on the current research and direct experiences in educational immersive spaces, this chapter will first define the security risks and offer real-world examples. Then, it will look at various potential social design interventions. "Social design" refers to protective measures created through awareness-raising among all participants, policy creation and implementation, human facilitation of teaching and learning in immersive spaces, and other efforts to improve and maintain the security for the socio-technical system, the institution of higher education, the learners, the faculty, and the larger cyber-sphere. These social design endeavors, one part of a larger 360 degree security approach, will improve security but never fully attain "perfect security" (a condition of no-risk). This chapter will include an international survey of instructors who teach in 3D immersive spaces to solicit their ideas about security and the social design of protective measures.

INTRODUCTION

With growing affordances for information transfer through the carrying capacity of the Internet, and the greater sophistication of 3D immersive technologies, many higher education courses, learning experiences and training exercises have moved to immersive 3D spaces. Learners themselves demonstrate a growing sophistication and comfort in such spaces, in the 15 years that virtual environments have been existent (Cikic, Grottke, Lehmann-Grube, & Sablatnig, 2008).

DOI: 10.4018/978-1-61520-891-3.ch005

This increase in the use of persistent and immersive virtual worlds provides many affordances for online learners. 3D spaces offer opportunities for spatial reasoning. They offer opportunities for multi-way communications among human learners, with automated (often very human-like) AI-agents. With their own digital physics and ecologies, the virtual environments may be dynamic and interactive; they may offer dynamic modeling of complicated systems with many changing elements and interactions (Colella, 2000). Here, the learning may be multi-sensory, full-surround, and focused within a particular context for situated learning. Learners may explore spaces for experiential discovery-learning; they may make decisions and see the results of those decisions in a simulation. They may collaborate with peers and consult with subject matter experts (SMEs). They offer persistence over time, for truly longitudinal learning and relationship-building.

These affordances in complex, interconnected socio-technical systems offer plenty of opportunities for security lapses and compromises. These risks may originate from the social aspects (the learners, the exchanged information, and the facilitation of teaching and learning) and the technological ones (the virtual environment, the scripted robots, and virtual creatures). These hazards may come from purposive attacks, unintended actions, accidents, and unintended synergies that may occur with combined actions. The origins of these risks are several-fold. The nature of 3D immersive spaces themselves carries inherent risks. Lapses may occur at any point of connectivity to the immersive spaces, and the more the connection points, the more potential there are for unintended risks. Security here may be understood in a multi-faceted and broad sense. This chapter will address what is socially controllable and what may have to be addressed through policy and technology (through design and the deployment of various technologies for systems maintenance, surveillance, record-keeping, and the maintenance of order). The social design aspect will touch on

issues of educational policymaking and enforcement, instructional facilitation, and technological oversight.

SOME CAVEATS

If security and surveillance are at one end of a continuum, at the other end would be the need for individual privacy protections. In M. Andrejevic's dystopian nightmare of a "digital enclosure," every human action is captured digitally and recorded (Andrejevic, 2007), in a panopticon society. Every person is theoretically trackable in wired and wireless spaces, and "black" information skimmers are alleged to be able to capture all electronic communications and sort through them for targeted messages and data (Bamford, 2008). The erosion of privacy is not the only concern. There are also risks of fomenting an unintended us-vs.-them between learners and the outside world beyond the confines of the controlled, private learning space.

Another caveat relates to the control-serendipity continuum. While control is sometimes linked with safety and security, excessive control leads to risks—of authoritarian approaches to a public architecture, of lack of chance-encounters, and of a lack of serendipity. There's potency in the interactions of the real moment that is unplanned:

The gesture has a spontaneity, a freedom, an unfiltered physicality in its instantaneous choice. There is a depth of communication in this moment-the split second of a photograph, the subtle timing of a comedian. These instants are not planned or contrived but quickly communicated through a developed intuition (Schkolne, 2002, p. 371).

Immersive spaces capture creativity in motion and mediate the transfer of complex knowledge.

This chapter will explore the research on security issues in immersive spaces and involve live actual security incidences in educational immersive learning spaces. This will offer some ideas how to socially design increased security in immersive learning. Social design here refers to protective measures stemming from awareness-raising among participants, policy creation and implementation, human facilitation of teaching and learning in immersive spaces, and other efforts to improve and maintain the security for the socio-technical system, the institution of higher education, the learners, the faculty, and the larger cyber-sphere. This strategy is seen as part of a 360° protective approach, including solid technological designs, virtual space management, and other endeavors. This chapter will also include the results of an international survey of instructors who teach in 3D immersive spaces that solicited their ideas of security and the social design of protective measures.

REVIEW OF THE LITERATURE

Safety and security have always been issues regarding the uses of the WWW and the Internet—regarding to personal safety, information protection, and infrastructure soundness. With the growing adoption and diffusion of immersive 3D technologies for learning, there have been growing concerns about how to secure this virtual space. The perception that immersive spaces may offer a growing venue for e-learning has encouraged the building of learner interfaces in virtual spaces to enhance the e-learning (Calongne, Endorf, Frankovich, & Sandaire, 2008, p. 188).

HUMAN RISKS

Those who run information technology (IT) systems suggest that even if a technology could be made failsafe (which categorically, it can't, based on the nature of code and the elusiveness of identifying hidden code functions), the human element introduces ever-present risks in a socio-technical environment where humans and machines interact.

Socio-technical designs consider both the technical and non-technical aspects of information systems (Siponen, 2001, pp. 106 - 107). Considering "the interconnected nature of both the system and people working within the organization" is a part of fourth-generation (4G) approaches to security policy (White & Rea, 2008, p. 59).

Swift trust has been found to be an assumption of many who take distance learning courses (Hai-Jew, 2007). Immersive virtual spaces are used to build trust for virtual team members: "3D virtual worlds and games may provide an alternate means for encouraging team development due to their affordances for facile communication, emotional engagement, and social interaction among participants" (Ellis, Luther, Bessiere, & Kellogg, 2008, p. 295). That early assumption of trust may not be desirable without some cautious hedging. This fast trust may raise the specter of fraud through malicious social engineering and the technological siphoning of knowledge or code or technological "cheats".

Impersonations have cost lost money in social networking sites (Sutter & Carroll, Feb. 6, 2009, n.p.), and the same scams may be easily transferred to 3D social spaces. Given the reality of "secondary markets" in virtual spaces, the spending of real money in and through virtual spaces (Guo & Barnes, 2007, pp. 69 – 76) has raised fears of financial fraud or the illegal gaining of another's property without paying for it.

"Cyberstalking" involves the seeking "to gain access to, or control over, an unwilling victim" in cyberspace (Burmester, Henry, & Kermes, 2005, n.p.). "Trolling" refers to the act of going online to cause grief to others. The posting of personal information online is highly discouraged, in part to head off potential physical and/or stalking risks.

Risks may come from within or from without. To borrow from the Prisoner's Dilemma theoretical, individuals may decide whether to cooperate or defect, to the relative benefit or detriment of others. Based on perceptions and people's interests, which are malleable, their attitudes and actions may change.

The porousness of the borders of immersive digital spaces allows for various participants who may have no formal role in the designed learning, and identity and verification are made tougher with the ease of creating new avatar identities. The human embodiment of digital avatars may not be the official learner, whether with or without the original avatar creator's permission.

Another aspect of "identity" is a psychological (individual-focused) and sociological (society-focused) one, where learners go online to reflect on and experiment with their sense of self in relation to others (Bers, 2001).

The immersiveness of the 3D spaces also may be intoxicating and may be addictive for some learners, given the rich aural, visual, and full-sensory aspects of such spaces. This risk involves "opportunity costs"—of foregone alternate options and choices in the real world while spending time and energy in the virtual. The new "immersive intelligence" enhances human imagination and perceptions:

There seems to be a correlation between immersive ideals and desires for extrasensory, distributed disembodiment, meaning a loss of cognitive body-image involving the expansion of boundaries. Immersive art fulfills the prosthetic task of artificially facilitating such an unrestricted state. The desire to exist in an anti- mechanistic state of expansion is temporarily and symbolically realized in engaging immersive art. In virtual immersion, conventional optic models may be surpassed (Nechvatal, 2001, p. 417).

Those who may be prone to parasocial relationships or other manipulations (Hai-Jew, 2009) may misread the synaesthetic media signals (and noise) and presume relationships with automated robots or mediated human-embodied avatars. Digital avatars have been designed to represent the human-embodied internal states through a greater range of expressiveness; these now blink and reflect some of the autonomic responses of the humans. Blinking animations on avatars (Takashima, Omori, Yoshimoto, Itoh, Kitamura, & Kishino, 2008) and avatar eye gaze control (Garau, Slater, Vinayagamoorthy, Brogni, Steed, & Sasse, 2003) have been found to raise people's senses of avatar realism.

Some are even emotional agents, with the ability to interact emotionally with a human whose own emotional reactions are captured and registered via camera. Animated conversational characters with dialogue as well as verbal and nonverbal behaviors (Gebhard, Kipp, Klesen, & Rist, 2003) offer automated interactions. People may engage with the automated interactions of artificial intelligence robots; they may interact with virtual artificial-life environments (where virtual creatures interact and change over time in an evolving digital biological system); they may engage real virtual crowds (Pelechano, Stocker, Allbeck, & Badler, 2008).

The growing sophistication of avatars has increased the human ability to empathize through mediated interactivity and the standing-in of avatars for other persons. Empathy is defined as the awareness of another's internal feelings, perceptions and intentions. Empathy enables people to vicariously respond to another via "psychological processes that make a person have feelings that are more congruent with another's situation than with his own situation" (McQuiggan, Rowe, & Lester, 2008, p. 1512).

Another human risk may not involve other people directly. "Simulator sickness" has been found to affect some who have gone online into immersive spaces. Their orientation and navigation may cause physical discomfort. Some researchers have found an increased incidence and severity of cybersickness among older visitors (Knight & Arns, 2006). Ergonomic stresses may be experienced in 3D virtual environments (De Sensi, Longo, & Mirabelli, 2007).

DATA RISKS

The information environment of a 3D immersive space involves interactions within that space and also between that space and other information spaces. Immersive worlds involve spin-off websites. They involve interactions between principals interacting via email, instance messaging, and portable devices. Nine out of 10 organizations faced information security incidences in 2005, according to the FBI in its *Computer Crime Survey* (Siponen, 2006, p. 40).

Being aware of the various information flows is an important part of promoting and maintaining security. Information may also be conceptualized as static (stored) and live (in transit); it may also by dynamic and evolving (being changed or acted on). The integrity of the information in its various forms will also be important to overall security. Information security has traditionally involved unauthorized and undesirable access to sensitive data. Information technology (IT) protections for data often involve the following:

Confidentiality, availability, integrity, and non-repudiation constitute the main requirements for *secure communication*. In an act of communication, the aim may not be to hide the act itself (this may be impossible); but the context of that act of communication needs to be confidential or un-touched (integrity) (Siponen & Oinas-Kukkonen, 2007, p. 62).

Confidentiality protects the privacy of the creators, users, and senders of information. Availability refers to the proper access to the necessary information for the individuals with the proper role profiles to have that access. Integrity refers to the non-tampering of particular information. Non-repudiation ensures that the integrity and origin of digital data may be proven or authenticated for genuine provenance or origins; non-repudiation ensures that those who are disputing the authenticity of a digital message or content cannot refute its validity (by limiting plausible deniability). The building of security structures that allow

for forensic investigations may help ensure that individuals cannot deny unauthorized access if they have engaged in that. Some information may be posted to threaten others; at a higher extreme, information may be used to lure or entice victims into "dangerous physical liaisons" (Burmester, Henry, & Kermes, 2005).

Intercommunications have to be protected in immersive spaces for them to be secure: "However, the communication channel must retain properties that duplicate those found in earlier modes of communication: secure and private communication, authentication of messengers, integrity of messages, and stability of the network" (Dawes, Bloniarz, Kelly, & Fletcher, 1999, p. 18).

Information loss may not primarily be an issue of technological security but may involve slippages by people in regular communications, with real-time interchanges. Communications channels between people are never fully purposive, and unintended information is often also conveyed. The practice of datamining (visual, behavioral, and otherwise) may result in rich harvests of unintended information.

The conduct of sociological, anthropological, ethnographic, social psychology, and other types of research in immersive spaces must follow the standards for human research, for the protection of all participants. There must be informed consent. Any potential duplicity of participants, leakage of private and personally identifiable information, and any potential harms will likely prevent or severely curtail such research.

In a higher education environment, that may involve confusions about the privacy of an online public classroom, with resultant potential Family Education Rights and Privacy Act (FERPA)-violations or other information compromises. One writer has asked what happens with online interactivity in light of federal open meetings laws? What happens with online crimes such as avatar harassment and assault? (Bugeja, 2008). Those are just some of the scenarios that highlight the lack of clarity regarding what is and is not privy online in immersive spaces.

People in real space have been known to lose memory devices with various types of important information. They've been known to lose or misplace laptops with private information. They've had large amounts of sensitive private information stolen from various computer systems. Immersive spaces involve the creation and deployment of data through displays and kiosks, automated agents, and live people. The inadvertent sharing of sensitive information may occur in immersive spaces as they do in real spaces.

High-tech data "scraping" involves the use of computer programs to extract data from a site, including protected or secure data. This sort of action, on the one hand, is seen as positive when it offers a constructive service. It is seen as negative when this results in the mass loss of private data, such as from social networking sites.

INSTRUCTIONAL FACILITATION RISKS

Some inherent risks of 3D spaces become clear with a simple oversight and perusal. One stems from the lack of pervasive awareness that most e-learning instructors have in learning / course management systems in terms of interactive messages. The ability to track user behaviors online and to archive their messages provides facilitator oversight. In immersive spaces, semi-private conversations may go on, and with that, potential exchanges that may involve personal harms or may compromise sensitive information. (Programs may be written for immersive spaces that track learner behaviors and messages, but these currently are not built into the immersive systems themselves.) Identities may be confusing in virtual space, with the ease of changing appearances, genders, and personae through digital morphing and "plasticity" (malleability).

3D environments also require a high learning curve to acclimate to the spaces and to learn the tools. These spaces call for learning and practice beyond formal learning spaces. Acclimating to an online immersive space may help users focus in the face of dynamic on-screen changes and to control their avatars more effectively. "All of these simultaneous visual, audio, cognitive and motor demands represent potential barriers to users, especially to those with a disability. Because an avatar's behavior in the world is visible to others, the fear of looking clumsy or behaving inappropriately may also constitute a significant barrier to participation" (Trewin, Laff, Cavender, & Hanson, 2008, p. 2728). Inherent barriers to the use of immersive spaces in higher education are compounded by security issues.

The disruptions from security problems may harm the cohesiveness of the online learning cohort. They may draw attention away from the authoritativeness of the curriculum and the human-embodied avatar, who is the instructor. Learners may experience negative reactions to adverse experiences—such as a compromise of their virtual identities. Security challenges may result in undesirable economic impacts to the institution(s) hosting the learning.

If assessments are done in the immersive spaces, that raises the specter of academic dishonesty. The danger in this relates to the dilution of the teaching and the learning and the risks of incorrect assessments. While academic dishonesty and plagiarism are not seen as traditional security issues, they are in the sense of lowering the efficacy of the designed online immersion for learning and skills acquisition. The facilitation should not cause undue fears, however, and should not overstate risks.

VIRTUAL ENVIRONMENT RISKS

The financial sustainability of virtual spaces may be yet another risk: "Is this virtual world real?

'Real' in the sense of a business that can sustain itself and/or grow and provide services? Or, is it fundamentally a high-tech Ponzi scheme: a pyramid operation in which the early users benefit from the later users, and the system grows until it runs out of new converts and implodes?" (Noam, 2007, p. 107). This potential Achilles heel is partially offset by the technological design of 3D objects that are portable off to 3D repositories and theoretically usable (and interchangeable) in other multiverses.

Given the openness of many immersive systems with digital objects that are not "locked down" or are prone to hacks, code innovations may be lost. Original digital objects may be compromised and reformed or disappeared. Virtual spaces may be tampered with, and digital objects or information may be exploited for different uses downstream. The protection of virtual property requires robust systems protections: "To protect virtual property, virtual environment systems will have to conform to certain requirements" (Cikic, Grottke, Lehmann-Grube, & Sablatnig, 2008).

Open-ended modeling tools affect cyber-world contents (Merrick & Maher, 2007). That open modding or end-user programming opens possibilities for the interruption of the learning experience. Griefers may add digital graffiti, change existing objects, swipe code, or destroy parts of the digital infrastructure of an online learning space. As found in simulations research, 3D immersive spaces may allow for the development and growth of incorrect mental models, without the direct correction of mistaken ideas. Unintended messages are a risk with all virtual designed experiences.

At the most extreme end is the risk of the use of an immersive, persistent space for "indoctrination, recruiting, rehearsing attacks, organization and communication by extremist groups" and terror (Mandal & Lim, 2008, p. 498). Immersive spaces may be used to spread political ideas, to organize; communicate and indoctrinate, rehearse attacks, and even launder money and finance terror.

DEFINING RISKS

Users of online immersive spaces may benefit from awareness-raising of risks. Identifying risks may require the reduction of natural defensive biases (Sherman & Cohen, 2002) for new perceptions. Risk management fundamentally involves the definition of risk—its various incarnations and the likelihoods. The traditional formula reads:

Risk = Probability x Consequence

Some risks may be anticipated; others may emerge whole as a "surprise." Higher education is moving into uncharted territories with the uses of immersive online spaces for learning and training. Their experiences may well help shape policies, practices, and case law that may have implications on the virtual environment's safety and security.

Between the human, data, learning facilitation, and virtual environment risks described above, the most high-cost ones would tend to be the human costs—in terms of time lost, damaged reputations, lost information, intellectual property compromises, wasted scripting hours, and inaccurate learning. At the core of the concerns for security is human well-being in the uses of immersive spaces and technologies.

There may be synergies between these various risks. For example, an identity compromise may lead to unauthorized sharing of information (a data risk), which may cascade to problems with the facilitation of learning. Unauthorized modding of the virtual environment may lead to negative learning in an experiential simulation. Parasocial relationships that morph into addictive human-machine or human-human ties may harm the virtual learning experience. In other words, compromises to security may have cascading effects and rippling social costs.

An insecure immersive space may involve risks to the people there, the information, the facilitation of learning, and the virtual environment. Based on cultural differences, contexts, and experiential savvy, different individuals and educational entities will likely come up with different

Figure 1. A visualization of the security risks in immersive 3D learning

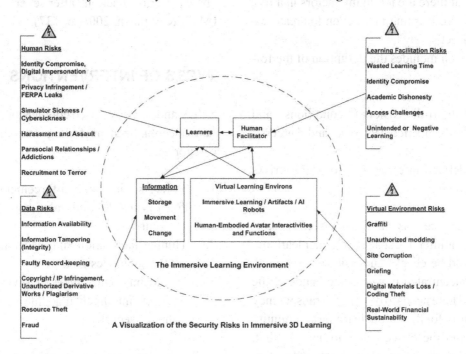

conclusions about what poses security risks. These local realities will inform decisions about which risks to anticipate and to face, and which to plan recoveries from. Figure 1 "a visualization of the security risks in immersive 3D learning" offers an integrative, contextualized conceptualization of current anticipated risks.

The origins of risk clearly come from a variety of sources: the underlying technologies, hackers, course instructors and learners, unofficial participants with malign motives, the larger economy, and / or a mix of synergistic effects (with unintended consequences).

Given the range of subject matters in higher education, it is important to note the variance in risk tolerance. Some content domains require lighter levels of safety and therefore entail higher risk tolerance. Sensitive simulations, trainings, and courses will require higher levels of safety and security and therefore have a much lower risk tolerance. Flexible immersive systems, in their continuing evolution, should be able to accommodate a range of types of training.

Finally, unknown or as-yet unforeseen risks will affect how this issue moves forward for those involved in immersive e-learning. Will there be coordinated social engineering and technological attacks for system takedowns? Will underlying virtual infrastructure codes be mimicked? Will there be new coded agents for attack or information siphoning or avatar impersonation?

SOME APPLIED PRINCIPLES

The design of socio-technical systems must consider the risks of so-called "human hazards" and "moral hazards" to lower risks and optimally prevent accidents or foreseeable risks. Those same preventive concepts apply to the design of online learning spaces. The setup of a virtual space for learning should consider security from the beginning of the design; additional measures may be evolved as the situation changes and also as new threats are anticipated and / or appear. Different types of interventions may increase the degrees of safety, but there are too many factors in a live and immersive learning interaction to create so-called "perfect safety".

Safety then includes the definition of the following:

- The multi-dimensional conditions and standards of safety (vs. risks and dangers), and
- The defined interventions to address risks and dangers

There must be reasonable principles in creating a secure immersive space for higher learning. There should be checks-and-balances in power, without concentrated power in the hands of the instructor. There needs to be general transparency about security for the virtual learning community members and the expectations to achieve that. Security involves a sense of well-being and protection from risk; security is a result of robust safety.

There must be high standards for suspicions and any sort of security-inspired enforcement, to protect individual freedoms (including that of privacy protections) from over-zealous endeavors. Excessive paranoia can lead to over-reactions and over-control in immersive spaces. For example, cultural differences or differences of opinions may create a perception of threat, and this may draw extra-curricular intrusions in immersive learning spaces. What may be considered protected information (for research and development, security, and academic research) may differ among participants.

A final principle is that of correctability and resilience in the aftermath of security breaches. How people may recover from unexpected events and "bounce back" may be affected by some mental and technological preparation. While not every contingency may be anticipated and protected against, a strong immersive space must be adaptable to different security breaches or disruptions. Technology may be used to support

"new patterns of action" after severe disruptions (Mark & Semaan, 2008, p. 137).

TYPES OF INTERVENTIONS

Safety and security-based counter-measures may be conceptualized as falling into three major categories.

1. Policy-setting and enforcement provides for a principle- and value-based approach to security.
2. Human facilitation and leadership focuses on the social design aspect.
3. The technological piece involves the use of code and intelligent machine affordances to enhance security.

These three elements need to be aligned and coordinated for highest effectiveness. No one approach will suffice because that will leave gaps in the overall protection. Table 1 addresses these Types of Interventions for a full approach to safety and security.

POLICY-SETTING AND ENFORCEMENT (RULES)

One approach that faculty in higher education have taken to strengthen security in immersive online spaces used for e-learning is to first shift legal responsibilities and potential liabilities. One endeavor requires students to sign waivers suggesting that they will not hold the instructor or university responsible for what happens to them online. Another professor advocated in a public conference in 2007 that faculty should get institutional review board (IRB) approval before requiring students to go into immersive spaces for their studies. Some universities have begun exploring changing online policies to clarify what learners' rights may be in 3D immersive social

Table 1. Types of interventions

Types of Interventions	Policy-Setting and Enforcement (Rules)	Human Facilitation and Leadership (Facilitation)	Technologies (Techno)
Actions	Learner signing of waivers Approval of Institutional Review Boards (IRBs) for immersive learner spaces University policies and practices Enforcement of the Terms of Service (ToS) or End User License Agreements (EULAs), and "griefer" banning The engagement of law enforcement for criminal behaviors	Empowerment of the virtual community Awareness-raising Open communications and transparency Development of community security mores and practices Power sharing among users / dilution of concentrated power Human proctoring of live user access	The "locking down" of particular digital elements Watermarking Datamining Surveillance and monitoring for system compromises Record-keeping and documentation Technological proctoring of live user access Computer forensics (and the preservation of relevant evidence) to track system compromises and anomalies

spaces. Having legal cover for the learning may not only enhance institutional and faculty protections but promote deeper understandings of potential risks. Well designed policies that are enforceable may strengthen the shared security and civility of online spaces.

Another strategy related to policy involves contacting the owners of various immersive sites to enforce their Terms of Service (ToS) or End User License Agreements (EULAs). Individuals found to harass others may be banned from a virtual immersive space. Often, sufficient evidentiary support must be submitted before any actions may be taken.

HUMAN FACILITATION AND LEADERSHIP (FACILITATION)

An instructor co-building a discovery learning space in the teen area of an immersive space took the space live with a middle school audience. In no time, a student had fashioned a digital gun for himself and ran around harassing his virtual schoolmate avatars. He also found an object that had been designed but not locked down and had fashioned it into something unrecognizable (Totten, Feb. 26, 2009). Designing for security for her also meant allowing up-front time for the young students to build their new avatars to their satis-

faction before launching into the learning, so the learners could actually focus and not unintentionally (or intentionally) undermine the immersive virtual learning. For newcomers to immersive spaces, the "dazzle" of the technologies may be overwhelming.

Positive social design may promote the security of virtual learning spaces through the empowerment of the virtual community of learners. Virtual communities require civic-mindedness to thrive. Moral values are embedded, even if they're not explicitly surfaced.

Raising the awareness of instructors, facilitators, and learners may encourage the co-evolving of group norms to promote individual and community-level security, as well as the security of the learning community within the larger multiverse. For example, being aware of what information should never be shared in an immersive virtual space may lower the incidences of fraud or information leakage or privacy compromise. Learners may become more aware of information provenance and judge the validity of information more effectively. They may develop stronger sense of self-control in virtual spaces.

They may have a clearer understanding of the limits of technology in terms of authenticating users, ensuring proper levels of authorized access, protecting coding, or ensuring secure information channels. They may be more aware of the manipulative elicitation of information. They may have a greater reluctance to give in to the "swift trust" often found in online interactivity but use a clearer sense of caution. Group norms may include a culture of security, which may involve more general awareness, effective general surveillance of anomalies, and more care for each other in incidences of cyber-bullying or harassment.

Instructor enthusiasm, tele-presence and high-interaction may create stronger rapport with learners. The multiple-user collective social presence may be more socially motivating to learners in virtual spaces. This high presence aligns with the digital space, where individuals embody their full-sensory avatars more fully.

In 3D spaces, it may help to have more open communications and transparency. There may be more affirmations and rewards of those who would surface signs of security compromises. Community memory may be enhanced, and learners may bring with them a record of trustful behaviors and a history based on past actions.

Learners may create a stronger sense of community "policing" and "sentinels" for corruption and notify the instructor or owners of the immersive spaces for helpful interventions. Users who are aware of possible recruiting for nefarious purposes may also be encouraged to speak up. A network of "tripwires" may be created to alert the community to security compromises, with timely reporting to responsible parties. There should also be security alerts among the members of the community. With the greater transparency should come enhanced power sharing. Concentrated power may lead to abuses in persistent social spaces.

There may even be human proctoring of live user access in high-value live immersive interactions, in the same way that high-value assessments are sometimes proctored (by both people and digital cameras). Indeed, some interactions may be more risk-tolerant than others.

Course housekeeping refers to the various tasks related to maintaining an e-learning space for learners. This involves the access of various individuals over time, the support they receive to support the learning, and the deployment of digital resources, for example. This also is a critical piece of ensuring continuing security—by ensuring that prior learners do not have the same levels of access in order to make changes to the shared course site.

A complex mix of learner motivations, cognitive and emotional outreaches, morals and ethics, and incentives may be brought into play to raise user awareness of security in IT security awareness (Siponen & Kajava, 1998, pp. 330 – 331).

TECHNOLOGIES (TECHNO)

Immersive spaces have differing functions to promote and enforce security measures. While digital elements may be locked down, these have been hacked before. While virtual learning spaces may be walled off and made inaccessible to others except by invitation, that does not necessarily stop imposters or those whose avatar access has been compromised. It's totally feasible that a course that meets in immersive spaces will have some events meeting in closed spaces, and other events meeting in more public ones, depending on the learning and the sensitivity of the information exchanged.

Digital objects may be watermarked for identification and possible tracking through immersive spaces or 3D object repositories. 3D spaces (whether through built-in technologies or third-party surveillance technologies) may afford datamining and surveillance of user behaviors and record-keeping of their actions—but at a price of compromising privacy.

Technologists who set up and run immersive systems may have a wide range of back-end tools to identify and stop abuses of the system. They may have forensics tools to capture information about abuses that may not be readily apparent on the user side. Insider abuses or unauthorized accesses may also be tracked.

Technology may "proctor" live user access to capture anomalies or identify particular threats. Artificial intelligence may capture and report on potential high-risk messages. Policies and social design should be aligned with technological capabilities for the best effects. Any computer forensic work that addresses issues of potential illegal activities will have to follow standards of digital evidence integrity and chain-of-custody that will stand up in a U.S. court of law.

It may be argued that all technological innovations are "dual use" (or "multi-use") in the sense that they may be used for the social good or for its opposite. Those tasked with creating security need to maintain a suspicious approach to all technologies and developments in order to probe potential vulnerabilities. In this sense, a technological race is constant and on-going, for the game-changing code or process that may mean access, system takeovers, decryption, and power—at the expense of mainstream security in virtual worlds.

The shape of this threat is changing, particularly with the identification of the so-called "targeted cyberweapon" Stuxnet Worm and its impact on supervisor control and data acquisition (SCADA) systems. This turn of events brought out the specter of potential state-sponsored hacking of systems for political aims, and its appearance changed the risk landscape for cyberspace by orders of magnitude. Researchers have long been warning about the weaponization of cyberspace, with techniques and codes being captured and used for various purposes (Clarke & Knake 2010).

ON BALANCE

These three elements—Policy-setting and Enforcement, Human Facilitation and Leadership, and Technologies may be considered multiple strands of an overall security strategy and approach. The policy offers legal and political cover for the security measures. The human facilitation

taps into the users to use live human intellect to protect the endeavors and resources. The technologies provide and protect the substructure on which the virtual is built. Without awareness, the policies themselves may not be applied. Without a technological system that can track and authenticate users, the policies of identity cannot be enforced. Without vigilant practitioners and learners, the policies and technologies may not be effectively used for immersive learning.

Even if all elements are in place and functioning accurately, there will be evolving and emerging security risks. Because of those concerns, it's important also to consider correctability and resiliency in the aftermath of security breaches.

POST-SECURITY-BREACH MITIGATION OF HARMS

There are actions that may be taken to make an immersive learning situation recuperable (of lost information or coding) and recoverable (bringing 3D spaces back online with the same level of learning value) somewhat easier. There may be plans put into place to mitigate the negative side effects of errors or security breaches. Expectations management among users may be modulated to ease shocks of security incidences.

Another approach may involve the creation of backups for the digital contents and their locations in the 3D space. This means keeping blueprints of the space and design specifics of each object. Users may port the digital objects into a separate discrete 3D repository in case that may be necessary. Having redundancy for textual information would also be helpful as an element of information management.

Arranging for separate communications channels in case the immersive system fails is also important to protect the facilitation of the learning. There are plenty of learning / course management systems and computer mediated communications systems that may enhance the record-keeping, information exchange, interactivity and learning by extending the capabilities of immersive spaces.

ONLINE SURVEY RESULTS

A brief survey "Security in 3D Immersive and Interactive Spaces in Higher Education" (See the appendix.) was created to surface faculty members' ideas of and experiences with security in immersive, persistent virtual worlds. This survey (created on the Axio™ Survey platform) was offered for three weeks in March 2009 and resulted in 23 completed surveys. The survey was publicized through various listservs for those who teach in immersive spaces.

The average time taken to complete the survey was 16 minutes and 31 seconds. More than half of the participants who responded had only been using immersive online spaces for teaching for 0 – 6 months. 26% had used them for between 19 – 24 months. 17% had used immersive spaces for more than two years. 4% had used it for between 7 – 12 months, and 4% had used it between 13 – 18 months. On the whole, the experiences of the people in this survey would fall on a bimodal curve,

with both "novices" and "experts" represented. Figure 2 "the length of experience with immersive spaces by survey respondents," shows this.

ONLINE SURVEY: DEFINING TYPES OF LEARNING IN IMMERSIVE SPACES

The types of learning designed in these immersive spaces revealed a broad range. Survey participants were asked to explain the types of learning they designed for 3D immersive spaces and to check all that applied. They were also given the opportunity to add additional learning not offered in the list. Their responses are included in Table 2. Table 2: "A Variety of Learning in 3D Immersive Spaces" has been organized by the order of popular-to-less-popular approaches based on the survey respondents.

The above responses show a wide variety of applied (and combined) teaching and learning strategies in immersive spaces. Understanding the various applications of immersive spaces in e-learning may provide insights for security gaps and risks. Some learning may involve the exchange

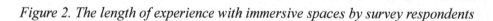

Figure 2. The length of experience with immersive spaces by survey respondents

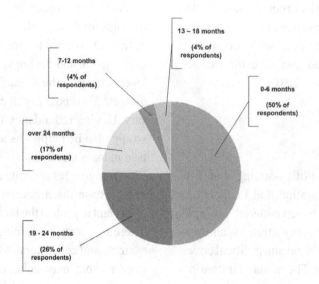

Table 2. A variety of learning in 3D immersive spaces

Self discovery learning	47.83%
Learner collaboration	39.13%
Skills based learning	39.13%
Simulation	34.78%
Practice	34.78%
Social learning	34.78%
Project-based learning	26.09%
Experiential learning	26.09%
Human facilitated learning	21.74%
Problem solving and decision-making	17.39%
Automated learning	13.04%
Role play	8.7%
Other	--*

* For "Other," respondents mentioned: "Virtual Architecture Design Learning Comments Text," problem based learning in the virtual world, and self-paced activities.

of patentable ideas or creations; some learning may involve simulated experiences (which may entail unintended "negative learning"); some learning may involve team collaborations where identities may be compromised or learners solicited into risky behaviors.

ONLINE SURVEY: DEFINING SECURITY ISSUES

The next question addressed the perception of security issues in online spaces. A number of responses equated online immersive security with safety in a face-to-face (F2F) classroom: "a 'safe' space which encourages free exchange of ideas and which is free from harassment, discrimination, or unwanted manipulation" and "the same way as anywhere else." Another wrote of the risk of endangering the "student experience." Others referred to the protection of digital property and "belongings".

Security was seen as physical safety for the digital avatars because these are stand-ins for the people behind them. The digital self should also be secure from others' manipulation. One respondent wrote:

There is much you can do (fly, skydive, surf), that might not be possible in RL (real life) without physical danger. You can try out social activities that you might not dare in RL (role playing games for example) with minimal emotional risk. The ultimate security in SL (Second Life) lies in 2 things: 1. ability to press quit at any time. 2. awareness that inventory & interactions are virtual. There are some aspects of SL that are not secure. Buildings are not secure, conversations in local chat are not secure, text that you write may be copied by others and disseminated [though against TOS (Terms of Service)]. On the other hand there are tools to provide reasonable security. Skyplatforms and IM provide some privacy. I believe that our ideas of security are overblown (tied to the cultures of litigation and therapy. In a new world where "privacy" is being redefined by the facebook (sic) generation, I hope we will become less concerned with security, when it isn't necessary.

Another looked at security as the protection of personal identity and details, in the real world. In-world risks have been identified as "gambling, child pornography, (and) pyramid schemes (that) have all appeared in Second Life™". The use of technologies for "cultural production" means that people use technologies to shape and understand the world and their places in it (Jones, 2000). There should not be negative "bleed-over" or harms from the digital world into the real. A project manager for the virtual world presence at a university (with responsibilities to support "faculty, administrators, students and staff" in the virtual world) suggested a diverse sense of security considerations:

I am not a security expert, but I think of this issue from two perspectives: (1) Does the student/

faculty member feel safe and secure in their ability to teach and learn in the environment, including: (a) security of their person (avatar) and objects and (virtual) possessions, (b) secure in their personal spaces, (c) secure in the knowledge that the university is taking necessary precautions to safeguard their work, give proper credit for actions/work performed, but not be unduly intrusive to their personal privacy (d) security of privacy, personal information and (e) secure communications. (2) Does the university have the ability to: (a) take the necessary precautions to assure all of the above, (b) protect their intellectual property (c) comply with existing laws and policies.

Another respondent pointed to the security of student anonymity enabled in immersive spaces. He or she pointed to online tools to restrict spaces to invited participants only and to ban "malicious users." This response suggested that there were sufficient tools to assure some kinds of identity assuredness and legitimate access.

ONLINE SURVEY: DEFINING RISKS

The next question asked respondents to define any risks they could see in 3D immersive spaces. This was phrased in a way to serve as a broad net to capture ideas.

One common perceived risk was that of non-participants interrupting a class. Cyberstalkers were also identified as a concern. Inappropriate exposure to contents "such as signage/imagery, language, or not fully-clothed or seductively clothed avatars" was also mentioned.

Another risk involved using excessive virtual social exchanges instead of "actual face to face social interaction" for learning outcomes, suggesting that virtual addictiveness could affect real-world F2F quality of life and learning. The hyper-realism of 3D immersive learning may lead to concerns for some individuals. This response seemed to refer to confusions between differentiat-

ing what is real and what is not. One respondent observed the risk of "becoming over involved in (the) environment separate from course activities (I know of this happening to 2 students, one of whom is now earning his living in SL and the other nearly suffered a nervous breakdown)."

The lack of sufficient funding for the development of immersive learning spaces was another concern. This suggests that clearer funding streams of virtual immersive endeavors may enhance their use for educational purposes.

Another respondent's response aligns with this concern:

3D immersive learning's risks mainly come from its newness. There are similar social and emotional risks as one finds entering a new culture (though you can always press quit). Like college abroad programs learning in SL may lead to:

1. *Confusing interactions until you understand the nuances of social norms,*
2. *If SL teachers are unfamiliar with the culture they may not be very good guides,*
3. *The lack of privacy and the possibility of making IM (instant messaging) mistakes are not unlike the risks we took when first using email (replying to all! when you meant to reply to one person),*
4. *Griefing is the real world experience of running into pan handlers or other surprising people on field trips (or anytime class is not in the sterile protection of classroom.*

Proper evaluation of actual learning is another danger, of "assuming value, without real measurement of outcome." This might suggest faculty may need more pedagogical design savvy and / or technological tools to achieve accurate assessment of learning outcomes.

The technological structure itself is seen as having been designed for a different purpose and therefore not having sufficient tracking or other security measures in place. "Many of the platforms for 3D immersive learning were designed for casual/entertainment use purposes, not for institutional use, and therefore do not provide the proper tools and data back-end (APIs or administrative tools) to allow institutions to ensure the above. In terms of liability, I am sure many platforms are being used in teaching and learning whereby instructors and institutions are unable to comply with existing laws."

The high technology requirements to run many of the immersive worlds pose a "major risk" that students will not have the required hardware according to another respondent. This person added: "All other risks seem to apply to other forms of learning and other uses of the Internet."

ONLINE SURVEY: SECURITY INCIDENCES

The next question addressed security incidences experienced in an immersive virtual world learning situation, if any. Quite a few respondents emphasized their newness in virtual worlds and added, "None yet."

A territorial sense of risk occurred for one respondent when some land next to theirs was developed in an unwanted way. This person wrote: "Islands created can be invaded by outside sources and develop next to you unless you have your own island....too much commercial selling of real money involved."

"Unkind" human-embodied avatars were experienced by students in Orientation Island and other areas of Second Life™. Another cited "griefing of all sorts too numerable to mention".

One respondent offered a litany of security incidences, which shows a broad range of concerns:

1. Students stumbled into sites that confused them or left them with questions
2. A griefer attempted to disrupt me when I was giving an SL presentation in front of a live audience

3. A student's heart was broken by an "sl boyfriend"
4. A meeting canceled because SL was not working

These were all learning experiences with analogues in RL (real life).

Data security, privacy issues, and institutional liabilities are issues of central concern for another respondent. This individual added: "We have had isolated incidents of "griefing" or troublemakers causing problems for classes, but these are few and far between. The most pressing issues are the institutional liability issues mentioned above - data security, (and) privacy issues, etc."

SURVEY: SOCIAL DESIGNS TO PROMOTE SAFETY

The last question read: "What sorts of 'social designs' do you use to promote safety in your immersive online learning? ("Social designs" refer to human facilitation, policy-setting and enforcement, awareness-raising and other designed strategies.) Please explain why."

Several respondents were encouraging of suggestions in this area but said that they didn't have anything to contribute at this time. Others suggested setting baseline understandings among learners.

You have to have some common starting point and rules when exchanging information between students online. Keep comments positive and the exchange in line with the education outcomes of the course.

One respondent wrote:

Before users are permitted access to our virtual space, they receive a notice in email and in the virtual space explaining that all applicable laws and university policies are in effect on our virtual campus. We have a "Public Safety" office on our virtual campus that explains what "griefing" is and provides strategies to deal with these incidents safely. We also provide contact information for reporting security incidents. One of the first things we teach students is how to escape unwanted or uncomfortable situations.

Another suggested basic information sharing: "Students are provided with information about risks and what to do but apart from that no action." Another quipped: "If you treat your students as adults, they will act like adults." Others suggested controlling those who have access to a course through SLOODLE (Second Life™ and Moodle™).

One explained a variety of strategies to promote safety for learners:

We discussed the "good" and "bad" of Second Life and compare it to the "good" and "bad" on the Internet or in any city. We explained the use of PG (parental guidance) and M (mature) areas in Second Life and noted that people from all of (sic) the world use Second Life. We explained how a user could report problems and block users from interacting with them. We created our own tutorials rather than having students explore Orientation Island. We asked students to create their accounts and when they arrived at Orientation Island they immediately teleport to our land for instruction and support. We also restricted access to our teaching area to the students, instructor, and instructional designer. It has been a really nice experience.

One sent students to a published book (Brian White's *Second Life: A Guide to your Virtual World*) in the first few weeks of class.

We discuss all of the issues I mentioned. I explicitly teach how to (a) quit and (b) teleport away from uncomfortable situations. As I said above, I see the use of VWs (virtual worlds) having the risks of a field trip and a travel abroad program. It is

important to provide students with an effective orientation so that they will be and feel safe in a new kind of learning space.

One suggested more robust administrative tools for virtual landowner controls. While user tracking is possible with additional scripting, this is not a common feature in the toolkit for most virtual world spaces.

DISCUSSION

The risk assessments seem to devolve into two general types of risks. High-criticality security issues may involve the loss of hundreds of human-hours of development work. They may involve the loss of intellectual property and digital items. They may result in the loss of privy information involving competitive advantage; they may involve economic fallouts. High criticality risks may discourage learners, faculty and administrators from using immersive spaces for higher education. Low criticality security risks may involve lesser losses (of the prior types mention) and less potent damages.

Such issues seem to be best addressed via policies and technologies. The companies or organizations that control the 3D immersive grid may bring authority, legal standing, high-level investigative access, and perspective to security issues.

Social design comes into play to support the human element in immersive interactivity and awareness-raising of anomalous behaviors. This assists in the identification of vulnerabilities. This supports the informing of the user public in strengthening protective measures. Socializing each generation of learners into security awareness, policies, and practices will require diligent efforts. Even if failsafe systems were ever created, the human piece requires the social design and outreach. The technological infrastructure should allow the creation of digital trails, user authentication, access controls, and archived histories of interactions. Using multiple approaches promotes "whole system" security, with fewer potential gaps.

A "security dividend" (that stems from safety and user confidence in immersive worlds) enhances e-learning in 3D immersive learning spaces. It lowers the transactional costs in the complex interchanges that occur with learning. It strengthens user trust and the reputations of these persistent metaworlds. It allows for more time and energy to be focused on the design and conduct of e-learning. It broadens the range of topics of what may be taught in this technological venue. It encourages risk-taking into untested realms of creativity (without fears that digital objects will be usurped, for example).

FUTURE CONCERNS

More work needs to be done on potential risks of immersive learning, with more research (both pure and applied), "red team" attacks on immersive systems, white-hat "ethical" hacks, and from-life learning, to test for vulnerabilities. Those who would "live dangerously" (within limits) in embodied avatars may be able to surface other learning. Because of the newness and amorphousness of this security concern in immersive spaces, much of the learning seems to draw from existing security issues in four-wall spaces, online learning scenarios, social networking sites, and virtual communities. More learning from direct 3D immersive spaces may offer fresh insights. More studies of people's experiences in immersive spaces (especially over time) would enhance the research literature. There needs to be research on the specifics of social design actions and how these mesh with the other modes of a 360° intervention: policy-setting and enforcement and technological robustness. Such information will have to be shared widely.

Immersiveness has been moving towards real spaces through digital installations, augmented reality, tele-collaborations, wearable computing, and the design of haptic / tactile devices. Interactive immersiveness is the zeitgeist of this phase of the Digital Age. Security will continue to be a concern in every form of immersive learning because of the known and unknown vulnerabilities stemming from people and the technologies. Auditing regularly will be critical to identifying security risks and violations, given the changing technological standards and systems and the changing faces of potential threats. This area will offer many possibilities for research and exploration.

CONCLUSION

Security is a deeply personal matter that affects learners' well-being and sense of safety; this affects user confidence in a virtual system and society. A sense of personal and group safety directly affects the risk-taking that learners will make in immersive spaces to acquire new relationships, knowledge and skills. Anticipating prospective risks in immersive spaces enhances e-learning in 3D spaces. Indeed, there is no single failsafe to achieve perfect safety for all users. Threat is an evolving state, and the nature of various threats will change and surprise those focused on security. Clearly, a combination of strategies (policy-setting and enforcement, human facilitation and leadership, and technologies) needs to be applied. Planning strategies to address these security risks may enhance the acceptance of these virtual world tools for learning purposes by lessening real and perceived risks. The uses of social design may offer a stop-gap and continuing safety measure to make virtual immersive spaces more inviting and supportive of learners now and into the future.

ACKNOWLEDGMENT

Thanks to all who participated in the online survey. I am appreciative of the work of the Second

Life®Users Group at K-State. I am grateful for the helpful comments of the anonymous respondents to the draft chapter and also Dr. Alan Rea's supportive and meticulous direction. "Social design" for security has evolved from years of work in various classrooms around the world, and I am grateful to my students for all that they've taught me. Thanks to R. Max, in the real and the virtual.

REFERENCES

Andrejevic, M. (2007). *iSpy: Surveillance and Power in the Interactive Era*. Lawrence, KS: University Press of Kansas.

Bamford, J. (2008). *The Shadow Factory: The Ultra-Secret NSA from 9/11 to the Eavesdropping on America*. New York: Random House.

Bers, M. U. (2001). Identity construction environments: Developing personal and moral values through the design of a virtual city. *Journal of the Learning Sciences, 10*(4), 365–415. doi:10.1207/S15327809JLS1004new_1

Bugeja, M. J. (2008). Second Life, revisited. Which should take precedence in a virtual-reality campus: Corporate terms of service or public-disclosure laws. *The Chronicle of Higher Education, 23–27.*

Burmester, M., Henry, P. & Kermes, L.S. (2005). Tracking cyberstalkers: A cryptographic approach. *ACM SIGCAS Computers and Society, 35*(3).

Calongne, C., Endorf, S., Frankovich, D., & Sandaire, J. (2008). A virtual environment for designing user interface prototypes. Consortium for Computing Sciences in Colleges. Rocky Mountain Conference. *JCSC, 24*(1), 188 – 195.

Cikic, S., Grottke, S., Lehmann-Grube, F., & Sablatnig, J. (2008). *Cheat-prevention and analysis in online virtual worlds*. Adelaide, Australia: E-Forensics.

Clarke, R. A., & Knake, R. K. (2010). *Cyber war: The next threat to national security and what to do about it*. New York: HarperCollins.

Colella, V. (2000). Participatory simulations: Building collaborative understanding through immersive dynamic modeling. *Journal of the Learning Sciences, 9*(4), 471–500. doi:10.1207/S15327809JLS0904_4

Dawes, S. S., Bloniarz, P. A., Kelly, K. L., & Fletcher, P. D. (1999). Some assembly required: Building a digital government for the 21st century. *1999 Center for Technology in Government*, (pp. 18).

DeSensi, G., Longo, F., & Mirabella, G. (2007). *Ergonomic and work methods optimization in a three dimensional virtual environment* (pp. 1187–1192). SCSC.

Ellis, J. B., Luther, K., Bessiere, K., & Kellogg, W. A. (2008). *Games for virtual team building*. *DIS 2008, Cape Town, South Africa* (p. 295). New York: ACM.

Garau, M., Slater, M., Vinayagamoorthy, V., Brogni, A., Steed, A., & Sasse, M. A. (2003). The impact of avatar realism and eye gaze control on perceived quality of communication in a shared immersive virtual environment, CHI 2003, Ft. Lauderdale, FL. *CHI Letters, 5*(1), 529–536.

Gebhard, P., Kipp, M., Klesen, M., & Rist, T. (2003). Authoring scenes for adaptive, interactive performances. In *AAMAS '03*, Melbourne, Australia, (pp. 725). New York: ACM.

Guo, Y., & Barnes, S. (2007). Why people buy virtual items in virtual worlds with real money. *The Data Base for Advances in Information Systems, 38*(4), 69–76.

Hai-Jew, S. (2007). The trust factor in online instructor-led college courses. *Journal of Interactive Instruction Development, 19*(3).

Hai-Jew, S. (2009). Exploring the immersive para-social: Is it *you* or the thought of you? *MERLOT Journal of Online Learning and Teaching, 5*(2).

Jones, S. (2000). Towards a philosophy of virtual reality: Issues implicit in 'Consciousness Reframed.' [Retrieved from JSTOR.]. *Leonardo, 33*(2), 125–132. doi:10.1162/002409400552388

Knight, M. M., & Arns, L. L. (2006). The relationship among age and other factors on incidence of cybersickness in immersive environment users. In *APGV*, Boston, Massachusetts, (pp. 162). New York: ACM.

Mandal, S., & Lim, E.-P. (2008). Second Life: Limits of creativity or cyber threat? IEEE. 498 – 503.

Mark, G., & Semaan, B. (2008). Resilience in collaboration: Technology as a resource for new patterns of action. In *CSCW '08,* San Diego, CA, (pp. 137 – 146). New York: ACM.

McQuiggan, S. W., Rowe, J. P., & Lester, J. C. (2008). The effects of empathetic virtual characters on presence in narrative-centered learning environments. In *CHI 2008 Proceedings: Character Development*, (pp. 1512), Florence, Italy.

Merrick, K., & Maher, M. L. (2007). Motivated reinforcement learning for adaptive characters in open-ended simulation games. In *ACE '07*, Salzburg, Austria, (pp. 127). New York: ACM.

Nechvatal, J. (2001). Towards an immersive intelligence. *Leonardo, 34*(5), 417–422. doi:10.1162/002409401753521539

Noam, E. M. (2007). The dismal economics of virtual worlds. *The Data Base for Advances in Information Systems, 38*(4), 107.

Pelechano, N., Stocker, C., Allbeck, J., & Badler, N. (2008). Being a part of a crowd: Towards validating VR crowds using presence. In *Proceedings of the 7th International Conference on Autonomous Agents and Multiagent Systems. International Foundation for Autonomous Agents and Multiagent Systems,* (pp. 136 – 142). New York: ACM.

Schkolne, S. (2002). Drawing with the hand in free space: Creating 3D shapes with gesture in a semi-immersive environment. *Leonardo, 35*(4), 371–375. doi:10.1162/002409402760181132

Sherman, D. K., & Cohen, G. L. (2002). Accepting threatening information: Self-affirmation and the reduction of defensive biases. *Current Directions in Psychological Science, 11*(4), 119 – 123. Retrieved Aug. 29, 2009, from http://www.jstor.org/stable/20182787

Siponen, M. T. (2001). An Analysis of the Recent IS Security Development Approaches. In Dhillon, G. (Ed.), *Information Security Management: Global Challenges in the New Millennium* (pp. 106–107). Hershey, PA: Idea Group, Inc.

Siponen, M.T. (2006). Secure-system design methods: Evolution and future directions. *IT Pro., 40.*

Siponen, M. T., & Kajava, J. (1998, 2002). Ontology of organizational IT security awareness—from theoretical foundations to practical framework. In *Enabling Technologies: Infrastructure for Collaborative Enterprises, 1998.* Stanford, CA. 330 – 331. Retrieved May 4, 2009, from http://ieeexplore.ieee.org/xpls/abs_all.jsp?arnumber=725713

Siponen, M. T., & Oinas-Kukkonen, H. (2007). A review of information security issues and respective research contributions. *The Data Base for Advances in Information Systems, 38*(1), 62.

Sutter, J., & Carroll, J. (2009, Feb. 6). *Fears of imposters increase on Facebook.* Retrieved Feb. 8, 2009, from http://www.cnn.com/2009/TECH/02/05/facebook.impostors/index.html

Takashima, K., Omori, Y., Yoshimoto, Y., Itoh, Y., Kitamura, Y., & Kishino, F. (2008). Effects of avatar's blinking animation on person impressions. In *Graphics Interface Conference,* (pp. 169 – 176), Windsor, Ontario, Canada.

Totten, I. (2009, Feb. 26). *Second Life Showcase.* Kansas State University Instructional Design Technology Roundtable Presentation.

Trewin, S. M., Laff, M. R., Cavender, A. C., & Hanson, V. L. (2008). *Accessibility in virtual worlds. CHI 2008 Proceedings: Works in Progress. Florence, Italy* (pp. 2728–2729). New York: ACM.

White, D., & Rea, A. (2008). Just trying to be friendly: A case study in social engineering. *Journal of Information Science and Technology, 4*(2), 59.

ADDITIONAL READING

Andrejevic, M. (2007). *iSpy: Surveillance and Power in the Interactive Era*. Lawrence: University Press of Kansas.

Balkin, J. M., & Noveck, B. S. (2006). *The State of Play: Law, Games, and Virtual Worlds*. New York: New York University.

Castronova, E. (2005). *Synthetic Worlds: The Business and Culture of Online Games*. Chicago: The University of Chicago Press.

Clarke, R. A., & Knake, R. K. (2010). *Cyber war: The next threat to national security and what to do about it*. New York: HarperCollins.

Dovey, J., & Kennedy, H. W. (2006). *Game Cultures: Computer Games as New Media*. New York: Open University Press.

Ludlow, P., & Wallace, M. (2007). *The Second Life Herald: The Virtual Tabloid that Witnessed the Dawn of the Metaverse*. Cambridge: The MIT Press.

Williams, J. P., Hendricks, S. D., & Winkler, W. K. (2006). *Gaming as Culture. Jefferson: McFarland & Company, Inc*. Publishers.

Williams, J. P., & Smith, J. H. (2007). *The Players' Realm: Studies on the Culture of Video Games and Gaming. Jefferson: McFarland & Company, Inc*. Publishers.

KEY TERMS AND DEFINITIONS

360-Degree: Involving all angles from a single point, suggesting inclusiveness.

Avatar: A digital personification or symbol of an individual or sentient form.

Datamining: The extraction of useful information from recorded contents of user interactions or other datasets.

Digital Enclosure: The concept that people may live in a physical space that is totally wired and recording all their decisions and actions; a conceptual digital "space" in which people's actions are recorded and observable.

Emo (emotional) Agent: An emotional agent or robot that may interact using emotions and affect with human users.

Grid: A network, a framework.

Griefing: Being a nuisance or trouble to others; causing annoyance through actions like graffiti-ing a site, scripting disrupting episodes in virtual worlds.

Haptic: Tactile, involving the sense of touch.

Human-Embodied: Driven by human intelligence and presence.

Immersion: Being deeply engaged or involved, full-sensory full-surround virtual environmental experience.

Interactivity: The interchanges and intercommunications between human-embodied digital avatars.

Open-Sim: An open-source non-proprietary simulation.

Panopticon: The concept of a living environment in which all actions are seen.

Parasocial: Resembling or imitative of a social relationship.

Parasocial Relationship: A one-way relationship between a person and a media figure or avatar.

Persistent: Lasting continuously over time (as in "persistent" virtual worlds).

Porous: Permeable, pervious (such as borders that are able to be passed through).

RL (Real Life): Actual real-world existence.

Robot: An automated or scripted persona or object in a virtual world.

Safety: Secure state-of-being.

Security: Freedom from danger.

SL (Second Life): A popular 3D virtual world populated by human-embodied and AI-driven avatars.

Social Design: The setup of policies, culture, awareness-raising, and social expectations for particular desired effects.

Surveillance: The monitoring or close observation of an individual or a group.

Synchronous: In real time.

Tracking: The recording of the actions and progress of an individual (or group) through virtual space.

APPENDIX

The following survey was deployed Mar. 9 – 31, 2009, and this was posted through the following venues:

- The Colleague-to-Colleague listserv (C2C) (c2c@list.jccc.edu)
- The DEOS listserv (deos@psu.edu)
- The Instructional Design Open Studio (IDOS) blog (http://id.ome.ksu.edu/blog/)
- Second Life Education Group (SLED) list (educators@lists.secondlife.com)
- Second Life Researcher List slrl@list.academ-x.com
- Presence PRESENCE-L@LISTSERV.TEMPLE.EDU
- Virtual Worlds VW@LISTSERV.EDUCAUSE.EDU

Security in 3D Immersive and Interactive Spaces in Higher Education (Survey)

I am collecting experiences that educators may have had with "security" in 3D immersive and interactive (learning) spaces in higher education for a forthcoming article or chapter. This survey consists of six brief questions. Please help me with this information collection.

Informed Consent

Description of Research and Procedures: The objective of survey is to gain a deeper understanding of potential security issues in 3D immersive spaces used for learning in higher education and possible social design mitigations against security risks.

Possible Risks or Discomforts: This study does not entail foreseeable risks or harms.

Benefits to the Participant: This research will contribute to the body of literature about ways to improve online learning and services, particularly in the 3D immersive realm.

Compensation: Participants will not be paid for their responses to this survey or telephone interview. There will be no monetary cost to this survey or telephone interview for their participation either.

Confidentiality of Research Information: No information will be released for non-research purposes. The self-identification information will not be cross-referenced with any other database of information. There will not be computerized tracking of respondents. Only necessary information will be collected. Data will be aggregated. Specific quotes may be taken from the interviews and surveys, but these will be used without identifiable descriptors and or only with participant agreement.

At the completion of the research, the digitized survey information will be securely stored and maintained for at least three years after the end of the study. The website that will host the survey will not maintain any identifiable records of participant responses.

Right to Withdraw: The survey respondent is under no obligation to participate in this study and is free to withdraw consent to participate at any time without penalty.

Summary of Results: A summary of the results (a research paper in digital form) will be supplied to any interested participants, at no cost, upon request and provision of a recipient's email address. The researcher's email will follow at the end of the survey.

Agreement to Participate in Online Survey: I voluntarily agree to participate in this research study and online survey. By completing the survey, I signify both my understanding of the informed consent and my voluntary agreement to participate.

This survey will not likely take more than 10 minutes to respond to.
Please participate only if you're 18 years old or older. Thank you.

The IRB Chairman at KSU may be reached as follows:
Dr. Rick Scheidt, IRB Chair
203 Fairchild, KSU
Manhattan, KS 66506
785-532-3224

Background Information

1. How long have you been teaching in 3D immersive spaces (like Second Life), in higher education?
    0-6 months
    7 - 12 months
    13 – 18 months
    19 – 24 months
    More than two years
2. What types of learning have you designed for 3D immersive spaces? Please check all that apply.
    Self-discovery learning
    Practice
    Social learning
    Learner collaboration
    Project based learning
    Automated learning
    Human-facilitated
    Skills based learning
    Simulation
    Experiential learning
    Role play
    Problem solving and decision making
    Other…

Survey Contents

3. How do you define "security" in 3D immersive learning spaces?
4. What risks do you see in 3D immersive learning? (Please write all that apply.)
5. What security incidences have you experienced in a learning situation or in relation to your teaching work in 3D immersive spaces, if any?
6. What sorts of "social designs" do you use to promote safety in your immersive online learning? ("Social designs" refer to human facilitation, policy-setting and enforcement, awareness-raising and other designed strategies.) Please explain why.

Chapter 6
"No Drama!"
A Case Study of Social Governance in Second Life®

Nola Johnston
BC Institute of Technology, Canada

ABSTRACT

This chapter argues that because in-world social relationships have value and impact on user experience, their security must be addressed by any group entering a virtual environment. Given the constraints imposed by legal structures, the coding of a world's architecture, and social norms and expectations, what options for management of social relationships are practical and effective? A case study of one social group in the virtual world of Second Life® offers a possible model. Elf Circle is a large group that has developed a comprehensive system of social governance—still evolving—to manage social relationships and protect its members. Its policies and procedures, and the reasons for them, are reviewed with the aim of providing some governance strategies that address common issues.

INTRODUCTION

When people talk about security for Rich Internet Applications (RIAs) such as virtual worlds, they are generally talking about protecting data and privacy. While critically important issues, these leave out a different kind of security—the social and emotional security of a person within those environments.

Does an individual feel safe and confident there, or frustrated, vulnerable, or threatened?

This chapter argues that because in-world social relationships have value and impact on user experience, their security must be addressed by any group entering a virtual environment. Given the constraints imposed by legal structures, the coding of a world's architecture, and social norms and expectations, what options for management of social relationships are practical and effective? A case study of one social group in the virtual world of Second Life® (SL™) offers a possible model. Elf Circle is a large group that has developed a comprehensive system of social governance—still evolving—to manage social relationships and

DOI: 10.4018/978-1-61520-891-3.ch006

protect its members. Its policies and procedures, and the reasons for them, are reviewed in this chapter with the aim of providing some governance strategies that address common issues.

Methodology

This study is based on interviews and my own experience: as with all Elf Circle members interviewed, I have been a member of the group since its inception and sit on both its primary governance bodies, High Council and High Circle. The interview with the owner of the group, Forcythia Wishbringer, was recorded via Skype. Other members provided written responses to a questionnaire (Appendix A), as did leaders of two other SL social communities. Respondents provided no personal identifying information, but their real avatar names are used.

Elf Circle members who are not part of governance and current or former members who disagree with its application were not interviewed. This is not because their opinions and experiences are not of value, but because the focus of the chapter is to examine the reasons for developing existing structures. A more in-depth exploration of the efficacy of the structure and its implications would be of considerable interest but would require a much longer document.

BACKGROUND

About Second Life

Second Life (www.secondlife.com) is not a game, but a platform owned by Linden Lab (LL). In-world content created by users (Residents) using the program's building and scripting tools provides amazingly diverse environments and activities. Basic user accounts are free, but the ability to display content created is tied to land ownership, i.e. rental of server space (Linden Lab, 2009a). Land is organized in 256 x 256 m blocks called regions (or "islands" or "sims", for simulators); individuals can lease entire regions or smaller parcels. Copyright resides with content creators, and an in-world economy (convertible to U.S. dollars) facilitates buying and selling of goods created by Residents. The potential of emergent virtual worlds such as SL is uncertain, their use is being explored actively by businesses, non-profits, and educators.

Virtual Worlds as Social Spaces

This chapter takes as a given two principles: first, that social relationships and the communities they inform within virtual reality are real (Pearce, 2009; Williams, 2006, 2007), and may persist across a range of online environments (Pearce, 2009), and secondly, that the economies of virtual worlds produce market, social (moral relationships based on reciprocity), and cultural (competencies, credentials, and artifacts of significance to a defined group) capital (Malaby, 2006). It follows from that position that these social and cultural relationships have value.

Although individuals enter them for different reasons (Bartle, 1996; Lastowka & Hunter, 2004; Whang & Chang, 2004; Yee, 2007), virtual worlds generally have a social component, even if it is not a formal goal. For example, because a virtual-world environment creates a sense of embodied presence that can affect how people interact by visually localizing individuals in a shared space (DiPaola & Turner, 2008; Gee, 2008; Noveck, 2004; Pearce, 2009; Slater, Sadagic, Usoh, & Schroeder, 2000) and may further naturalize interactions through the use of spatial sound (Yankelovich, 2007), people tend to spend informal time socializing and networking before and after virtual meetings (Linden, 2009; Linden Research, 2009).

In a social context, avatars have a "real and persistent identity within an online universe" (Ludlow & Wallace, 2007) and may express distinct personas or explore their identity (Pearce, 2009; Taylor, 2006); online social relationships are real and for some the liminal nature of interactions may actually serve to make them more intense (Williams, 2006). Group identity frames individual identity (Pearce, 2009), and both are dynamically and contextually formed by interaction with and within the game (Consalvo, 2009; Taylor, 2009). Virtual worlds are a locus for emergent cultures (Ludlow and Wallace, 2007; Meadows, 2008; Pearce, 2009; Shirky, 2003).

Social relationships can replicate the kind of stresses and conflicts found in the real world; a relationship breakup can be emotionally catastrophic whether the environment is virtual or real, and can seriously stress a community if members feel compelled to take sides. Individuals may have different goals or expectations, which may or may not match those experienced in the real world or in other virtual worlds (Lessig, 2006; Ludlow & Wallace, 2007; Pearce, 2009), and thus lead to conflicts. Additional stresses may result from factors indigenous to virtual environments.

Deviant Behavior

Although virtual worlds are notable for their culture of kindness and altruism (Boellstorff, 2008), visitors do face threats, some relating to conflicts informed by social and technical relationships and some resulting from deliberate intent (griefing).

Griefing

Griefing refers to disruptive attacks by avatars that harm the experience and enjoyment of others. True griefing is intentional and involves deliberate attacks or harassment. Minor offenses such as littering (leaving objects on others' land) or indecency (manifesting mature/adult content in regions classified as PG, which means General in SL) may be deliberate but can also occur by accident or because people don't know local rules or how to use the interface.

Avatars can be trapped in containers by "caging" devices or attacked by weapons scripted to use a push attack (i.e., fire invisible objects that take advantage of the system of physics applied by SL's coding to push an avatar). Although these attacks do no real harm, they may be distressing to "newbies" (new users) who do not know how to escape them. For this reason, non-consensual physical attacks are prohibited by Linden Lab except in areas designated as "unsafe," which allow a simulation of death (the avatar will run out of "health" and be teleported home) and are often reserved for combat.

Linden Lab actively works on mechanisms to minimize and contain damage from indirect assaults on the SL "grid" (Linden, 2009b) and reports serious Denial Of Service (DOS) attacks to the FBI (Au, 2008).

The level of anonymity possible and the consequent disinhibition resulting from it (Boellstorf, 2008; Lessig, 2006; Williams, 2000) may partially explain why griefing is likely to occur in virtual worlds, but this may also relate to identity construction: "For some, it's the only way they can think of to build their virtual persona" (Ludlow & Wallace, 2007). Categorization models of players may vary (Bartle, 1996; Foo, 2004; Whang & Chang, 2004; Yee, 2007), but griefers represent a particular user type and may be part of a griefer culture/community (Foo, 2004; Ludlow & Wallace, 2007; Whang & Chang, 2004). Punishment is generally ineffective at rehabilitation, because it only works if the individual cares about consequences (Williams, 2000). Groups can ban a griefer from their lands, but the griefer can simply move on to other areas; if banned from the world, the anonymity typical of virtual worlds may allow them to return using a different avatar.

It is important to recognize the potential social impact of griefing and understand its consequences as real. Users may have a significant emotional investment in their avatar and their in-world experiences (Boellstorff, 2008; Meadows, 2008; Pearce, 2009). Although online interactions are by definition virtual, and in Second Life neither avatars or belongings can be harmed in a permanent way, the associated emotional experiences can be very real to the victim of an attack, even when purely text-based (Dibbell, 1993; Williams, 2000), and may in fact be more psychologically harmful than an offline equivalent (Williams, 2006). Forcythia Wishbringer, owner of Elf Circle group, notes that in-world experiences of assault can be intensified by an individual's personal history (F. Wishbringer, personal communication, April 29, 2009).

Governance within Second Life

The evolution of structures of governance in online applications is generally a work in progress that meshes public and private rules and remedies to address specific needs (Cannataci & Mifsud-Bonnici, 2007). Within Second Life, formal governance of social relationships exists at three levels: that of the code, that of the system (the legal framework implemented by Linden Lab) and the governance practices of individual groups.

Governance by Code

The idea that cultural structures and governance of virtual environments are defined by code is well established (Bartle, 2006; Lessig, 2006). The technical structure of a virtual environment defines and shapes the reality of that environment—including cultural and governance practices—by making some things possible and others impossible. In SL, for example, communication with large groups of people is facilitated by the Group function: anyone in a Group can easily send an IM to all members. But at the same time, the Group function limits communication, because no avatar may belong to more than 25 groups. No one can get around this constraint: until the code changes, it is as immutable as a law of nature, and will define and limit possibilities for both individual experience and community governance.

Such constraints can be problematic. Who writes the code? Are they accountable for its consequences? What are their goals? Code functionally defines social relationships, but the people who write it don't necessarily have social management knowledge and skills that would allow them to create viable structures that encourage community development and health (Ludlow & Wallace, 2007).

Governance by Law

Linden Lab's Terms of Service (Linden Lab, 2009c), a legal document that all users must agree to as part of entering the world, sets out the conditions for participation in Second Life. Its Community Standards (Linden Lab, 2009d) define general rules for behaviour by prohibiting certain classifications of activities, including intolerance, harassment, assault, disclosure (of other Residents' personal information or communications), indecency, and disturbing the peace. An Abuse Reporting system enables Residents to lay complaints. Linden Lab will investigate and, based on the severity of the offense, use sanctions ranging from warnings and suspensions to account cancellation. Complainants are not told how their issues are resolved, an approach that protects privacy but provides little satisfaction.

Linden Lab takes a generally hands-off approach to direct governance. Philip Rosedale, its CEO, said, "[O]ur feeling is... that we should aggressively move into code anything we can, because of the enhanced scalability it gives us. And we should execute policy outside of code only when absolutely necessary or unfeasible." (Lessig, 2006) LL's approach to difficult issues is therefore often reactive; activities such as gambling and content relating to child pornography were prohibited explicitly when issues arose from in-world activities. LL enforces policies if they discover contraventions, but generally relies on Resident reporting to find them, which can result in inconsistencies. Some legal issues are devolved entirely: Linden Lab grants copyright over all content created within SL to the creators, but will not enforce copyright law or adjudicate violations, advising Residents with copyright disputes to file a complaint under the Digital Millennium Copyright Act. Many virtual world owners take a similarly hands-off approach (Castronova, 2006; Ludlow & Wallace, 2007). The opacity of judicial process and the devolution of enforcement to Residents has left many users of SL dissatisfied (Boellstorff, 2008; Ludlow & Wallace, 2007).

Governance by Community

In the "real" world, social organizations create security for members by defining and maintaining order through sets of rules and sanctions which govern external and internal interactions (Brenner, 2008). But real-world legal structures may not adequately address the specificity of online deviant behaviour, generating a need for alternative remedies (Williams, 2006) In order to protect community cohesion (Williams, 2000; 2007) many communities, including Elf Circle, have set up internal governance systems to augment those provided by Linden Lab's code and legal systems.

ELF CIRCLE

About Elf Circle

The Elf Circle (EC) group, formed in 2006, is owned by Forcythia Wishbringer. Its membership at the time of writing is 1750+ avatars and growing. It is associated with a publicly accessible land base comprised of 40 directly connected regions joined together to form a High Fantasy Continent. Other groups in the same area raise the total of fantasy-themed regions to 80+ (Figure 1).

Elf Circle's mission, stated in its Charter (Elf Circle, 2009), is "to provide a safe, enjoyable experience for everyone." All policies and practices are designed to support this goal. The Charter reinforces Linden Lab's Community Standards

and sets out prohibitions against specific behaviours deemed as harmful to EC's goals. Associated regions in the continent must adhere to Charter rules.

Wishbringer owns the "core" sims within the fantasy continent. Most land is rented to tenants; approximately 25% is reserved for public use, providing oceans, greenspaces, and centres for activity, such as the Castle (a large meeting space with group information), the Drum Circle (a dance and socialization space), a Library, and a Market for vendors.

Elf Circle hosts a range of activities including concerts, dances, competitions, classes, and social subgroups. It participates in real-world fundraising events; in 2009 its Circle of Life team raised L$886,061 (approximately US$3420) for the American Cancer Society's Relay for Life in Second Life campaign (American Cancer Society, 2009).

Governance is designed to facilitate such activities while protecting the community against

Figure 1. Elf Circle is a large social group within Second Life. Its lands adhere to a high fantasy theme and its members participate in a wide range of social and creative activities intended to develop and reinforce community; this shows part of a build made by the Elf Circle team for the American Cancer Society's Relay for Life in Second Life fundraising campaign. ©2009 Nola Johnston. Used with permission.

external and internal threats. Queen Forcythia Wishbringer, head of a benevolent monarchy, is advised by a High Council of selected avatars and supported by two volunteer services: the Greeters, who welcome and educate visitors, and the Guardians, who enforce rules and protect the community from griefers.

The next sections will outline some of the modifiers affecting governance and show how EC's approach addresses the problems these constraints create.

External Modifiers of Governance Practice

Smith (1998) lists four conditions that increase conflict within groups: an open, heterogeneous population, lack of shared goals, asymmetrical power structures, and strategies for dealing with dissent that lack full consensus. This is significant for Elf Circle, which has a diverse membership and is constrained by coded structures that enforce asymmetry in power and opacity in process.

Power Relationships, Code and Legal Structures

Contemporary governance theory argues that governance is most effective when networked, involving participation from a multiplicity of stakeholders, and negotiated through consensus (Mayntz, 2003). But certain structures of governance may be enforced or prevented by the architecture of the world (Lastowka & Hunter, 2004; Lessig, 2006). As Richard Bartle points out in his hierarchy of levels of constraint (Bartle, 2006), the developers of a virtual worlds are gods in their relationship to that world because they control its physics and cannot abrogate that power even if they want to.

In the case of Second Life, the ability to enforce rules is defined by the program architecture and Linden Lab's legal framework in terms of individual ownership of land and groups. Landowners and Group owners are the only ones who have legal standing, though they may assign management abilities to others. Alternative forms of governance and ownership in SL can be explored, but they cannot be enforced: a group may set up a democratic structure, but if a dispute occurs only the official landowner as recognized by LL will have any real power, and there is no mechanism in code or LL's legal framework to protect the interests of non-owners. In any case, as Desmond Shang (the leader of another large SL social group) points out, true democracy is impossible in a world in which anonymity is the rule and one individual may control multiple avatars (D. Shang, personal communication, April 17, 2009).

Ironically, Elf Circle was originally formed because of a conflict over ownership. The owner of another fantasy-themed group shared governance to some degree with Forcythia Wishbringer, who legally owned most of the land base that the group was associated with. Wishbringer paid for these regions with her own money, augmented by rentals and group donations. The group owner and his supporters believed that the lands morally belonged to the group, not Wishbringer, and expected control over all decisions relating to them as well as to the group itself. Wishbringer and her supporters believed that the legal landowner who paid the bills had primary rights over the land, and should also therefore have some authority over the group associated with those lands.

When disagreements arose as to the direction of the group, compounded by issues of trust over finances, different perspectives on ownership and rights, the impossibility of full transparency with regard to financial issues or governance, and the legal structure and policies imposed by Linden Lab, the issue exploded, and Wishbringer was removed from governance of the group and then from the group itself when she publicly took issue with her removal. Wishbringer then created Elf Circle group and removed the lands she owned, leaving the original group with only one region. Many members of the original group migrated to

Elf Circle at this time; others remained or kept dual memberships. Both groups survived this split and currently have healthy membership levels.

A significant cause of the split was a dissonance between the understanding and actuality of power relationships over land. Some individuals attributed power to the group owner because of his association with the group he had created, but Linden Lab's legal structures gave it absolutely to another individual because of her status as landowner. The problems that led to this irreconcilable conflict are one of the reasons that Elf Circle has the governance structure it does, assigning absolute authority of group and lands to the individual who has legal standing with Linden Lab.

Transparency and the Legitimacy of Authority

The UN Development Program lays out 5 basic requirements for good governance, including participation, transparency, and accountability (Abdellatif, 2003). Extensive research shows that the way in which decisions are made, not just outcomes, will significantly affect perceptions of legitimacy of authority (Mertins, 2008). Individuals are more likely to perceive a process as fair if they are given a voice and treated with dignity, and are more likely to perceive governance as legitimate if they perceive procedures as fair (Lind & Earley, 1992; Lind, Tyler & Huo, 1997). If information on trustworthiness is not available, judgments are made based on perceptions of procedural fairness (Van den Bos, Wilke, & Lind, 1998). The group engagement model argues that if people are given fair process and treated with dignity and respect, their status and self-definition will be affirmed and cooperation within the group will be enhanced (Tyler & Blader, 2003).

Linden Lab's code and legal framework explicitly limit options for transparency. Only Linden Lab can access user data, including communication logs. Individual avatars may be wholly anonymous in-world if they so choose. Publicly

sharing personal information or logs of communications without permission is prohibited by the Community Standards. It is therefore almost impossible to acquire "hard evidence" in a dispute to prove the rights of one side or the other, and information that is acquired can rarely be shared.

In a world that limits transparency how can legitimacy of governance be established? Experience confers some authority (Boellstorf, 2008). The interplay between social capital (reciprocity in actions) and cultural capital (acquired competencies) is one way of generating trust (Malaby, 2007). But if a platform's code, legal structures, and corporate policies are the sole arbiters of practice, it is very difficult for communities to develop systems of trust and enforcement (Ludlow & Wallace, 2007). Yet as seen in the experience of EC's formation, factors relating to trust and legitimacy can have a very real effect on the viability of a group.

Elf Circle's Solution

Partly because of the experiences associated with its formation, Elf Circle deliberately harmonizes its governance practices with Linden Lab's situation of authority with the individual. The owner of the group, Forcythia Wishbringer, is the ultimate authority for all decisions relating to the group, its governance, and the core lands associated with it.

While Wishbringer holds all legal power, a High Council chosen from other landowners and significantly active volunteers advises on policy. High Council was created to "help develop the whole Elf Circle culture" because Wishbringer believed that "a world that several people helped to create the social structure for would be a much more exciting, viable world... I felt we needed to have more than just one person giving their opinion." She looked for "intelligent people who didn't think exactly like me," who had "different skills, a different outlook." (F. Wishbringer, personal communication, April 11, 2009) Having an advisory body spreads responsibilities over more people and thus incorporates a level of diversity and flexibility that is likely to produce a more viable and adaptive organization (Smith, 1998).

Wishbringer is the final arbiter of all issues, and she makes a point of responding to all communications from members. Any sanctions against an avatar may be appealed to her. For the most part she is willing to give offenders against EC rules one or more chances to change behaviour. Although there is no system of democratic representation, public "town hall" meetings are held at least twice a year so that she can respond to questions and critiques.

High Council recognizes that "their ability to enforce laws is limited by their ability to persuade people to adhere to them" (Bartle, 2006); governance requires "Consent of the governed. Persuasion. Compromise. Ownership." (P. Aquitaine, personal communication, April 26, 2009) It therefore considers issues carefully and takes time to develop responses, sets up clear policies and procedures, and tries to be absolutely consistent in their application. Members of all governance bodies are expected to model appropriate behaviour and thereby group values.

Given structural legal limitations on transparency, this approach will not prevent some members for thinking (and saying, sometimes in very confrontational ways) that the governance of EC is arbitrary, biased, and unjust, but the relatively slow, careful and consistent process of adjudicating disputes does mitigate some of the worst attacks. It also serves to help prevent High Council from becoming reactive in its decisions.

Elf Circle is not democratic, but its structure harmonizes with practical realities. Legitimacy is asserted through the establishment and enforcement of values-based social norms, recognizing that the ability to elicit agreement will be substantially informed by the quality of the social capital—the "moral relationship of mutual obligation" (Malaby, 2006)—within the group.

Internal Modifiers of Governance Practice

No community can exist without conflict (Castronova, 2006). Interviewees noted that a number of common and predictable issues can cause serious social problems: miscommunication, lack of information, issues of process, limited time and resources, slow decision making, conflicts of interest, potential abuses of power, and favoritism. Many of these are generated by conflicting social norms or conflicting expectations of reality: "The world doesn't work the way I want it to!" (A. Goodliffe, personal communication, April 16, 2009).

Social Norms

Beyond law, all communities have social norms that define what is acceptable and what is not (Lastowka 2009; Lessig, 2006). Some are clearly defined through rule sets and some are more subtle and unspoken—the choice of what to wear in a particular context, for example. Restaurants may post "no shoes, no service" signs. An invitation to a neighbour's barbecue may not lay out rules of dress, but nonetheless some kinds of clothing will be clearly more appropriate than others, and you will likely be given some odd looks if you turn up in formal wear.

In similar ways, social norms vary between in-world communities, and between in-world communities and the real world (Lessig, 2006; Ludlow & Wallace, 2007; Pearce, 2009). Communities in virtual worlds are emergent (Meadows, 2008; Pearce, 2009) and thus in a constant process of defining their cultures. The difficulty for newcomers is in learning and understanding what norms apply in a specific context. When customs are not firmly and explicitly established, conflicts can arise over what is acceptable behaviour. A well-known example from the World of Warcraft (Meadows, 2008) describes the griefing of a funeral held in honor of a player who had passed away in the real world. Those attending the in-world funeral expected real-world codes of respect to apply to it; those who griefed it expected World of Warcraft combat norms to apply, because the funeral was held within the game.

Expectations

Individuals may bring a number of problematic expectations with them when they enter a new environment, some but not all relating to social norms and problems can arise when these expectations are not met. Virtual worlds are confusing—they are both noticeably different from reality and weirdly similar. It may seem at first to be just a strange game played by invented personas, but then they may discover that the bonds and emotions of social relationships developed with other avatars are exactly those felt in real-world relationships (Castronova, 2006; Ludlow & Wallace, 2007; Meadows, 2008; Pearce, 2009; Taylor, 2006). In-world experiences may resemble real-world experiences, but take a very different twist; you may be harassed, but then be rescued by someone who drops in like a superhero and magically ejects the offender from a region. Many real-world social structures defining status (age, wealth, position, etc.) disappear in SL, but new ones arise. Such disjunctions open new opportunities but can also be very disorienting.

Some common problematic expectations relating to virtual worlds include:

- "Normal" real-world capabilities, policies, and procedures may not transfer to a virtual world because of technical limitations or legal structures. Technical limitations on the number of avatars in one area might prevent large gatherings; legal limitations might require a group to set up a waiver system in order to share logs of meetings; limitations on the number of groups one can belong to and the number of roles within a group may determine administrative structures.

- In the real world, people generally know the difference between public and private spaces. Homes are private; parks are public; schools and offices are somewhere in between, open with some restrictions. Perceptions in virtual worlds can vary widely because a commonly understood definition of public and private space does not yet exist. Many users, especially newbies, believe that if a space can be accessed it is public, because virtual reality is not "real," but Residents who find strangers entering their virtual homes uninvited may feel quite differently about it. Elf Circle's Charter defines entering locked areas as trespassing and requests visitors to ask permission to visit homes where people are in residence.

- Individuals define griefing differently (Ludlow & Wallace, 2007): griefers often argue that it's "just a game" (Whang & Chang, 2004) or that anything allowed by software is permissible (Mistral, 2009). Others regard activities as griefing if social rules of etiquette and fairplay are contravened (Foo, 2004), leading them to expect sanctions to be applied regardless of whether formal rules are broken.

- "The pesky thing about rights is that they keep coming up. Players keep claiming that they have them." (Koster, 2000) Lastowka and Hunter (2004:51) note that "Just as new residents bring with them expectations about property, they bring expectations of other human and constitutional rights." These expectations may not mesh with reality. EC is a privately-owned social group operating on privately-owned lands, with a Charter that lays out its governance structure, yet some members still expect fully democratic procedures and a degree of control of its governance and are angry when these are not provided. Members sometimes expect issues to be dealt with much more quickly than is practical in an organization run by volunteers with diverse real-world schedules and responsibilities.

- Virtual worlds attract international users, who may bring varying expectations and social norms with them (Boellstorff, 2009; Smith, 1998; Williams, 2006). "[A]gain and again, people inhabiting avatars inevitably arrive at the conclusion that they have rights, often based on the rights they are accustomed to enjoying in their real-world cultures. American players, for instance, expect the right to free speech as well as self-determination." (Pearce, 2009) Users may also bring cultural expectations from other online environments; gamers may expect an environment with defined goals and the mechanisms to achieve them, newcomers from combat worlds may expect combat and aggression to be generally acceptable.

- Expectations of appropriate social interaction can be a source of misunderstandings and conflict. Some residents may be hampered in communication because they are not using their native language. Some users—Au (2008) estimates 5 to 15%—are disabled in real life and may have limitations that affect their interactions. Second Life has a significant population of Residents on the autism spectrum, because its architecture makes it easier for these users to interact and socialize effectively (Au, 2008; Boellstorff, 2008).

Elf Circle's Solution

Elf Circle's response to the problem of variable expectations is to find ways to increase community cohesion, with an emphasis on establishing and protecting core values. The lack of democratic representation may actually assist in this, as per

Clay Shirky's assertion that the rights of a "core group"—those who "care most about the integrity and success of the group"—trump individual rights in some situations, because primacy of the group's rights is necessary to the survival of the group itself (Shirky, 2003).

Clearly Define Goals and Values and Focus Activities on Them

Conflicts easily arise when the goals of individuals or the goals of members vs. administrators vary significantly, as is likely in a diverse population with varying social norms and expectations (Smith, 1998). At the same time, Celia Pearce's work on the D'ni Diaspora (Pearce, 2009) establishes that online communities can be strong entities capable of transferring and surviving across multiple environments, and notes that "One of the key findings of the study is the important role of values in group cohesion." (Pearce, 2009)

Elf Circle's Charter establishes an explicit set of values, reflected in its goals of providing a "safe, enjoyable experience" to members and visitors. Tolerance, respect for others, creativity and activities that help create a beautiful, dynamic and peaceful environment for the greater good of the community are encouraged and respected (Figure 2).

EC members are encouraged to develop activities and hold events for the benefit of the group. This is important because the social interactions between individuals in the context of the group are what Pearce describes as an intersubjective flow that defines both individual and group identity: "[I]n the course of the study, it became very clear that (1) group and individual identity were inextricably linked, and that (2) individual identity evolved out of an emergent process of social feedback." (Pearce, 2009). A sense of responsibility to the community is important in reinforcing community values (Pearce, 2009; Tyler & Blader, 2003), and Elf Circle encourages this through its use of volunteers.

Figure 2. Elf Circle's Castle provides a meeting place for public events. Information on Elf Circle, including its Charter, is available from notecard givers in annex wings from the Castle itself. ©2009 Nola Johnston. Used with permission.

Define Rules through Charter

Written rules help a community maintain its integrity of purpose (Bruckman, 1996): they define social norms, harmonize expectations and thus increase individuals' understanding of and commitment to the community. Elf Circle's Charter (Elf Circle, 2009), provided to all members when they join the group, codifies its values. Definitions of inappropriate behaviour are specified in some detail in order to avoid conflicts in expectations.

Educate Members and Visitors: Greeters

Greeters are an on-call volunteer corps who "welcome and guide visitors, answer questions about Elf Circle and the Elven Continent, and ensure interested persons understand and agree to Charter prior to joining" (P. Aquitaine, personal communication, April 26, 2009). Greeters go through rigorous training to make sure they understand Elf Circle and their role. Greeters do not have the authority to refuse membership; if they have concerns, applications are referred to Wishbringer.

Enforce Rules: Guardians

Elf Circle Guardians are an on-call volunteer corps created to enforce Charter rules, a recognition that social norms do not always ensure compliance with rules or group safety (Lessig, 2006). EC members are required to call for Guardian help on EC Group IM (Instant Messaging) channel when griefed, and are prohibited from retaliating, as some griefers attempt to lure their victims into counterattacking and breaking SL rules, thereby leading to LL taking action against them (Foo & Koivisto, 2004).

Guardians respond to minor infractions by providing a notecard copy of Charter and a warning. Stronger sanctions are applied only if a person continues to break the rules. For serious, persistent or obviously intentional incidents of griefing a security system allows avatars to be ejected and/or banned from EC lands. Complex or delicate issues are referred to High Guardians, a small council which develops Guardian policy and training, or, if they relate to EC policy, to High Council. All avatars have a right to appeal sanctions taken by Guardians to Wishbringer, who makes final judgments and is the only person empowered to remove membership rights. It should be noted that only a handful of avatars have ever been banned or had membership rights removed for offenses other than intentional griefing.

By deliberate policy, Guardians do not police and respond only to calls for assistance. This recognizes the delicate balance between providing governance and exerting control, as well as the potential problems caused by differing views on legitimate governance (Williams, 2007). "Should people in EC come to the belief that the Guardians are present to handle perceived internal threats (i.e. dissenters), there will be an exodus of active people within EC" (S. Brown, personal communication, April 20, 2009).

A prospective Guardian must go through a comprehensive training process (Appendix B) that reviews common problems and emphasizes non-confrontational techniques for dealing with them. A substantial part of Guardian training is learning how to distinguish genuine griefers from clueless newbies. Diplomacy and the respectful treatment of others is emphasized. "…[T]he example is set by person after person after person, and then modeled, of how to help others without offending them."

Wishbringer notes that the clear and consistent combination of education and enforcement, which deals quickly and efficiently with serious incidents but also enables the potential integration of offenders into the community, has had positive results—around 30 deliberate griefers have joined the EC community after being dealt with diplomatically (F. Wishbringer, personal communication, April 11, 2009).

No Drama

Because Elf Circle recognizes the right of its members to enjoy a safe environment (Williams, 2007) and includes emotional safety within that remit, it limits free speech. Charter prohibits forms of speech likely to be contentious and disruptive: verbal harassment, obscene language, religious recruitment, and political activities.

It also explicitly prohibits behaviour defined as drama: "Individual disputes will occur, but airing them in a public venue such as Elf Circle chat or Drum Circle or another public event is prohibited, as this can impact the enjoyment of others." Sanctions will be applied when a request to desist is repeatedly ignored. The rule against drama recognizes how easy it is for interpersonal conflicts that usually affect only a few people to make an environment uncomfortable for others, or even to escalate until they split a group.

Do not Become Involved in Interpersonal Disputes

One of the keystones of Elf Circle's approach to governance is that it will not become involved in interpersonal disputes. This is because Linden Lab's technical and legal frameworks make it impossible to fully access and share information, and thus also make it impossible to adjudicate conflicts fairly. Its position is that when effective, transparent participation is precluded, official involvement can actually escalate disputes until they become dangerous to group cohesion, as people take sides on not just the rights and wrongs of the original conflict, but also on how the group governance system dealt with it.

Members with disputes that involve TOS/CS contraventions are referred to the Linden Lab Abuse Reporting system and policies. Members who have disputes with others that do not involve TOS/CS contraventions may be dealt with through other mechanisms; for example, any complaints of renters against their neighbours will be dealt with by the landowner. If a private dispute is aired in Elf Circle's public venues the airing will be dealt with as drama; the content of the original conflict will not be addressed in any way.

The policy of refusing to address interpersonal conflicts may give some avatars the feeling that their grievances have not been dealt with justly; however, it recognizes practical limitations on group governance and is designed to break a cycle of offense, retaliation, and counter-retaliation, and thus minimize disruptions to the community overall.

Minimize Regulation

"More laws and regulations don't solve problems—instead people only begin to find contradictions in the laws and argue them." (S. Brown, personal communication, April 20, 2009) The Simple Rules strategy in contemporary management theory (Davis, Eisenhardt & Bingham, 2009) reinforces this, arguing that while an organization must have some structure to function efficiently, too many rules impede flexibility. Rules that are too specific can be confusing or lead to more issues simply because there will always be things that they don't cover (Suler, 1996).

Elf Circle minimizes its rules and keeps them general rather than specific. Rules are usually formed only "in response to an issue that has not been able to be resolved without having a rule." (F. Wishbringer, personal communication, April 11, 2009) When possible, existing rules are applied, rather than creating new ones. Problems with an aggressive vampire game were dealt with by applying rules against non-thematic activity rather than banning members of vampire groups, thus avoiding a backlash suffered by other communities who banned avatars (S. Brown, personal communication, April 20, 2009).

When possible, the group uses the mechanics of the world to enforce behaviour and maintain order without resorting to direct enforcement. There were consistent problems with complaints of non-members using the EC public sandbox (building area) to create content that did not conform to EC thematic requirements. EC's solution to the problem was not to increase enforcement, but to use land settings to limit the sandbox use to EC members only.

This approach of setting rules but not micromanaging has generally been effective in avoiding significant social problems and preventing backlash.

Policy into Practice: Issues of Deception, Drama, and Free Speech

Interpersonal disputes in a virtual world can be every bit as ethically and procedurally complex as those in the real world. What if one discovers that the person one had been having virtual sex with—and had married—is a different gender than one thought they were? A survey conducted in mid-2007 showed that 23% of Residents used an avatar that did not match their gender, so "Unsurprisingly, one of the most common ethical dilemmas in Second Life is whether a gender cross-dresser should feel obliged to reveal his or her real-life sex to a virtual world romantic partner" (Au, 2008:79; see also Lastowka & Hunter, 2004).

When a member of Elf Circle discovered that a former romantic partner had deceived them as to their gender, the person deceived demanded that Elf Circle take action against the deceiver. High Council refused, on the grounds that its consistent policy is never to intervene in interpersonal conflicts. But because the deceiver was a member of High Council, there was suspicion among some that this decision resulted not from policy but from favoritism.

The victim of the deception and some supporters began to speak out against the perpetrator at public events on EC lands and through EC Group IMs. Individual EC members who were not part of the system of governance asked them to stop; when they did not, complaints against their actions were lodged with Wishbringer. The individuals concerned were warned that they must stop interrupting others' enjoyment of activities or face sanctions. Any who did not comply were eventually removed from the Elf Circle group and banned from the EC lands.

Ultimately an avatar representing himself as a lawyer for a free-speech group raised the suggestion that legal action might be taken against Elf Circle, and met with Wishbringer and some members of High Council to make a presentation challenging its actions. Elf Circle's response (presented by a member who is a lawyer in real life) stated that it was a privately-owned group exerting its policies with respect only to privately-owned lands and group communication mechanisms, that its Charter prohibited discussing contentious issues in public EC venues, and that SL's Terms of Service and Community Standards prohibit verbal abuse, harassment, and publicly discussing an avatar's real-life identity. No legal action was ever taken against Elf Circle.

This conflict raised some interesting issues. Although it was clear to everyone that a deception had indeed taken place, it was not so obvious that Elf Circle could or should take action against the deceiver. The deceived avatar argued that the deceiver had demonstrated unethical behaviour that, because EC represented strong ethical values, warranted their removal from Council. The deceiver had voluntarily stepped down from Council for some months, but the deceived avatar wanted them permanently banned from any participation in governance. Some High Council members questioned whether a real-world social organization would take (or be expected to take) such action against a board member who misrepresented their gender if the deception was not germane to the activities of the group and their function within it.

During the process of entering SL you must choose a gender, so most people quickly understand that gender is fluid in a virtual world. There are no mechanisms in SL to confirm gender or identity; only Linden Lab has access to that kind of information. Members of EC's High Council took the position that in such a context individuals, not EC's governance bodies, must take responsibility for their personal relationships and any issues arising out of them.

Gender issues in virtual worlds are complex to begin with, but this dispute became more complicated when it morphed into a conflict over free speech, pitting the right of an individual to speak against the right of a group to protect itself against the consequences of such speech, a common tension in virtual environments (Mnookin,

2001). Elf Circle's policies always reinforce the primacy of the group in such conflicts: its position is that any member may say anything they like privately, but if they speak about contentious issues in a public space belonging to Elf Circle they must stop if asked to do so. Its reasoning is that at best public disputes are disruptive to the peaceful enjoyment of the lands, and that at worst they can escalate until the community is seriously damaged or destroyed. Sanctions are applied when it is necessary to protect the cohesion of the group, not to punish offending individuals. In this case the deceived avatar and their supporters suffered sanctions not because they complained about how the deceived was treated, but because they repeatedly did so at public social events in EC lands and refused to stop when asked to do so.

EC's prohibitions against drama and refusal to address interpersonal disputes recognize the ease with which one can be drawn into a dispute between individuals, especially in a social context, and are intended to prevent escalations. It is possible that by prohibiting public conflict issues may be driven to fester under the surface, undermining the group's health and viability, but so far the strategy seems to be generally effective at maintaining a strong community.

The Experience of Other Communities

Caledon

The Independent State of Caledon is a 19th Century Steampunk Victorian nation-state owned by Desmond Shang (http://www.caledonwiki.com). Its 45 regions comprise a vibrant and creative community with wide-ranging activities.

Caledon's Covenant lays out "'common law' expectations of the residents" that are in place "just in case someone really decides to push it, and for the literalists that need to read that stuff in black and white" and Shang sees himself as "a sort of civil servant." The Covenant includes a statement of Avatar Rights that outline social expectations in a positive way and acts as "a check and balance against heavy-handed management". True griefers are dealt with expeditiously, but Shang uses a light touch and will not deal with social conflicts unless rules are broken. When asked to deal with disputes, he is often "purposefully slow to respond" in order to provide a cooling off period.

Caledon does not manage social interaction to the degree that Elf Circle does. Public debates on contentious issues are permitted because "I feel that individuals do have specific rights to their thoughts and opinions, and that being able to air these is far healthier than otherwise," though he acknowledges that this approach has "caused me a little bit more trouble than it has solved in the short run."

Dream Travelers

Dream Travelers is a non-profit umbrella group with two subgroups, Shockproof (for stroke survivors) and Brigadoon Explorers (for those on the autism spectrum). The groups were founded by The Sojourner ("Soj") in order to provide support to members of these groups "along with their loved ones and caretakers" (D. Bernstein, personal communication, April 24, 2009), and after Soj's death in May 2008, they have continued under the direction of Dorie Bernstein and Golda Stein. The group is associated with three sims, has a public sandbox, and holds regular classes and discussion groups on topics relating to the Dreams mission or SL in general. A current project is to build a walk-through interactive model of the brain that offers information on strokes, autism, and other brain-related issues.

Dreams' governance structure is simpler and less formal than that of Elf Circle and Caledon, reflecting the fact that the group is much smaller, but is similar in approach. Rules are made by the estate leaders and an advisory council. A security/

janitorial staff enforces them, assisted by council and teachers. Building is restricted building to group members except for the Sandbox, an action that "creates a containment field" for many griefing abuses. Griefers are dealt with quietly, by banning and using the Abuse Report mechanism.

The overall policy is "to quietly deal with problems as they arise and find a solution that will be most beneficial to the involved parties." The administrators do not respond to interpersonal disputes in any way unless the disputes are "adversely affecting the group" (D. Bernstein, personal communication, April 24, 2009).

Governance Strategies

While the three groups have some significant differences, their overall approach to governance is notably consistent. All set out a code of conduct relating to their goals and have adapted it based on experience. All have developed enforcement systems but take a hands-off approach as much as possible. None will address interpersonal conflicts unless group rules are broken. All sometimes receive complaints that they are not interventionist enough.

All three groups acknowledge that the the wealth of alternatives provided by SL and consequent power of a member to go elsewhere if they disagree with a group's governance is a check on overbearing administration. The inability to transfer cultural and social capital (goods and friendship) between virtual worlds can act as an inhibitor preventing people from leaving worlds they are unhappy with (Balkin, 2004; Lessig, 2006), but within SL there are a wide range of communities representing diverse interests and opinions, so an individual can leave one group and join another without losing belongings or friends.

All interviewees were asked to make recommendations for governance practices in Second Life and other virtual worlds; these follow.

Planning

Make sure you understand the world you will be operating in. Research its social norms and its technical and legal structures, especially around group management and communication. Policies should only by set by persons who are familiar with both the organization and with the virtual world and its requirements and limitations, and should harmonize the goals and needs of the group with the realities of the world. Determine if existing real-world policies and practices can be transferred into the virtual world, and how to deal with those that cannot. Consider if and how to maintain the image of an organization, business or brand, and develop relevant rules and procedures if necessary. Clarify members' responsibilities with regard to representing the group when at work or at play.

"Don't manage social interactions, as much as possible." (D. Shang, personal communication, April 17, 2009) When planning governance, define what consequences, good or bad, might follow from trying to manage social interactions—or not doing so.

A group must have resources to do what it wants to do; be practical and realistic. Look for ways for group members to contribute to the community, and provide mechanisms for recognition of in-world skills. (Note that options for contributions must be well thought out since new problems can arise when not all contributions can be accommodated.)

A group's success should not depend on one person. Make sure knowledge and responsibility are shared and that a system for transferring authority (and ownership, if necessary) is in place in the event of an emergency. On the other hand, remember that the more people that are involved in governance, the more time will be required for governance. Text-based interaction will take much longer than voice chat (but minutes of meetings can be logged and shared more easily).

Applied Governance

Define your values. Write a mission statement to provide a context for the group and a code of conduct that sets the rules in terms of that context. Define how due process will work when rules are broken. Make sure there is a fair system for appeal. Make the system of governance as transparent as possible, given legal and technical constraints. Develop an efficient mechanism for communicating with members and educating them about the world as well as expectations of them.

Do not create a rule unless absolutely necessary, and keep rules general and flexible rather than specific. "You shouldn't set a new rule when an existing one will serve" because new rules may cause unexpected problems (A. Goodliffe, personal communication, April 16, 2009). In a social environment it is likely that every time a rule is created there will be a backlash.

Be prepared for unexpected trouble. "There will always be loopholes and unexpected scenarios." (F. Armistice, personal communication, April 30, 2009) "SL is like any group of people on the internet, volatile and unpredictable. You are opening yourself up to any number of publicly embarrassing incidents." (A. Goodliffe, personal communication, April 16, 2009)

Recognize that "even people of goodwill inadvertently behave indiscreetly in an unfamiliar place. ...It takes a long time to learn how to behave in a virtual world." (P. Aquitaine, personal communication, April 26, 2009)

If possible, make sure there is always someone available to deal with issues, preferably inworld. Emphasize diplomacy over policing; respond to issues rather than looking for them. Provide training for those responsible for education and/ or enforcement.

Be consistent. "Tell what you're going to do, do it, and continue to do it." (D. Bernstein, personal communication, April 24, 2009) "Treating them right over a long period means that I have some margin for error going forward." (D. Shang, personal communication, April 17, 2009).

Some Additional Considerations

Virtual worlds can be very strange to newcomers, so it's important to include time for orientation. "Just coming into Second Life is an emotional shock." (F. Wishbringer, personal communication, April 11, 2009) Provide time to explore and preliminary social interactions before expecting people to accomplish tasks. Provide familiar visual metaphors as a starting point; use a traditional meeting room before holding a meeting suspended in mid-air.

Virtual worlds have distinct cultures—be aware of those in the world you are entering and carefully consider how the culture you are creating within the world fits in (Rufer-Bach, 2009). "Any policy you wish to transfer needs to be revisited to be sure it's appropriate for the environment." (D. Bernstein, personal communication, April 24, 2009) "You have to build your culture, and if you don't have a real life culture that people all understand and agree on, then it's not going to work that well." (F. Wishbringer, personal communication, April 11, 2009)

Although some level of discipline can be imposed on existing members of a real-world business/organization moving into a virtual world, the behaviour of natives of that world cannot be coerced effectively.

In social worlds, social relationships are paramount. "My advice to anyone who wishes to establish an SL society is that it is all about relationships." (S. Brown, personal communication, April 20, 2009)

Virtual worlds provide a sense of social presence that can generate problems of the same sort that exist in the real world. For example, conflicts on issues relating to proximity can arise which can be mitigated if the group puts buffer zones between spaces leased to members for "homes."

FUTURE RESEARCH DIRECTIONS

As shown, social relationships are fundamental within virtual worlds, but long-term research and analysis of their function and governance is needed as individuals and organizations move into such environments in greater numbers and their use becomes more commonplace. The scope of this investigation was limited; the experience of a wide range of groups should be compared and evaluated, together with the contextual effects of varying goals. The role and effects of dissent as a modifier should be included in wider studies.

Although considerable work exists in this area, further thorough examinations of the details in which the differences between immersive virtual environments and real worlds come into play in the practice of governance would be useful. What are the effects of expectations that do not match the environment? How is status determined? What establishes legitimate authority under a virtual world's constraints? How do cultural activities and rituals affect governance? How does the concept of social capital (Malaby, 2006) play into governance?

Elf Circle is not a democracy. Research has explored the results of some experiments with democracy in online environments, but could further examine the specifics of attempts within immersive virtual worlds, for example by considering how social presence affects the implementation of such structures, or how structures adapt in relation to constraints that apply in specific environments.

The experience of virtual world residents on the autism spectrum and their intersection with a world's general population offers the potential for study. What are the implications of their experiences with regard to social governance? Other defined user groups may offer useful insights as well.

CONCLUSION

Constraints on governance may be determined by external factors such as code or legal structures or internal factors such as social norms and expectations. This chapter posed a question: given the range of issues that a group may face in a virtual world and the constraints that may apply to their management, what options for governance of social relationships are practical and effective? Elf Circle's approach, based on clear goals and values and a good understanding of the practical limitations that affect their pursuit, has on the whole been very successful. Its Charter is respected and has been emulated by other groups (F. Wishbringer, personal communication, April 11, 2009). The fact that the group is consistently growing in the presence of viable in-world alternatives can be taken as an indicator that the majority of members accept and support its structure; more people join the group for what it provides than leave it because they are dissatisfied with its governance.

It is important to recognize that EC's success in governance occurs within a specific context that involves a range of modifiers, so it cannot be taken as a recipe that will work for every group in every virtual world. For example, Elf Circle's goals of providing a universally safe and pleasant experience for members and visitors lead it to exert higher levels of control over behaviour than other communities might find necessary. Williams (2007) notes that formal systems of community regulation are not necessarily more effective in curtailing deviance than informal vigilantism; EC's success in using it effectively is informed by its association with a limited land base and its goals of providing a safe experience only in relation to that land base.

Finding the right balance when deciding when and when not to manage dynamic social relationships is a complex process, and every community must evaluate its needs and the applicability and effectiveness of the governance choices it makes. The general principles derived from Elf Circle's

experience, however, are adaptable and provide a useful model for any group seeking to form a community in a virtual world.

REFERENCES

Abdellatif, A. (2003, May). *Good governance and its relationship to democracy and economic development.* Global Forum III on Fighting Corruption and Safeguarding Integrity, Seoul, Korea. Retrieved April 23, 2009 from http://www.pogar.org/publications/governance/

American Cancer Society. (2009). *Relay For Life of Second Life team totals.* Retrieved October 3, 2009 from http://main.acsevents.org/site/TR/RelayFor-Life/RFLFY09RFLorg?sid=70525&type=fr_info rmational&pg=informational&fr_id=19490

Au, W. J. (2008). *The making of Second Life: notes from the new world.* New York: HarperCollins.

Balkin, J. M. (2004). Law and liberty in virtual worlds. [Retrieved from Business Source Complete, EBSCO.]. *New York Law School Law Review. New York Law School, 49*(1), 63–80.

Bartle, R. A. (1996). *Hearts, clubs, diamonds, spades: players who suit MUDs.* Retrieved April 2, 2009 from http://www.mud.co.uk/richard/hcds.htm

Bartle, R. A. (2006, September 4). Why governments aren't gods and gods aren't governments. *First Monday* [Online], *0*(0). Retrieved April 21, 2009 from http://firstmonday.org/htbin/cgiwrap/bin/ojs/index.php/fm/article/view/1612/1527

Boellstorff, T. (2008). *Coming of age in Second Life: an anthropologist explores the virtually human.* Princeton, NJ: Princeton University Press.

Boellstorff, T. (2009). Virtual worlds and futures of anthropology. *AnthroNotes, the Museum of Natural History Publication for Educators.* Retrieved September 21, 2009 from http://www.anthro.uci.edu/faculty_bios/boellstorff/boellstorff.php

Brenner, S. W. (2008). Fantasy crime. *Vanderbilt Journal of Technology and Entertainment Law, 11*(1). Retrieved April 13 2009 from http://works.bepress.com/susan_brenner/

Bruckman, A. (1996) Finding one's own in cyberspace. *Technology Review Magazine.* Retrieved September 24, 2009 from http://www.cc.gatech.edu/~asb/papers/old-papers.html

Cannataci, J. A., & Mifsud-Bonnici, J. P. (2007). Weaving the mesh: finding remedies in cyberspace. [Retrieved from Business Source Complete, EBSCO.]. *International Review of Law Computers & Technology, 21*(1), 59–78.. doi:10.1080/13600860701281705

Castronova, E. (2006). *Synthetic worlds: the business and culture of online games.* Chicago: Chicago University Press.

Consalvo, M. (2009) There is no magic circle. *Games and Culture.* DOI: 10.1177/1555412009343575 Retrieved September 21, 2009 from http://gac.sagepub.com/cgi/content/abstract/1555412009343575v1

Davis, J.P., Eisenhardt, K.M. & Bingham, C.B. (2009). Optimal structure, market dynamism, and the strategy of simple rules. *Administrative Science Quarterly, 54*(3), 413-452. Retrieved October 4, 2009 from Business Source Premier. EBSCO.

Dibble, J. (1993) *A rape in cyberspace.* Retrieved April 22, 2009 from http://www.juliandibbell.com/texts/bungle_vv.html

DiPaola, S., & Turner, J. (2008). Authoring the intimate self: identity, expression and role-playing within a pioneering virtual community. *Loading.* Retrieved September 21, 2009 from http://journals.sfu.ca/loading/index.php/loading/issue/view/4/showToc

Elf Circle. (2009). Retrieved October 15, 2009 from http://www.slhighfantasy.com/site/

Foo, C. Y. (2004). *Redefining grief play.* Other Players conference on multiplayer phenomena, Copenhagen, December 6-8, 2004. Retrieved April 23, 2009 from http://www.tu-chemnitz.de/phil/medkom/mn/spive/index.php?option=com_docman&task=cat_view&gid=18&Itemid=33

Foo, C. Y., & Koivisto, E. M. (2004). *Grief player motivations.* Other Players conference on multiplayer phenomena, Copenhagen, December 6-8, 2004. Retrieved April 23, 2009 from http://www.tu-chemnitz.de/phil/medkom/mn/spive/index.php?option=com_docman&task=cat_view&gid=25&Itemid=33

Gee, J. P. (2008). Video games and embodiment. *Games and Culture.* DOI: 10.1177/1555412008317309 Retrieved September 21, 2009 from http://gac.sagepub.com/cgi/content/abstract/3/3-4/253

Koster, R. (2000). *Declaring the rights of players.* Retrieved April 22, 2009 from http://www.raphkoster.com/gaming/playerrights.shtml

Lab, L. (2009a). *Purchasing land.* 2009. Retrieved October 7th, 2009 from http://secondlife.com/land/purchasing.php

Lab, L. (2009b). *Open Source FAQs.* Retrieved October 6th, 2009 from http://secondlifegrid.net/technology-programs/virtual-world-open-source/faq

Lab, L. (2009c). *Terms of service.* Retrieved October 15, 2009, from http://secondlife.com/corporate/tos.php

Lab, L. (2009d). *Community standards.* Retrieved October 15, 2009, from http://secondlife.com/corporate/cs.php

Lastowka, F. G., & Hunter, D. (2004). The laws of the virtual worlds. [Retrieved from Business Source Complete, EBSCO.]. *California Law Review, 92*(1), 3–73. doi:10.2307/3481444

Lastowka, G. (2009). Rules of play. *Games and Culture*. DOI: 10.1177/1555412009343573 Retrieved September 21, 2009 from http://gac.sagepub.com/cgi/content/abstract/1555412009343573v1

Lessig, L. (2006). *Code and other laws of cyberspace, version 2.0*. New York: Basic Books. PDF version retrieved August 25, 2009 from http://codev2.cc/

Lind, E. A., & Earley, P. C. (1992) Procedural justice and culture. *International Journal of Psychology, 27*(2), 227. (AN 5777083) Retrieved from Business Source Complete, EBSCO.

Lind, E. A., Tyler, T. R., & Huo, Y. J. (1997). Procedural context and culture: variations in the antecedents of procedural justice judgments. [Retrieved from Business Source Complete, EBSCO.]. *Journal of Personality and Social Psychology, 73*(4), 767–780. doi:10.1037/0022-3514.73.4.767

Linden, A. (2009, March 19). *Three questions for Diane Berry, CEO of TMPA on an event in Second Life*. Blog entry posted to https://blogs.secondlife.com/community/workinginworld/blog/2009/03/19/three-questions-for-diane-berry-ceo-of-tpma-on-an-event-in-second-life

Linden Research, Inc. (2009) *How meeting in Second Life transformed IBM's technology elite into virtual world believers*, [case study]. Retrieved April 13, 2009 from http://secondlifegrid.net/casestudies

Ludlow, P., & Wallace, M. (2007). *The Second Life Herald: the virtual tabloid that witnessed the dawn of the metaverse*. Cambridge, MA: The MIT Press.

Malaby, T. M. (2006). Parlaying value: capital in and beyond virtual worlds. *Games and Culture, 1*(2), 141–162..doi:10.1177/1555412006286688

Malaby, T. M. (2007). Contriving constraints (the gameness of Second Life and the persistence of scarcity). *Innovations, 2*(3), 62–67..doi:10.1162/itgg.2007.2.3.62

Mayntz, R. (2003) *From government to governance: Political steering in modern societies*. Paper presented at the IOEW Summer Academy on IPP, Würzburg, Germany, September 7-11, 2003. Retrieved October 16, 2009 from http://www.ioew.de/fileadmin/user_upload/DOKUMENTE/Veranstaltungen/2003/SuA2Mayntz.pdf

Meadows, M. S. (2008). *I, avatar: the culture and consequences of having a Second Life*. Berkeley, CA: New Riders.

Mertins, V. (2008). *The effects of procedures on social interaction: a literature review*. Discussion Papers 200806, Institute of Labour Law and Industrial Relations in the European Community (IAAEG). Retrieved April 2, 2009 from http://ideas.repec.org/p/iaa/wpaper/200806.html

Mistral, P. (April 2, 2009) FrizzleFry interview part 2. *The Alphaville Herald/Secondlife Herald*. Retrieved April 22, 2009 from http://foo.secondlifeherald.com/slh/2009/04/frizzlefry-interview-part-2.html#more

Mnookin, J. (2001). Virtual(ly) law: the emergence of law in an on-line community. In Ludlow, P. (Ed.), *Crypto Anarchy, Cyberstates, And Pirate Utopias*. Cambridge, MA: The MIT Press.

Noveck, B. S. (2004/2005). The state of play. [Retrieved from Business Source Complete, EBSCO.]. *New York Law School Law Review. New York Law School, 49*(1), 1–18.

Pearce, C. (2009). *Communities of play: emergent cultures in multiplayer fames and virtual worlds*. Cambridge, MA: The MIT Press.

Rufer-Bach, K. (2009). *The Second Life Grid: The Official Guide to Communication, Collaboration, and Community Engagement.* Indianapolis, IN: Wiley Publishing.

Shirky, C. (2003). *A group is its own worst enemy.* Retrieved September 15, 2009 from http://www.shirky.com/writings/group_enemy.html

Slater, M., Sadagic, A., Usoh, M., & Schroeder, R. (2000). Small-group behavior in a virtual and real environment: a comparative study. [Retrieved from Business Source Complete, EBSCO.]. *Presence (Cambridge, Mass.), 9*(1), 37–51.. doi:10.1162/105474600566600

Smith, Anna DuVal. (1998). Problems of conflict management in virtual communities. In P. Kollock and M. Smith (Eds.), *Communities in Cyberspace.* New York: Routledge. Prepublication draft, retrieved March 30, 2009 from http://www.advs.net/cinc.htm.

Suler, J. (1996). *The bad boys of cyberspace: deviant behavior in online multimedia communities and strategies for managing it.* Retrieved April 29, 2009 from http://www-usr.rider.edu/~suler/psycyber/badboys.html

Suler, J. (1996). *The psychology of cyberspace.* Retrieved April 29, 2009 from http://www-usr.rider.edu/~suler/psycyber/badboys.html

Taylor, T. L. (2006). The assemblage of play. *Games and Culture.* DOI: 10.1177/1555412009343576. Retrieved September 21, 2009 from http://gac.sagepub.com/cgi/content/abstract/1555412009343576v1

Taylor, T. L. (2009). *Play between worlds: exploring online game culture.* Cambridge, MA and London, England: The MIT Press.

Tyler, T., & Blader, S. (2003). The group engagement model: procedural justice, social identity, and cooperative behavior. [Retrieved from Business Source Complete, EBSCO.]. *Personality and Social Psychology Review, 7*(4), 349–361. doi:10.1207/S15327957PSPR0704_07

Van den Bos, K., Wilke, H. A. M., & Lind, E. A. (1998). When do we need procedural fairness? The role of trust in authority. [Retrieved from Business Source Complete, EBSCO.]. *Journal of Personality and Social Psychology, 75*(6), 1449–1458. doi:10.1037/0022-3514.75.6.1449

Whang, L., & Chang, G. (2004). Lifestyles of virtual world residents: living in the on-line game "Lineage." [Retrieved from Business Source Complete, EBSCO.]. *Cyberpsychology & Behavior, 7*(5), 592–600. doi:.doi:10.1089/1094931042403091

Williams, M. (2000). Virtually criminal: discourse, deviance and anxiety within virtual communities. [Retrieved from Business Source Complete, EBSCO.]. *International Review of Law Computers & Technology, 14*(1), 95–104.. doi:10.1080/13600860054935

Williams, M. (2006). *Virtually Criminal: Crime, Deviance and Regulation Online.* London: Routledge.

Williams, M. (2007). Policing and cybersociety: the maturation of regulation within an online community. *Policing and Society, 17*(1), 59–82.. doi:10.1080/10439460601124858

Yankelovich, N. (2007). *MPK20: Sun's virtual workplace* [Video]. Retrieved October 15, 2009 from http://research.sun.com/projects/mc/video/MPK20-oct2007.mov

Yee, N. (2006). Motivations of play in online games. [Retrieved from Business Source Complete, EBSCO.]. *Cyberpsychology & Behavior, 9*(6), 772–775..doi:10.1089/cpb.2006.9.772

ADDITIONAL READING

Au, W. J. (2008). *The making of Second Life: notes from the new world.* New York: HarperCollins.

Balkin, J. M. (2004). Law and liberty in virtual worlds. [Retrieved from Business Source Complete, EBSCO.]. *New York Law School Law Review. New York Law School*, *49*(Issue 1), 63–80.

Bartle, R. A. (2004). *Designing Virtual Worlds*. Berkeley: New Riders.

Bartle, R. A. (2006, September 4). Why governments aren't gods and gods aren't governments. *First Monday* [Online], Volume 0 Number 0. Retrieved April 21, 2009 from http://firstmonday.org/htbin/cgiwrap/bin/ojs/index.php/fm/article/view/1612/1527

Boellstorff, T. (2008). *Coming of age in Second Life: an anthropologist explores the virtually human*. Princeton, Oxford: Princeton University Press.

Brenner, S. W. (2008). Fantasy crime. *Vanderbilt Journal of Technology and Entertainment Law*, Volume 11, Issue 1. Retrieved April 13 2009 from http://works.bepress.com/susan_brenner/

Cannataci, J. A., & Mifsud-Bonnici, J. P. (2007). Weaving the mesh: finding remedies in cyberspace. [Retrieved from Business Source Complete, EBSCO.]. *International Review of Law Computers & Technology*, *21*(Issue 1), 59–78.. doi:10.1080/13600860701281705

Castronova, E. (2006). *Synthetic worlds: the business and culture of online games*. Chicago: Chicago University Press.

Castronova, E. (2007). *Exodus to the Virtual World: How Online Fun is Changing Reality*. New York: Palgrave Macmillan.

Dibble, J. (1993) *A rape in cyberspace*. Retrieved April 22, 2009 from http://www.juliandibbell.com/texts/bungle_vv.html

Koster, R. (2000) Declaring the rights of players. Retrieved April 22, 2009 from http://www.raphkoster.com/gaming/playerrights.shtml

Lastowka, F. G., & Hunter, D. (2004). The laws of the virtual worlds. [Retrieved from Business Source Complete, EBSCO.]. *California Law Review*, *92*(Issue 1), 3–73. doi:10.2307/3481444

Lessig, L. (2006). *Code and other laws of cyberspace, version 2.0*. NY: Basic Books. PDF version retrieved August 25, 2009 from http://codev2.cc/

Life, S. Official websites include https://secondlife.com. https://blogs.secondlife.com/, and http://secondlifegrid.net/.

Ludlow, P. (Ed.). (2001). *Crypto anarchy, cyberstates, and pirate utopias*. Cambridge, MA and London, England: The MIT Press.

Ludlow, P., & Wallace, M. (2007). *The Second Life Herald: the virtual tabloid that witnessed the dawn of the metaverse*. Cambridge, MA and London, England: The MIT Press.

Malaby, T. M. (2006). Parlaying value: capital in and beyond virtual worlds. *Games and Culture*, *1*(2), 141–162..doi:10.1177/1555412006286688

Malaby, T. M. (2007). Contriving constraints (the gameness of Second Life and the persistence of scarcity). *Innovations*, *2*(3), 62–67..doi:10.1162/itgg.2007.2.3.62

Meadows, M. S. (2008). *I, avatar: the culture and consequences of having a Second Life*. Berkeley, CA: New Riders.

Mertins, V. (2008). *The effects of procedures on social interaction: a literature review*. Discussion Papers 200806, Institute of Labour Law and Industrial Relations in the European Community (IAAEG). Retrieved April 2, 2009 from http://ideas.repec.org/p/iaa/wpaper/200806.html

Noveck, B. S. (2004/2005). The state of play. [Retrieved from Business Source Complete, EBSCO.]. *New York Law School Law Review. New York Law School*, *49*(Issue 1), 1–18.

Pargman, D. (2000) *Code begets community.* Retrieved April 29, 2009 from http://xml.nada. kth.se/~pargman/thesis/

Pearce, C. (2009). *Communities of play: emergent cultures in multiplayer fames and virtual worlds.* Cambridge, MA and London, England: The MIT Press.

Rymaszewski, M., Au, W. J., Wallace, M., Winters, C., Ondrejka, C., & Batstone-Cunningham, B. (2007). *Second Life: The Official Guide.* Indianapolis: Wiley Publishing.

Salen, K., & Zimmerman, E. (2004). *Rules of Play: Game Design Fundamentals.* Cambridge, MA: MIT Press.

Smith, J. H. (2002) *The Architecture of Trust.* Retrieved April 29, 2009 from http://www.itu. dk/people/smith/pages/aot.htm

Suler, J. (1996). The psychology of cyberspace. Retrieved April 29, 2009 from http://www-usr. rider.edu/~suler/psycyber/psycyber.html

Suler, J. *The Psychology of Cyberspace.* Retrieved April 29, 2009 from http://www-usr.rider. edu/~suler/psycyber/psycyber.html

Taylor, T. L. (2009). *Play between worlds: exploring online game culture.* Cambridge, MA and London, England: The MIT Press.

Terra Nova. A Weblog About Virtual Worlds. Terra Nova authors include scholars and practicioners from a variety of disciplines. http://terranova. blogs.com/

Williams, M. (2006). *Virtually Criminal: Crime, Deviance and Regulation Online.* London, New York: Routledge.

APPENDIX A: QUESTIONNAIRE

I would particularly like to thank those Second Life avatars who generously contributed their time and thoughts to this project: Pericat Aquitaine, Fredrich Armistice, Dorie Bernstein, Susan Brown, Armandi Goodliffe, Desmond Shang, and Forcythia Wishbringer.

Elf Circle respondents were sent the following questionnaire. Wishbringer was interviewed by Skype using an expanded version; the owners of the other social groups were given versions without the questions on Elf Circle, though background information on its governance structure was provided to them for context. Other than Wishbringer, all interviewees submitted responses by email or in-world notecard or Instant Message. Only avatar names identified the respondents, and no real-life information about them was required of them.

Questionnaire

Thanks for participating in this interview! If you only have time to answer some of these questions, the ones in the last section (on Governance) are the most important.

Elf Circle

- From your point of view, why is EC structured as a benevolent monarchy?
- What are the benefits and disadvantages of this structure?
- When and how should a new rule be created? Under what circumstances would you choose not to set a rule?
- Do you have any comments on how Elf Circle's system of governance was developed?
- How would you describe the High Council and its purpose?
- How would you describe the Guardians and their purpose?
- How would you describe the Greeters and their purpose?
- Why has such a comprehensive system of rules, education and enforcement developed?
- Why do Guardians and Greeters go through such comprehensive training processes?
- What do you observe about people's emotional investment in SL in general and EC in particular?
- Do you think that emotional investment affects their behavior either positively or negatively?
- Why is Elf Circle's system generally so successful?

Types of Problems

Note that in this chapter I am attempting to explain how and why certain kinds of problems arise, and how an organization can effectively deal with them through governance, rather than analyzing the specific mechanisms of individual problems. Although I will raise specific issues as examples of the kinds of problems that can be encountered, I will not be giving names or details on them. For example, I will mention that free speech vs. drama has been an issue, but will avoid giving any particulars beyond those needed to set the context in general as an interpersonal conflict. If you give details of specific problems in your responses and I quote you, any such details will be removed before publication.

- What are typical issues that cause problems?
- Do issues fall into typical categories? If so, what?
- Are problems predictable or unexpected?
- Can you give examples of unexpected problems? How were they solved?
- Which issues have been the hardest to deal with? Were they predictable or unexpected?
- Did policy change as a result?

Governance

I am particularly interested in where similarities and differences between RL and SL experiences occur, and your advice on setting up effective systems of governance for social groups in a virtual environment.

- Do you think that real-world policies and rules can be transferred into SL directly?
- If not, what kind of policies don't transfer, and why? What are the differences between RL and SL?
- What advice would you give any organization or business entering SL about managing the social interactions of their members, both internally and externally? (e.g. within the group, or in interaction with the larger SL public, especially if the group has a formally structured interaction with the public, as it would for example if it was a business trying to reinforce its brand or a non-profit trying to educate people)
- Do you think that technology (what it allows you to do and prevents you from doing) can guide/define social interactions and governance? Does it affect the governance of EC? How?
- To what extent do you think that problems in EC are caused by differences in people's expectations?
- Are they differences because of differences between real-world cultures, or because of differences between SL cultures, or between real-world and SL expectations?
- Examples?
- In a virtual world, how do you establish legitimate authority?
- How do you think trust plays into governance?
- Elf Circle's authority is challenged from time to time. Do you think that it would be challenged in the same world if this was a face to face group? If not, what are the differences and why are they there?
- What is the biggest challenge to EC's authority in governance?
- How can that challenge be addressed?
- Is there anything else you'd like to comment on? Are there any questions that you think I should have asked, but didn't?

APPENDIX B: ELF CIRCLE GUARDIAN TRAINING

Elf Circle Guardians go through a comprehensive training process designed to ensure that they fully understand the culture of Elf Circle and their duties in relation to it, that they demonstrate a significant level of commitment to Elf Circle, and that those who are inappropriate for the work are weeded out. A strong focus is ensuring that they understand that in doing Guardian work they are representing Elf

Circle, not themselves. Greeters go through a similar training process for similar reasons. The full training process usually takes an individual 2-3 months at the Initiate level and 2-5 months at the Apprentice level.

The Guardians hold weekly meetings, and use formal ceremonies as signifiers of accomplishment when candidates for membership complete different levels of training, as a means of reinforcing camaraderie and group cohesion.

Initiates

Initiates must attend 5 training sessions; the introduction, Charter, code of conduct, ethics, and basic anti-griefer tactics. If they wish to continue further they are made Apprentices and assigned to a mentor (an experienced Guardian who has gone through mentoring training in addition to the standard training).

Apprentices

Mentors introduce a range of topics to their Apprentices, using resources provided or developing their own materials. Required sessions include rules and procedures for dealing with griefers and other social issues. Less obviously, they include "how-to" information on sports such as archery or formal combat and how to greet newcomers and make them welcome.

Additional sessions are offered for in-depth training on different topics; an Apprentice can specialize but is expected to choose a good selection from anti-griefer, greeter, sporting, or roleplay streams.

In order to graduate and become a full Guardian, an Apprentice must have their mentor's approval, complete an assigned task (often something that helps familiarize them with the lands), and plan and host a public event. The intent of the latter is to provide a supportive environment that encourages the Apprentice to try something new, contribute to the community, and show leadership and organizational skills. Finally, a "live fire" session tests their ability to respond effectively and appropriately to unexpected scenarios.

When they successfully meet all requirements, they will be promoted to guardian and provided with tools that will allow them to deal with griefers.

Chapter 7
Sociable Behaviors in Virtual Worlds

Francisco Grimaldo
Universitat de València, Spain

Miguel Lozano
Universitat de València, Spain

Fernando Barber
Universitat de València, Spain

Juan M. Orduña
Universitat de València, Spain

ABSTRACT

When simulating three-dimensional environments populated by virtual humanoids, immersion requires the simulation of consistent social behaviors to keep the attention of the users while displaying realistic scenes. However, intelligent virtual actors still lack a kind of collective or social intelligence necessary to reinforce the roles they are playing in the simulated environment (e.g. a waiter, a guide, etc). Decision making for virtual agents has been traditionally modeled under self interested assumptions, which are not suitable for social multi-agent domains. Instead, artificial society models should be introduced to provide virtual actors with socially acceptable decisions, which are needed to cover the user expectations about the roles played in the simulated scenes. This chapter reviews the sociability models oriented to simulate the ability of the agents that are part of an artificial society and, thus, interact among its members. Furthemore, it also includes a full description of a social model for multi-agent systems that allows the actors to evaluate the social impact of their actions, and then to decide how to act in accordance with the simulated society. Finally, the authors show the social outcomes obtained from the simulation of a particular 3D social scenario.

INTRODUCTION

Three-dimensional environments have significantly evolved since their beginning in the late sixties. The continuous increase of the available hardware as well as the improvement of the graphic software, in parallel with the evolution of computer networks, have brought virtual environments closer to the physical world; as science fiction already envisioned (Stephenson, 1992). 3D virtual

DOI: 10.4018/978-1-61520-891-3.ch007

worlds are at the cutting edge of the evolution of the Internet towards the new Web 2.0. Some well-known examples of such kind of applications are Massively Multiuser Virtual Environments (e.g. World of Warcraft (Blizzard Entertainment, 2009), SecondLife® (Linden Lab, 2009)...). The aim of these applications is the immersion of the users within a fictitious world. However, apart from the classical goal of immersive technologies (achieved by means of virtual reality devices such as data gloves or head-mounted displays) these 3D worlds aim at achieving the user's mental immersion by populating virtual worlds with synthetic actors, whose animated behavior resembles their equivalent in reality.

The simulation of virtual worlds is a current research topic with a great number of problems to be tackled. One of them is the challenge of populating virtual worlds with autonomous agents emulating human behaviors. Besides showing a good graphical appearance, these virtual actors must perform like-life behaviors. The behavioral animation requires the development of intelligent systems that can simulate believable behaviors for the 3D characters. This challenge involves dealing with perception, motor or animation control, goal selection, action planning and communication skills to interact with other characters or users. Therefore, this complex problem has led to the integration of different artificial intelligence techniques that reproduce intelligent skills such as autonomy, reactivity, pro-activity and sociability (Wooldridge, 1995).

Day after day, virtual worlds are incorporating new services that not only complement the originals located in the real world but also create a hybrid total experience of the physical and virtual reality, also known as interreality (Kokswijk, 2007). Consequently, the incorporation of social skills in the behavioral animation of different kinds of synthetic characters is a keystone in the development of last generation 3D virtual worlds (Williams *et al.*, 2006; Yee *et al.*, 2007). These social synthetic characters could be used to im-

prove the user's mental immersion in Massively Multiuser Virtual Environments (Rehm & Rosina, 2008). Additionally, they could be used to model different behaviors in crowd simulations, in order to evaluate the overall impact of different policies in critical circumstances such as catastrophic events (Pelechano *et al.*, 2008).

The complexity of the behavioral animation requires splitting the problem and managing each part independently. Since virtual actors should have a reactive nature, which can be easily recognized by the users or other actors, this feature is usually considered crucial for providing credibility. According to this, the literature of virtual humans contains a high number of works focused on reactive skills (Reynolds, 1987). Secondly, proactive behaviors require the use of planning or decision making mechanisms that introduce a new intelligence layer to be integrated. Hence, there is a significant reduction in the number of works covering both behavioral aspects (Funge *et al.*, 1999). Finally, social behaviors are rarely considered, as they add a new complex problem to be integrated (Reilly, 1996). Sociability refers to the ability of agents, which are part of an artificial society, to interact among them. Some works have faced sociability by providing synthetic characters with skills such as navigation (Helbing & Molnar, 1995), emotions or affection (Lim & Aylett, 2009). Nevertheless, intelligent virtual actors still lack a kind of collective or social intelligence beyond these agent-centered skills. As virtual humans usually play a role in the simulated environment (e.g. a waiter, a guide, etc.), they generate certain expectations associated with their activities and their relationships with the rest of agents in the scene, including the user. However, virtual characters' decision-making has generally been modeled under self interested assumptions, which are not suitable for multi-agent domains. Instead, artificial society models should be introduced to provide virtual actors with socially acceptable decisions. Actors need to evaluate the social impact of their actions to decide how to act in accordance with the society. However, social decision-making entails complex cognitive processes that require an abstract knowledge of the elements of the environment. Different works have proposed the inclusion of semantic information in virtual environments (Badler *et al.*, 2000; Farenc *et al.*, 1999). Regardless of the nature of the application, the definition of a basic semantic knowledge will benefit the production, the visualization and the interaction associated to 3D virtual worlds. Moreover, the possibility of reusing ontological descriptions previously designed also constitutes an interesting feature that approaches virtual worlds to the field of the Semantic Web (Grimaldo *et al.*, 2008b).

In the next section, we analyze the social decision-making techniques currently proposed and their evolution. We also review the literature around social virtual agents, as a specific use case. Then, we focus on MADeM (Multi-modal Agent Decision Making) (Grimaldo *et al.*, 2008a), a new open-source project based on the Multi-Agent Resource Allocation theory (Chevaleyre *et al.*, 2006), that provides a robust social simulation tool. MADeM is able to simulate different kinds of societies (e.g. elitist, utilitarian, etc), as well as social attitudes of their members such as, egoism, altruism, indifference or reciprocity. All these features are evaluated from the results obtained in the Virtual University Bar, a social simulation environment designed as an interesting example to evaluate the features provided by the MADeM

system. The chapter ends with a discussion about the future lines of research and the general conclusions.

Background

Social and organizational models are being studied under the scope of multi-agent systems (MAS) in order to regulate the autonomy of self-interested agents. Nowadays, the performance of MAS is determined not only by the degree of deliberativeness but also by the degree of sociability. In this sense, sociability points to the ability to communicate, cooperate, collaborate, form alliances, coalitions and teams. Being assigned to an organization generally occurs in Human Societies (Prietula, 1998), where the organization can be considered as a set of behavioral constraints that agents adopt (e.g. by the role they play) (Dignum & Dignum, 2001; Hübner *et al.*, 2002).

Figure 1 shows the spectrum obtained between rational agents and social agents. The intelligent behavior provided by rational agents is not enough in environments with shared resources. On the one hand, self interested agents (i.e. agents devoted to accomplish a set of goals) easily come into conflicts in a resource bounded environment even though their goals are compatible. The conflicts are generally derived from the implicit competition produced when situating different agents in a shared environment with a finite number of resources. Coordination techniques can help in

Figure 1. From Rational agents towards social agents

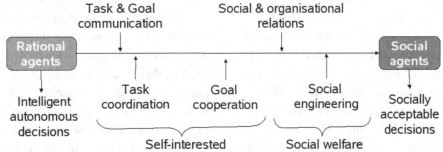

this context to avoid the behavioral inconsistencies produced when displaying the animation of groups of virtual actors. Task and goal passing techniques are nomally used to provide a certain degree of coordination in this context. Furthermore, the agents must be also prepared to cooperate themselves when sharing the same goals, which is also a normal group state.

On the other hand, socially intelligent agents are autonomous problem solvers that have to achieve their goals by interacting with other similarly autonomous entities (Hogg & Jennings, 2001). Bearing this in mind, multi-agent systems are normally referred to as societies of agents, and provide an elegant and formal framework to design social behaviors for autonomous agents.

The definition of a proper MAS organization is not an easy task, since it involves dealing with three main dimensions: functioning, structure, and norms (Hübner *et al.*, 2002). On the one hand, as functionality is normally required, the MAS generally aims at achieving the best plans and cover aspects such as: the specification of global plans, the policies to allocate tasks to agents, the coordination of plans, etc. (Decker, 1998; Tambe, 1997). On the other hand, there are systems that are focused on defining the organizational structure (i.e. roles, relations among roles, groups of roles, etc.) and try to accomplish their global purpose whereas the agents follow the obligations/permissions their roles entitle them (Ferber, 1998; Fox *et al.*, 1998).

From behavioral animation area, much research has been done in virtual agents for the last few years (Badler *et al.*, 1993; Reynolds, 1987; Thalmann & Monzani, 2002). The pioneer work of Dimitri Terzopoulos showed how to design a natural ecosystems animation framework with minimal input from the animator (Tu & Terzopoulos, 1994). He simulated *Artificial fishes* in virtual underwater worlds. However, human behavior is clearly different and more complex to emulate. In (Raupp & Thalmann, 2001; Thalmann & Monzani, 2002) the goal is to design controlled agents with a high

degree of autonomy. These agents are an extension of the Belief-Desire-Intention (BDI) architecture described in (Rao & Georgeff, 1991), and they include internal states such as emotions, reliability, trust and others. Emotional architectures have been also applied to virtual agents (animals and humans) to manage sociability and rationality and to produce believable groups of synthetic characters (Delgado-Mata & Aylett, 2004; Prada & Paiva, 2005).

Social reasoning has been extensively studied in multi-agent systems in order to incorporate social actions to cognitive agents (Conte & Castelfranchi, 1995). As a result of these works, agent interaction models have evolved to social networks that try to imitate the social structures found in real life (Hexmoor, 2001). Social dependence networks allow agents to cooperate or to perform social exchanges attending to their dependence relations (i.e. social dependence/power (Sichman & Demazeau, 2001)). Trust networks can define different delegation strategies by means of representing the attitude towards the others through the use of some kind of trust model (e.g. reputation (Falcone *et al.*, 2004)). Finally, agents in preference networks express their preferences (normally using utility functions) so that personal attitudes can be represented by the differential utilitarian importance they place on the others' utilities. Following this preferential approach, the MADeM (Multi-modal Agent Decision Making) model (Grimaldo *et al.*, 2008a) is a market-based mechanism for social decision making, capable of simulating different kinds of social welfares (e.g. elitist, utilitarian, etc.), as well as social attitudes of their members (e.g. egoism, altruism, etc.). It considers multi-modal decisions as those that are able to merge multiple information sources received from the group. Hence, MADeM agents express their preferences for the different solutions considered for a specific decision problem using utility functions. Thus, coordinated social behaviors such as task passing or planned meetings can be evaluated to finally obtain socially acceptable behaviors. The next section fully explains the MADeM procedure as well as its implementation as an open-source library over Jason (2009), a well-known multi-agent programming framework.

THE MADEM MODEL

The MADeM model provides agents with a general mechanism to make socially acceptable decisions. In this kind of decisions, the members of an organization are required to express their preferences with regard to the different solutions for a specific decision problem. The whole model is based on the MARA (Multi-Agent Resource Allocation) theory (Chevaleyre *et al.*, 2006). Therefore, it represents each one of these solutions as a set of resource allocations. Thus, the definition domain of MADeM is composed by the following elements:

A set of agents $\vec{A} = \left\{ a_1, \dots, a_n \right\}$ where each a_1 represents a particular agent involved in the decision. A vector of weights $\vec{w} = w_1, \dots, w_n$ is associated to each agent representing the internal attitude of the agent towards other individuals.

A set of resources $R = \{r_1, \dots, r_m\}$ to be allocated by the agents, where each r_i represents resources in the form of *task(slot)*, where the *slot* is a parameter that needs to be assigned in order to execute the *task*. Then, it identifies each one of the solutions for a specific decision problem as an allocation P of elements (either agents or objects) to task-slots as follows:

$$P = \{t_1\left(s_1\right) \leftarrow e_1, \dots, t_1\left(s_n\right) \leftarrow e_n, t_2\left(s_1\right) \leftarrow e_{n+1}, \dots, t_m(s_n) \leftarrow e_{n*m}\}$$

A set of utility functions $U = \{U^1, U^2, \dots, U^q\}$. These utility functions will be used to evaluate the allocations from different points of view. Additionally, each agent will have a vector of utility weights $\vec{w}_u = w_{u1}, \dots, w_{uq}$ representing the importance given to each point of view in the multi-modal agent decision making.

- A collective utility functions $Cuf = \{elitist, egalitarian, utilitarian, Nash\}$, representing the social welfare of the simulated society, that is, the type of society where agents are located.

MADeM uses a market-based winner determination problem to merge the different preferences being collected according to the kind of agent or society simulated. The details of the whole decision making procedure are explained in the following subsection.

Decision Making Procedure

MADeM uses one-round sealed-bid combinatorial auctions to choose among different solutions to a decision problem. Auctioneer and bidder roles are not played by fixed agents throughout the simulation. Instead, every agent can dynamically play each role depending on his/her needs or interests. For example, an agent would be the auctioneer when he wanted to pass a task to another agent. On the other hand, agents receiving the auction would bid their utility values provided that they were interested in the task being auctioned. Thus, MADeM lies in between centralized and distributed market-based allocation.

An overview of the multi-modal decision making procedure followed by the agents is shown in Figure 2. This procedure is mainly based on the following steps:

Auctioning phase: This phase is carried out by a single agent (a_1) who wants to socially solve a decision problem (e.g. where to sit). This agent then constructs the set of allocations representing all the possible solutions for the problem ($P_1, P_2, \dots, P_m$). These allocations have the form of task slots assignations such as $itAt(Obj_m) \leftarrow table_1$. Next, he auctions them to

Figure 2. MADeM Procedure

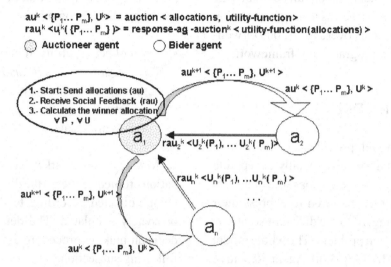

a particular group of agents, that we call the target agents. Each auction also includes a single type of utility function that the agent is interested in evaluating from the others ($au^k(P_1, P_2, ..., P_m, U^k)$). As complex decisions require taking into consideration more than one point of view, the auctioneer agent can start different auctions for the same set of allocations (au^1 through au^q).

Bidding phase: Since the auctioneer informs about both the task slot allocations and the utility functions being considered, bidders simply have to compute the requested utility functions and return the values corresponding to each auction back to the auctioneer ($rau_i^k = U_i^k(P_1), ..., U_i^k(P_m)$).

1. *Winner determination phase:* In this phase, the auctioneer selects a winner allocation for each launched auction. To do this, he uses a classical winner determination problem. Afterwards, he chooses one final winner allocation among these auction winners using a multi-modal decision making process. Thus, the final winner allocation will represent an acceptable decision for the society being simulated. The details of these calculations are fully described in the next section.

Winner Determination Problem

Once bidders have answered to an auction call (no answering means no preference, therefore, utility zero) the auctioneer agent has the utility values ($U_i(P_j)$) given by each bidder ($i \in A$) to every allocation being evaluated (P_j). Equation 1 groups these utility values in a set of vectors, one for each allocation.

$$\overrightarrow{U(P_j)} = U_1(P_j), ..., U_n(P_j) \qquad \forall j \in [1..m]$$

$$(1)$$

Remember that every agent had an associated vector of weights representing its attitude towards the other individuals ($\vec{w} = w_1, ..., w_n$). According to it, the auctioneer weighs the utility vectors in equation 1 doing a component by component multiplication with the attitude vector as shown in equation 2.

$$\overrightarrow{U_w(P_j)} = \overrightarrow{U(P_j)} * \vec{w} \qquad \forall j \in [1..m]$$

$$(2)$$

Attitude weights are used to model the social behavior of the auctioneer agent. For example, a whole range of behaviors between egoism and altruism can be modeled using the vector of equation 3, where $p=0$ represents the previous behavior, $p=1$ represents total altruism and $p=0.5$ represents an egalitarian behavior or indifference between oneself and the rest of the agents.

Egoism – Altruism:

$$\vec{w} = p,...,p,1-p,p,...,p \quad w_i = 1-p, w_{j \neq i} = p, i = Myself \tag{3}$$

It is also possible to model reciprocal attitudes by means of the vector $\vec{w}$. A simple example is shown in equation 4, where weights are based on the interchange of favors between agents.

$$Reciprocity: w_i = \frac{Favors\_from(i)}{Favors\_to(i)} \tag{4}$$

In order to socially behave, the auctioneer agent attends to the social welfare value when selecting the winner allocation of each auction. Therefore, the winner determination problem chooses the allocation that maximizes the welfare of the society (equation 5).

$$\forall k \in [1..q]$$

Auction Winner:

$$P_{wk} \quad \leftrightarrow \quad sw\left(P_{wk}\right) = \max_{j \in [1..m]} sw\left(P_j\right) \tag{5}$$

To compute the social welfare of an allocation, the auctioneer uses Collective Utility Functions (CUFs) and the weighted utilities defined in equation 1 (as shown in equation 6). MADeM allows selecting among different CUFs when evaluating the social welfare of an allocation. At the moment, four CUFs have been integrated in MADeM, each one related to a kind of society: utilitarian, egalitarian, elitist and Nash.

$$sw\left(P\right) = cuf\left(\overrightarrow{U_w\left(P\right)}\right) where$$

$$\begin{cases} cuf_{utilitarian} = \sum u_w(i) \\ cuf_{egalitarian} = min\left\{u_w(i)\right\} \\ cuf_{elitist} = max\left\{u_w(i)\right\} \\ cuf_{Nash} = \prod u_w(i) \end{cases} \tag{6}$$

An agent can ask other agents about different points of view (e.g. efficiency, tiredness, etc). In order to do this, he performs several auctions with different types of utility functions (see parameter U^k in Figure 2). Once all these auctions have been resolved, the auctioneer has the winner allocation for each point of view and the social welfare obtained provided that allocation is adopted (see equation 7).

$$\left\{au^1\left(P_1,...,P_m,U^1\right) \rightarrow \left(P_{w1},sw\left(P_{w1}\right)\right),...,au^q\left(P_1,...,P_m,U^q\right) \rightarrow \left(P_{wq},sw\left(P_{wq}\right)\right)\right\} \tag{7}$$

Lastly, the MADeM final winner allocation is that which maximizes the welfare of the society after having multiplied it by the corresponding utility weight $\vec{w}_u$, as shown in equation 8:

Final Winner:

$$P_w \quad \leftrightarrow \quad sw\left(P_w\right) = \max_{k \in [1..q]} w_u\left(k\right) * sw\left(P_{wk}\right) \tag{8}$$

J-MADeM: MADeM over Jason

This section describes how the MADeM model can be used by an agent programming language to make socially acceptable decisions available to agents eventually part of an organization. Among several languages for agent programming, we have chosen the AgentSpeak language (Rao, 1996) and its open source interpreter Jason (Bordini *et al.*, 2007) to program this kind of social agents. This choice was made because the language is based on the well known BDI architecture and the interpreter can be easily customised to include the MADeM support. The coupling of MADeM with Jason is inspired in other extensions of Jason, in particular J-MOISE+ (Hübner *et al.*, 2007) and hence the name J-MADeM, as it joins Jason and MADeM.

The J-MADeM is built upon the *Jason Communication Infrastructure*, thus extending the communication level options available in Jason with a set of modules that provide agents with the built-in feature of performing MADeM decisions. Figure 3a illustrates how these components are integrated into Jason. The J-MADeM basically offers to the AgentSpeak programmer: (i) an agent architecture that Jason agents can use to carry out their own MADeM decisions, (ii) an interface to develop utility functions that can be used along with the MADeM model and (iii) a set of internal actions to manage the parameters of these kinds of decisions.

The *J-MADeM Agent Architecture* extends the *Jason Agent Architecture* in order to incorporate all the necessary modules that allow MADeM decisions to be automatically carried out. The main components of the *J-MADeM Agent Architecture* are shown in the figure 3b, where we can identify the following elements:

- **MADeM Parameters:** This data storage contains the MADeM context currently defined for the agent. Essentially, it stores the personal weights, the utility weights, the collective utility function and the bid timeout to be used in future MADeM decisions.
- **Decision Launcher:** This module starts the MADeM process for a particular decision. Firstly, it stores the MADeM context for this decision into the *Decision Data* storage, thus allowing other decisions to be concurrently performed with different MADeM parameters. Secondly, it auctions each of the allocations being considered as solutions to the target agents.
- **Decision Data:** This data storage holds all the information related to the MADeM decisions still in process. Therefore, it contains their MADeM context, their considered allocations and the preferences received for each of them.
- **MADeM Communication Module:** This module extends the Jason agent com-

Figure 3. (a) Overview of the J-MADeM architecture and (b) detailed view of the J-MADeM Agent Architecture.

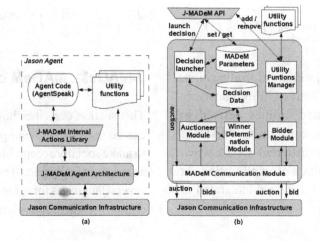

munication module in order to deal with MADeM messages. When it receives a MADeM auction, it invokes the *Bidder Module* to get the agent's preferences over the considered allocations. On the other hand, when it receives a MADeM bid, it informs the *Auctioneer Module* about the received preferences.

- **Bidder Module:** This module manages the reception of a MADeM auction. It extracts the considered allocations and bids for them according to the agent's preferences. To express these preferences it relies on the utility values provided by the *Utility Functions Manager*.

- **Utility Functions Manager:** This component acts as an interface between the built-in MADeM mechanism and the user defined *Utility Functions*. Thus, it is in charge of locating and invoking them in order to calulate the agents' utilities for the set of considered allocations.

- **Auctioneer Module:** This module manages the reception of MADeM bids. It extracts the sender's preferences and stores them into the *Decision Data*. As soon as the preferences from all the target agents have been received, it calls the *Winner Determination Module* to solve the decision.

- **Winner Determination Module:** This module solves the MADeM winner determination problem using the information stored into the *Decision Data* for the decision being resolved (i.e. considered allocations, agents' preferences, personal weights, utility weights, social welfare…). Once resolved, it notifies the agent about the winner solution.

For a complete description of the utility function interface and the set of internal actions refer to the J-MADeM documentation available at the Jason website (Jason, 2009).

APPLICATION EXAMPLE

In this section, we show how we have integrated MADeM into a multi-agent framework oriented to simulate socially intelligent characters in 3D virtual environments. This framework is developed over Jason (2009), so that the J-MADeM library is used to provide BDI agents with the ability to perform MADeM decisions. Figure 4 depicts the architecture of the system, which can be basically divided into two parts:

- The *Semantic Virtual Environment* uses ontologies to define the world knowledge

Figure 4. Multi-agent simulation framework

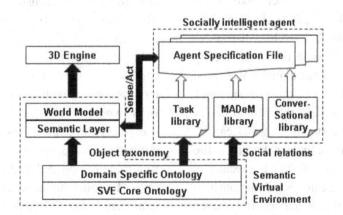

base (i.e. the object taxonomy and the object interrelations) as well as the set of all possible relations among the agents within an artificial society. The environment is handled by the *Semantic Layer*, which acts as an interface between the agent and the world, thus sensing and executing the actions requested by the agents. The animation system – virtual characters, motion tables, etc. – is located at the *3D Engine* that can extract graphical information from the *World Model* database in order to perform visualization.

- *Socially intelligent agents* receive sensorial information from the *Semantic Layer* and compute the appropriate sequence of actions in order to achieve their goals. The agent's finite state machine is defined in the *Agent Specification File*. It calls the following libraries to enrich agent behavior: the *Task Library*, that contains the operators that sequence the actions needed to animate a task; the *J-MADeM Library*, that provides the agents with the mechanisms to make social decisions; and finally, the *Conversational Library*, that contains the set of plans that handle the animation of the interactions between characters (e.g. ask someone a favor, planned meetings, chats between friends...).

In order to test MADeM, we have created a virtual university bar where waiters take orders placed by customers. The typical objects in a bar, such as a juice machine, behave like dispensers that have an associated time of use to supply their products (e.g. 2 minutes to make an orange juice) and they can only be occupied by one agent at a time. Therefore, waiters should coordinate to avoid conflicts. Additionally, agents can be socially linked using the concepts defined in the ontology (Grimaldo *et al.*, 2008b). For example, waiters and customers create social relationships with their friends and this social network is used

when deciding whether to do favors, to promote social meetings, etc.

Waiters serve orders basically in two steps: first, using the corresponding dispenser (e.g. the grill to produce a sandwich); and second, giving the product to the customer. For each task, a waiter evaluates whether to carry out the task against the chance to pass it to another waiter and perform his next task. That is, tasks are always auctioned using MADeM before their execution in order to find good social allocations. When calling MADeM, waiters take into account three points of view (i.e. utility functions): *performance*, *chatting* and *tiredness*. First, the performance utility function aims at maximizing the number of tasks being performed at the same time and represents the waiters' willingness to serve orders as fast as possible. Second, social behaviors defined for a waiter are oriented to animate chats among its friends at work. Therefore, the social utility function evaluates social interest as the chance to meet a friend in the near future, thus performing a planned meeting. Third, the tiredness utility function implements the basic principle of minimum energy, widely applied by humans at work. Finally, the type of society being simulated for waiters is elitist. That is, waiters will choose those allocations that maximize the utility functions previously defined.

On the other hand, customers place orders and consume them when served. Now, we are interested in animating interactions between customers that are consuming with their friends. Therefore, customers call MADeM to solve the problem of *where to sit*. In this case, the task slot being auctioned is the place where to sit and the candidates being evaluated are all the tables in the environment as well as the bar. Customers consider two points of view when calling MADeM: *sociability* and *laziness*. The social utility function defined for customers assigns a maximum value to a table provided that there is a friend sitting on it. To consume standing up at the bar is not considered of social interest at all, hence, its utility value is defined as zero. The laziness utility function evaluates each table according to their distance to the customer and, opposite to sociability, standing at the bar is now considered the best option. The type of society being simulated for customers is utilitarian, therefore, customers will choose those allocations that maximize the addition of the utility values previously defined. For a full description of the utility functions used by waiters and customers see (Grimaldo *et al.*, 2008a).

Results

In order to verify the social outcomes obtained with MADeM agents, we have simulated different types of waiters serving customers (see Figure 5 for a snapshot of the running 3D virtual environment). The results shown in this section correspond to simulations where 10 waiters attend 100 customers.

As we have previously mentioned, we have modeled an elitist society of waiters within which agents consider three points of view (i.e. performance, sociability and tiredness), each of them represented by its own utility function. In this context, utility weights can be adjusted to create different types of social waiters. For example, a *coordinated* waiter could be an agent that chooses its decisions following performance 75% of the times and following sociability or tiredness in the rest of the situations. The vector of utility weights for a *coordinated* waiter would then be

$$\overrightarrow{w_u} = 0.75, 0.125, 0.125,$$ where each component represents the importance given to each utility function being evaluated. Similarly, we have defined *social* waiters as agents with the following vector of utility weights $\overrightarrow{w_u} = 0.125, 0.75, 0.125$ and *egalitarian* waiters as agents with

$$\overrightarrow{w_u} = 0.125, 0.125, 0.75.$$

Table 1 summarizes some performance results obtained with *coordinated*, *social* and *egalitarian*

Figure 5. 3D virtual university bar environment

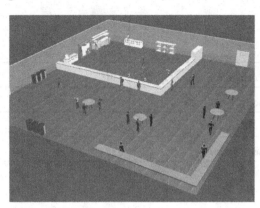

waiters against *self-interested* waiters with no social mechanism included. Firstly, column *Tasks/s* results from dividing the total number of actions performed by all the waiters by the amount of time needed to serve all the customers. Secondly, column $\overline{NChats}$ is the average number of chat actions carried out by each waiter. Thirdly, column σ_{NTasks} shows the standard deviation in the number of actions performed by each waiter. According to these results, *coordinated* waiters perform better (see higher values in column *Tasks/s*) since the majority of conflicts caused by the use of the same dispenser (e.g. the coffee machine) are resolved with specialization, that is, by passing the task to another waiter already using the dispenser. On the other hand, *social* waiters take more time to serve customers but animate a greater number of chats among friends (compare the average number of chats being animated in column $\overline{NChats}$). *Egalitarian* waiters look at the tiredness utility function and try to allocate the task to the least tired waiter, therefore, the standard deviation in the number of tasks performed by each agent tends to zero (see column σ_{NTasks}). Finally, *self-interested* waiters demonstrate to perform worse than any kind of social waiter. As these agents are unable to do task passing nor

133

Table 1. Performance results of different types of waiters

Agent	Tasks/s	$\overline{NChats}$	σ_{NTasks}
Coordinated	0,91	5	6.73
Social	0.65	29.4	4.37
Egalitarian	0.62	6.6	2.74
Self-interested	0.17	-	-

chatting, columns σ_{NTasks} and $\overline{NChats}$ are not considered.

Besides the possibility to define the importance of each point of view through the vector of utility weights $\overrightarrow{w_u}$, MADeM allows for the definition of a vector of personal weights $\overrightarrow{w}$ that models the attitude of an agent towards the other individuals. Table 2 shows the task passing results obtained for the defined waiters using the models of attitude considered previously: indifference, reciprocity, altruism and egoism. In this table, column $\overline{Favors}$ refers to the average number of favors (tasks) exchanged between the agents and column σ_{Favors} refers to the standard deviation in the number of favors. Agents using *indifference* do not apply any modification over the utilities received. Therefore, we consider the results of this attitude as the base values to compare with for each type of waiter. *Reciprocity* weights utilities attending to the ratio of favors already done between the agents. This attitude produces equilibrium in the number of favors exchanged as it can be seen in column σ_{Favors}. *Altruism* has been implemented in such a way that the weight given to oneself utilities is 0.25 whereas the weights for the rest of the agents are 0.75. As expected, altruist agents do more favors, since the importance given to the other's opinions is three times the importance given to their own opinion (see high values for the average number of favors exchanged $\overline{Favors}$). On the other hand, *egoism* weights are 0.75 to oneself and 0.25 to the others, thus, agents rarely do favors (see low values in column $\overline{Favors}$).

Agent's preferences can sometimes go against personal attitudes. For example, whereas *reciproc-*

Table 2. Task passing results for different personal weights

Attitude	Coordinated		Social		Egalitarian	
	σ_{Favors}	$\overline{Favors}$	σ_{Favors}	$\overline{Favors}$	σ_{Favors}	$\overline{Favors}$
Indifference	7.57	6.9	3.52	8.7	7.58	13.6
Reciprocity	1.15	8.8	1.76	7.8	2.4	15.5
Altruism	5.94	17	6.66	12.7	4.44	17.9
Egoism	1.41	0.7	0.81	0.4	0.47	0.1

ity tries to balance the number of favors, tiredness tends to assign tasks to the least tired waiter (see the greater σ_{Favors} for egalitarian waiters). Another example is *egoism* applied to *egalitarian* waiters, in this case no task at all is passed among the agents ($\overline{Favors} = 0.1$). However, agent's preferences can also empower personal attitudes. For instance, *altruism* applied to *coordinated* waiters produces a high level of specialization. This type of agents produces big values for σ_{Favors} as the agents already using a dispenser (e.g. a juice machine) keep on getting products from the dispenser following both an altruist and a coordinated behavior that reduces collisions for the use of an exclusive resource. Despite this issue, personal weights have demonstrated to produce similar effects on the agents regardless of the kind of waiter being considered (i.e. *coordinated, social* or *egalitarian*).

Unlike waiters, customers make decisions within a utilitarian society where they consider two points of view: *sociability* and *laziness*. Figure 6 shows the behavior obtained with different types of customers. We compare two metrics: the mean number of social meetings performed among the customers and mean distance covered to consume. Lazy customers, with low utility weights for sociability, most of the time choose to consume at the bar or to sit at a nearby table (see point $\overrightarrow{w_u} = 0.3, 0.7$). Therefore, the mean distance to the consuming place is short but only a few social meetings are animated. On the other hand, social customers, with higher utility weights for sociability, perform more social meetings but they also need to move longer distances to find their friends.

Points $\overrightarrow{w_u} = 0.6, 0.4$ and $\overrightarrow{w_u} = 0.7, 0.3$ in figure 6 correspond to some examples of social customers.

FUTURE RESEARCH DIRECTIONS

3D virtual worlds have significantly evolved since their beginning. However, users often point to their lack of immersion due to the great number of uninhabited scenes or to the elementary interactions between avatars and autonomous humanoids. Currently, synthetic actors still need to incorporate a broad range of social techniques to enhance their behavioral animation, which will

Figure 6. Lazy vs. social customers

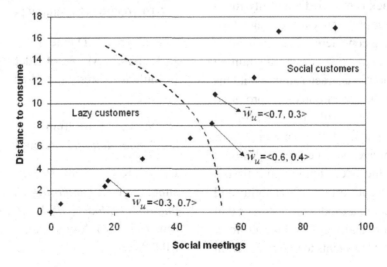

finally improve the mental immersion of the user within 3D virtual worlds.

Therefore, future work in this research area must cover the integration of new social techniques in the agent decision making, such as the one presented in this chapter. This goal must lead the researchers to look for the synergy among computer graphics, artificial intelligence and social sciences. This sort of socially intelligent actors will be useful to populate professional environments such as a 3D e-government office (where autonomous humans can socially follow the protocols between the administration and the citizens) as well as entertainment scenes such as the virtual bar showed in this chapter.

CONCLUSION

This chapter has presented a new social decision-making technique to provide 3D virtual agents with consistent social behaviors suitable to be animated. Firstly, we have analyzed the literature and evolution of social decision-making in multi-agent domains. Then, we focus on MADeM and its integration into Jason (J-MADeM), a new open source library oriented to create different types of simulated societies. The main feature of J-MADeM agents is that they are able to merge several points of view received from other agents. This social feedback is modeled via utility functions that express the preferences of each agent for every solution being considered. The application example presented aims at incorporating human style social reasoning for character animation. This way, we evaluate the social outcomes provided by the J-MADeM. The results obtained for the virtual university bar show how two groups of socially intelligent agents can consider different points of view in their decision making: first, a team of waiters using performance, sociability and tiredness; and second, a model of customer that evaluates sociability and laziness. Furthermore, this example allows the agents to manage several

personal and collective utility functions as well as a set of weights (personal and utility-based) in order to perform elaborated social simulations.

ACKNOWLEDGMENT

This work has been jointly supported by the Spanish MEC and European Commission FEDER funds under grants Consolider Ingenio-2010 CSD2006-00046 and TIN2009-14475-C04-04.

REFERENCES

Badler, N., Bindiganavale, R., Bourne, J., Palmer, M., Shi, J., & Schuler, W. (2000). *A parametrized action representation for virtual human agents* (pp. 256–284). Cambridge, MA: MIT press.

Badler, N., Philips, C., & Webber, B. (1993). *Simulating Humans: Computer Graphics, Animation and Control*. Oxford, UK: Oxford University Press.

Blizzard Entertainment. *World of warcraft*. (2009). Retrieved February 2009 from http://www.worldofwarcraft.com.

Bordini, R. H., Hübner, J. F., & Wooldrige, M. (2007). *Programming Multi-Agent Systems in AgentSpeak using Jason*. Chichester, UK: Wiley. doi:10.1002/9780470061848

Chevaleyre, Y., Dunne, P. E., Endriss, U., Lang, J., Lemaitre, M., & Maudet, N. (2006). Issues in multiagent resource allocation. *Informatica*, *30*, 3–31.

Conte, R., & Castelfranchi, C. (1995). *Cognitive and Social Action*. London: UCL Press.

Decker, K. S. (1998). Task environment centered simulation. In *Simulating Organizations: Computational Models of Institutions and Groups* (pp. 105–128). Menlo Park, CA: AAAI Press / MIT Press.

Delgado-Mata, C., & Aylett, R. (2004). *Emotion and action selection: Regulating the collective behaviour of agents in virtual environments* (pp. 1304–1305). AAMAS.

Dignum, V., & Dignum, F. (2001). Modelling agent societies: Co-ordination frameworks and institutions. In P. Brazdil & A. Jorge, (Eds.), *Procs. of the 10th Portuguese Conference on Artficial Intelligence (EPIA'01)*, (LNAI 2258, pp. 191-204). Berlin: Springer.

Falcone, R., Pezzulo, G., Castelfranchi, C., & Calvi, G. (2004). Why a cognitive trustier performs better: Simulating trust-based contract nets. In *Proc. of AAMAS'04: Autonomous Agents and Multi-Agent Systems*, (pp. 1392–1393). New York: ACM.

Farenc, N., Boulic, R., & Thalmann, D. (1999). An informed environment dedicated to the simulation of virtual humans in urban context. In P. Brunet & R. Scopigno, (Eds.), *Proc. of EUROGRAPHICS"99, 18*(3), 309–318. London: The Eurographics Association and Blackwell Publishers.

Ferber, J., & Gutknecht, O. (1998). A meta-model for the analysis and design of organizations in multi-agents systems. In *Proc. of the 3rd International Conference on Multi-Agent Systems (ICMAS'98)*, (pp. 128–135). Washington, DC: IEEE Press.

Fox, M. S., Barbuceanu, M., Gruninger, M., & Lon, J. (1998). An organizational ontology for enterprise modelling. In *Simulating Organizations: Computational Models of Institutions and Groups* (pp. 131–152). Menlo Park, CA: AAAI Press / MIT Press.

Funge, J., Tu, X., & Terzopoulos, D. (1999). Cognitive modeling: knowledge, reasoning and planning for intelligent characters. In *Proc. of SIGGRAPH'99*, (pp. 29–38). New York: ACM.

Grimaldo, F., Lozano, M., & Barber, F. (2008). MADeM: a multi-modal decision making for social MAS. In *Proc. of AAMAS'08: Autonomous Agents and Multi-Agent Systems*, (pp. 183–190). New York: ACM.

Grimaldo, F., Lozano, M., Barber, F., & Vigueras, G. (2008). Simulating socially intelligent agents in semantic virtual environments. *The Knowledge Engineering Review, 23*(4), 369–388. doi:10.1017/S026988890800009X

Helbing, D., & Molnar, P. (1995). Social force model for pedestrian dynamics. *Physical Review E: Statistical Physics, Plasmas, Fluids, and Related Interdisciplinary Topics, 51,* 4282. doi:10.1103/PhysRevE.51.4282

Hexmoor, H. (2001). From inter-agents to groups. In *Proc. of ISAI'01: International Symposium on Artificial Intelligence.*

Hogg, L. M., & Jennings, N. (2001). Socially intelligent reasoning for autonomous agents. *IEEE Transactions on Systems, Man, and Cybernetics, 31*(5), 381–393. doi:10.1109/3468.952713

Hübner, J. F., Sichman, J., & Boissier, O. (2002). A model for the structural, functional, and deontic specification of organizations in multiagent systems. In G. Bittencourt & G. L. Ramalho, (Eds.), *Procs. of the 16th Brazilian Symposium on Artifical Intelligence (SBIA'02)*, (LNAI Vol. 2507, pp. 118-128). Berlin: Springer-Verlag.

Hübner, J. F., Sichman, J. S., & Boissier, O. (2007). Developing organised multi-agent systems using the Moise+ model: Programming issues at the system and agent levels. *International Journal of Agent-Oriented Software Engineering, 1*(3/4), 370–395. doi:10.1504/IJAOSE.2007.016266

Jason. (2009). Retrieved 2009 from http://jason.sourceforge.net/.

Lim, M. Y., & Aylett, R. (2009). An Emergent Emotion Model for An Affective Mobile Guide with Attitude. *Applied Artificial Intelligence Journal, 23*, 835–854. doi:10.1080/08839510903246518

Linden Lab. (2009). *SecondLife®*. Retrieved February 2009 from http://secondlife.com/.

Pelechano, N., Allbeck, J., & Badler, N. I. (2008). *Virtual Crowds: Methods, Simulation, and Control*. San Francisco: Morgan & Claypool Publishers.

Prada, R., & Paiva, A. (2005). Believable groups of synthetic characters. In *Proc. of AAMAS '05: Autonomous Agents and Multi-Agent Systems*, (pp. 37–43). New York: ACM.

Prietula, M., Carley, K., & Gasser, L. (1998). *Simulating Organizations: Computational Models of Institutions and Groups*. Menlo Park, CA: AAAI Press / MIT press.

Rao, A. S. (1996). AgentSpeak(L): BDI agents speak out in a logical computable language. In S. Verlag, (Ed.), *Proc. of MAAMAW '96*, (LNAI 1038, pp 42–55).

Rao, A. S., & Georgeff, M. P. (1991). Modeling rational agents within a BDI-architecture. In *Proc. of KR '91: The 2nd International Conference on Principles of Knowledge Representation and Reasoning*, (pp. 473–484). San Mateo, CA: Morgan Kaufmann publishers Inc.

Raupp, S., & Thalmann, D. (2001). Hierarchical model for real time simulation of virtual human crowds. *IEEE Transactions on Visualization and Computer Graphics, 7*(2), 152–164. doi:10.1109/2945.928167

Rehm, M., & Rosina, P. (2008). SecondLife® as an Evaluation Platform for Multiagent Systems Featuring Social Interactions. In *Proc. of AAMAS '08: Autonomous Agents and Multi-Agent Systems*, (pp 1663–1664). New York: ACM.

Reilly, W. S. N. (1996). *Believable Social and Emotional Agents*. PhD thesis, School of Computer Science, Carnegie Mellon University, Pittsburgh, PA, USA.

Reynolds, C. (1987). Flocks, herds and schools: A distributed behavioral model. In *Proc. of SIGGRAPH '87*, (pp 25–34). New York: ACM.

Sichman, J., & Demazeau, Y. (2001). On social reasoning in multi-agent systems. *Revista Ibero-Americana de Inteligencia Artificial, 13*, 68–84.

Stephenson, N. (1992). *Snow crash*. New York: Bantam Books.

Tambe, M. (1997). Towards flexible teamwork. *Journal of Artificial Intelligence Research, 7*, 83–124.

Thalmann, D., & Monzani, J. (2002). Behavioural animation of virtual humans: What kind of law and rules? In *Proceedings of Computer Animation* (pp. 154–163). Washington, DC: IEEE Computer Society Press.

Tu, X., & Terzopoulos, D. (1994). Artificial fishes: physics, locomotion, perception, behavior. In *Proc. of SIGGRAPH '94*, (pp. 43–50). New York: ACM.

van Kokswijk, J. (2007). *Digital Ego: Social and Legal Aspects of Virtual Identity*.

Williams, D., Ducheneaut, N., Xiong, L., Zhang, Y., Yee, N., & Nickell, E. (2006). From Tree House to Barracks: The Social Life of Guilds in World of Warcraft. *Games and Culture, 1*, 338–361. doi:10.1177/1555412006292616

Wooldridge, M. J., & Jennings, N. R. (1995). Intelligent agents: Theory and practice. *The Knowledge Engineering Review, 10*(2), 115–152. doi:10.1017/S0269888900008122

Yee, N., Bailenson, J. N., Urbanek, M., Chang, F., & Merget, D. (2007). The Unbearable Likeness of Being Digital: The Persistence of Nonverbal Social Norms in Online Virtual Environments. *Cyberpsychology & Behavior, 10*(1), 115–121. doi:10.1089/cpb.2006.9984

ADDITIONAL READING

Bartle, R. A. (2003). *Designing Virtual Worlds. New Riders.*

Moulin, H. (1991). *Axioms of cooperative decision making.* Cambridge University Press.

Osborne, M. J. (2004). *An Introduction to Game Theory.* Oxford University Press.

Chapter 8
Establishing Social Order in 3D Virtual Worlds with Virtual Institutions

Anton Bogdanovych
University of Western Sydney, Australia

Simeon Simoff
University of Western Sydney, Australia

ABSTRACT

An important security aspect of Virtual Worlds (in particular Virtual Worlds oriented towards commercial activities) is controlling participants' adherence to the social norms (rules of behavior) and making them follow the acceptable interaction patterns. Rules of behavior in the physical world are usually enforced through a post factum punishment, while in computer-controlled environments we can simply block the actions that are inconsistent with the rules and eliminate rule violations. In order to facilitate enforcing the rules in such automatic manner and allow for frequent rule changes, the rules have to be expressed in a formal way, so that the software can detect both the rules and the actions that can potentially violate them. In this chapter the authors introduce the concept of Virtual Institutions that are Virtual Worlds with normative regulation of interactions. For development of such systems the authors employ the Virtual Institutions Methodology that separates the development of Normative Virtual Worlds into two independent phases: formal specification of the institutional rules and design of the 3D interaction environment. The methodology is supplied with a set of graphical tools that support the development process on every level, from specification to deployment. The resulting system is capable of enforcing the social norms on the Virtual Worlds' participants and ensuring the validity of their interactions.

INTRODUCTION

Every day in the physical world we participate in a number of institutions. Once we enter a work place, shop or university we realize the change of the context and start obeying the rules of the environment we have entered. Our behavior is highly influenced by these rules, which range from not strictly enforceable and rather implicit social conventions (like etiquette) to more explicit and usually strictly controlled instructional *norms* (like having to walk through a metal detector in

DOI: 10.4018/978-1-61520-891-3.ch008

an airport or to pay for the purchased items before exiting a shop).

The *institutions* are trusted third parties, which establish the rules of the interactions and administer strict control in regards to their enforcement (North, 1990). The establishment of the institutions helps in reducing the complexity in the decision making of the participants as well as in increasing the trust between individuals and improving the security of their interactions (Schotter, 1981). Government is one of the most prominent examples of an institution. The rules it tries to enforce are various laws present in the country the government is representing.

In human societies there are two available rule enforcement mechanisms: preventive measures, which prevent the rule violation from happening; and sanctions, which are used to punish the rule violator (Fehr & Fischbacher, 2004). While all the possible efforts are put into developing preventive measures, the physical world is so complex that it is impossible to prevent many rule violations from occurring. Therefore, the majority of the rule-control mechanisms used in the physical world is sanction based. The rule enforcement mechanisms of a government, for example, include the employment of armed forces like police or the army.

The *participants* of non-gaming *Virtual Worlds* like Second Life also have to deal with institutions when they access virtual classrooms, sell virtual goods or attend research conferences. Unlike the physical world the environment of a Virtual World is both computer-controlled and computer-generated. Furthermore, the complexity of a Virtual World is much lower than the complexity of the physical world. In such environments it is more efficient to employ preventive rule enforcement measures rather than use sanctions. The institutional rules of a Virtual World can potentially be expressed in a formal way and their enforcement can happen automatically by blocking all the actions that are inconsistent with the institutional rules.

Despite such exciting prospects, Virtual Worlds in their current form are rather anarchical environments developed on an ad-hoc basis. Instead of being properly formalized and automatically enforced, institutional rules are often assumed to be part of the common sense knowledge of the users. Some of them are expressed in the terms of services of a particular software product. When it comes to regulation, the rules are still often enforced in a sanction-based manner: by issuing warnings to the rule violators or even banning them if the violation reoccurs. To our knowledge, none of the existing Virtual Worlds offers a centralized technological solution that would enable structuring the interactions of participants and establishing social order in an automatic manner. Moreover, there is no widely used methodology being employed by Virtual Worlds developers that is structured around formalizing the rules of participants' interactions. Even for those cases where the rules of behavior are controlled by the code of the software, having no clear methodology and no formal representation of the rules makes it extremely difficult to introduce rule changes in the system.

Many existing Virtual Worlds are developed for engaging users into some sort of entertainment activities where participants value their virtual experience because of the freedom of interactions, and lack of norms and boundaries. Introducing the explicit social norms and the computational control of those might not be an appropriate measure for such environments. However, Virtual Worlds also proved to be a very promising technology for so-called "serious games" in domains like electronic commerce, education, tourism, etc. In these domains the absence of formal rules of behavior and reliable methods to enforce those is rather unfortunate and is, in our opinion, one of the key contributors to the present low acceptance of the Virtual Worlds technology by the industry. Therefore, the remainder of the chapter is focused on developing technological facilities for structuring the interactions of participants (the term "*participants*" is used throughout the chapter to refer to both human users and computer-controlled characters participating in a Virtual World through their avatars) in the Virtual Worlds oriented towards 'serious' games, not the general purpose Virtual Worlds.

A key contribution of this work is the concept of *Virtual Institutions*. The key idea behind Virtual Institutions is to treat *Virtual Worlds* as *Normative Multiagent Systems* (Boella, Torre, & Verhagen, 2007) that cater for mixed society of software *agents* and humans. Normative Multiagent systems is a field of research within Artificial Intelligence that suggests to treat complex computational systems as societies of autonomous entities (agents) which abide by a formally defined set of social norms and interaction protocols. The implementation focus of Normative Multiagent Systems is on programming the environment in terms of the rules of behavior of participants and acceptable interaction protocols rather than on modeling the behavior of individual agents. Such focus permits ignoring the internal architecture of the individual agents' architecture and concentrate on the system design instead.

Conceptually, *Virtual Institutions* are Virtual Worlds with normative regulation of interactions. Technologically, the current implementation of the Virtual Institutions concept incorporates a three-layered deployment framework and a design methodology. The methodology separates the development of Virtual Worlds based on the concept of Virtual Institutions into two independent phases: specification of the institutional rules and design of the 3D interaction environment. It is supplied with a set of graphical tools that support the development process on every level, from specification to deployment. The proposed approach is not only useful for helping humans to establish social order in Virtual Worlds but also for helping autonomous agents to reduce the uncertainty about the world, understand and learn the rules of the interactions and interpret the actions of the others. Although in the current form Virtual Institutions are only concerned with establishing explicit rules they can also be employed for establishing implicit social conventions.

Further in this chapter we present the concept of Virtual Institutions, establish the case in favor of defining and operating Virtual Worlds as Normative Multiagent Systems, outline extensive details of the Virtual Institutions Methodology that should be used for design of Normative Virtual Worlds and describe the deployment architecture we have developed. The presentation is concluded by illustrating the Virtual Institutions concept with an example, summarizing the contribution and outlining the directions of future work.

VIRTUAL INSTITUTIONS

Virtual Institutions is a paradigm that facilitates establishing social order in Virtual Worlds. The concept of Virtual Institutions is defined as follows:

Virtual Institutions are 3D Virtual Worlds with normative regulation of interactions.

More precisely, we propose to separate the development of Virtual Worlds based on the concept of Virtual Institutions into two independent phases: specification of the interaction rules and design of the 3D Interaction environment. For producing more efficient designs such separation is widely used in architecture (Maher, Simoff & Mitchell, 1997), from where we adapt elements of activity/space modeling applied to Virtual Worlds. Apart from design efficiency, in our case this separation has the following advantages:

- It helps in achieving clear distribution of the development tasks between system analysts and designers;
- Explicitly focusing the attention of system analysts on interactions enables them to analyze the system in details and elicit substantial requirements specification before creating the visualization, which is useful

for detecting critical issues and errors at an early stage;

• It makes the specification of the interaction rules independent of particular Virtual Worlds technology used for the visualization of the system, permitting a quick and easy portability to new visualization platforms.

To be able to support the conceptual separation between the design of a Virtual World and normative control of the interactions within this space we conceptually model Virtual Institutions as two conceptual layers: Visual Interaction Layer and Normative Control Layer.

The Visual Interaction Layer maps to the domain of 3D Virtual Worlds. It is concerned with audio and visual aspects of the multimedia, as well as with visualization of the interactions of participants in the 3D Virtual World.

The Normative Control Layer maps to the domain of Normative Multiagent Systems. Electronic Institution (Esteva, 2003) is the particular type of a normative multiagent system that we employ for this case. An Electronic Institution is understood as a computational environment that is enacted in accordance with a certain formal specification. The specification includes common language, a hierarchy of acceptable roles, the role flow policy, norms of behavior and interaction protocols. In the Normative Control Layer we employ Electronic Institutions for enabling institutional control of the interactions within the Visual Interaction Layer.

Not every Virtual World requires normative control of interactions as well as not every physical world institution needs 3D Visualization. Systems that involve high degree of interactions, which need to be structured in order to avoid violations, may need institutional modeling. From these, only institutions, where 3D visualization of active components is possible and beneficial, are worth visualizing in Virtual Worlds.

Systems that could benefit from both interaction control and 3D visualization, provided by

the concept of Virtual Institutions, should be built following the Virtual Institutions metaphor, presented in the next section.

Virtual Institutions Metaphor

Virtual Worlds are inspired by the metaphor of architecture. They often employ physical structures like buildings, rooms, walls, etc. to represent different kinds of activities and to separate them from one another (Russo Dos Santos et al., 2000). The metaphor of architecture is convenient as humans are mostly familiar with the concept of a building. Therefore, the metaphor of architecture seems like a good choice for Virtual Institutions and can be applied to the same (or an even wider) range of problems that we are concerned within this chapter. However, Virtual Worlds that are expected to support normative regulation of interactions require the introduction of some design constraints to the metaphor used by such Virtual Worlds.

Virtual Institutions can be viewed as a virtual space which we call 3D Interaction Space. This space can correspond to an arbitrary 3D Virtual World populated by avatars and various objects. Inside the 3D Interaction Space a set of buildings are located, where each of the buildings represents an Electronic Institution. The appearance of the 3D Interaction Space outside the buildings can be arbitrary and the behavior of avatars is not controlled by the institutional norms. However, there are restrictions on appearance and interactions inside the buildings.

As it is hard to provide a physical metaphor for the 3D Interaction space we introduce some sort of a substitute. We present the metaphor of a garden, as a place surrounding the institutional buildings. This metaphor is well known to humans as gardens often surround residential buildings in the physical world. In this way the 3D Interaction Space can be described as the combination of the garden and institutional buildings.

Employing the building metaphor for the visualization of an institution is motivated by the

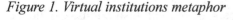

Figure 1. Virtual institutions metaphor

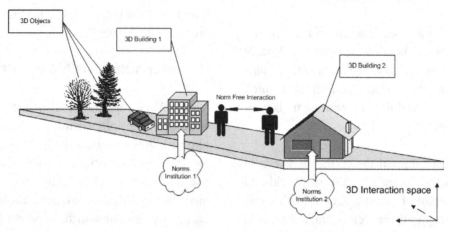

fact that many institutions familiar to the participants from the physical world (like universities, courts, banks etc.) also have a brick and mortar representation. As in the physical world the walls of a virtual building create visible boundaries for norm enactment.

Each institutional building is associated with its unique set of interaction rules, which are controlled by the specification of the corresponding Electronic Institution. The participants are visualized as avatars and each of them is assigned with at least one role. Only participants with specific roles can enter the institutional buildings and once there should act according to the specification of the corresponding institution. The concept of a role is widely used in Virtual Worlds. In many game based Virtual Worlds a role reflects the fact of being a part of a selected group and determines different abilities of the participants associated with it. In non-game based Virtual Worlds the role is normally used to distinguish between fee-paying subscribers and participants with trial membership.

Further elaborating the metaphor, we see each of the institutional buildings being divided into a set of rooms that are separated from each other by walls and doors. The doors are opened or closed for a participant depending on the role and the institutional state. Walls and doors are often employed in the physical world to restrict access to

some activities; hence, this choice of metaphors is consistent with physical world institutions.

Figure 1 outlines the details of the Virtual Institutions metaphor presented so far. With the help of the 3D Virtual Worlds technology the metaphor of Virtual Institutions can be visualized. All of the concepts contributing to the metaphor (Garden, Buildings, Rooms, etc.) will have their respective graphical representations inside the resulting 3D Virtual World.

The findings in the area of Virtual Worlds design research suggest that during the construction of a 3D representation of a Virtual World, it is important to keep the benefits of traditional 2D interface design in mind (Bowman, Kruijff, LaViola, & Poupyrev, 2001). Participating in a 3D environment, where users can manipulate 3D objects, does not necessarily mean exclusion of 2D interface elements. In fact, the interaction with 2D interface elements offers a number of advantages over a 3D representation for particular tasks (Nielsen, 1998). Most efficient selection techniques, for instance, are widely realized in 2D, whereas, the selection process in a 3D user interface must consider the user's viewpoint and distance to the object.

Based on these findings we suggest enhancing the Virtual Institutions metaphor with two additional components (which in the resulting

Virtual World will be visualized as additional 2D elements). The first component is a map of the 3D Interaction space, which inside a building is transformed into a building map. The map metaphor is widely used in various Virtual Worlds to assist navigation through the virtual space. Virtual Worlds can be harder to navigate than the physical worlds, and employment of maps proved to be very useful in Virtual Worlds (Darken & Sibert, 1996). Consequently, as Virtual Institutions are visualized as Virtual Worlds, we introduce maps navigational maps of Virtual Institutions.

Another additional component that contributes to the overall metaphor and which is also visualized in 2D is what we call "backpack with obligations". Electronic Institutions provide technological facilities for participants to collect obligations while acting inside the institution. If a participant does not fulfill some obligations, the institution may impose some restrictions to participant's activities. We introduce the backpack metaphor to inform participants about the reasons for imposed restrictions and to provide them with convenient facilities to visualize their commitments (so that enforcement of restrictions can be promptly avoided). This metaphor is taken from military-oriented games, in which it is usually the case that a player is given a mission, which in turn consists of a set of submissions. Any time during the game, the player can click on his/her backpack to see the mission related details. In a similar way, the backpack can be used in Virtual Institutions to show the acquired obligations to the participants.

Next we describe the components of each of the Virtual Institutions conceptual layers in terms of the new metaphor.

Visual Interaction Layer

Visualization of the Virtual World and its participants as well as providing the participants with interaction facilities is associated with the following set of concepts.

3D Interaction Space

It represents the generated 3D Virtual World, and there is no possibility for participants to move beyond it. The only way to leave it is by disconnecting from the Virtual World client. Once someone enters it, he/she will become embodied as an avatar and will be physically located inside. To enhance the believability of the visualization the space is usually populated with a number of various 3D objects, depending on the domain of the virtual institution(s) in it. In the default case, a 3D Interaction Space is decorated as a garden, where the objects enhancing the believability are trees, bushes, cars etc. A special type of object inside a garden is the building, which metaphorically represents the institution. Agents enter the institution by entering the building. Anywhere outside the institutional building interactions among participating avatars are not regulated and every event that happens inside this space is immediately visualized without any prior validation. In other words the space outside the buildings is the unregulated part of the virtual world.

Institutional Building

An institution is represented as a building in the 3D Interaction Space, and the interactions within the building are regulated by the specified institutional rules. The Electronic Institution is seen as a computational infrastructure that establishes a set of norms on the behavior of participants, who can be either humans or autonomous agents. Every event that a participant requests through an input device (typically but not limited to pressing keys on the keyboard or operating with the mouse) is first sent to the institutional infrastructure for validation. If the institution permits event's execution - the corresponding action is performed and visualized, otherwise the event is blocked and dismissed. The institution provides context-based explanations of the reasons why the event can not be processed.

Each institutional building has a single entrance door, through which the participants can enter it.

Avatars

The participants of the 3D Interaction Space are visualized as *avatars*. We distinguish between the following two types of avatars: avatars for users (the institution customers) and avatars for the institutional employees. For the users' avatars an initial set of default appearances is provided, but those appearances can be changed later. The institutional employees are usually represented by autonomous agents that play internal roles in the corresponding Electronic Institution. They are assumed to have similar appearance which goes inline with the dress code of the institution they are employed with. As mentioned earlier outside the institutions the avatars are free to execute any possible action (the set is limited by the functionality of the respective virtual world) and their communication is not moderated by any of the institutions. Once they enter the institutional building they can only execute the actions that are permitted by the corresponding institution for the role in which they have entered. In some of the rooms it is allowed by the institution to split the user into several alteroids (avatars). The concept of an *alteroid* is similar to the concept of a thread in object-oriented programming. Splitting into alteroids for an agent means that two instances of the given agent are created inside a transition, which can simultaneously move into two different scenes and act there independently. Each time a new alteroid is created a user should decide which to choose to control and a new autonomous agent is executed to take control over the one that was controlled before. This functionality allows a user to employ autonomous agents for performing some routine tasks on user's behalf, while the user may be involved into some other activities.

Rooms

Every institutional building consists of a set of rooms, each one representing a different activity. The rooms are supposed to be represented as a set of rectangular boxes closed by walls from every side. Each of the rooms has at least one door, through which it can be entered. Once a participant enters a room, the only possibility for the corresponding avatar to move outside the room boundaries is to walk through one of the doors embedded into the walls of the room. To be able for a user to instantly move from one room to another it is necessary for those two rooms to be connected via a door. Unlike in many Virtual Worlds, in Virtual Institutions it is not always the case that a user can enter the room through a door and then will be able to exit it through the same door. On the contrary, when the room is entered the entrance door may be automatically locked for the user. This depends on the specification of the underlying Electronic Institution, whether it allows the backward movement between the rooms or not. In order to provide a consistent experience to the users we suggest that system designers should include the backward movement everywhere where it is possible.

Doors

The Doors are used to connect different rooms in the institutional building. The institutional rules and the execution state determine which agents (avatars) depending on their role can progress through the door. This is strictly controlled by the Electronic Institution.

Map

In order to simplify the navigation of the users, every institution is supplied by the map of the building. The map usually appears in the upper-right corner of the screen as a semitransparent schematic plan. Each of the available rooms is shown on the map and the human-like figures show every user the positions of all the alteroids a user is associated with. While moving through the institution the positions are updated accordingly.

Backpack with Obligations

While acting in an institution a user may acquire some commitments. An example of such a commitment may be that a user who just won the auction will not be able to directly leave the institution, but is committed to visit the payment room before leaving. These commitments are expressed in the specification of the underlying Electronic Institution and are fully controlled by the system. In order to have a simple way to present those commitments to a user we use the metaphor of a backpack used in many computer games. The backpack is usually present in the lower right part of the screen and a user may decide to hide it or show it back after hiding. Clicking on the backpack will result in a user being presented with the textual list of the acquired commitments.

Events/Actions/Messages

Although, we anticipate that the users may use all sorts of different devices for navigating virtual worlds, in a standard case a participant of a 3D Interaction Space is able to control the avatar and change the state of the Virtual World by pressing keyboard buttons, moving a mouse or clicking mouse buttons. Those physical actions executed by a user in the real world generate events inside the Virtual World, which are then visualized as actions executed within the 3D Interaction Space. The events that a user is trying to execute inside an institutional building are not directly visualized. Before visualization every event is transformed into a message understandable by the institution and sent to the institutional infrastructure for validation. The action is performed only if a given message is consistent with the current state of the institution and it is not against the institutional rules to visualize the corresponding action.

Normative Control Layer

The description of the Visual Interaction Layer provided the explanation of the Virtual Institutions metaphor in terms of the Virtual Worlds domain. In order to explain how the institutional control of the processes inside the Virtual World is achieved we next present the mapping of the concepts presented above to the domain of Electronic Institutions. Further in this section we provide an explanation how each of the concepts described in the previous section is expressed in terms of Electronic Institutions.

A detailed explanation of the components constituting an Electronic Institutions specification is presented in (Esteva, Cruz, & Sierra, 2002). Figure 2 presents a short overview of the mapping between the concepts of Electronic Institutions and the corresponding concepts of the Virtual World.

Institutions

In Virtual Institutions every building is seen as an institution. This metaphor is borrowed from the physical world, where most of the institutions are brick and mortar. Entering or exiting such an institution changes the behavior of participants, including their conversation style. Most of the processes inside each brick and mortar institution are controlled by the institutional infrastructure.

Scenes and Transitions

Scenes and Transitions in Virtual Institutions are represented as rooms and corridors. A scene in Electronic Institutions is seen as the protocol that describes a basic activity. By giving a brick and mortar representation to this concept we suggest representing each of such basic activities as a separate physical room inside the institutional building.

Figure 2. Mapping between 3D virtual worlds and electronic institutions

Specification Element	Example	Virtual World Element	Example
Scene	RegistrationRoom	Room	
Transition		Room/No representation	
Connection	(Receptionist) Guest	Door	
Number of participants	Max 30	Size of the room	
Agent	Guest	Avatar	
Message	(inform (? RoomManager) (all Buyer) closed)	Action	
Root Scene	root	Room/No representation	
Exit Scene	exit	Garden	
Obligations	((obl !x (inform (!x buyer) (?y buyer_ac)(payment !price)) buyer-settlement))	Backpack	
Performative Structure	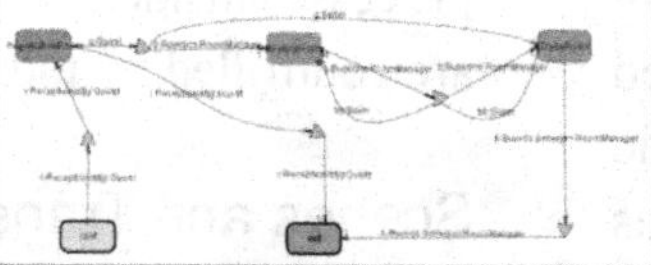	Map	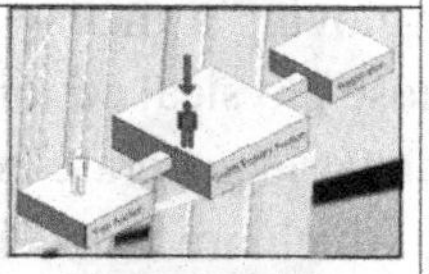
Data Types in Ontology	Desk	3D Objects or No Representation	

Transitions in Electronic Institutions serve the purpose of a middle point between two different scenes and sometimes are used for synchronization of agents. In a case when a transition is used for synchronization purposes we suggest to visualize it as a room of a special kind. Probably the most appropriate appearance for such a room would be a waiting room similar to the waiting rooms in the airports. That's the place where participants will have to wait for someone else to join them if the institution demands so.

In the Electronic Institutions specification for each of the scenes the number of participants for each of the accepted roles is always specified. We use this information to determine the "size" of the room in terms of the units of the Virtual World. The more avatars can enter the scene the bigger it should be. Hence, the size of the room is proportional to the sum of the maximum number of participants of all accepted roles.

Performative Structure and Virtual Institution layout

The original idea behind the Performative Structure is to define the main activities and specify the role flow of participants between those activities (scenes). The closest concept present in the Virtual Worlds domain is the map of the building. As it naturally happens in the Virtual Worlds, the map for each of the participants is personalized. The participants are usually only interested in the places that they can access and have much less interest in the rest. This allows us to personalize the map in a way that only the scenes that a participant is able to access are visualized there.

Every Performative structure contains special types of scenes called "root" and "exit". These scenes are not associated with any processes inside the institution and cannot have a protocol specified for them. The root scene only serves the purpose of being the entrance point into the institution. In some cases when a root scene is connected to more than one transition it is useful to visualize it as a small room with a set of doors. Otherwise, when there is only one transition connected to it we suggest avoiding creating unnecessary rooms and do not visualize it. The entrance door of the institution in this case will lead straight into the

room connected to the root scene via the first transition.

The exit scene defines the exit point. It is never visualized. Reaching the exit scene means leaving the institutional building. So, once a participant walks through a door that corresponds to the connection leading to the exit scene, the corresponding avatar will be located outside the institutional building and the exit door will be closed (as there can be no return connection from the exit scene).

Connections

The connections in the Performative Structure graph are used to determine the flow of participants between a scene and a transition. In the Virtual World we see them visualized as doors connecting different rooms. Many connections should not be visualized at all. For example, when in the specification there are several incoming connections that define entering a scene by the agents playing different roles, there is no need to create a separate door inside the corresponding rooms for each of them. In such a case only one door will be present and all the agents will use the same door for entering the room.

In the case when a transition is not visualized all the connections leading to it should not be visualized too. In such situation the rooms that are connected with each other via this transition will have a direct door connection.

Obligations

The obligations the participants acquire in an institution are represented as the backpack, which on opening displays the textual description of the obligations.

Data Types in Ontology

To be able for the agents operating in an Electronic Institution to "understand" each other it is necessary for them to establish common language.

Therefore, the ontology defines a set of data types that the agents should operate with (by sending messages to each other). The majority of the Virtual Worlds inhabitants are humans, who usually are pretty good in establishing a common language without any ontological help. Mixed societies of agents and humans are a different ball game. The data types in the ontology are used to describe objects that the participants operate while interacting inside the institution. Although some data types may refer to intangible concepts, the majority of them should be represented as 3D objects. Associating data types from ontology with 3D models in the Virtual World helps autonomous agents to recognize these objects, manipulate them, track actions upon them and refer to them in conversations with humans.

Virtual Institutions Methodology

For building Virtual Institutions we propose using the Virtual Institutions methodology outlined in Figure 3. This methodology covers the whole development process and is also supplied with the tools for deployment of Virtual Institutions. This methodology should be employed by system architects and software developers (both are further called users). In general, applying Virtual Institutions methodology requires 7 steps to be accomplished:

1. Eliciting Specification Requirements.
2. *Specification* of an Electronic Institution.
3. *Verification* of the specification.
4. *Automatic Generation* of the corresponding 3D environment.
5. *Annotation* of the Electronic Institution specification with components of the 3D Virtual World.
6. *Integration* of the 3D Virtual World and the institutional infrastructure.
7. Enabling Implicit Training.

Completing the above steps will result in defining both Normative Control Layer and Visual Interaction Layer of the corresponding Virtual Institution. As shown in Figure 3, the specification requirements for the Normative Control Layer are derived on Step 1 of the methodology. The Normative Control Layer is created on Step 2 and Step 3. The development of the Visual Interaction Layer is completed after applying Step 4, Step 5 and Step 6. In case a system designer wishes to enable programming agents through implicit training mechanisms Step 7 should also be completed. Next we present a detailed overview of each of these steps.

Step 1. Eliciting Specification Requirements. The initial step of the methodology is the analysis of the application domain by system architects with the goal to elicit specification requirements. This

Figure 3. Methodology steps

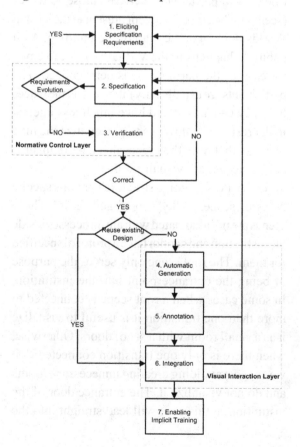

step should result in the creation of the Software Requirements Document. In this document the key activities, roles of the participants and basic scenarios are outlined. The suggested methods for eliciting system requirements are interviews, questionnaires as well as other means of applied exploratory and descriptive research. Once the specification requirements are established, Step 2 should be used to formalize them. A detailed methodology for completing this step is outlined in (Bogdanovych, Rodriguez, Simoff, Cohen, & Sierra, 2009).

Step 2. Specification. In the current technological solution, this step is conceptually the same as specifying the institution using the Electronic Institutions methodology (Arcos, Esteva, Noriega, Rodrguez-Aguilar, & Sierra, 2005) and should also be executed by the system architects. It establishes the regulations that govern the behavior of the participants. This process is supported by ISLANDER (Esteva et al., 2002), which permits to specify most of the components graphically, hiding the details of the formal specification language and making the specification task transparent. The specification is determined by the following sets of rules:

- Conventions on language, labeled as "Dialogical Framework", which specify the roles allowed for participants, the relationships amongst those roles and a common language.
- Conventions on interactions, labeled as "Scenes", which define conversation protocols for a group of roles, where a protocol is defined as a final state machine. Each scene requires a definition of its participating roles and their population, its conversation protocol, and the states at which the participants can either leave or enter the conversation. The scenes of an institution define the valid interactions that the participants are allowed to have and set the

context wherein the exchanged illocutions must be interpreted.

- Conventions on activities, labeled as "Performative Structure", which determine the types of dialogues in which participants can be engaged. Once the key activities (scenes) are identified, the role flow between different scenes is set. Each of the scenes is further associated with an interaction protocol, where a protocol is defined as a final state machine.
- Conventions on behavior, labeled as "Norms", which determine the consequences of participants' actions in different scenes. These consequences are regarded as commitments acquired while acting in the environments and have to be fulfilled later on. These commitments restrict future activities of the participants. They may limit the possible scenes that can be entered and possible actions that can henceforth be executed.

If during the formalization it became evident that the system requirements elicited on Step 1 are insufficient or if for some other reason their evolution is required, the system architect has a choice to return to Step 1 for refining the system requirements. If no requirements evolution is necessary and the specification of the system is complete, its validity should be ensured on Step 3 of the methodology. For additional technical details of Step 2 see (Esteva, 2003).

Step 3. Verification. One of the advantages of the formal nature of the methodology is that the specification produced on the previous step can be automatically verified for correctness by ISLANDER. The tool verifies the scene protocols, the role flow among different scenes and the correctness of norms. This verification is static in nature, meaning that the specification has to be finalized before the verification can take place (in contrast to trying to verify on the fly during the specification process). The verification starts with the validation of the correctness of the protocol defined by each scene. This includes checking that the state graph of each scene is connected, that each state is reachable from the initial state and that there is a path from each state to a final state. It is also ensured that the messages associated to the arcs of the state graph are correct with respect to the Dialogical Framework.

The Performative Structure establishes how participants can legally move between different scenes. As we do not want them to get blocked in any scene or transition it is verified that from each scene and transition participants always have a path to follow, and that from any scene or transition there is a path to the final scene (so that all participants can leave the institution).

Finally, ISLANDER checks whether the norms are correctly specified and whether the participants can fulfill their commitments. As commitments are expressed in terms of actions that have to be carried out in the future, it is verified that those actions can be performed. For instance, if there is a norm that defines that a participant has to pay for acquired products, it is checked that from the scene where the products are purchased there is a path that allows reaching the payment scene.

The verification permits to detect errors in the institutional rules before starting the design and development of the Visual Interaction Layer. If such errors are found, the developers should go back to Step 2 to correct those. If the specification contains no errors there are two options how to proceed. If there is an existing design that fits the Electronic Institutions specification, i.e. the 3D visualization of the environment has already been created for an earlier design, then the developers may skip the next two steps and continue with Step 6. Otherwise, the generation step (Step 4) should be executed.

Step 4. Automatic Generation. On the generation step the 3D Virtual World and its floor plan can be created in a fully automatic way. Not only the institutional specification defines the rules of the interactions, but also helps to understand which

visualization facilities are required for participants to operate in the institution. Some elements of the specification have conceptual similarities with building blocks in 3D Virtual Worlds, which makes it possible to create an automatic mapping between those. On this step of the methodology the Electronic Institution Specification is automatically transformed into the skeleton of the Virtual World. The scenes and transitions are transformed into 3D rooms, connections become doors, and the number of participants allowed to be in a scene determines the size of each room.

A method used for the automatic generation step is described in (Drago, Bogdanovych, Ancona, Simoff, & Sierra, 2007). After finishing this step the generated visualization has to be annotated on Step 5.

Step 5. Annotation. A fully immersive and visually rich Virtual World cannot be automatically created just on the basis of this specification. In order to make the generated skeleton appealing it has to be enriched with additional graphical elements on the annotation step. These additional elements include textures and 3D Objects like plants, furniture elements etc.

Apart from the elements defined in the Performative Structure most of the components of the Electronic Institutions specification do not require visualization. Such components are ignored on the generation step. In some situations, however, the visualization of these components is useful. For example, data types defined in the ontology can be represented by 3D objects. If this is the case, on the annotation step a system designer should create 3D models for these objects and manually insert them into the corresponding rooms.

This step of the methodology does not usually require the involvement of the system architects and should rather be executed by software developers and graphic designers. After this step the user can return to Steps 1 and 2 to refine the specification requirements or the specification itself, or can continue with Step 6. More details about the annotation step can be found in (Bogdanovych, 2007).

Step 6. Integration. On the integration step the execution state related components are specified. This includes the creation of the set of scripts that control the modification of the states of the 3D Virtual Worlds and mapping of those scripts to the messages, which change the state of the Electronic Institution. Firstly, the scripts that correspond to the messages from the agent/institution protocol need to be defined. These include entering or leaving a scene or transition, entering or leaving an institution, etc. Next, the scripts that correspond to the specific messages defined in the ontology on the specification step must be created. In case there were any 3D objects representing the ontology data types, the actions upon which require validation - the mapping between these objects and the corresponding data types in the ontology has to be established.

Making the integration a separate step of the methodology stimulates the development of the scripts in the form of design patterns, which are generic enough to be reused in other systems.

After accomplishing this step the generated 3D Virtual World is ready to be visualized and the Virtual Institutions infrastructure will be executed to take care of the validity of interactions between participants, verify the permissions of participants to access different scenes and make sure that all the institutional norms and obligations are imposed. This step is particularly important for the case when the system requires using an already existing design. For existing designs the integration step cannot happen automatically and, currently, manual integration is the only possible way to enable the technological connection between the Visual Interaction and Normative Control layers.

Similar to the previous step, integration should be conducted by software developers. After this step the user can return to Steps 1 and 2 to refine the specification requirements or the specification itself, or can continue with Step 7. Additional details of the integration step are presented in (Bogdanovych, 2007).

Step 7. Enabling Implicit Training. Virtual Institutions provide unique facilities for development of autonomous agents. We propose the method of Implicit Training (see (Bogdanovych, Simoff, & Esteva, 2008) for details), which is a central technology behind the decision making of the autonomous agents in Virtual Institutions. With the help of Implicit Training the agents can learn sophisticated human-like behaviors from observation of human actions in the 3D environment. Following this approach in many cases it becomes much more efficient to train the autonomous agents than to program them. In contrast to programming, such approach is much less resource consuming and a lot more flexible.

In case of Implicit Training the Normative Layer of Virtual Institutions forms the basis for the decision graph of the agent, where possible illocutions become the nodes of this graph. For each of those nodes it is possible to specify whether implicit training is conducted or not. This process is completed on the Enabling Implicit Training step of the methodology.

Deployment

Applying the Virtual Institutions Methodology described in the previous section results in the creation of the Electronic Institution Specification (the central component of the Normative Control Layer) and the 3D model of the Virtual World (containing the institutional building that represents this specification). The logical connection between the two layers is achieved on the integration step. In order to maintain this connection and make the Virtual Institution functional an additional software layer was required. In this section we present the resultant architecture for deployment of Virtual Institutions.

Our deployment architecture consists of three independent layers as shown in Figure 4. First layer here is the Normative Control Layer. It uses the

AMELI system (Arcos et al., 2005) to regulate the interactions of participants by enforcing the institutional rules established on the specification step. AMELI maintains the execution state of the institution and uses it along with the specification to guarantee that participants' actions do not violate any of the institutional constraints. Each participant is introduced into the institution via an institutional agent called "governor". The governor blocks the actions that are inconsistent with institutional rules and explains those rules to the respective participant on demand.

Second layer is the Communication Layer. Its task is to causally connect the institutional infrastructure with the visualization system and transform the actions of the visualization system into messages, understandable by the institutional infrastructure and the other way around. This causal connection is achieved via the Causal Connection Server (Bogdanovych, Berger, Sierra, & Simoff, 2005), which uses the Action-Message table created on the integration step to establish the mapping between actions of the Visual Interaction Layer and messages of the Normative Control Layer. The causal connection is happen-

ing in the following way: an action executed in the 3D Virtual World (that requires institutional verification) results in a change of the institutional state in the AMELI layer, as well as every change of the institutional state is reflected onto the 3D Virtual World and changes its state.

The third layer, the Visual Interaction Layer, is used to visualize the 3D Virtual World for the users. The 3-layered approach not only supports the conceptual subdivision of a Virtual Institutions into the Normative Control Layer and Visual Interaction Layer as it was presented in the previous section, but also has a number of practical benefits:

1. The interactions inside the 3D Virtual World become structured, secure and predictable, as everything that needs control is verified by AMELI and will happen as specified.

2. The Visual Interaction Layer can be easily replaced (i.e. when a more advanced visualization platform appears on the market) with minimal changes required for the rest of the system.

3. The changes in the Normative Control Layer can be automatically reflected onto the

Figure 4. Runtime architecture

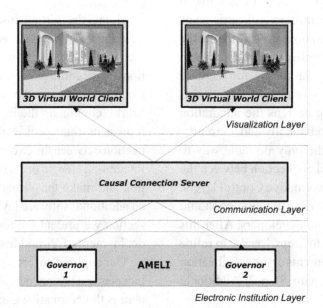

Visualization layer or will require minimal manual adjustment.

4. A number of different visualization platforms (possibly implemented via different technologies) can be simultaneously connected to the Causal Connection Server and share the same institution.

5. Some of the software agents that do not interact with the humans can directly connect to the institution via the Normative Control Layer and operate (interact) there, keeping their observable presence (room location, actions within the room, etc) in 3D, so that other participants (humans) will be able to observe their presence and actions in the 3D Virtual World. This is important in terms of awareness and consistency of the environment, and markedly differentiates the Virtual Institutions technology.

CONCEPT ILLUSTRATION: TRADING INSTITUTION

In order to illustrate the concept of Virtual Institutions let consider the following scenario.

Scenario: *Imagine a fishmonger who is very interested in contemporary art. He is a regular*

customer of a Virtual Institution and uses its fish market auction for buying and selling fish. One of the rooms in this institution serves as the gallery for graffiti posters. The artist is present in the room and is looking forward to conversations with visitors. The fish monger enters the poster exhibition and spends his time browsing through the art works, while his other alteroid, driven by an autonomous agent, participates in the fish market auction and buys fish on his behalf.

Institution Formalization

In this section we demonstrate how the formal specification of the Trading Institution from the above described scenario can be created using the ISLANDER tool (Esteva et al., 2002). The specification of the Trading Institution forms the basis for the Normative Control Layer of the corresponding Virtual Institution.

Dialogical Framework

The specification starts by defining the roles of the accepted participants. Each role specifies a pattern of behavior within the institution. The participants can play multiple roles at the same time and can change their roles. There are two types of roles:

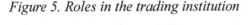

Figure 5. Roles in the trading institution

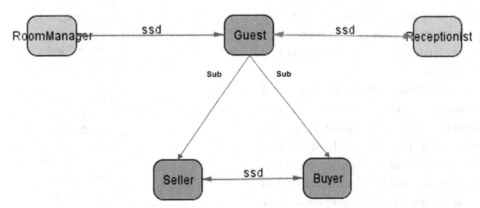

internal roles - played by the staff agents to which the institution delegates its services and tasks, and external roles - performed by external agents.

Figure 5 outlines the relationships amongst the roles in the Trading Institution.

"Receptionist" and "RoomManager" are internal roles in this institution, while the rest are external roles. The Receptionist is an institutional employee, whose task is to greet external participants and verify their registration details. The RoomManager is another employee responsible for starting the interactions in the Meeting Room and controlling the execution of each auction conducted in the Trading Room.

All of the external participants are playing the role "Guest". This role has two subroles: "Buyer" and "Seller". This fact is expressed in Figure 5 by two arrows marked as "Sub". Having subroles for a given role means that in the Trading Institution each Guest can become a Buyer or Seller as a result of some action (i.e. entering correct registration details) and these roles will be accepted everywhere where the "Guest" role is accepted.

The two-directional arrows marked with "ssd" (static separation of duties) in Figure 5 define incompatibility between roles. In our case, once a user has entered the Trading Institution as a Guest it is not possible for this user to become a Receptionist or RoomManager. And vice-versa, a Receptionist or RoomManager cannot change their roles to become a Guest or any of its subroles. The same condition is true for Buyer and Seller. A Guest who has registered as a Buyer cannot be a Seller anymore. This security feature of linking identities to roles in each moment of time during the operation of the institution is a trade off limitation.

Once the roles of the participants are defined in order for them to be able to interact with each other we need to define a common ontology, acceptable illocutionary particles, valid communication language expressions and content language.

The ontology defined within the Dialogical Framework specifies the acceptable data types

and functions (structuring the message content) that can be used inside the illocutions uttered by participants. There are standard data types: Integer, Float, String, Agent, etc. which can be instantly used. Other data types, which are compositions of the basic data types, can also be defined. The ontology used for the Trading Institution is shown in Figure 6.

This ontology specifies a single custom data type "Good", which is a tuple of the following form: (goodID: float; goodName: String). The rest of the ontology components are functions to be used in the illocutions inside scene protocols. These functions in our example are marked with an "f" symbol and include: accept, approached, closed, etc.

The illocutionary particles for this institution include: "inform" and "request".

The communication language used by the agents consists of the expressions of the following form:

Figure 6. Ontology used for the trading institution

156

(i (α$_i$, r$_j$) β,γ,τ)

In this expression:

i - is an illocutionary particle (e.g. request, inform);

α$_i$ - can be either an agent variable or an agent identifier;

r$_j$ - can be either a role variable or a role identifier;

β - represents the addressee(s) of the message and can be:

- (α$_k$, r$_k$) the message that is addressed to a single agent.
- r$_k$ the message that is addressed to all the agents playing the role r$_k$.
- "all" the message that is addressed to all the agents in the scene.

γ - is an expression in the content language;

τ - can be either a time variable or a time-stamp.

An example of an expression pattern sent by a Guest agent to a Receptionist in the Registration Room looks like:

(request(?x Guest)(!y Receptionist)(login ?user ?pwd))

This particular expression means that agent "x" playing the role Guest sends a login request to agent "y" with user identifier and email address as the parameters of this request.

In this expression "?x" stands for a free occurrence of the variable and "!x" is its application occurrence, which means that it has to be replaced by the last bound value of variable "x".

Figure 7 shows the components of this regular expression. The dialog window on the left hand side illustrates the possible illocutionary particles that are defined in the Trading Institution. These include "request" and "inform". For an agent to be able to construct an expression as in the equation above, the "request" illocutionary particle should be defined in the Dialogical Framework of the institution.

The "Function type" dialog window in Figure 7 illustrates the definition of the "login" message inside the ontology. This definition simply specifies the number of parameters (two) and their type (both are of type String).

Figure 7. Illocutions, content language and communication language

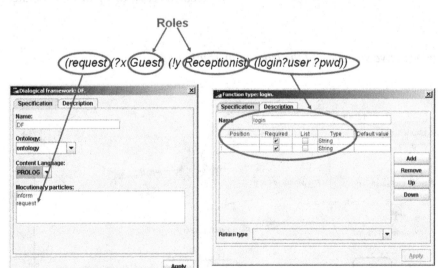

Performative Structure

The Performative Structure defines the relationships between basic activities (scenes) of the institution. These relationships can be: causal dependency (e.g. a Guest agent must go through the registration scene before going to any further scenes); synchronization points (e.g. synchronize a Buyer and a Seller before starting a negotiation scene); parallelization mechanisms (e.g. a Buyer agent can go to multiple auction scenes); choice points (e.g. a Buyer leaving the registration scene can choose which auction scene to join); the role flow policy (which participants can access which scenes depending on their roles). Figure 8 outlines the Performative Structure of the Trading Institution.

The rectangular shapes in Figure 8 represent scenes, the arcs connecting them are connections and triangular shapes are transitions. Three of the scenes "Registration", "Meeting" and "Trade" in this Performative structure are functional components. Another two scenes: "root" and "exit" are only used to show the entrance point (root scene) and exit point (exit scene) of the institution processes. When an agent joins the institution it is immediately moved to the root scene. Reaching the exit scene means leaving the institution.

The transitions are used for rerouting agents between scenes and for agent synchronization. Most of the transitions in Figure 8 are marked with an "x" symbol (exclusive choice point), which means that the agents can only follow one path from such a transition. One of the transitions doesn't have this symbol (choice point). This is because with this transition it is permitted for an agent to follow multiple paths. In the particular case of the Trading Institution the choice point transition connects MeetingRoom and TradeRoom scenes. A Buyer agent is allowed to perform the stay-and-go operation in the TradeRoom (which will be further shown in the protocol of this scene). This means that the Buyer agent can split into alteroids inside this transition. There is also another type of transitions - the synchronization and parallelization point available in Electronic Institutions (this type wasn't used in our example). Such transitions can be used to force splitting agents into alteroids or force synchronization for agents with different roles.

The TradeRoom scene's appearance differs slightly from the rest of the scenes and appears to be slightly "bumpy". This illustrates that for this scene it is allowed to have multiple executions. To have multiple executions means that a number of instances of a scene with the same protocol are created, each of them is associated with a state

Figure 8. A performative structure of the trading institution

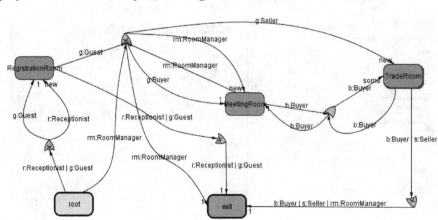

and the agents can join or leave these instances depending on the state and permissions.

The labels indicated above the connections define the role flow of participants. In the case of the Trading Institution the following role flow dynamics are possible:

Agents with the "Guest" role can access the RegistrationRoom scene from the root through a corresponding transition. After successful admission in the RegistrationRoom in the next transition Guests can change their role and become either Buyer or Seller. If the admission wasn't successful - the Guests are not allowed to enter any further scenes and can only leave the institution.

If admitted as Buyers, Guests change their role and can enter the MeetingRoom. From the MeetingRoom Guests can move to the TradeRoom and then either leave the institution or return back to the MeetingRoom. The label "some" on the arc connecting the TradeRoom with the corresponding transition shows that a Buyer can enter more than one instance of the TradeRoom scene.

If a Guest agent is admitted as a Seller, it can create a new instance of the Trade room and conduct an auction there. The Sellers are not allowed

to enter the MeetingRoom and from the RegistrationRoom can only go to the TradeRoom or exit.

Agents with the "Receptionist" role activate the RegistrationRoom scene. This is expressed by the label "new" on the incoming connection into the RegistrationRoom. Before the scene is activated other participants cannot enter it. As the task of the Receptionist is to control the registration of the guests, from the RegistrationRoom it can only exit the institution and cannot access any other scene.

Agents with the "RoomManager" role activate the MeetingRoom. They can only access this scene. When the MeetingRoom scene is terminated the RoomManager agent can exit the institution through the corresponding transition.

Scene Protocols

The RegistrationRoom scene is used for letting the Guest agents identify themselves. It accepts only one "Receptionist" agent and twenty "Guest" agents to be simultaneously present within this scene. The protocol for the RegistrationRoom scene is presented in Figure 9. This figure also

Figure 9. Scene protocol for RegistrationRoom

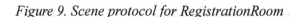

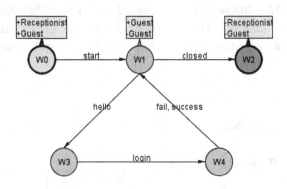

start: (timeout[0])
hello: (request(?x Receptionist)(?y Guest) hello)
login: (inform (!y Guest) (!x Receptionist) (?login ?pwd))
success: (inform (!x Receptionist) (!y Guest) success)
failure: (inform (!x Receptionist) (!y Guest) (fail?reason))
closed: (inform (?x Receptionist) (all Guest) closed)

shows the illocutions that may trigger the state changes in the scene.

This protocol outlines 5 different states through which the RegistrationRoom scene can evolve (W0 - W4). State W0 is the initial state. As soon as the scene is activated it is switched into W0. In this state the agents with roles "Receptionist" and "Guest" can enter the scene. This is expressed through the labels "+Receptionist" and "+Guest" above the state.

As a result of a timeout ("start" illocution) the scene will immediately change its state to W1. While the scene is in this state all the agents with the role "Guest" can enter or leave this scene.

The final state of the scene (the state in which scene is destroyed and can not be accessed anymore) is "W2". This state can be reached from state "W1" through "closed" illocution. This illocution occurs when a Receptionist sends the "closed" message to all Guests. In the final state all the agents are forced to leave. The fact that all of them are indeed able to do so is expressed by the labels "-Receptionist" and "-Guest" above the state W2.

The registration process happens between states W1, W3 and W4. Each of the Guest agents that enter the scene while it is in W1 state will receive the identification request from the Receptionist ("hello" illocution). As the result of this illocution the scene will evolve to state W3. The Guest should respond with its login and password

by sending the "login" illocution. This will change the state of the scene to W4.

If the registration details of the Guest are acceptable - the Receptionist will inform the Guest about it by executing the "success" illocution. If the registration details sent by the Guest are incorrect - the Guest will be notified about the failure to register ("fail" illocution) and can try to register once again. Either of these two illocutions will change the state of the scene to W1.

Notice that while RegistrationScene is in states W3 and W4 it is impossible for any agent to leave or enter the scene.

The MeetingRoom scene is to be used for social interactions between Buyers. The protocol and illocutions for this scene are presented in Figure 10.

It consists of two states (W0 and W1). In state W0 agents with roles "RoomManager" and "Buyer" can enter the scene and agents with the role "Buyer" can leave the scene. It is allowed to have 1 receptionist agent and up to 50 Buyers inside the scene. The scene will evolve to the state "W1" when a RoomManager agent will decide to destroy the scene by sending the "closed" illocution. In this case all the agents will be forced to leave the scene and the scene will be terminated. Such simple protocol is due to the fact that in the particular implementation we are not concerned with controlling the socially acceptable behavior of the agents and no restrictions are imposed on how they interact in the MeetingRoom scene.

Figure 10. Scene protocol for MeetingRoom

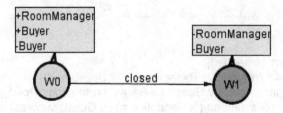

closed: (inform (?x RoomManager) (all Buyer) closed)

The TradeRoom scene is used for conducting different kinds of auctions following the downwards-bidding protocol. The protocol for the TradeRoom scene and the corresponding illocutions are presented in Figure 11.

This scene has six possible states. In the initial state (W0) agents with the role "Buyer" and agents with the role "Seller" can enter the scene. From the initial state the scene can evolve to the state W1. This happens as the result of a Seller notifying all the Buyers that the auction is about to start by executing the "start" illocution. While the scene is in this state Buyers can enter and leave the scene.

The final state of this scene may be reached from state W1 through the "closed" illocution. This illocution is executed in case a Seller has no more products to sell and decides to close the auction and destroy the corresponding scene.

When a Seller decides to submit a good to be sold at the auction, the state of the scene is changed from W1 to W3 by sending the "startRound" illocution. Here the good being sold, initial price for the good and the time for the auction are announced. In the downward bidding auction the price is constantly decreasing from the initial price to the lowest price a Seller is ready to accept. This process is expressed through "newPrice" and "decreasePrice" illocutions. The bidding time is divided into 100 segments. Each 1/100 of the bidding time the timeout ("newPrice" illocution) is red and the scene evolves to W4. The price is then updated by the Seller and the scene reverts to W3.

The buyers are to react to the price changes and as soon as they see the price they are ready to pay - they should notify the Seller that they are ready to accept the current price. If a buyer agent accepts the price, it executes the "accept" illocu-

Figure 11.Scene protocol for TradeRoom

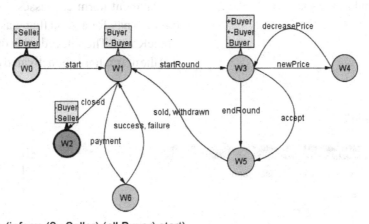

start: (inform (?x Seller) (all Buyer) start)
closed: (inform (!x Seller) (all Buyer) closed)
startRound: (inform (!x Seller) (all Buyer) (startRound ?good ?price ?bidding_time))
endRound: (inform (!x Seller) (all Buyer) (endRound))
sold: (inform (!x Seller) (all Buyer) (sold !good !y !price))
withdrawn: (inform (!x Seller) (all Buyer) (withdrawn !good))
newPrice: timeout[!bidding_time/100]
decreasePrice: (inform (!x Seller) (all Buyer) (updatePrice ?price))
accept: (request (?y Buyer) (!x Seller) accept)
payment:(request (?y Buyer) (!x Seller) (payment ?price))
success: (inform (!x Seller) (!y Buyer) success)
failure: (inform (!x Seller) (!y Buyer) (failure ?reason))

tion and terminates the auction. As the result, the scene evolves to the state W5. It will also evolve into W5 if none of the buyers have decided to accept the good within the given time frame or if the seller decides to finish the round for some other reason ("endRound" illocution).

At the end of the auction the seller either announces the winning Buyer ("sold" illocution) or withdraws a good from the auction ("withdraw" illocution). As a result of this, the scene reverts to the state W1, where Buyers can enter and leave and a new auction round for another good can be initiated by the seller.

Notice that in states W1 and W3 all participants playing the role Buyer can exercise the stay-and-go operation (this is expressed in the scene protocol with the label "+-Buyer" above the corresponding states). Such label in a scene means that the scene is in an acceptable state for agents to split into alteroids. If an agent decides to execute the stay-and-go operation then one of the alteroids remains in the original scene and all other alteroids can leave the scene and move somewhere else.

Norms

Norms define the consequences of agents' actions within the institution. Such consequences are captured as obligations. "Obl(x; φ; s)" means that agent x is obliged to do "φ" in scene s.

Norms are special types of rules specified by three elements:

- **Antecedent:** the actions and Boolean expressions over illocution scheme variable that provoke the activation of the norm.
- **Defeasible Antecedent:** the actions that agents must carry out in order to fulfill the obligations.
- **Consequent:** the set of obligations expressed as pairs of scene and illocution schema.

In the trading institution there is only one Norm present (paymentNorm). This norm is presented in Figure 12.

Payment norm expresses the obligation of a buyer to pay for a good that was purchased in the TradeRoom. The antecedent in this norm specifies that the norm should be activated in the TradeRoom

Figure 12. Norm example

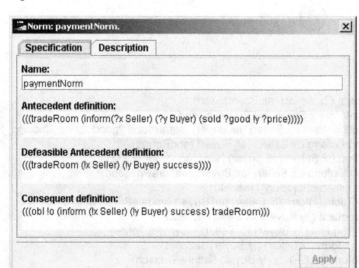

scene as soon as a seller announces that a particular good was sold to a given buyer. Once the antecedent is fired - the buyer acquires an obligation to commit the action expressed in the defeasible antecedent. The defeasible antecedent outlines the actions that should be done to withdraw the acquired obligation. In our case the obligation can only be withdrawn if in the TradeRoom the buyer agent receives a confirmation about successful payment. The consequent shows the actual obligation the agent acquires when the antecedent is fired. In our case this obligation is not something the buyer agent has to do, but something its actions will trigger.

Norms provide an additional mechanism to control the validity of agent interactions. One of the intentions behind introducing this formalization element into Electronic Institutions was to facilitate control over the obligations an agent may acquire while moving through different scenes. For example, it is possible to have an institution similar to the Trading Institution, where payment would be completed not in the TradeRoom but in another scene. Apart from norms in this case there is no mechanism to actually control that the pay-

ment was made, while with the use of norms it is possible to establish such inter-scene validation.

Visualization

The Visual Interaction Layer of the Trading institution corresponds to the 3D Virtual World outlined in Figure 13. The Virtual World contains a landscaped garden, within which the institutional building is located. The building consists of five rooms, three of which correspond to Registration, Meeting and Trading scenes in the Electronic Institution specification. The other two rooms represent the transitions connecting these scenes in the specification. The rooms are separated by doors, where doors are either locked or open for a participant depending on its role and the state of the scene.

The Virtual World for this institution is automatically generated from the Electronic Institution specification. In the Visual Interaction Layer the Electronic Institution specification determines the skeleton of the Virtual World. In the Normative Control Layer the specification serves as the basis for the execution of the infrastructure, en-

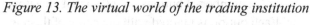

Figure 13. The virtual world of the trading institution

forcing the interaction constraints, controlling the state of conversations, and providing permissions for different roles.

The Performative structure forms the basis for the map of the institution and the 3D model of the institutional building. Each of the scenes ("Registration Room", "Meeting Room" and "Trade Room" in this case) lay the foundations for the generation of the 3D models of the rooms. The size of each room is determined by the maximal number of participants specified for each scene. The root and exit scenes do not have any visual representation. Transitions are transformed into special types of rooms (corridors) connecting the scenes. Connections (arcs of the Performative Structure graph) are represented as doors. Each door is initially locked, and will be opened as soon as the participant is granted the permission to enter the corresponding scene or transition by the institution.

After the automatic generation the rooms in the newly created Virtual Institution are not furnished, however, the doors, transitions and door labels are present. This institution is fully functional, which means that all the security issues of the institution will be imposed (e.g. permissions, protocols, obligations). The agents are able to freely interact and take part in conversations; the consistency of those conversations and interactions with the institutional rules is guaranteed by the infrastructure and the possibility to split into alteroids is also granted. To make the institutional building visually appealing the textures and additional objects are added at a later stage.

Each participant enters the system appearing as an avatar in the garden. The initial role given to each of the participants is "Guest". As defined in the specification any "Guest" can enter the institution. Therefore, the entrance door of the institutional building is always open for all avatars. Entering the institutional building for an avatar means entering the Registration Room. The "root" scene and the transition connecting it to the "Registration" scene are not visualized.

After successful registration in the Registration Room the participant's role changes and, depending on this new role, appropriate doors are open. Opening of the doors happens independently for each particular avatar, and the same doors may be locked for a different avatar if respective permissions are not granted.

Once inside the institutional building a participant moves throughout its different rooms. The Registration Room serves as a reception desk. Once the desk is approached a participant is welcomed into the institution by the Receptionist agent and asked to enter login and password details to be able to proceed further. Figure 14 illustrates the Registration Room.

From the Registration Room every participant can either leave the institutional building by walking back through the entrance door into the garden or enter the corridor (transition) behind the registration room, which connects it to the Meeting Room. The door that connects the corridor with the Meeting Room is initially locked. Only when the user is correctly identified as a "Buyer" this door will be unlocked. If the user is identified as a "Seller" the door will not be open, as Sellers are not permitted to enter the Meeting Room. The exit door from the corridor in this case will contain a number of buttons on it (as in an elevator). Each button is marked with the name of the auction currently conducted inside the Trading Room. Pressing a button results in teleporting the Seller into the selected instance of the Trading Room.

The interior fragment of the Meeting Room is presented in Figure 15. To match the scenario presented above, the room is decorated as a graffiti poster gallery. The posters are presented in a conventional way (hanging on the walls) as it is usually done in physical world galleries. The participants of the gallery are represented as avatars. The avatar controlled by an autonomous agent has a robot-like appearance. All the other avatars are human participants with customizable appearances.

Figure 14. Registration room inside the trading institution

Figure 15. Meeting room inside the trading institution

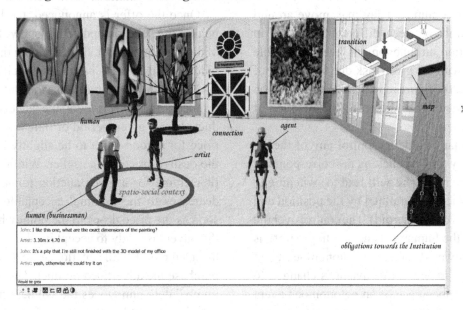

Additionally to the main 3D part, the Virtual World is enhanced with some two-dimensional elements. The chat window serves the purpose of the communicator between participants. To reduce the information overload and engage people into spatial interactions the maximum audibility distance is specified. Only the avatars within the audibility distance can participate in a conversa-tion. The avatars that are not within this distance cannot "hear" the conversation. Due to this fact, the female-looking avatar present in the left part of the window is not disturbed with the conversa-tion between the artist and the fish monger. This approach also provides means to address privacy issues: humans can clearly observe the participants of each conversation and may not give away secure information if there are undesirable participants present.

Another important 2D part of the interface is the map of the institution. It is only visible if the mouse pointer is moved to the right border of the screen. The large rectangular blocks represent rooms and the smaller ones correspond to transitions. The solid figure with the arrow on top of it displays current location of the human-driven avatar within the institution. The non-solid figures represent the autonomous agents that are in the participant's subordination. As it was already mentioned, Virtual Institutions permit situations where a participant can split herself/himself into a number of alteroids. Only one of the alteroids can be controlled by a human and all the others are controlled by autonomous agents. Autonomous agents act autonomously trying to fulfill the task specified by a human. They may move around and even walk between different rooms. If in some situation an autonomous agent is unable to proceed with the given task due to the lack of intelligence, the figure representing this agent on the map starts to blink attracting the attention of the human.

The human is able to control any of the alteroids at any time by clicking the corresponding figure on the map. This will lead to switching to a different view (determined by the position and head rotation of the alteroid). The control over the avatar that the human was controlling before is automatically passed on to an autonomous agent and the appearance of this avatar is changed to the default appearance of an autonomous agent (robot look). In the given scenario the autonomous agent (non-solid figure) represents the fish monger in the fish market auction, while the fish monger drives the avatar (solid figure) through the Meeting Room.

The backpack with obligations is another two-dimensional element of the user interface. It helps the human to remember the obligations towards the institution that have to be fulfilled. The backpack automatically opens and the pending obligation is displayed if the situation of not fulfilling an obligation makes it impossible to proceed to another scene or state in the institution. The participant can also see the obligations on demand by clicking on the backpack icon.

As it is expressed in the institutional specification, the Trading Room is allowed to have multiple executions. Therefore, it is represented as a number of similar rooms placed on top of each other. Inside each of these rooms a different type of auction is conducted. One such auction is shown in Figure 16. The room instance is functioning as a fish auction. A seller is conducting an auction with lobsters being the current offer. The buyers are located around the seller's desk, waiting for an acceptable price. The red (dark in grey scale printing) robot on the left hand side is the fishmonger's autonomous agent from our scenario.

Once the offer is announced, the big screen behind the seller is updated to show the picture of the current product, the remaining time left for bidding and current price. As specified in IS-LANDER the auction follows the Dutch auction protocol. In this protocol the auction is conducted for a given period of time and the initial price for a good is set to be slightly higher that the desired price of the seller. Within the given time frame for a given auction round the price decreases to the minimal acceptable price. As soon as the price drops to the point when one of the buyers is ready to accept it - the buyer raises his hand to notify the auctioneer that he wants to purchase the advertised product. The auctioneer immediately announces the winner and if there are still any goods lefts to be sold - continues with the next round. After a successful purchase the buyer who won the previous round is required to approach the seller and finalize the purchase. The obligation to pay for the good is assigned to the buyer by the institution and can be observed through the buyer's backpack. Until this obligation is fulfilled this buyer will be unable to leave the institution. The product that was not sold during the round is withdrawn from the auction.

Figure 16. Trading room inside the trading institution

CONCLUSION AND FUTURE WORK

We have presented the concept of Virtual Institutions, which are 3D Virtual Worlds with normative regulation of participants' interactions. The concept of Virtual Institutions includes two logical levels: Visual Interaction Layer (responsible for the visualization of participants and for providing them with interaction facilities inside the space of the Virtual Institution) and Normative Control Layer (responsible for establishing and controlling the enforcement of the interaction rules within the Virtual Institution).

The design of these two logical levels is covered by the Virtual Institutions Methodology. To support this methodology we have developed a feasible and economically efficient technological solution, which utilizes two existing technologies - Electronic Institutions technology and Virtual Worlds technology and includes tools for formalization and deployment of Virtual Institutions.

The majority of existing virtual worlds are developed on an ad-hoc basis. Virtual Institutions is one of the first formal methodologies that addresses in a more systematic way the development of Virtual Worlds. As a formal methodology, it

has a number of advantages. Firstly, employing formal methods forces the system designer to analyze the system in details before implementing it. Secondly, it permits to detect the critical points and errors at an early stage. Thirdly, the methodology clearly distinguishes and separates the two important aspects of the design of a virtual institution: the design of institutional rules and the design of institution visualization in Virtual Worlds. As a result these two processes can be run in parallel. Another advantage of using this methodology is that the supplied tools make the development faster, helping to achieve some tasks automatically. Moreover, due to this distributed multilayer architecture possible updates of the system can be accommodated faster. This in combination with the execution infrastructure permits a quick and easy portability of the system to new visualization platforms.

In their current form Virtual Institutions do not allow violating the institutional rules, however, to facilitate learning of the rules by the users it is often required to enable violation of some of the non-critical rules. In our further development of the Virtual Institutions we have focused on enabling such "soft norms" and their enforcement through sanctions.

REFERENCES

Arcos, J. L., Esteva, M., Noriega, P., Rodrguez-Aguilar, J. A., & Sierra, C. (2005). An Integrated Developing Environment for Electronic Institutions. In Unland, R., Klusch, M., & Calisti, M. (Eds.), *Agent related platforms, frameworks, systems, applications, and tools* (pp. 121–142). Birkhaeuser Basel.

Boella, G., van der Torre, L., & Verhagen, H. (2007). Introduction to normative multiagent systems. *Normative multi-agent systems* (pp. 71–79). Internationales Begegnungs- und Forschungszentrum fuer Informatik (IBFI), Schloss Dagstuhl, Germany.

Bogdanovych, A. (2007). *Virtual institutions*. Doctoral dissertation, University of Technology, Sydney, Australia.

Bogdanovych, A., Berger, H., Sierra, C., & Simoff, S. (2005). Narrowing the Gap between Humans and Agents in E-commerce: 3D Electronic Institutions. In *Proceedings of the 6th International Conference on Electronic Commerce and Web Technologies (EC-Web '05)* (pp. 128–137). Berlin: Springer- Verlag.

Bogdanovych, A., Rodriguez, J. A., Simoff, S., Cohen, A., & Sierra, C. (2009). Developing Virtual Heritage Applications as Normative Multiagent Systems. In *proceedings of Agent Oriented Software Engineering Workshop (AOSE 2009)* organized by AAMAS 2009 (pp. 121–132). Berlin: Springer.

Bogdanovych, A., Simoff, S., & Esteva, M. (2008). Training Believable Agents in 3D Electronic Business Environments Using Recursive-Arc Graphs. In *Third international conference on Software and Data Technologies* (ICSoft 2008) (pp. 339–345). INSTICC.

Bowman, D. A., Kruijff, E., LaViola, J. J., & Poupyrev, I. (2001). An Introduction to 3-D User Interface Design. *Presence (Cambridge, Mass.)*, *10*(1), 75–95. doi:10.1162/105474601750182333

Darken, R. P., & Sibert, J. L. (1996). Wayfinding strategies and behaviors in large virtual worlds. In *Chi '96: Proceedings of the SIGCHI conference on human factors in computing systems* (pp. 142–149). New York: ACM Press.

Drago, S., Bogdanovych, A., Ancona, M., Simoff, S., & Sierra, C. (2007). From Graphs to Euclidean Virtual Worlds: Visualization of 3D Electronic Institutions. In G. Dobbie (Ed.), *Australasian Computer Science Conference (ACSC2007)* (Vol. 62, pp. 25–33). Ballarat Australia: ACS.

Esteva, M. (2003). *Electronic institutions: From specification to development*. Doctoral dissertation, Institut d'Investigaci'o en Intellig`encia Artificial (IIIA), Spain.

Esteva, M., de la Cruz, D., & Sierra, C. (2002). ISLANDER: an Electronic Institutions editor. In *First international conference on Autonomous Agents and Multiagent Systems (AAMAS 2002)*, (pp. 1045–1052). Bologna: ACM Press.

Fehr, E., & Fischbacher, U. (2004). Social Norms and Human Cooperation. *Trends in Cognitive Sciences*, *8*(4), 185–190. Available at http://dx.doi.org/10.1016/j.tics.2004.02.007. doi:10.1016/j.tics.2004.02.007

Maher, M. L., Simoff, S., & Mitchell, J. (1997). Formalizing Building Requirements Using an Activity/Space Model. *Automation in Construction*, *6*, 77–95. doi:10.1016/S0926-5805(96)00171-9

Nielsen, J. (1998). *2D is Better Than 3D*. Jakob Nielsen's Alertbox.

North, D. C. (1990). *Institutions, Institutional Change and Economic Performance*. Cambridge, UK: Cambridge University Press.

Russo Dos Santos, C., Gros, P., Abel, P., Loisel, D., Trichaud, N., & Paris, J.-P. (2000). Mapping Information onto 3D Virtual Worlds. In *Proceedings of the International Conference on Information Visualization* (pp. 379–386). Washington, DC: IEEE Computer Society.

Schotter, A. (1981). *The Economic Theory of Social Institutions*. Cambridge, MA: Cambridge University Press.

ADDITIONAL READING

Arcos, J. L., Esteva, M., Noriega, P., Rodrguez-Aguilar, J. A., & Sierra, C. (2005). An Integrated Developing Environment for Electronic Institutions. In Unland, R., Klusch, M., & Calisti, M. (Eds.), *Agent Related Platforms, Frameworks, Systems, Applications, and Tools, Whitestein Book Series* (pp. 121–142). Birkhaeuser Basel.

Cascio, J., Paffendorf, J., Smart, J., Bridges, C., Hummel, J., Hurtsthouse, J., and Moss, R. (2007). Metaverse Roadmap: Pathways to the 3D Web. Report on the cross-industry public foresight project, July 4, 2007.

Damer, B. (1998). Avatars! Exploring and Building Virtual Worlds on the Internet. Peachpit Press, 1998.

Esteva, M., de la Cruz, D., & Sierra, C. (2002). ISLANDER: an Electronic Institutions editor. In First International Conference on Autonomous Agents and Multiagent systems, pages 1045–1052, Bologna. ACM Press, 2002.

Rodriguez-Aguilar, J.A. (2003). On the design and construction of agent-mediated electronic institutions, volume 14 of Monografies de l'Institut d'Investigació en Intelligència Artificial. Consejo Superior de Investigaciones Científicas, 2003.

Weiss, G. (1999). Multiagent Systems: A Modern Approach to Distributed Artificial Intelligence. MIT Press, 1999.

Chapter 9
Property–Based Object Management and Security

Torsten Reiners
Curtin University of Technology, Australia & University of Hamburg, Germany

Sascha Wriedt
University of Hamburg, Germany

Alan Rea
Western Michigan University, USA

ABSTRACT

The hype of Second Life is over. But the experience of this truly exciting period lives on in many disciplines and research areas, which are developing emerging technologies in virtual, as well as augmented worlds. And as is the rule with new forming developments, the path is not yet determined and weaves through different stages and platforms, calling for additional prototypes to understand the true impact of virtual worlds, Web 3D, or Augmented Reality. Using broad strokes and looking for a common denominator, most people conclude that it is Web 2.0 with all its (social) functionality and 3D objects as the embodiment of virtual existence. Many publications discuss Web 2.0 features and applications, but most do not focus on the 3D objects in the context of virtual worlds and their implications. In this chapter, the authors examine and observe what (virtual) objects are, as well as which properties should be used for inter-world interoperability. The past technological implementations demonstrate that protecting digital media (i.e. music and video) is an endless endeavor and that no security feature is simultaneously unbreakable and usable. This does not need to be the case for 3D virtual objects because we can learn from the past and achieve a new level of protection in a rising media. In this chapter the authors propose such a solution by putting forth a general 3D object understanding that includes a look at virtual worlds such as Second Life with a feasible concept of object security. They suggest that with a new framework objects can be secured and promote additional growth within, and among, virtual worlds. They propose a Global Object Management System (GOMS) architecture as a potential solution to this challenge.

DOI: 10.4018/978-1-61520-891-3.ch009

1 INTRODUCTION

When we think about security in virtual worlds, our first inclination might be how we login into the system and verify our identity. This single-factor authentication by username and password is meant to protect our identity, and privileges in the world. However, we are also protecting the true value of the virtual world avatar: its owned objects. Of course we can consider the experiences through play (Castronova, 2003) as well, but what we might value the most is not just the avatar (and by extension, us) but owned objects (e.g., property) (Horowitz, 2007). Of course these objects can be placed in the virtual world, worn on the avatar, or stored in a virtual inventory, but they generally exist in a single virtual world. Depending on the world, users might have invested massive amounts of real or virtual money, or copious amounts of time to upgrade items. Because of these investments, securing virtual objects within specific worlds, and potentially transferring them to others (in the case of virtual world closure, user choice, etc.) is quite an important issue now and in the future as we see greater virtual market penetration via 3D environments.

Managing objects is already a critical need even with the majority of current virtual worlds as closed environments. In closed environments avatars and objects are restricted to just one environment and a direct transfer is seldom possible or even favored. Even though the object encoding standard for the graphical representation of objects (nodes, edges, textures) is shared, additional scripting or environment specific modifications cannot be exported. Virtual worlds, such as World of Warcraft (Blizzard Entertainment, 2010) or Habbo Hotel (Habbo Hotel, 2010), do not allow object imports to protect the in-world market. In these worlds, providers place the objects in the virtual environment's economy, and offer them in specialized stores or reward users after they complete a series of tasks (e.g. quests). There are some trades completed in marketplaces like eBay, but many times these violate the specific virtual world's Terms of Service (TOS). Within a virtual game realm, there are reasons for this control, such as the provider needing to control the game flow, balance, and economy. Virtual worlds are different. Development over the last few years indicates a stronger desire for object interchange between virtual worlds (Watte & Systems, 2009). In order to effectively facilitate this interchange, the interoperability of objects beyond the specific world's aspects and controls is crucial. In other words, users' objects need to retain privileges, functionality, and interaction with the chosen virtual world environment whenever possible. We propose that the replacement of the current paradigm of environmentally-controlled static objects with dynamic objects that communicate their properties, much as newer object oriented programming languages.

1.1 Discussion of Crucial Terminology

Before continuing, we need to define our terminology for this chapter as our use of interpretation of terms might be different. We use the term *object* for virtual (digital) objects in virtual worlds. Note that the analogy to the object model as used in programming languages like C++ or Java basically matches our concept of object representation: Objects behave according to their code, interact by messages, and are related by a dynamic reference graph with relations as part of a larger semantic network (cf. Section 2.2). Objects belonging to an avatar are stored in an individual *inventory* or general storage facilities (*repository*). *Properties* specify the object; this is also called metadata (Baca, 2008) or capabilities (Scheffler et al., 2008). The creator, owner, or user of an object is represented in virtual worlds by *avatars*. Note that in our understanding, *users* on social networks like Facebook or Flickr are as well using (multiple) avatars to represent their *identity*. We do adhere to the term avatar for the virtual representation of one user and ignore possible multiple identities (c.f. post-modern identity theory) depending on the current control. We use the term *users*, even though in virtual environments, this does not imply only humans but could stand for an object, which acts like or on the behalf of the real world person. Therefore, everything being said about the user is also valid for objects. Objects require access rights and privileges to interact in the environments. This is a critical distinction for us as we use the term *access* with respect to resources in the environment rather than access to the environment (*authentication; identity verification* of the real user). We use the term *group* to describe a collection of users (and ultimately objects), whereas we use the term *entity* for user, group, or object.

1.2 Moving from Avatar to Object

Pushing the awareness away from the avatar-centered perspective in virtual worlds toward the object itself is the underlying theme throughout our discussion, as well as our proposed architecture. In every context, researchers talk about the experiences in virtual worlds (Gregory et al., 2009), how users represent themselves (Ducheneau et al., 2009), how communication is taken to a higher level (Reiners et al., 2009), and how students explore and even create their learning material (Erlenkötter et al., 2008). But the object, the true building block of every idea, plays just a minor supporting role in most research and discussions. Obviously, the creations are demonstrated in words and images, and used to emphasize the new learning experience, but rarely does research examine securing the creations, neither archiving nor transferring them to other platforms. Perhaps most researchers consider this the work of the hosting organization, but we would argue this is not the case.

Most users would agree that objects are critical for the immersive experience; otherwise, virtual worlds would be full of avatars with nothing to do (and some might argue avatars would not even

exist). Users from around the world have already created over a billion Second Life objects, but these are objects stored on closed servers with access only by specialized software with limited options for local copies and transfer to other environments. This paradigm extends to many other worlds as well. We argue that although the concentration is on the avatar for identification, the value of objects is often underestimated. In this chapter, we explore the object itself and describe the minimal requirements for relevant properties in secure (multi-) environments. By examining the importance of objects and illustrating the need to control and manage every aspect, we are able to create the foundation on which we design our concept that defines how one can manage and secure not only the objects themselves but also increase the potential for the inter-world transfer of objects.

We must stress that although we accentuate the importance of identity security, authentication, and trusted networks, we do not discuss detailed technical aspects, but remain at a high-level discussion. Our lack of discussion in this area is not meant to slight its importance, nor does this mean that we do not address methods to secure objects like digital watermarking; however, we provide only references for algorithmic or implementation details as these are far beyond the scope of this chapter, but not our overall research agenda; see Section 6 with suggestions for further reading.

1.3 Chapter Organization

Our discussion on object properties and management, security issues, and the proposed Global Object Management System (GOMS) architecture is presented in the remainder of the chapter. In Section 2 we discuss the object itself and focus on the properties (2.1), as well as on the object management (2.2). We also discuss and create an advanced object design for objects, and offer supporting examples. Section 3 centers on security concerns and proposed object protections. Second

Life (3.2), and briefly its open source counterpart OpenSim (3.3) and Project Wonderland (3.4), are examined as examples of current object handling, and throughout we examine management and security challenges. This discussion leads to Section 4 in which we put forth our suggested architecture. We conclude the chapter (Section 5) with a look to future research milestones and a summary of our lessons learned to date. Virtual worlds and the 3D Web are still in their infancy and demand more research on object handling, encoding, and especially security. We believe the demand for inter-world exchangeability will supersede the current closed world's approaches resulting in additional compatibility and interoperability questions, as well as potential benefits and challenges with interblending cultures and societies.

2 OBJECTS AND THEIR IMPORTANCE

Shifting the focal point from an avatar-centered perspective towards objects requires a well-founded model to encode objects including their properties, security, and robustness for inter-world transfers. Although the encoding of objects and their interdependencies is the subject of several standards and publications, we outline generic properties and influences on the objects and their management which have to be considered in a secure environment no matter what the encoding (Section 2.1). This model inevitably demonstrates potential security risks without reducing arguments for specific standards or shortfalls of other approaches. In addition, we expand the object-oriented concept where all information and functionality is part of the object itself and not induced by the environment. This facilitates the integration of security provisions and enhances the portability and compatibility. The described model is used in Section 3 to analyze different worlds, and is represented in our discussions of Second Life, OpenSim, and Project Wonderland.

However, the model could be applied to any virtual world's objects.

2.1 Object Properties

Information describing an object is referred to as meta-data (Baca, 2008). Dublin Core, EXIF, or XMP are a few specifications to annotate objects like websites or images with further information like size, format, or content; see Wikipedia (2010) for a current list. For 3D objects, standards like X3D (Web 3D Consortium, 2010), O3D (Google Code Labs, 2010), XML3D (Slusallek, 2010), or COLLADA (COLLADA, 2010) provide elements (e.g., XML-tags) to describe properties in the object itself. Here, we discuss the objects from a formal perspective with respect to required functionality incorporating elements from various sources (c.f., in virtual worlds, on the Web, or in applications), but neither from the perspective of virtual worlds nor including a broad coverage of elements. The proposed list is not complete but does demonstrate major categories that need to be adapted within an object and its anticipated application in order to work within our proposed architecture.

We propose that all objects can be classified by their properties into the following categories: *metadata, physical, appearance, function, environment, relation,* and *social.* Figure 1 represents these categories in a general sense; Table 1 describes the categories in more details.

Depending on the environment and usage of objects, further properties need to be added; requirements of being within a certain proximity of the object, having a certain state to interact with an object (e.g., avatar has to sit on the driver seat to operate the vehicle), having certain qualifications, and so on. ***Interaction*** of objects is encoded using the *relation, function,* and *environment* properties and allows for dynamic systems; i.e. by providing a server based semantic network for the object relation. Interaction as well as access are encoded in the object and therefore

Figure 1. Properties describing the object. For each property, only examples of elements are shown

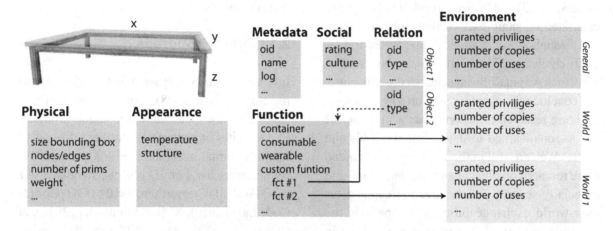

Table 1. Short explanation of the object properties

Property	Description
Metadata	Further information describes the object in more details, which cannot be assigned to other categories. This is general (e.g., name, date of creation), context-dependent (e.g., e-learning, specialized application), or classification (e.g., keywords based on ontologies, field of study). With respect of improving interaction of objects, linking external information resources (e.g., databases, knowledge information systems) to define proper reaction on the behalf of the involved objects are intended; see also the description for *interaction* following the table.
Physical	Objects used in environments that represent (virtual) physical spaces, such that physical properties reassure adequacy of the objects in that environment; e.g., burning torches require oxygen and even virtual life might need food to stay alive. Proper physical behavior requires parameters, e.g., to detect collision of objects (*size*), to determine the capability of floating (*density*), or balancing objects (*weight*). Technical parameters like number of prims, nodes, or surfaces allow an estimation of the complexity and, therewith, the applicability.
Appearance	The object's representation for the avatar; e.g. material with its sensory perception and other haptic experiences. Appearance and physical properties are discriminated as appearance is related to the user (represented by the avatar) and physical to the environment; whereas avatars are considered as objects under the direct users' control. Precisely, properties encode, e.g., observed temperature (based on environment or self-regulated like an oven), structure (rough surface vs. smooth), interpretation of objects being worn (costumes).
Function	Specify how the object can be used by other objects or avatars; e.g. container to store other objects, vehicle for avatars, or food to eat for more energy. Besides some predefined attributes like wearable or consumable, custom functions are the key to an unlimited (interactive) virtual world. Interfaces (*sensors*) monitor the environment for occurring events and trigger assigned functions; e.g. collision, touch by an avatar, or progress of time.
Environment	Link object properties to an environment and need to be specified for each object instance throughout the full lifetime. Examples are granted privileges to access, modify, or transfer the object on individual or group level, number of allowed copies, or restrictions where and how often the object can be used (required, e.g., in virtual games where player buy food items to regain energy for their avatar by using the object in parts or completely fall as well). In addition, the access rights for functions (see *functional properties*) follow the same idea: the object grants (or denies) access to roles, groups, or individual users depending on environment as well as other attributes like time, cost or ownership of objects; see also *relation*.
Relation	Define relations to other objects and used mainly to encode possible interaction. Relations are encoded comparable to semantic networks, where the type of relation as well as the related object is given. For example, a door requires a particular key; it would be specified here with the type *open/close* and the object identifier of the key. Instead of relations to specific object, we could use concepts: A wine bottle requires an object representing the concept of a *drinking container (glass)* for the relation *pour*.
Social	Describes the context of objects; e.g. rating and cultural adequacy. Social properties are required to prevent conflicts where objects should not be presented to certain cultures or religions, or being next to another object; e.g. the kindergarten next to the red light district would be a bad choice. The terms describing context should be mapped against ontologies.

provide the foundation for an inter-environment tool.

Unfortunately, current environments use proprietary encodings and, therefore, are not compatible. For example, there is no common language among all worlds; Second Life uses its own script language, Linden Scripting Language (LSL) with scripts being stored as part of the objects (Linden Lab, 2010a), while Project Wonderland does not yet support in-world functions, but uses precompiled cells on the server-side (Retha, 2008). As a result, functions are linked to their (compatible) environment. Later alternatives could include a code conversion or general scripting language with distinct APIs for each world (i.e., internal object support). Another weakness with respect to security surfaces in Second Life. Access to functions is controlled by the function itself with implementations for each role. Instead of bundling multiple roles into one function (e.g. touching an object causes different reactions for creator and general users), the execution right should be controlled by environmental properties and environment specific grants for each entity.

In addition to compatibility problems among the environments, we need to address the relational complexity between objects; i.e. as the information is stored within the object itself. To limit the object's size, only non-general relations or relations concerning the main purpose of the object should be stored in the object. As a general rule for every function involving two or more objects, there is also a relation defined. That is, for example, the key to a door or specific tires for a vehicle. For the sake of generality, external semantic networks with allowed interactions between objects are accessible by the object. Note that the security of a system is increased if object interaction is restricted to semantically correct ones, assuming that objects are specified correctly (c.f., Section 3). Another important application of relations is about referring to alternative (e.g., other media formats, alternative representation) or modified objects (versioning) (c.f., Section 2.2).

The proposed categories with exemplary properties are visualized for three different objects in Figure 2. Although demonstrating the idea of how to encode objects, we do not intend to be accurate in the syntax; i.e. neither the parameters for functions, fully specified relations, nor the reference of relation types to functions are shown for the sake of readability. Properties in the first two categories should be self-explanatory. For example, the property temperature indicates if objects are heat-sources or depend on the temperature of the environment. The car (*trabbi*) is ambivalent and could be either dependent on the environment (parked car on the street) or self-heating (engine and a/c is running). Here, we declared the *trabbi* to be the first case and would model its components (engine, a/c) to be heat sources, with both objects being related to the car in the category relation. In environment, the overall number of *trabbis* is unlimited (inf.), although some virtual worlds like Second Life explicitly restricts the count to 50 to increase its value. Moreover, defined functions, as well as general operations are granted or denied to entities: the *chair* is not visible to the avatar Tyke McMillan. In Second Life the car can only be driven by owners, whereas everyone can sit in it. Finally, relations are defined; i.e., the object *chair* can be transported by the object *trabbi*, and the attendant is able to load the object. Note that the object *attendant* does not have a relation to drive the object *trabbi*, therefore we assume either that the *attendant* cannot drive the *trabbi* (even in case of being the owner) or that specific rules in the server-based semantic network exist on a general level to restrict this relation.

2.2 Object Management

Over their lifetime, objects can face several risks from multiple sources that target flaws in the object design, application, and handling. The best analogy is found in the software industry, where developers try to stay ahead of hackers by regular software updates to fix security breaches

Figure 2. The overview shows three different objects with their properties as well as the interdependencies encoded in the property relation.

		chair	trabbi	attendant
Metadata	name	chair	trabbi	attendant
	oid	001_000101_00000000012345_00002000	011_000100_00000000021234_00000001	001_000100_010101010122222_10000000
	classification	furniture, wood	car, plastic, GDR	person, company
	ontology	chair -> furniture -> object	trabbi -> car -> vehicle -> object	attendant -> person -> mammal -> object
Physical	bounding box	60x60x140	360x150x150	90x70x180
	weight	3	600	85
	prims	13	9	1
	state	solid	solid	solid
	density	0,8	5000	1,3
	buoyant force	x,y	x,y	x,y
Appearance	temperature	warm, env.	cold, env.	warm, self
	structure	rough wood	glass, plastic, rubber	soft skin
Function	container	no	yes	no
	consumable	no	no	no
	wearable	no	no	no
	functions			
	id, env, code	sit_on, general, { ... }	sit_in, general, { ... }	walk, general, { ... }
	id, env, code	sit_on, SL, { ... }	drive, SL, { ... }	dance, SL, { ... }
	id, env, code		load, SL, { ... }	
Environment	general			
	#uses	1	1	1
	#copies	inf.	inf.	1
	priviliges	execute{sit_on}	execute{put_obj_on}	execute{open}
	mode	allow	allow	allow
	id	creator, owner, *Tyke McMillan*	all	owner
	Second Life			
	#uses	1	1	1
	#copies	inf.	inf.	10
	priviliges	transfer, execute{sit_on}	execute{put_obj_on}	execute{put_into}
	mode	allow	allow	allow
	id	owner	all	owner
	priviliges	visibility	take, transfer, drive	visibility
	mode	deny	allow	allow
	id	Tyke McMillan	owner	all
	priviliges		execute (load, transport)	
	mode		allow	
	id		owner, group(MOVETEAM)	
Relation	oid	trabbi		load trabbi
	type	transport →		←
	oid			sit_in trabbi
	type			←
	oid			transport trabbi
	type			←
	oid			sit_on chair
	type		←	
Social	rating	moderate	moderate	moderate
	culture	-	GDR, nostalgia	-

(left margin, rotated: name instead of iD used)

(resulting from development errors) and adapting to changed environments (new technology). To improve security, we investigate relevant factors regarding the object management and increase awareness of possible issues about security while demonstrating the importance to have an object-oriented design in a multi-environmental context to include identity, transfer between two or more entities, visibility, or access. We are aware that the list is not complete and specialized worlds or applications require additional parameters, which have to be carefully considered in the same context with respect to security.

Object security originates in the system design and every non-considered possible breach or missing information can later be used to manipulate the objects, their relation, or interaction. The robustness to new contexts is important as a change of context might reveal information or grant access to invalid entities in a multi-world setting. In addition, the design determines the versatility (to include the combination or communication across environments) and API of objects. Of course, another risk is the user itself. The object needs protection against manipulation, distribution (creating copies, transfer), or loss. The entertainment industry constantly attempts, with doubtful success, to limit the number of digital copies for music and movies using special codices, DRM (Digital Right Management [Zeng et al., 2006]), or specialized software. Although not a focus on this discussion, DRM is a good example for existing secure technological solutions and their limitations. Additionally, trusted computing achieves a sophisticated level of security by involving the whole system; the application is distrusted by the general users as their decision is passed to others (Kabus, 2009). It also increases administrative overhead in case of multiple devices or change of hardware and software. We must learn from past mistakes and we believe our framework embodies these learned lessons in its approach.

In the following sections, we identify several factors influencing object design and its security. Protecting objects requires knowledge of what to protect, where objects are applied and what kind of interaction is allotted. We discuss factors like identity, privileges, transfer, or tracking from an object-oriented perspective. Even though the list encompasses the most important items, we are aware that it could be extended in order to consider other models to encode objects.

2.2.1 Object Identification and Privileges

Objects require unique *identification* on a global level. In Figure 2, we used Unified Resource Identifier (URI, Berners-Lee et al., 2005) with the scheme http://obj_id.net/objid to reference the object (domain, global unique identifier). Additional possible encodings are the country code of the creator (3 hexadecimal digits), unique identification of the original environment (6), time stamp (15) and unique object number in this environment (9): *objid*=001_000100_01 23456789ABCDE_01234567; see also UUID (Universal Unique Identifier, Leach et al., 2005) or DOI (Digital Object Identifier, International DOI Foundation, 2010; commonly known in the research community for bibliographic references) for schemes to code persistent identification.

Availability describes the quantity of objects (overall or within an environment), while *uniqueness* guarantees that two different objects never have the same identifier. While availability is merely verifying that the number of existing objects is not above a given (global) boundary, uniqueness raises certain (philosophical) questions: what makes an object unique? What qualifies the assignment of new identifiers? Are modified objects new unique objects with new identifier or can we consider them to be the same as before? Nevertheless, we suggest a simplified approach: An object is the same as long its physical structure is unmodified, e.g., parts, edges, nodes, or surfaces are constant in number and position. On the other hand, any change of the physical structure results in a new object, whereas the original is copied for references and versioning (c.f., Section 2.2.2). For example, if a car is painted green, it is still the same object. If the car is modified by a new body, we consider it to be a different (and, therefore, new) object. Both objects store references to each other for traceability, such that modifications can be resolved to the very first original object.

Access and interaction depends on the *privileges* granted to entities. For conformance, interchangeability, and security, *basic* privileges need to be globally defined, whereas the environments guarantee the compliance of privileges and their correct implementation (c.f., Section 3.1). We distinguish *basic* (e.g., transfer, modifying, touch, and visibility) and *user-defined* (e.g., driving or using an object in a certain way) privileges in our architecture because the latter usually require a specific function to define the privilege implications in the environment. Object privileges are specified by parameters such as:

1. **Identities**: Comma separated list of identities that defines the entities for which the given privileges are relevant. In addition to entities, roles can be used (e.g., *all, none, creator, owner,* or *user*).

2. **Privileges**: Comma separated list of privileges based on a global dictionary.

3. **Allocation**: The keywords *deny* or *allow* either grant or revoke the privileges.

4. **Time Validity**: Time period during which the privileges are granted or revoked. For example, major content is only visible for the group *adult* between 10pm and 4am.

Each custom function (property *function*) as well as environment (property *environment*) has its own set of independent privileges. With respect to administrative overhead, objects assign privileges to roles or groups rather than individual avatars or objects. However, in cases with high demands on personalization or security, individually granted privileges are the first choice. If privileges depend highly on the environment and offered object functionality, a basic set might be limited to privileges like access, transfer, visibility (e.g., research department, where visitors are not allowed to see everything), mobility (allowed to move the object), delete, take, or modify the object.

Objects allow different **roles** (e.g. *creator, owner,* or *user)*. In contrast to the general al-

location of roles to users and groups, objects are treated as equivalent and are able to be creators, owners, or users (e.g., an aerial scanner which creates and sends out drones to collect data). In this case, either the creator of the scanner (scanner follows instructions implemented by its creator) or the scanner itself (fully in charge of the process [e.g. autonomous and intelligent software agents]) is the creator of the drones.

The argumentation is diverse if we look at multiple entities being creators for the same object. How would we share responsibility? Are creators responsible for their part or the whole object? Can every creator modify all parts or only their own? Can one creator restrict the access for other creators of the same object? It might be possible to model multiple creators but for practicality and acceptance, we need a simple and intuitive concept. For that reason, we allow for the role *creator* only one avatar or object. To allow collaborative work, the responsible creator needs to assign privileges like *object modification*.

Every object is owned by (multiple) entities. Note that multiple owners share the object equally with the same privileges. For example, revenues or votes for decisions are equally distributed to all owners rather than using different shares similar to shareholders in publicly tradable companies. If such functionality is required, it can and should be implemented as a custom function. Comparable with reality, multiple ownerships are valid even for objects taken into the inventory of one avatar; the access on the other hand might be restricted. The first owner is always equal to the creator, who also sets the initial privileges. Whether an owner is able to change or pass privileges depends on the granted rights.

Last, we have the role *user* to control interaction with the object based on privileges and functionality. This role is used to explicitly limit the access to specific entities; not specified ones are not allowed to get privileges granted. Only owners are special as they cannot be excluded from the role user.

2.2.2 Object Access and Transfer

Privileges grant *access* to objects and define the interaction, which are either default functions or functions defined in the object (*functional*). Besides using privileges, the access to objects can rely on other objects being owned by the entity; e.g., key cards to open doors. The relation of objects can be defined in two ways: by object identifier or object metadata. The first approach is about higher security as the creator defines the *lock* and *key* by object identifier (key) in the relation properties of the lock; see example in Figure 3. Access to the lock is only possible if the key is owned and carried (on the avatar or in the inventory) by the authorized entity. (Unmodified) copies are also eligible as they are cross-referenced with the original; here the creator keeps responsibility for allowing copies. Using common metadata description is less secure as other avatars can create objects with matching properties. Examples for scenarios are clothing, extensions for rooms, or food items in role games.

Especially in scenarios where the objects are subjected to high security, invisibility to non-authorized users is the safest solution (Wright & Madey, 2008a). The idea of granting *visibility* rather than access relies in the general server-client-architecture, where non-visible objects are not transferred to the client and, therefore, are safe against most attacks. Another example how visibility can be used, is set in a theater. While objects on stage are visible but not accessible, stage-hands need to (re-)build the stage setting without being visible. This can be solved using different spaces; that is, the visibility of the avatars (being objects) and all objects for the next scene is denied for everyone but stage workers, who setup the stage. During a break, the visibility is flipped with the current stage.

We distinguish two kinds of *transfer*. *Passing* is about changing the ownership by giving objects to one or more entities. *Copying* is about replicating an object and passing the new object. A change of ownership denotes several considerations about rights, privileges, and properties. It goes without saying that with lacking privileges or access to the objects, neither passing nor copying is possible. First, the entity triggering the transfer must have adequate privileges and be the owner. In case of multiple owners, it has to be sufficient that one owner passes the object without getting approval of all. The trust for correct decisions was approved by granting the privilege in the

Figure 3. Demonstrating object visibility and access. In Scenario a), Tyke is in front of the door but does not have the key. Therefore, the door is looked. In Scenario b), Tyke has the key and can open the door. In Scenario c), Phillip has the key, but the visibility of the door is not granted to him and, therefore, the key not usable to get on the other side of the wall.

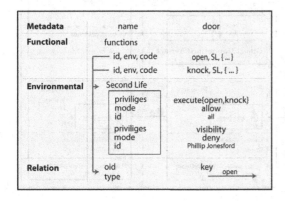
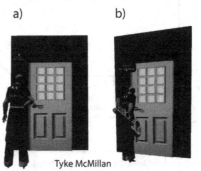

first place. Note that it is technically possible to ask all owners before transferring the object, but would result in long delays even if everyone would agree on the transfer; e.g. delays through operative tasks, holidays, or sickness. Second, the mapping of properties and privileges for the next (new) owner needs to be specified. That is, the current owner has to define for every property or privileges how these are passed and if the new owner is able to change or pass these to the next owner. For example, a shop owner is allowed to personalize and sell tickets (even though he is not the creator) to someone else, who is not allowed to modify the ticket afterwards, e.g., date or category; see Figure 4.

Copying involves the creation of new objects and, therefore, requires an additional consideration: who becomes the creator of the copy? Basically, it is either the creator of the original object or the entity who initiated the copy process. In our opinion, the second concept is superior as the latest responsibility for the object is visible; see also object traceability to guarantee references to previous creators. Note that the access for the original creator has to be granted through privileges as well. This allows, given the right privileges, to prevent even updates or other access (like revoking the object) by the creator and, therefore, keeping object static; e.g. in test scenarios where updates would change the outcome. Another plausible idea might be an empty creator field to differentiate copies from originals; if the creator is kept in the trace. Copying also requires verification of availability.

1. **Unlimited Object Quantity, Restricted Environment:** The entity requests to copy a limited object, which is either authorized

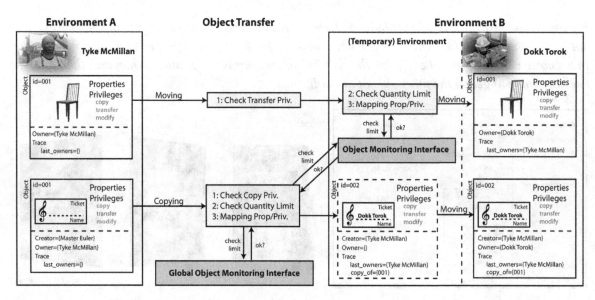

Figure 4. Transfer of objects. In the upper part, Tyke McMillan transfers an object to Dokk Torok who is not allowed to pass it further on to others. Both have no privileges to make copies or perform modifications. Quantity is verified locally within the new environment. The lower part demonstrates copying, where Tyke McMillan owns a ticket that can be copied but not given away (that is, the blank ticket stays with Tyke McMillan). Tyke has the right for modification, i.e. inserting a name on the ticket. Quantity is checked on global and local level as a new object is created. Note that functions (inserting names while copying) and properties (creator, trace) are not shown with all details.

or denied based on the total count of currently existing objects in the environment, including inventories. Therefore, environments have to monitor object counts and apply control mechanisms like *first come, first serve* or *hierarchical structures,* where certain entities overrule concurrent copy requests; e.g., requests by avatars outvote requests by objects.

2. **Limited Object Quantities:** Albeit the object knows its own maximum number of existing copies, a superior authority needs to monitor the overall existence of limited objects in all environments. In general, a trusted server is used, where copy requests are handled similar as in environments.

In both cases, we need to discuss the influence of the previous owner or (original) creator. In several scenarios, influences are welcomed by new owners (e.g., updating functionality) or previous owners (e.g., retrieving rented objects after a predefined time period). Many recent cases illustrate that buying objects in Internet stores do not imply unrestricted ownership, such as Amazon deleting E-Books on the Kindle (June, 2009), or Apple reserving its right to access and revoke applications on the iPhone (von Lohmann, 2010). The (negative) feedback towards (unknown) surveillance by companies/governments enforces exigencies of rules for inter-entity access to be followed: transparency, revocation of access privileges, and traceability of all performed procedures.

The object transfer is also restricted by rules (e.g., no allowed copies), technical properties (e.g., the object format is not compatible with another environment), or the environment itself (no export from closed environments). In addition, the properties can change over time and/or environments; examples are price or age of the object influencing the functionality. For the sake of interest, we should briefly discuss the relevance to use standards for encoding object details. Without questioning, standards are superior to proprietary

formats in case that objects are not supposed to be limited to one platform; the number of import and export filters is reduced, redundancy and transfer errors are avoided, structural errors of the format are found faster, and documentation and tutorials are generally available. Over the last years, several standards, specifications, or proposals for standards were developed, for the purpose of object storage or security, the format is not relevant and we consider the objects to be binary files.

2.2.3 Object Information, Tracking, and Quality

The *Metadata* represents additional information. Depending on the virtual environment it can be generated automatically or has to be specified by the entities themselves. Further information about the object is given by building *inheritance trees* where properties (e.g., functional, environmental, and relation) are selected and merged for child objects. New objects can also be created by combining objects. In contrast to inheritance, the objects are kept as they are and combined to larger ones; i.e. by defining their relative position to each other as well as the interaction of components. Examples are the combination of vessel and crane (ship being able to (un)load storage without external equipment) or tires for vehicles, where the relative position is as important as the type and the granted rights for tire changes.

Objects need and should (if not otherwise specified) *trace* all occurring changes, modifications, and relations to other objects. Generally speaking, the information about the object is stored as part of the object; whereas the environment is responsible for maintaining the trace. Note that the mechanism has to be used with caution, as the trace might flood the object and cause huge object size. Versioning corresponds to keeping track of copied and modified objects. The trace within objects can be used to recreate every previous version; assuming that the trace is copied for every new version of an object. We discriminate the following information types, whereas further are defined by each environment. Information is stored with timestamp, environment, and involved entities.

1. **Trace:** Keep trace of originating object in case of copying, change of owner, or modification of major properties (e.g., regarding grants or functions). The information here is, e.g., required to trace object history, versioning, inheritance, or ownership.
2. **Function:** Allow functions to write to the trace log.
3. **Detail**: Keep track of any modification of the object; e.g., movements, interactions with other entities, or modifications of less relevant properties.
4. **Debug:** Include further information to debug specific scenarios or tracing errors. Here, information about the environment is included to reconstruct specific settings.

Persistence is the "characteristic of data that outlives the execution of the program that created it" (Wikipedia, 2010). To transfer this to our scenario, the secure and unchanged storage of objects has to be guaranteed. First, each environment has to take care of this, as well as the Global Object Database; see Section 4. This requirement is in line with specifications for databases. On the other hand, virtual objects are part of shared environments with interaction while the owner is offline. Assuming correct grants, the object changes are in consent with the owner. Changes are communicated and stored in form of single messages (based on time intervals or occurring events) or cumulated reports being send to the owner. If an object state needs to be kept, either the grants must be very restrictive or replicated to a secure environment.

Finally, the *context* and *quality* of objects is specified by several properties. The context is characterized by, e.g., community appropriate-

ness, compatibility, and collaboration, whereas the quality has to be seen with respect to the context as well as the user's expectation. Security in this context comprises the *price-quality-relation* such that the risk of overpricing or deviation in promised functionality is reduced; i.e. as uncountable projects (starting with Second Life to Linux to Gimp to OpenOffice) and repositories demonstrated the effect of motivation and believe in sharing by containing high-quality objects being available for free download.

Community Appropriateness accentuates the context of objects in relation to specific communities. Objects placed in an environment by the user require certain guarantees about the neighbors' behavior with respect to quality, kind, or appropriateness. For example, the virtual representation of a company has a showroom with replicas of the real world toys being produced. It is seldom appreciated if, e.g., a strip club or shop for nude skins opens in the neighborhood. Without further discussion where to draw the line between appropriate and inappropriate, certain mechanism should allow guarantees about (visible) neighboring objects. Another property for community security is about internationalization and consideration of cultural aspects of the intended users. First, objects as well as their human readable properties need be available and extensible in multiple languages. Second, the different interpretation of an object from culture to culture needs be considered at all times, either by warnings, limited access, or masking for certain users; e.g. not showing objects in a store by hiding or replacing.

Compatibility has to be approached by three different directions: (1) Can objects be combined and work in a given environment (intra-compatibility; e.g., combining two objects as a group and forming a new object)? (2) Can an object be used in any environment without losing its functionality? (3) From a plain technical perspective, can the encoding of object information and functions be readable and either be applicable or executable (we believe so). While general properties and structure can be transferred to different formats without a problem, it might not apply to functions where inter-language transfer is rather complex and involves high risks of errors.

Collaboration on the one hand is the communication between objects (e.g. interaction between agents) and describes the way objects can handle given problems and tasks together. On the other hand it stands for the possibilities of one or more avatars editing (e.g. building, designing an object) or using (e.g. driving a virtual car with both avatars being able to control the car) objects simultaneously.

3 SECURITY ASPECTS

3.1 Risks and Protection

The previous section illustrated key requirements for objects in a multi-virtual world setting. Obviously, every item on the list is vulnerable to harm, either via criminal intent or by accident. Even though criminal minds will find ways to overcome almost any security barrier given time, it is important to increase the required maximum effort, while not interfering with the handling, features, preventing the application from effectively running. As mentioned previously, it is not our intention to describe the technology, but to increase the risk awareness in order for users to think about precautions. In the following section, we browse through all object related aspects and describe options for protection. Note that this is by far not complete and does not consider all components to initiate an attack. For example, we do not discuss visualization protection, where the object can be extracted from the graphics card memory, scanned from the monitor, or intercepted by knowing the rendering algorithms in open source software. If the viewing of objects needs to be secure, closed (and proprietary) software is needed on protected systems. Figure 3 shows an

example for a shop, where intruders manipulated the items in various ways.

However, objects need to be transferred and stored on local media for individual repositories in order to maintain backups of objects and their associated intellectual property. Therefore, our main concerns are related to (illegal) copies and modifications of digital objects. This is comparable with DRM in the music industry or eBook handling, where companies need to prevent illegal copies by means of linking (to specific hardware) or determent (inscription with traceable information about the buyer). For 3D objects similar ideas can be used to integrate the cases above for a secure system.

3.1.1 Object Identification and Privileges

Observing a specific environment, the ***uniqueness*** of ***identifier*** and control of objects is done efficiently by internal object servers and databases. With multi-environments, we require global servers and either standards used by all environments or dedicated mapping functions with respect to objects and their properties. The global object server is used to register new objects, verify identity, validate the integrity, and protocols in their location. In addition, asymmetric encryption (key pair; c.f. Furht et al. (2005)) is used to link the creator to the object as well as guaranteeing the unsophisticated content and meta-data. Here, the hash code and certificates for the environment (virtual world, application, and inventory) are used on trusted systems with respect to security (c.f. Torres Padrosa (2009) with focus on DRM). Like DRM, the platforms are licensed and verified for modification (e.g., malware) before objects are imported. In addition, digital objects are encrypted to prevent unauthorized copies and to allow distribution on public channels or media. Encrypted objects are matched with certificates based environment and users and can include further limitations like export or time of availability. Certificates restrict the usage of objects and check the adherence of *availability* by limiting the issuance.

3.1.2 Object Identification and Privileges

Observing a specific environment, the ***uniqueness*** of ***identifier*** and control of objects is done efficiently by internal object servers and databases. With multi-environments, we require global servers and either standards used by all environments or dedicated mapping functions with respect to objects and their properties. The global object server is used to register new objects, verify identity, validate the integrity, and protocols in their location. In addition, asymmetric encryption (key pair; c.f. Furht et al. (2005)) is used to link the creator to the object as well as guaranteeing the unsophisticated content and meta-data. Here, the hash code and certificates for the environment (virtual world, application, and inventory) are used on trusted systems with respect to security (c.f. Torres Padrosa (2009) with focus on DRM). Like DRM, the platforms are licensed and verified for modification (e.g., malware) before objects are imported. In addition, digital objects are encrypted to prevent unauthorized copies and to allow distribution on public channels or media. Encrypted objects are matched with certificates based environment and users and can include further limitations like export or time of availability. Certificates restrict the usage of objects and check the adherence of *availability* by limiting the issuance.

Granting *privileges* follows a hierarchical top-down order. The *role* creator has all privileges by default and can appoint new owners and users including their privileges. Based on the privileges, owners are allowed to add additional owners and users, while users are generally not allowed to add additional entities to the object. Note that it should not be technically restricted, but the owner or creator should decide on this in principle. Another

exception to this approach is that the owner can reduce the privileges of the creator to forbid access or visibility. The privileges are not defined by certificates but stored within the object. Encrypted hash codes are used to check for modification. Keeping the privileges accessible for inspection has advantages user with sufficient rights can be contacted and misuse is reduced by visibility of names. The security relies on the encryption and the integrity of the environments. Certificates are used from a global server, which could also be used for verification against a central database with all privileges.

3.1.3 Object Access and Transfer

Again, we have to distinguish passing and copying. *Passing* implies an authentication of the user and its certificates (i.e. being the owner and allowed to transfer the object) as well as a substitution of ownership and location of the object. If ownership is passed, the existing certificate for the original owner is invalidated such that objects cannot be used anymore; e.g., import into and use in (uncertified) environments would fail. *Copying* initiates the creation of a new object with instantiation of properties. Most important is the verification on allowed availability of copies. Here, the global server controls to total count as objects only know about the limit but not the concurrently existing objects.

Legal copies can be secured and monitored. However, what about illegal processes like stealing, plagiarism, alternating? Objects are digital assets and can simply be copied. Therefore, if the environment is not protected or objects are stored on public servers, stealing equals a simple copying process. The encryption (i.e. if the environments are running on trusted systems) of objects and certificates secures the objects sufficiently, such that hacking is not in proportion to the value of the objects and they become a less attractive target, or perhaps become more attractive yet unobtainable. On non-secure systems, object information might be extracted while being processed so there is not much that can be done about this but to require a secure environment before sending certificates for encryption. The same applies for alternating between types of systems, as it requires decryption and verification using the certificate.

Plagiarism is another issue as someone rebuilds objects or distributes slightly modified objects as their own. Here, watermarks (also called tattoos) can be used that are integrated into the object and allow identification and therefore tracking of the original creator. The disadvantage of watermarks in 3D objects is their robustness compared to watermarks for images (Eshraghi & Samavati, 2007). We also need to differentiate between private users who are interested in modeling their reality by creating replicas from the real world (and do not sell and distribute them afterwards) and the professionals who build their business on brand replicas; e.g. car or sport brands. We do not intend to discuss laws and existing cases as this

is different in almost every country. Nevertheless, on important security concern is to protect objects from unauthorized copying (even though we know from movie and software piracy that the race cannot be won) and to identify copied objects.

3.1.4 Object Information, Tracking and Quality

Modification covers almost all cases shown in Figure 5 but copying and stealing. Protection is only possible, if an intruder has no direct access to the object including its meta-data and properties. Any part that is not allowed to be modified without permission has to be signed. However, if objects can be transferred out of a secure environment (e.g. the users' hard disk), the object content is readable and could be used for a new object. Encryption of the object prevents any access without having the right certificate. Certificates do not have to cover the whole object and might be associated with or

Figure 5. Possible manipulations in a virtual world store, if we do not have a sound security concept

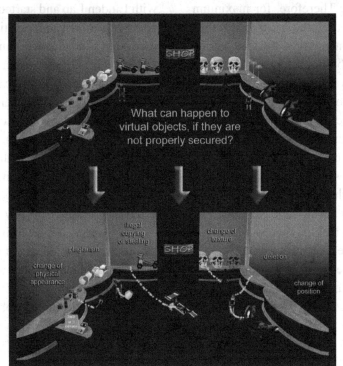

exclude components. For example, a virtual house needs modifiable surfaces to decorate the walls, but perhaps the floor layout cannot be modified.

The major crux with all of this is that every component must act jointly. Transferring a secure object to an (assumed safe) environment also initiates the certificate delivery to decode the object. It would be realistic to hypothesize that the user is neither aware of the ambidextrous behavior nor would he notice the operations on the object. Comparable back doors (as well as other issues like compatibility problems of asset and application) existed with DRM for music and caused its decline: using non-digital media after decoding and compression to dissolve watermarks created DRM-free copies. We have already mentioned the counterpart where programs read the graphic card memory. The computer industry already has different solutions to provide secure platforms, e.g. trusted computing (Trusted Computing Group; 2010) or trusted networks (Open Trust, 2010).

Systems are as secure as their weakest component because someone can enter the system and change behavior. Therefore, for maximum security, we need secure (and trusted) systems. We have covered some issues to demonstrate important issues to be considered in an open inter-world setting. Even though arguments about open source and free objects abound and should be considered, it is necessary to provide protection against users not following a codex, but instead cause harm by stealing, changing or deleting. Even within a secure system, it is always given to open objects and share code and design, and strongly supported by the authors. Nevertheless, companies relying on making money within virtual worlds must have a means to protect assets and intellectual property, in order to have the confidence that they can participate in and thrive in virtual worlds, as well as expand their virtual world offerings.

3.2 Examples in Real Environments

In this section we examine Second Life (and to a short extent OpenSimulator and Project Wonderland) to provide contemporary examples of object handling. We are not going to cover every aspect about object handling but want to provide a rough understanding about what happens in 3D worlds. Sure, there are almost uncountable other worlds (see KZero (2009) and Virtual World Review (2010) for an overview) each with unique object handling and protection. We decided on Second Life as it is the most popular one with respect to in-world development of objects and on the other two as they provide a very good platform to implement our concept. Also these worlds provide opposites like closed vs. open world, entertainment vs. business context, single grid vs. multi-grid, and so on; but this would not be part of the following discussion.

3.2.1 Second Life

Second Life was started in 1999 by Philip Rosedale with Linden Lab and started much of the interest about second (virtual) realities not only in popular media but also scientific journals; cf. (Linden Lab 2010d). The success was primarily related to the immense possibilities for customization of one's avatar, environment, as well as the intricate economic system and ability to communication and interaction with others in a free to form environment unlike games with their codified rules. It should be noted that Second Life participates in many research projects supporting virtual worlds and has contributed greatly to various disciplines in this respect; however, it is still considered a closed world as avatars and content is still not freely exchangeable. Still, we can benefit from a brief discussion in terms of how this virtual world manages its multitude of objects.

3.2.1.1 Object Identification and Privileges

Second Life uses the Universal Unique Identifier (UUID, Linden Lab, 2010b): a 128-bit *identifier* following standards by the Open Software Foundation. This approach provides for a large range for UUIDs, as well as rules for creating unique UUIDs, such that the likelihood of unintentionally assigning the same one twice is very rare. Thus, no central server for coordination is needed, providing a less complex mechanism. Using this approach, the closed Second Life system can validate new UUIDs and prevent identifier collisions.

Second Life further protects objects in its system by operating all of the virtual world servers and allows limited access only after authentication. We should note that this approach might be modified and relaxed somewhat with Second Life offering new servers users can buy and use behind organizational firewalls with proposed full access to hosted islands at the administrative level (Linden Lab, 2010c) and continuing development on the Open Grid Protocol (Linden Lab, 2009a). However, this would most likely be cost prohibitive to most individual users.

In Second Life, objects have creators (the very first owner without additional rights compared to owners) and owners; access control for *user* can only be done within scripts. That is, *privileges* to functions are part of the scripted function and changes require programming knowledge. Another example is using the internal function to move objects (non-physical ones, as others can be moved by just applying force to them). This feature is either implemented as a function including permission for entities or granted by selecting an option to allow moving objects by anybody.

Another privilege is given through parcel management, which restricts access but not visibility if it is on an island with public access rights. In Second Life, to provide protection (access and visibility), objects require an isolated island not attached to others. The roles and capabilities in Second Life allow specifying users within groups, but with respect to objects, it provides only transfer to groups (and not roles within the group), access to manipulation as moving, copying, editing, and setting the object for sale. Other object related capabilities are indirectly controlled through parcel management, where settings specify who can create new or return existing objects. All of this leads to some particularly challenging security and access issues in Second Life. As described in the following section, the limitations are quiet high and limit the flexibility as well as the security. That is, secure and public areas have to be clearly separated (i.e. due to visibility issues) and user specific access is limited to roles and capabilities or requires specific scripts (compared to user role or having object-related privileges that can be granted to users).

3.2.1.2 Object Access and Transfer

One of Second Life's main features is the economic system, where users buy and sell objects and land. As a result, the transfer of objects is closely associated with sale prices; however, the price does not affect the transfer itself. The transfer is limited to the role *owner* as users are handled within scripted functions and the creator is considered to be owner as well. Privileges for the next owner cannot be specified beyond very restricted limits (Linden Lab, 2009b). The next owner gets either full access and modification rights to the object, is only allowed to create further copies, or has to keep it as it is. The next owner is selected by passing the object to another entity (in Second Life restricted to avatars), whom receives the object with the chosen rights. Second Life does permit an option, where the object can be copied by everybody who also gains full access by this. From a security perspective, this is unacceptable as it provides unlimited copies in an uncontrolled manner.

Second Life tracks three privileges that can be passed to the next owner: 1) modify (change everything about the object), 2) copy (create unlimited copies of an object), and 3) resell (next owner can sell the object). If copy and sell are activated, the next owner can copy and sell the object as well, causing an uncontrolled distribution with possible enormous economic damage. When a person passes objects without copy permission this implies that the object is given away without any possibility to retake it. Users in Second Life can create temporary objects with a built-in destruction timer and Second Life provides visible options to encode this in functions. Temporary objects and areas that clear themselves after a certain time endangers persistence as the world is changeable without real control; even though the objects are returned to the owners' inventory. Note that scripts have their own permissions similar to object permissions so this framework can be extended here as well.

3.2.1.3 Object Information, Tracking and Quality

Second Life uses properties for objects in order to support the advanced physical engine and provide a true immerse feeling for users. Nevertheless, restrictions apply as some properties are not permitted to be changed to provide more straightforward realistic modeling: Object weight is determined by size rather than being able to specify concrete mass, flexible objects cannot be physical, and objects cannot be connected to others; e.g. connecting a rope to a hook or having a realistic towing bar. Programming manipulation allows implementing these elements but only with detailed effort and advanced knowledge about the system. In addition, objects lack information for retrieval, usage, and relation. Besides object name and description, no further object information can be assigned by developers such as meta-data, cultural, or social appropriateness, as well as (semantic) relationship to other objects. Although verification for object placement in a certain area can be based on age, ethics, or culture on a higher level, by having underlying ontologies or rule-based systems, this is unfeasible because with over a billion hardly-specified objects, object

retrieval is comparable to finding the infamous needle in a hay stack.

Please note that users can create objects in-world or with external applications like Blender to allow for detailed object parameters. However, once imported, these objects are stored in-world on Linden Lab servers and come under the same restrictions as objects created in-world; moreover, an export out of Second Life for further modification is currently not anticipated. Applications do exist (e.g., Second Inventory) that permit backups of completely owned objects (with full access rights) in the avatar's inventory to external storage devices, but not of islands or specified objects in the world (even user-owned). Nevertheless, the security is minimal for controlling access to objects and producing (unauthorized) copies because other software can download whole islands even though it violates Second Life's ToS. Another program, Open Source viewer, can access all in-world information to visualize objects and, therefore, can create digital replicas. Currently, there is no mechanism to encrypt objects or require certificates to validate object ownership. This makes the protection of intellectual property a challenge.

Except for the ToS prohibition in Second Life against external copy tools there are no features or controls in place to help creators properly protect their objects. However, Linden Lab is aware of the problem and is considering several changes, especially because everything digital faces the risk of being somehow copied (Linden Lab, 2009c). Some form of an approved rights management program could make large strides towards a safer environment for Second Life creators.

Ultimately, Second Life is a pioneer in Virtual Worlds, but its closed-world system leads to many object management shortcomings in terms of access, interoperability, and security. Objects are for in-world usage with limited inter-world transfer possibilities. Although server-based storage and execution of scripts lends itself to high-level protection, it also leads to a very restricted access to specific object properties. Moreover, security is not part of the object design (besides the ownership and passed rights for the next owner) but requires individual implementation using internal scripting language. Relation and context-based properties are not implemented and object naming and tagging is not enforced which results in the difficult retrieval of objects. Security can be implemented but requires programming knowledge and loyalty to the Second Life environment as the restrictions cannot be ported to other virtual worlds.

3.2.2 OpenSimulator

OpenSimulator (also called OpenSim) started in 2007 and is an Open Source 3D application server to create a virtual world being compliant with Second Life viewers (using the same protocols for the client-server communication and grid management) and also resembles many other aspects (OpenSimulator, 2010a). Nevertheless, OpenSimulator is by far more than just a re-written Second Life server as it provides a larger functionality, while giving full control over the server through local installations (behind the firewalls of organizations) and unrestricted interfaces to integrate further applications. In addition, the functionality can be extended by loadable modules, multiple protocols providing communication beyond the OpenSimulator grid, users have full control over their objects, and in-world scripting is not limited to one proprietary language but can be, e.g., LSL, Jscript, C#, Yield Prolog, or VB.Net (OpenSimulator, 2010c).

In contrast to Second Life, OpenSimulator can be installed on individual computers, providing the user with all rights for administrating the system; including access to the virtual objects for, e.g., backup. The same advantages are given in the so-called grid-mode (depending on the access rights assigned to the individual users) where multiple instances are connected to a larger virtual world and, from a technological perspective, several servers are used to distribute the required workload. Individual servers are set up for the management of users, grid, assets, inventory, messaging, and regions. It is anticipated (and done in first experiments) to connect the OpenSimulator grid to the Second Life grid and allow traversal of avatars from one world to the other (Linden Lab, 2008). But so far, the teleport works just for the avatar without any objects including the appearance of the avatar itself. However, object transfer between OpenSimulator and Second Life is subject of further research; a detailed description can be found in Sequeira (2009); whereas security is not the main concern in this work.

The similarity (and compatibility) of OpenSimulator to Second Life with less administrative limits and less costs for maintaining land, OpenSimulator is an interesting test and development platform for users as content (objects) can be exported to Second Life; i.e. if LSL was used as the script language (Winkler, 2010, Vilela et a., 2010, Novak, 2010). Note that OpenSimulator is still development in process and while it proofed its robustness in real-life projects, many aspects like full support of LSL are not yet implemented to their full extent. From a research and educational perspective, the missing economical support might be of little relevance, but companies with ambitions to make revenue are not able to use OpenSimulator for their productive installation. Another problem in OpenSimulator, which might be the result of the current status as alpha version and still in development, is the missing terms of services and the therewith the problem of defining and claiming copyrights.

The security of objects is similar to Second Life. Objects are transferred to the client for visualization (while objects with no access are kept on the server in Project Wonderland) and allow access to the object structure through this. Encryption and further protection through tracking and watermarking are mentioned as possible extensions but not yet specified with any means. Note, that the storage of objects is different in Second Life (file system) and Open Simulator (database). The architectural design of OpenSimulator provides a great basis for concepts like we suggest in Section 4 as the server structure already separates different responsibilities.

3.2.3 Project Wonderland

Project Wonderland is an Open Source collaborative 3D virtual world implemented in Java and designed as a server-client-architecture. Until 2010, the project was funded by Sun Microsystems (Oracle, 2008) who intended to develop a robust, secure, reliable, scalable, and functional environment for organizations to improve communication among distant partners, but also to work collaboratively together by having all common desktop tools like OpenOffice available. The funding was stopped during the acquisition of Sun by Oracle and is continued (by the same team) as Open Wonderland (Open Wonderland, 2010; Korolov, 2010) with the same focus.

Project Wonderland is built on top of the 3D engine jMonkeyEngine and the game server Project Darkstar. The virtual world is internally described by a (3D) scene graph with the node *world* as the root and all other *cells* hierarchically organized from the root down. *Cells* are the objects described as the volume they take in the virtual world. A cell can contain further cells and can be positioned, rotated, or scaled. To each cell (which could be a TV set), capabilities are assigned to describe what can be done with the object. This is comparable to the functions used in our object model. The cells' initial state is stored in a hierarchy of XML-files (also called Wonderland File System), which describes the cell structure and the containing components, modules, and artworks. The cells can be created by every user and dynamically loaded into the world. Simple editing is possible since version 0.5, such that location is not necessarily set in the XML file but using graphical interfaces.

Security is a major aspect for Project Wonderland. The Open Source approach allows an installation behind corporate firewalls and the extensive APIs can be used for integration of the existing authentication and identity management of the business. The objects are secured by (hierarchical) access control lists to control visibility, interaction, and editing. For Project Wonderland, a DAC implementation with focus on simplicity exists. The *Discretionary Access Control* (DAC) restricts the access to objects for users or groups, similar to the UNIX model (Wright & Madey, 2008); i.e. passing the rights down in the hierarchy. The access permissions can be passed on to other users. WonderDAC has three user groups (*owner, group, everyone*) with two permissions (*interact, alter*). The authors keep the complexity (and therewith the granularity for access rights) low in favor of acceptance. Thus, objects with no interact permission will not be visible to avatars. Note, that without permissions, objects are not submitted to the clients to increase security. Further security features like encryption or prevention of stealing objects is not (yet) implemented, even though DAC can be used to restrict access by unauthorized users.

Second Life and Project Wonderland are targeting different users. While Second Life is focused on in-world activities using the provided tools, connectivity to external applications is very limited due to the restricted interfaces. Project Wonderland, on the other hand, allows import of most formats and (almost) unlimited extensibility by further modules. The main target groups are (business) teams working on real-life projects like meetings for brainstorming, presentations, or product development. To provide a virtual counterpart for an office setting, Project Wonderland allows inclusion of desktop applications like OpenOffice or Internet Browser. Second Life also allows the projection of web sites (including interaction), but is not supporting collaborative work as the interaction is local to the client.

Creation or modification of objects in-world is not possible and reduces its value especially for users without experience in using external programs for modeling. Second Life and Open-

Simulator already have full editors allowing everyone do be creative. Same applies to in-world scripting, which is currently in early development in Project Wonderland but will provide a more flexible way of extending the functionality compared to Second Life as different programming languages without restrictions will be supported. Other missing features are, for example, personal inventories, exchange of objects between avatars, or an economical system and in-world currency; but with Project Wonderland still in development (current version 0.5), the chances of improvement are high. With respect to our concept for object security, Project Wonderland provides an ideal experimental environment.

4 CONCEPT FOR OBJECT SECURITY

Virtual worlds have been around for some time, yet the research centering on object security in multi-environment conditions is still quite undeveloped. As we noted earlier in the chapter, securing objects in single environments is mainly done through restricting access by authentication and access control lists, while the multi-environment focus on the transfer of objects is mainly centered on standards discussions; cf. Hurlimann (2009) and OpenSimulator (2010b). Industry to date is interested more in protecting music and movies, instead of 3D objects in virtual worlds. Numerous publications and research streams cover watermarking, encryption, and signatures, but almost none focus on 3D object security in multi-environments. More needs to be done on how we can guarantee that objects are unique or limited to a certain count. Note that we are aware of the influence of market shares and revenues involved in the entertainment industry for music and movies versus 3D-objects in virtual worlds.

Moreover our concept may not shake the view of the (virtual) worlds because we cover known technologies from other fields and existing environments, but we integrate them into a trusted network of objects and certificated environments. Our research argues that people need to be aware of security, and be aware that playing in and learning about virtual worlds has to mesh with the business needs for serious applications. We should also emphasize that our research does not move away from the concepts and philosophy of open objects, but many users are hesitant to fully use virtual worlds because they do not want to lose their ideas and properties. We realize there needs to be a balance between freedom and security.

Our proposed architecture uses technology already implemented within the Internet, for data protection, or digital right management to manage objects in multi-environments. Our concept surrounding the protection of objects includes encryption, certificates, safe and trusted environments, trusted networks, and therefore participation of environment providers to implement this support and protection. In terms of our ongoing research, we have initiated the implementation of the *Global Object Management System* and currently conducting our first experiments with mobile applications. Our concept of securing objects demonstrates that we are able to protect our work, transfer it to other environments, and by this improve their overall value of objects. In addition, secure objects will create new marketplaces as companies can control the penetration of the market by limiting objects (e.g., collectibles with increased value) or prevent plagiarism and manipulation, thereby protecting copyright and intellectual property.

Our architecture combines several ideas common to digital goods controls on the Internet (images, movies, books, or music), as well as virtual worlds (OpenSimulator, Project Wonderland), in conjunction with encryption and security concepts (PGP, watermarks, DRM). The following sections describe our concept and some implementations of GOMS, how it can be integrated in virtual environments, and what current research questions on which we are currently focusing. With respect to underlying technologies, we refer to a collection of books and papers for further reading at the end of our chapter.

4.1 Global Object Management System Architecture

This section outlines our system architecture created to handle digital objects and provide (if requested and anticipated by the object) a secure exchange between different environments. We discuss it in this section realizing that the presented system is reduced to elementary components to visualize the idea, while keeping the complexity low (cf. Section 4.2 and Figure 14).

Figure 6 shows a possible exchange of objects passing through different devices and platforms. In this example, Torsten buys the object *chair* (originally created by Torsten's Second Life avatar Tyke) and keeps the copy on a mobile device (1). For this example, we assume a global limit of four objects *chair*; including the original in the store. With respect to the environments, we assume the blackberry to be certified and secure, while the iPhone and Notebook are not certified. Torsten has no privileges besides transferring the object to other devices (2) or environments (3). In *Second Life*, Tyke (the next owner of the object) is

allowed to create copies (up to a given limit) and passes two newly created *chairs* to Phillip (4) in the same environment. Phillip keeps one version in his personal inventory (7, transfer) and transfers one version to the mobile device of his (real-life) user Sascha (5, transfer); with no privileges for Sascha to do any modifications to the object. Later, Sascha intends to give another copy of the object to his colleague Alan as a present (6). Unfortunately, we have created two extra copies of the object *chair* since the first transfer (in total, there are already four *chairs* in the system) and reached the upper boundary; preventing us from actually giving Alan a copy of the *chair*. Note that Alan's mobile device is a secure environment and, therefore, objects are verified and checked against limits thereby stopping the transfer. However, on unsecure devices, this might not be checked, but the object would be protected by encryption, thereby stopping the transfer as well; cf. Section 4.1.3 and 4.1.4. In conclusion, we have to deal, for example, with unsecure (in the following called uncertified) environments, change of ownership, checking the availability of objects, and securing the transfer.

Figure 6 also includes transactions that may result in possible GOMS security risks: These include (a) authentication, (b) secure transfer of

Figure 6. Example for the turnaround of an object passing through several certified and non-certified systems and environments.

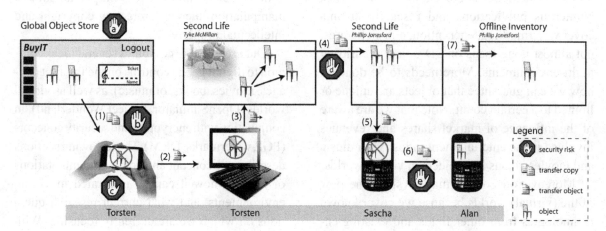

objects, (c) protection of objects on non-trusted devices, (d) multiplying and transferring objects, and (e) guaranteeing the given limit of existing objects in the system. Our example demonstrates the need for GOMS to control security of the object and its properties (e.g., scripts or meta-data), keep track of objects (e.g., ownership, count, or location), entities (users, avatars, environments), and regulate processes (transfer, copy, filter, transformation). By using strict authentication, key-pair encryption, hash codes, and certificates for environments, we build a network of trusted components, in which object security can be controlled and guaranteed to a certain extent. This is similar to the trusted computing framework and its strong hierarchical approach to secure systems all the way from hardware to applications, which guarantees non-manipulated systems (Trusted Computing Group, 2010).

In case of missing privileges and certificates, the encrypted objects are not usable on, for example, Torstens' mobile devices (non-trusted system), even though the devices can pass the digital files on to other users and avatars. Alan, on the other hand, owns software which is trusted and able to decode objects for visualization if his device has the appropriate object permissions and access. For the sake of completeness, we call objects **invalid** if the object is modified and not yet verified for correctness by GOMS or transferred from an uncertified environment without being completely encrypted. Otherwise, objects are considered to be **valid**. The object is valid as long as it is only in certified environments, whereas GOMS is required to verify availability, which cannot be done otherwise; cf. Section 4.1.4.

Multiple ownership of objects does not imply that all owners have their individual copy, considering that the same object cannot exist more than one time; for example, a unique piece of artwork. It merely means that the object should be simultaneously accessible by all owners. In this situation, GOMS keeps track of transfers, knows about the current owner (of the *physical*

object) and location (device), and supports communication and exchange of objects. In addition, GOMS acts as a global object server providing access to replicas of objects if, local repositories or inventories are offline. Figure 14 in Section 4.2 shows the major components and processes of GOMS, and the following subsections (4.1.1-3) describe details about how GOMS handles potential security risks and required processes.

4.1.1 Authentication

Granting access to objects, servers, environments, or functionalities can be implemented in many ways. In this case we need to control the access to system components (e.g., accessing a store), allowed functionality within the components (e.g., browsing the catalog, buying objects, (unrestricted) transfer to other systems), or the privileges being granted for specific objects. *Access control lists* (ACL) are the common solution to control access. Similar to the UNIX file system, ACL govern distinct access on different levels (*read, write, execute*) for different user groups (*owner, group, everyone*). Whereas the level of detail can vary in other systems, here access is granted to identities. For example, Second Life uses *creator* and the permission to *transfer* or *copy* objects, whereas visibility (read) is not realized.

For the sake of completeness, we mention other concepts but will not go into further details because we use privileges to encode access to objects. The other concepts are *role based access control,* (RBAC, users or groups have assigned roles with specific access to resources), *discretionary access control* (DAC, restricting the access to objects for users or groups, similar to Unix models [cf. Wright & Madey, 2008a]), *mandatory access control* (MAC, also called non-discretionary access control, which uses multi-level security), *capability-based security* (CBS, in which the user needs capabilities to access or interact with referenced objects according to the rights of the capability, [cf. Scheffler, 2008]), and *rule-based access control* (RuBAC, *a* set of rules that defines the access to resources [cf. Techtopia, 2009]) for further information about this subject.

In addition to different models for controlling the access, we need to specify the kind of authentication, such as providing proof that one is the authorized individual. Basically, the spectrum varies from single factor authentication of username-password with different exigencies for the password quality up to multi-factor authentication with combined biometric identification, password authentication, and device credentialing (Vielhauer, 2005). With respect to object security, we will later describe key-pair encryption with secret and public keys. If a message or object is encrypted with the public key, it can only decoded by the matching secret key, therefore identity is proven by owning the correct key (in addition to keeping the secret key, the validity of the public key is also verified by trusted networks [Haenni and Jonczy, 2007]). On the other hand, the secret key can be used to sign messages (encryption), with the public key as the matching counterpart for decryption or identity check, respectively (cf. Ferguson et al. (2010) for more details on key pair encryption).

4.1.2 Encryption

In case of secure environments (e.g., object stores, mobile devices, virtual worlds), the interception of objects during transfer is the most likely attack vector against content. Secure connections (e.g. virtual private networks (VPN) or secure protocols

like SSL) and authentication of communication partners are critical protections to prevent attacks (e.g., man-in-the-middle). In addition, the objects require encryption in case of illegal acquisition so that the objects are of no value for the attacker since they are undecipherable (cf. Cole (2009) for an overview for network security). Figure 7 depicts the processes for authentication and secure transfer in open networks. In this example, the user requests access via a mobile device using login and password (1), which is authenticated by the identity server (2). Furthermore, a secure channel is established (4) to transfer (6) the requested object (5). Note that this example excludes the GOMS encryption visualization and focuses on the authentication and transfer.

Advanced protection is required when objects are in open (non-certified and non-trusted) environments; e.g. Torstens' mobile device in Figure 6. In this is situation, object access, in conjunction with any modifications, duplications, or usages, needs to be prevented. Objects have properties and content with discerned access levels that need to be maintained. In many cases, it might be expedient to allow readability of properties for retrieval or classification. Nevertheless, the integrity of the object has the highest priority and requires several mechanisms that must be included in the security model.

Depending on the kind of object (free vs. payment, open code vs. hidden code), the content may or may not be visible. One option would be the inclusion of previews while the full content is kept encrypted without the required matching

Figure 7. Authentication and secure transfer of objects; encryption is not shown here

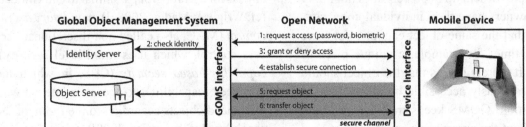

keys or certificates. Previews could also censor adult themes until required authentication had occurred. Integrity is assured by encrypted hash codes, which are inserted by GOMS or respective environments using their secret keys. Note that in open (uncertified) environments encryption can, and perhaps should, be used on the whole object (to include properties and content) in order to prevent any access. The object would be stored on the device without further application or usage. One scenario to use this approach would be the backup on (public) storage places to distribute the risk of data loss. Further description on hash codes is discussed below within the context of object transfer (cf. Section 4.1.3 covering object transfer).

Another context for objects is a secure, certified, and trusted environment. Here, the content is (in certain boundaries) protected against external risks and can be decrypted by entities with sufficient privileges. Figure 8 demonstrates the practice of certificates where requested objects (1) are encrypted and wrapped in envelopes (2) before being transferred to the requesting environment. Not shown in Figure 8 is the identity authentication illustrated in Figure 7, with which the enveloped is addressed and sealed. Just as with public key encryption, the envelope can only be opened with a matching certificate. The corresponding certifi-

cate (matching the previously encoded object) is requested (4), personalized (5), and sent back (6) to open the envelope (7). The personalization includes further details on what the identity is permitted to do. In our model this concerns access to properties and content as privileges (regarding the object) are part of the object itself. In step (7), it is important that the environment is trusted and verification holds against attacks and security holes. Much of this is accomplished in the system framework as trusted systems require a complete stack of authenticated components, from hardware to the high-level software application. The object can be decoded by opening the envelope with the certificate and decrypting the content. Further regulation of privileges is done by the environment, which guarantees the object security and blocking of attacks from internal and external threats and unauthorized access.

In general, the current active environment is responsible for the security of the object before, during, and after the transfer to new environments. This holds true for certified environments that are part of the complete GOMS architecture. Nevertheless, we must consider uncertified environments, as well as two modes of connectivity: online and offline. Being online is straightforward as the transfer involves GOMS, which tracks and maintains identities, certificates, object states, and

Figure 8. Using certificate to protect objects from being used in environments other than certified ones

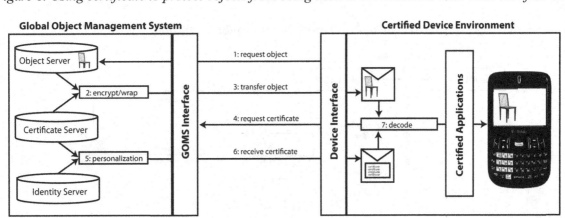

availability. Therefore, the object can be transferred via GOMS to perform all checks (cf. Section 4.1.3). However, offline transactions require further precautions. If objects are moved to uncertified environments, they are wrapped with an envelope using the public environment key (issued by GOMS during certification). The following actions would be performed for increased object security:

- **Content Encryption:** The environment creates a symmetric key to encrypt the content. The key itself is stored (with the object) and encrypted for each identity having access rights (defined by the privileges) with the corresponding public key. This encryption allows decryption by different entities without distributing the actual key; c.f. Figure 9.
- **Property Encryption**: Encryption similar to the key for content, but designed either for all properties as a whole or each individual property to provide selective access control. This key can be valuable if one wants to keep general information for the object accessible for search engines while other properties are kept secret.
- **Integrity**: Maintaining an object's desired state and behavior is most important in uncertified environments to protect against modifications, as well as achieve access

in secure environments. Encrypted hash codes provide fast verification against unauthorized modifications by recalculating and comparing the hash code to the decrypted matching public key hash code. Deviations result in invalid objects.

Modification should also be considered using hash codes to assure integrity. If online, each modification can be verified by GOMS (including privileges) which will create and sign new hash codes. Offline hampers the process, but with change and revision tracking in place (including prove of identity), GOMS can use this information to later verify, approve, and assign new and valid hash codes to the object.

We illustrate this procedure in Figure 10 as follows: (1) Calculate hash codes for different parts of the object, thereby identifying the corresponding hash code (for which modifications are anticipated). (2) Re-calculate the current hash code (HC_{TR1}). (3) Copy the original content to the trace for later verification, reconstruction, and protocol of modification. (4) Perform the modifications (here *Stuhl* to *Chair*). (5) Calculate the new hash code (HC_{TR2}). (6) Sign both (old and new) hash codes with the private key such that GOMS can verify the identity by using the matching public key. (7) Add the signed hash codes to the list of hash codes. (The list contains the original hash code and two for each modification).

Figure 9. Access to encrypted content by multiple entities using encryption of onetime keys

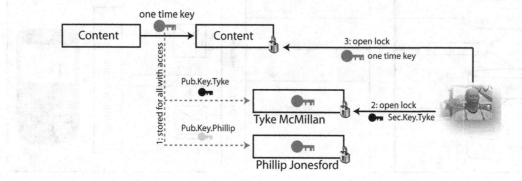

Figure 10. Protection of integrity if accessible properties are modified in uncertified environments. The approval is done by GOMS. Here, the hash codes are given for the name, content, and overall object

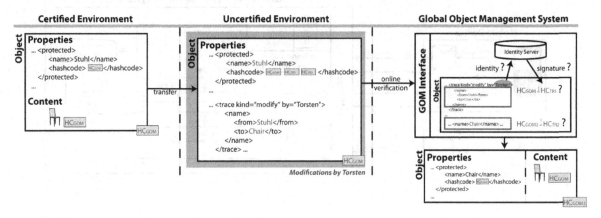

GOMS completes the online verification as well. Here, the signed hash codes (calculated and signed by the identity who did the modifications) are compared to the ones from GOMS (HC_{TR1} with HC_{GOM} and HC_{TR2} with HC_{GOM2}). If the hash codes do not match, the object is considered invalid (assuming that someone did [unauthorized] modifications). Otherwise, the modification is accepted and the object is compressed by removing hash codes and recalculating the overall object hash code once again.

Object are deemed invalid if re-calculated hash codes do not match the signed hash code in the object, or if there is a list of hash codes for any part (implying that modifications of the object were not verified; cf. Section 4.1.3) Although certified environments might be able to provide functionality for integrity verification, they cannot control limitations on the count of objects unless being connected to GOMS (cf. Section 4.1.4).

4.1.3 Transfer of Objects

Without distinguishing between copy and move, there are eight kinds of transfer in GOMS, that are either offline or online, as well as all combinations of certified and uncertified environments. As discussed previously in the chapter, transfer

between uncertified environments cannot be controlled in either connectivity mode. All that can be assured is to protect the content through encryption and rely on later GOMS verification. Transferring objects from certified to uncertified environments while being offline can be done by encrypting required parts (content), guaranteeing integrity through hash codes (mainly properties), and wrapping the object in an envelope (requiring a certificate or matching key to open the envelope again).

Figure 11 depicts the online transfer of objects from certified to other environments via GOMS. The wrapped object (1, using the private key of the environment) is transferred to GOMS (2) where it is first unwrapped (3) and checked against several criteria (4). GOMS serves as storage facility for all objects including information about their current location, quantity, and ownership. GOMS also verifies if objects are valid and have not been manipulated by unauthorized entities. Therefore, each incoming object is checked for its expected **location** (problems might result from transfers to non-certified environments), its **validity** (certified environments can invalidate objects if they are deleted or show manipulations), **integrity** (hash codes have to match the content and properties), and **quantity** (does a copy exceed the maximum

Figure 11. Process of verifying the transferred object

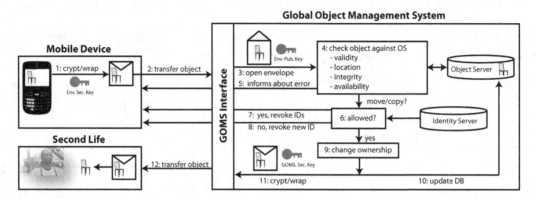

number of globally available objects). The checks also include verifying and processing the modifications still being encoded in the objects (cf. 4.1.2).

If checks fail, the transfer is cancelled and the initiating environment is informed to revoke the copied object or inform the user (5). Problems with the object are then handled by the environment itself or the object is send to GOMS for repair. If the transfer is allowed (6, the object can be copied or moved, including the privileges of involved identities), the source as well as new object id in the originating environment is revoked (7, object is invalid), otherwise the transfer is cancelled and the id of the new object is revoked (8). Having the environment revoke objects is necessary because moving and copying objects can leave objects in the cache, and the objects need to be declared as invalid (responsibility of the environment, whereas GOMS would not further issue certificates for these objects). The ownership is modified and the privileges are updated. Finally, the object is encrypted, wrapped (11), and sent to the destination environment, which could be the same as the originating one (12). In addition, the object database is updated according to the object properties and content (10). Information about the transfer is associated with the object for later traceability, with information such as environments, type of transfer, involved identities, and changed ownership.

Copied objects reference their source via the identifier in the trace; cf. also Figure 4. This ensures that the source identifier of a copied object is not removed (loss of all references). The identifier is also duplicated in the object with the second identifier being signed by GOMS as with the hash codes. As a result, GOMS is able to recognize copies and their origin. During the checks (cf. Figure 11), the trace is updated according to the signed source identifier (cf. Figure 12).

4.1.4 Uniqueness of Object Identifier and Limited Quantity

Our proposed architecture combines two philosophies: global server-based management and simultaneous self-sustaining objects. We have chosen this approach to strike a balance between handling and security. The previous sections provided an overview about security and transfer procedures, but did not discuss the concept of securing uniqueness and boundaries on limited objects. Again, the main concern is that objects can originate from uncertified environments where online-connection to GOMS is not guaranteed at all times. Therefore, new objects are considered to be invalid as long as they are not verified and approved by GOMS.

If we assume that an object is created in an uncertified system (e.g., XML-editor), it is not

Figure 12. Securing integrity of identifier and inheritance tree during copy

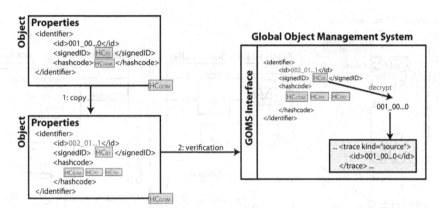

possible to define unique identifiers without contacting GOMS; thus the creator program might define its own identifier. The identifier is flagged as temporary (either by parameter or the missing signed hash code [by GOMS]) and has to be later adjusted by GOMS (e.g., using an [Web] service or importing it into a certified environment). While the object is part of GOMS, the object server keeps track of the unique identifier such that it is not re-assigned as long as the object is still used. The identifier can be re-used if objects are permanently removed.

In addition to managing the uniqueness of objects, GOMS controls limits on objects. First, the usage of objects relies on certificates (certified environments) and strict encryption of critical parts in uncertified environments. Second, the validity and integrity of objects is approved only by GOMS (by hash codes), which is also keeping track of all objects and their count. Thus, GOMS holds limits by not validating new objects or by restricting issued certificates. Let's have a look at another example: Protection against stealing. When objects leave a certified environment, they require proper protection by having them *sealed* (signed) and/or encrypted with the corresponding secret key of the owner. Protection against modification is given by hash codes while stealing is

prevented by (1) encryption and (2) the challenge of seal removal from the original owner. This is especially true if copied and passed along to someone else within uncertified environments. Here, the transfer has to be later authorized by GOMS involving authentication by both (new and old) owners.

Figure 13 depicts the verification process from a higher system level. Here, if an object is copied several times within an uncertified environment, the verification during import will either result in acceptance or rejection of the object. The verification of ownership is not shown in Figure 13, but is part of Step 3. In general, the imported object (1, 5, and 7) is first verified by GOMS (2 and 8; requiring an online connection) regarding the different criteria (3): validity, expected location (here, objects should be reported to have left a certified environments before or the last know environment is contacted to verify the transfer), integrity, ownership, and availability. The outcome of the verification results either in decrypting the object by passing a certificate to the environment (4) or rejecting the object. Most important in this context is the UUID, the ownership, the trace of the object to verify transfers, and signatures as well as hash codes (cf. our discussion in the previous sections).

Figure 13. Import of (non-approved) copies into certified environments

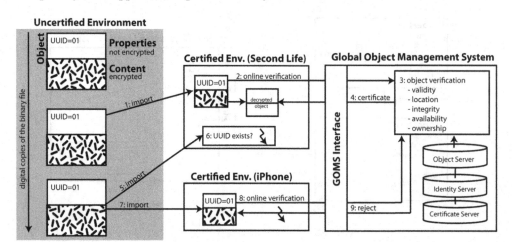

4.2 GOMS Architecture in an On-Going Research Project

GOMS is research in progress. Thus, several components exist mere as experimental prototypes rather than releasable modules. But the implementations so far demonstrate that we are pursuing a promising research stream with the architecture and able to provide a secure environment for critical projects in an emerging field. All of the previously described concepts are building blocks for GOMS, with the overall schematic illustrated in Figure 14. There are additional modules here not discussed in this chapter because they do not directly deal with object security management. These modules are primarily the filters (import, export, conversion) and the databases for building the (semantic) network of objects. The following list presents a short overview and description of the modules:

Figure 14. Modules of the Global Object Management System and currently applied test environments in the ongoing research project

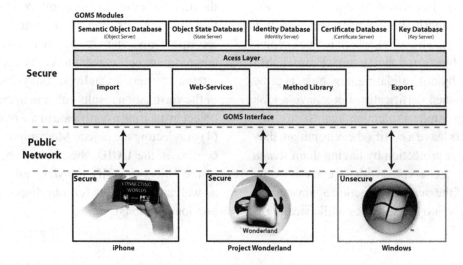

- **Environments**: We focus currently on three environments, one of which is simply the uncertified Windows file system to verify the security of objects. The others are Project Wonderland, where we have the highest degree of flexibility for experiments in virtual worlds and the IPhone with a self-developed mobile store for 3D objects. We consider the last two environments to be secure and trusted. OpenSim is a further candidate currently being considered to expand the number of environments.

- **Databases**: GOMS requires storage of objects, certificates, and identities. Here, we use different database models with respect to the stored data. The core component is the development of a **Semantic Object Database**, which does not follow the relational database model but builds networks representing the relations of the objects (cf. Aust and Till, 2009). This database stores the actual object and uses the information in the properties (and especially relations) to build a network of objects. In combination with *intelligent* import filters to analyze tags with respect to concepts (including WordNet), we are able to build automatic relations and increase the value of the network (cf. Boese, 2010). Other databases we use are the **Object State Database** (information about identifier, validity, location, and ownership), the **Identity Database** (information about all entities including groups), the **Certificate Database**, and **Key Server**. The object and object state databases are separated for performance reasons, whereas the second one contains operative data for repetitive request, while the first is rather seen as a data warehouse and advanced requests. Note that we consider database and server to be synonymous as the databases include technology to access them via network and

to process requests in a more advanced way than just returning the results.

- **Export and Import**: Controlling all incoming objects and requests including the described verification on validity (cf. Section 4.1.3) and converting (if possible) of objects during export to a specific environment. Here, it might be important to emphasize again, that compatibility in multi-environments is as problematic as security. We use an object model, where the multitude is encompassed but limits still exist especially with respect to functionality. If conversion is not possible, export might be denied. The filtering and conversion process is not further described here as this is only of minor relevance for security.

- **Web-Services**: Most of the functionality should be accessible by other applications in their simplest form. Precisely, GOMS provides services to verify the validity and integrity of objects, to retrieve objects from the (semantic) network, convert objects, and other functions.

- **Interfaces**: Communication to environments and applications is established through the GOMS Interface (also responsible for establishing a secure communication channel). The databases are accessed via an Access Layer controlling requests for data; if more than one database is involved.

The above modules were not discussed in this chapter as they do not immediately apply to object security. Although they are critical for smooth GOMS operation, they are not application here. Additional discussions of the GOMS architecture as it relates to object security within e-learning (Reiners et al., 2005; Reiners & Suhl, 2007) are available. With respect to our ongoing research, we are currently implementing the next version of the encryption model for a larger experimental setting. We do want to note that an initial experiment using the iPhone produced promising results that confirm the malleability and functionality of the GOMS architecture to adapt to various media while controlling the flow of objects. More about the GOMS architecture and our research is available at our website (http://www.virtual-object-security.org).

5 CONCLUSION

Based on the Gartner Hype Cycle, (public) virtual worlds are far beyond their *peak of inflated expectations* and expected to reach the *slope of enlightenment* within the next years with some fields like education already well beyond this point. During the gold-rush atmosphere the speed of development resulted in numerous virtual environments and uncountable amounts of objects with little concern about security for the objects, but finding (economical) applications. However, it seems that with the revival of 3D entertainment and the shift to a 3D Web, where virtual worlds and Web 2.0 define the common denominator, it is more or less a matter of time. Add to this the importance of security not only of the environment and avatar (through authentication) but also the objects, which are the essential building blocks for a dynamic and living environment.

In this chapter, we proposed a different approach for encoding virtual objects following the object oriented programming paradigm. All information is stored within the object, such as privileges for access and behavior functionality. We illustrated contemporary approaches, such as in Second Life to demonstrate the comprehensiveness of current and coming applications, always keeping in mind the need of object security and exchange between different environments. In addition, we sketched our GOMS architecture consisting of trusted environments and interconnected servers to guarantee object security. We picked major processes to demonstrate the

object handling with transfer, integrity, and availability. Key components of GOMS are the encryption, usage of hash codes, and wrapping in sealed envelopes requiring certificates to be opened again. This approach follows accepted security standards currently used in digital right management implemented, with arguable success, in the entertainment sector. We are aware that our approach involves obstacles and should be used with care in real-life scenarios. Nevertheless, security for objects must happen in various contexts so that an overlay of encryption and trusted environments is accepted as standard procedure rather than the alternative of unauthorized copies or access.

GOMS is ongoing research and its implementation in process. Select components exist and function well. This encourages us to continue on our path. The demand for security exists and we propose our solution to redefine the object and its handling. Coming from an educational background, we are concerned with (maybe minor) cases from creating objects in classroom or exams up to innovative product development in distributed virtual teams, where, for example, prototypes of new engine concepts (in form of 3D objects) are exchanged via the Internet and could be illegally acquired. However, in business, a breach of object security would be more dire. The loss of intellectual property or trade secrets could cause an economic catastrophe if the invention becomes public before securing, e.g., patents. GOMS is a systematic approach to guard against this occurring so that organizations can innovate in virtual realms knowing that intellectual property encapsulated in objects will be protected by the very system they use to create objects.

6 ADDITIONAL READING

Numerous publications and research streams cover watermarking, encryption, and signatures, but almost none focus on 3D object security in multi-environments. More needs to be done on how we can guarantee that objects are unique or limited to a certain count. We mentioned and used various technologies, which are important for the global object management system but beyond the scope of the paper. We suggest the following sources as a starting point to dive deeper into the subject (of which some were already cited in the chapter): Encryption in general (Ferguson et al., 2010; Schneier, 2007; Furht et al., 2005), Pretty Good Privacy (PGP; Garfinkel, S.), network security (Cole, 2009; Ciampa, 2009), Digital Right Management (Torres Padrosa, 2009; Zeng et al., 2006), digital watermarking (Eshraghi & Samavati,, 2007; Ho et al., 2009; Cox et al., 2007).

Virtual worlds go e-learning. The major application for virtual worlds is education, i.e. distance/blended learning or classes requiring a certain amount of travel (geography, analyzing different cultures), bringing alive history (visiting sites, rebuilding the past), visualize scientific experiments (physical settings for gravity, teaching astronomy), or interacting in role plays (theatre, discussions, psychology). The number of papers is endless; some examples (among our very own publications) are Dreher et al. (2009a), Dreher et al. (2009b), Reiners et al. (2009), Gregory et al. (2009), Daniels Lee (2009), and Jäger & Helgheim (2009)). But virtual worlds spread to almost every field, some resources (without referencing further individual publications) are the Journal of Virtual Worlds Research (http://jvwresearch.org), Virtual Worlds News (http://www.virtualworldsnews. com), the reports from KZero (http://www.kzero. co.uk), and the blogs of and about virtual worlds or their (e.g., Second Life at http://blogs.secondlife.com and http://nwn.blogs.com). For new ideas, even novels can provide some background (Stephenson, 1994). Last, we should have a short look at virtual worlds and their objects. Especially, as virtual objects are getting valuable and sell for over $330.000 USD (Jones, 2010); see also Muttik (2008), Sastry (2007), and Lee (2009).

7 REFERENCES

Aust, T., & Sarnow, M. (2009). *Entwurf und Implementierung einer Medien-Datenbank-Middleware mit integrierten Semantischen Netzen* (engl.: Design and Implementation of a Media-Database-Middleware with Integrated Semantic Networks). Diploma Thesis.

Baca, M. (2008). *Introduction to Metadata*. Getty Research Institute.

Berners-Lee, T., Fielding, R., & Masinter, L. (2005). *Uniform Resource Identifier (URI): Generic Syntax*. Retrieved May 15, 2010, from http://tools.ietf.org/html/rfc3986

Blizzard Entertainment. (2010). *World of Warcraft Community Site*. Retrieved May 15, 2010, from http://www.worldofwarcraft.com

Boese, S. (2010). *Entwicklung und Umsetzung einer konzeptualisierten Speicherung von Dokumenten in einer semantischen Datenbank* (engl.: Development and Implementation of a Conceptualized Storage of Documents in a Semantic Database). Diploma Thesis.

Castronova, E. (2003). *The Price of 'Man' and 'Woman': A Hedonic Pricing Model of Avatar Attributes in a Synthethic World*. CESifo Working Paper Series No. 957. Retrieved May 15, 2010, from http://ssrn.com/abstract=415043

Ciampa, M. (2009). *Security+ Guide to Network Security Fundamentals*. Course Technology.

Cole, E. (2009). *Network Security Bible* (2nd ed.). Chichester, UK: Wiley.

COLLADA. (2010). *COLLADA: Digital Asset and FX Exchange Schema*. Retrieved May 15, 2010, from http://collada.org

Cox, I., Miller, M., Bloom, J., Fridrich, J., & Kalker, T. (2007). *Digital Watermarking and Steganography* (2nd ed.). San Francisco: Morgan Kaufmann.

Daniels Lee, P. (2009). Using Second Life to Teach Operations Management. *Journal of Virtual Worlds Research, 2*(1), 3–15.

Dreher, C., Reiners, T., Dreher, N., & Dreher, H. (2009a). 3D Virtual Worlds as Collaborative Communities Enriching Human Endeavours: Innovative Applications in e-Learning. In *Proceedings of IEEE DEST, TD-001252* (2009).

Dreher, C., Reiners, T., Dreher, N., & Dreher, H. (2009b). Virtual Worlds as a Context Suited for Information Systems Education: Discussion of Pedagogical Experience and Curriculum Design With Reference to Second Life. *Journal of Information Systems Education, Special Issue, 20*(2), 211–224.

Ducheneaut, N., Wen, M., Yee, N., & Wadley, G. (2009). Body and mind: A study of avatar personalization in three virtual worlds. In *27th Annual CHI Conference on Human Factors in Computing Systems (CHI 2009)*, April 4-9; Boston, MA.

Erlenkötter, A., Kühnlenz, C.-M., Miu, H.-R., Sommer, F., & Reiners, T. (2008). Enhancing the class curriculum with virtual world use cases for production and logistics. In *Proceedings of E-Learn 2008: World Conference on E-Learning in Corporate, Government, Healthcare, & Higher Education,* Las Vegas, (pp. 789–798).

Eshraghi, M., & Samavati, F. F. (2007). 3D watermarking robust to accessible attacks. In *Proceedings of the First International Conference on Immersive Telecommunications* (Bussolengo, Verona, Italy, October 10 - 12, 2007). Brussels, Belgium: ICST (Institute for Computer Sciences Social-Informatics and Telecommunications Engineering).

Ferguson, N., Schneier, B., & Kohno, T. (2010). *Cryptography Engineering: Design Principles and Practical Applications*. Chichester, UK: Wiley.

Furht, B., Muharemaqic, E., & Socek, D. (2005). *Multimedia Encryption and Watermarking*. Berlin: Springer.

Garfinkel, S. (1994). *PGP: Pretty Good Privacy*. Sebastopol, CA: O Reillly.

Google Code Labs. (2010). *O3D API: Google Code*. Retrieved May 15, 2010, from http://code.google.com/apis/o3d

Gregory, S., Reiners, T., & Tynan, B. (2009). Alternative realities: Immersive learning for and with students. In Song, H. (Ed.), *Distance Learning Technology, Current Instruction, and the Future of Education: Applications of Today, Practices of Tomorrow* (pp. 245–272). Hershey, PA: IGI Global.

Gütl, C., Chang, V., Kopeinik, S., & Williams, R. (2009). 3D Virtual Worlds as a Tool for Collaborative Learning Settings in Geographically Dispersed Environments. In *Conference ICL2009*, September 23 -25, Villach, Austria

Habbo Hotel. (2010). *Habbo Hotel US: Make friends, join the fun, get noticed!* Retrieved May 15, 2010, from http://www.habbo.com

Haenni, R., & Jonczy, J. (2007). A New Approach to PGP's Web of Trust. In *EEMA '07, European e-Identity Conference*. Retrieved May 15, 2010, from www.iam.unibe.ch/~run/download.php?pdf=HJ07

Ho, A. T. S., Shi, Y. Q., Kim, H. J., & Barni, M. (2009). *Digital Watermarking: 8th International Workshop, IWDW 2009*, Guildford, UK, August 24-26, 2009, (LNCS on Security and Cryptology, 5703). Berlin: Springer.

Horowitz, S. J. (2007). Competing Lockean Claims to Virtual Property. *Harvard Journal of Law & Technology, 20*(2), 443–458.

Hurliman, J. (2009). *Approaching Virtual World Interoperability*. Retrieved May 15, 2010, from http://software.intel.com/en-us/blogs/2009/02/18/approaching-virtual-world-interoperability

International, D. O. I. Foundation. (2010). *The Digital Object Identifier System*. Retrieved May 15, 2010, from http://www.doi.org

Jäger, B., & Helgheim, B. (2009). Role Play study in a Purchase Management class. In Molka-Danielsen & Deutschmann, M. (Eds.), *Learning and Teaching in the Virtual World of Second Life*. Trondheim, Norway: Tapir Academic Press.

Jones, R. (2010). New Record for most expensive virtual object – $300,000USD. *MetaSecurity: Security of Virtual Worlds*. Retrieved May 15, 2010, from http://metasecurity.net/2010/01/05/new-record-for-most-expensive-virtual-object-300000usd

June, L. (2009). *Amazon remotely deletes Orwell e-books from Kindles, unpersons reportedly unhappy (update)*. Retrieved May 15, 2010, from http://www.engadget.com/2009/07/17/amazon-remotely-deletes-orwell-e-books-from-kindles-unpersons-r

Kabus, P. (2009). *A Network-Agnostic and Cheat-Resistant Framework for Multiplayer Online Games*. Ph.D. Thesis, Technical University of Darmstadt, Germany.

Korolov, M. (2010). *Laid off Wonderland developers to continue project*. Retrieved May 15, 2010, from http://www.hypergridbusiness.com/2010/02/laid-off-wonderland-developers-to-continue-project

KZero. (2009). *Q4 2009 Universe chart: Teens and Adults*. Retrieved May 15, 2010, from http://www.kzero.co.uk/blog/?p=3976

Leach, P., Mealling, M., & Salz, R. (2005). *A Universal Unique Identifier (UUID) URN Namespace*. Retrieved May 15, 2010, from http://www.ietf.org/rfc/rfc4122.txt

Lee, C.Y. (2009). Understanding Security Threats in Virtual Worlds. *AMCIS 2009 Proceedings*. Paper 466.

Linden Lab. (2008). *Open Grid Public Beta begins today*. Retrieved May 15, 2010, from http://blogs.secondlife.com/community/features/blog/2008/07/31/open-grid-public-beta-begins-today

Linden Lab. (2009a). *Extend SL: Open Opportunities for Virtual Worlds*. Retrieved May 15, 2010, from http://develop.secondlife.com/extend-sl/open-grid-protocol

Linden Lab. (2009b). *Next-owner permissions FAQ*. Retrieved May 15, 2010, from http://wiki.secondlife.com/wiki/Next-owner_permissions_FAQ

Linden Lab. (2009c). *Linden Lab Official: About CopyBot, similar tools, and the Terms of Service*. Retrieved May 15, 2010, from http://wiki.secondlife.com/wiki/Linden_Lab_Official:About_CopyBot,_similar_tools,_and_the_Terms_of_Service

Linden Lab. (2010a). *LSL Portal: Second Life WiKi*. Retrieved May 15, 2010, from http://wiki.secondlife.com/wiki/LSL_Portal

Linden Lab. (2010b). *UUID: Second Life Wiki*. Retrieved May 15, 2010, from http://wiki.secondlife.com/wiki/UUID

Linden Lab. (2010c). *Introducing the Second Life Enterprise Beta: Second Life Lives Behind-the-Firewall*. Retrieved May 15, 2010, from http://work.secondlife.com/en-US/products/server

Linden Lab. (2010d). *Linden Lab: Makers of Second Life*. Retrieved May 15, 2010, from http://lindenlab.com

Muttig, I. (2008). *McAffee*. Retrieved May 15, 2010, from http://www.mcafee.com/us/local_content/white_papers/threat_center/wp_online_gaming.pdf+virtual+world+object+security

Novak, T. P. (2010). *eLab City: A Platform for Academic Research on Virtual Worlds*. Retrieved May 15, 2010, from http://elabresearch.ucr.edu/blog/uploads/publications/Novak_2010_JVWR.pdf. Submitted to Journal of Virtual Worlds Research Open Wonderland (2010). *Open Wonderland*. Retrieved May 15, 2010, from http://openwonderland.org.

OpenSimulator. (2010a). *Main Page: OpenSim*. Retrieved May 15, 2010, from http://opensimulator.org

OpenSimulator. (2010b). *The OpenSim Hypergrid*. Retrieved May 15, 2010, from http://opensimulator.org/wiki/Hypergrid

OpenSimulator. (2010c). *Scripting Languages: OpenSim*. Retrieved May 15, 2010, from http://opensimulator.org/wiki/Scripting_Languages

OpenTrust. (2010). *Trusted Networks*. Retrieved May 15, 2010, from http://www.opentrust.com/en/market/trusted-networks

Oracle (2010). *Project Wonderland: Go ahead, make a scene*. Retrieved May 15, 2010, from http://labs.oracle.com/spotlight/2008/2008-08-19_project_wonderland.html

Reiners, T., Dreher, C., Büttner, S., Naumann, M., & Visser, L. (2009). Connecting Students by Integrating the 3D Virtual and Real Worlds: We Need 3D Open Source Spaces to Keep Socialization, Communication and Collaboration alive. In T. Bastiaens et al. (Eds.), *Proceedings of World Conference on E-Learning in Corporate, Government, Healthcare, and Higher Education 2009* (pp. 3125-3126). Chesapeake, VA: AACE.

Reiners, T., Sassen, I., & Reiß, D. (2005). Ontology-based Retrieval, Authoring, and Networking. In G. Richards (Ed.), *Proceedings of World Conference on E-Learning in Corporate, Government, Healthcare, and Higher Education 2005*, (pp. 2349—2354). Chesapeake, VA: AACE.

Reiners, T., & Suhl, L. (2007*). eMANGO: eContentplus EU-Proposal*. Working Paper. University of Hamburg.

Retha, A. (2008). *Notes on Wonderland Cells on the Client and Server*. Retrieved May 15, 2010, from https://elgg.leeds.ac.uk/bms4a2r/weblog/11190.html

Sastry, A. (2008). Security in Virtual Worlds: Blurring the Borders. *Technewsworld*. Retrieved May 15, 2010, from http://www.technewsworld.com/rsstory/59399.html?wlc=1275089297

Scheffler, M., Springer, J. P., & Froehlich, B. (2008). Object-Capability Security in Virtual Environments. *Virtual Reality Conference, IEEE VR '08*, (pp. 51—58). DOI: 10.1109/VR.2008.4480750.

Schneier, B. (2007). *Schneier's Cryptography Classics Library: Applied Cryptography, Secrets and Lies, and Practical Cryptography*. Chichester, UK: Wiley.

Sequeira, L. (2009). *Mechanism of three-dimensional content transfer between the OpenSimulator and Second Life grid*. Master Thesis, Universidade de Trás-os-Montes e Alto Douro.

Slusallek, P. (2010). *XML3D*. Retrieved May 15, 2010, from http://www.xml3d.com

Stephenson, N. (1994). *Snow Crash*. New York: Penguin.

Techtopia. (2009). *Security + Essentials*. Retrieved May 15, 2010, from http://www.techotopia.com/index.php/Security%2B_Essentials

Torres Padrosa, V. (2009). *A DRM Architecture Based on Open Standards: Contribution to an Architecture for Multimedia Information Management and Protection Based on Open Standards.* Berlin: VDM Verlag Dr. Müller.

Trusted Computing Group. (2010). *Home of TCG.* Retrieved May 15, 2010, from http://www.trustedcomputinggroup.org

Vielhauer, C. (2005). *Biometric User Authentication for IT Security: From Fundamentals to Handwriting.* Berlin: Springer.

Vilela, A., Cardoso, M., Martins, D., Santos, A., Moreira, L., Paredes, H., et al. (2010). Privacy challenges and methods for virtual classrooms in Second Life Grid and OpenSimulator. In *2010 Second International Conference on Games and Virtual Worlds for Serious Applications*, (pp. 167—174).

Virtual Worlds Review. (2010). *Virtual Worlds Review.* Retrieved May 15, 2010, from http://www.virtualworldsreview.com/info/categories.shtml

von Lohmann, F. (2010). *All Your Apps Are Belong to Apple: The iPhone Developer Program License Agreement.* Retrieved May 15, 2010, from http://www.eff.org/deeplinks/2010/03/iphone-developer-program-license-agreement-all

Watte, J., & Systems, F. (2009). Virtual World Interoperability: Let Use Cases Drive Design. *Journal of Virtual Worlds Research, 2*(3), 3—13. Retrieved May 15, 2010, from https://journals.tdl.org/jvwr/article/view/727/526

Web 3D Consortium (2010). *X3D for Developers.* Retrieved May 15, 2010, from http://www.web3d.org/x3d

Wikipedia (2010). *Metadata Standards.* Retrieved May 15, 2010, from http://en.wikipedia.org/wiki/Metadata_standards

Winkler, S. E. (2010). Licensing Considerations for OpenSim-Based Virtual Worlds. *Journal of Virtual Worlds Research, 2*(4), 3—16. Retrieved May 15, 2010, from http://journals.tdl.org/jvwr/article/view/871/636

Wright, T. E., & Madey, G. (2008). *Discretionary Access Controls for a Collaborative Virtual Environment.* Technical Report. Retrieved May 15, 2010, from http://www.cse.nd.edu/Reports/2008/TR-2008-12.pdf

Wright, T. E., & Madey, G. (2008). *WonderDAC: An Implementation of Discretionary Access Controls within the Project Wonderland CVE.* Technical Report. Retrieved May 15, 2010, from http://www.cse.nd.edu/Reports/2008/TR-2008-15.pdf

Wright, T. E., & Madey, G. (2008). Discretionary Access Controls for a Collaborative Virtual Environment. *The International Journal of Virtual Reality, 9*(1), 61–71.

Zeng, W., Yu, H., & Lin, C.-Y. (2006). *Multimedia Security Technologies for Digital Rights Management.* New York: Academic Press.

Chapter 10
X3D:
A Secure ISO Standard for Virtual Worlds

Joerg H. Kloss
X3D Consultant and Expert, Germany

Peter Schickel
Bitmanagement Software GmbH, Germany & Web3D Consortium, Germany

ABSTRACT

This chapter discusses the topic security in standard based virtual worlds with emphasis on X3D as the international ISO/IEC standard for Virtual Worlds. The general security challenges in persistent and economic virtual environments are addressed as well as the importance of standardization and security as the two key success factors for reliable, cost-effective and long-term attractive Virtual World (VW) platforms. Different actual standardization approaches are compared to the established X3D format that follows a clear security standardization path. Based on the Internet standard XML the specific advantages of X3D are emphasized, such as seamless integration into Web applications and deployment of generic XML tools. The generation of encrypted and signed X3D binary files is demonstrated according to the XML Security Recommendation of the W3C consortium. In a practical session the appliance of security approaches to concrete X3D implementation projects is described from the perspective of Bitmanagement, a market leader for interactive Web3D graphics software.

INTRODUCTION

X3D is a powerful description language and open data format for high-end real-time 3D graphics, animation and interaction dedicated to Web-based and other professional 3D applications. It is an international ISO/IEC standard, designed and maintained by the Web3D consortium, with origins

in the VRML standard, and widely-used within different scopes, like e.g. scientific visualization, virtual and augmented reality, geographical information systems and Virtual Worlds. Due to its specific characteristics as a human readable web description language like XHTML, the Web standard X3D offers similar advantages, but is confronted with challenges like security. In consequence the current specification for HTML 5 states that embedding 3D imagery into XHTML

DOI: 10.4018/978-1-61520-891-3.ch010

documents is the domain of X3D, or technologies based on X3D that are namespace-aware (W3C, 2009).

If it comes to the question of security in X3D-based Web applications and VW's there are many issues similar to those with other VW technologies and approaches, some that are related to the general discussion of the World Wide Web Consortium (W3C) standards, and some others that are quite specific to X3D itself. Further on there are individual security solutions developed by companies working with X3D day-to-day. This chapter will shortly address some of these different aspects, but will focus on the X3D specific approaches and will present a concrete example of the security solution applied by the 3D viewing technology company Bitmanagement. The reader gets an approximate overview about security aspects in VW's, becomes acquainted to the specific approaches in X3D, and finally learns how security is applied to real-world X3D applications today.

BACKGROUND

The question of security in VW's is manifold. This is even more comprehensive when it comes to persistent VW's that include economic systems with virtual currencies, which are connected to real-world markets and money. And it applies likewise to massively multiplayer online games (MMOGs), social as well as corporate worlds. With the rise in success, members, virtual goods and economical power of a VW, also the potential for misuse and attacks increases. The list of possible risks is long and in no case complete: avatar identity fraud, theft of virtual and intellectual properties, disclosure of private data, cheating in trading and by illegal object duplication, harassments and threats to minors, vulnerabilities to platforms by spam and denial of service (DoS) attacks and so on.

Most of these challenges are not even fully captured yet, and cannot be solved just technically.

Furthermore, many VW's are based on closed systems with individual architectures as well as proprietary data formats, which makes it even harder to define, apply, and establish a general security approach of trust.

INDUSTRY STANDARDS AND PROPRIETARY TECHNOLOGY

However, with a reliable, independent, and transparent standard, investments into VW's could become more 'secure' also from an economical point of view. To overcome the prevailing multitude of proprietary technologies and privately held platforms, different standardization approaches are currently under development (Behr, 2009).

SUN Darkstar

A popular virtual worlds server is provided by the Darkstar project from SUN (SUN, 2009). In a strategic whitepaper SUN confirms that due to major technical differences of virtual worlds platforms open standards are needed in this domain and states that X3D is one possible solution here (SUN, 2008).

Google O3D

With a focus on 3D Web graphics Google released their proprietary browser plug-in "O3D" (Google, 2009b). Their target audience are JavaScript programmers who need the flexibility of a low level graphics API. However it does not provide a method to define the content in a declarative way. Application developers have to use JavaScript code to manipulate the behavior of their content, which is considered slow, because it needs to be interpreted at runtime. With regards to security there is no specific encryption path foreseen as all parts of the application logic and behavior have to be entirely programmed in JavaScript.

Khronos WebGL

The Khronus consortium and Mozilla are working on a interface for "Accelerated 3D on the Web" (Khronos, 2009), called WebGL. It is a JavaScript binding to OpenGL ES 2.0 for Rich 3D Graphics, that is likely to be supported soon in Browsers such as Google Chrome, Mozilla and Opera. As it is based on Javascipt as well it is bound to the same drawbacks in terms of performance and encryption.

OpenSim and Second Life

Following the proprietary Second Life architecture the OpenSource server "OpenSIM" offers compatibility between OpenGrids, and also a limited form of teleporting (Opensimulator, 2009). As the software is still in its infancy (alpha version) further topics such as encryption and security have probably not been addressed yet.

MPEG-4 and MPEG-V

The Metaverse group of the Motion Picture Experts Group (MPEG, 2009) suggests a rough draft for a "MPEG-V" standard that also tries to cover miscellaneous interfaces between the virtual and the physical world. MPEG-4 already incorporates X3D since 2004. the abstract specification for X3D(ISO/IEC 19775) was first approved by ISO. Later in 2005 the XML and classic encoding was approved.

Flash and PaperVision

Adobe flash (Adobe, 2009) is a very popular proprietary multimedia platform. In the latest flash version 10 simple 3D transformation and objects can be viewed, especially for the purpose of graphical user interface design. However it is possible to produce astonishing 3D effects with the help of the papervision project PaperVisionX.

Silverlight

Microsoft Silverlight (Microsoft, 2009) is a proprietary web browser plugin that enables features such as animation, vector graphics and audio-video playback similar to flash. So far the 3D graphics support is very limited.

IBM and the Emerging 3D Internet

IBM recently is investigating the emergence of the 3-D Internet with the main aim to help their employees work together in a better way. Sametime3D is one of their research lab projects for exploring new ways of collaboration with virtual worlds. It is partially based on IBM's Lotus and Linden Lab's Second Life technology. IBM internally uses virtual worlds to conduct research, host events, and to acclimate new employees (IBM, 2009). A similar approach to provide 3D meetings and conferencing tools is done by the California based company Integrated Virtual Networks (IVN), that is creating IP for live video avatar communication in virtual worlds (IVN, 2009).

Nevertheless, all of these approaches are still far away from international accepted standards, and therefore offer only a weak basis for decisions about long-term investments into VW's. Moreover the current endeavors for standardization are focused on elementary requirements, like interoperability between VW's, compatibility of 3D assets and teleporting of avatars. Advanced topics like seamless integration into existing Web environments, efficient conversion and reutilization of existing 3D models, as well as security of 3D applications are usually not in the focus of those discussions, yet.

THE ISO STANDARD X3D AND ITS HISTORY

The X3D standard can be used for a variety of secure 3D applications as it features also interactive functionality. Therefore it is not only a 3D format, in addition it is a programming language that provides an event mechanism called "routing". Here events can be passed from sensors (e.g. a proximity sensor that measures the proximity of a pilot avatar to an object) via routes to the event-in interface of a leaf in the scene graph. If a event is received here it dynamically changes the scene graph at the time of the next drawing cycle. So many interactive scenarios can be programmed that are especially important for the interaction of avatars in VWs. This fact distinguishes X3D from other pure 3D data storage formats. Many larger companies put a lot of emphasis to this fact and are not even allowed to use any other format than an ISO standard by company regulations as it is important to them that the software is running for many years in a reliable way. Especially, if you are looking for a robust 3D technology this is a big plus for a company decision. Also it is possible to express every X3D file in the VRML notation - a human readable format called X3D classic encoding. This notation helps a lot in understanding the source tree for a 3D world. Any engineer can understand the underlying structure of the 3D world and can therefore follow and even change the functionality of the world. This is not possible in a closed system where the content author has to rely on authoring tools only. Usually such proprietary systems offer merely limited functionality to manipulate and change the 3D scene graph. In addition in X3D three dimensional single objects can be described as well as interactive virtual worlds.

The technology necessary for virtual worlds has been standardized with a consortium of talented experts for more than a decade. We will see the history of the X3D standard in the following lines in order to understand the evolution of a standard. Within this evolution process nearly all requirements for virtual worlds and interaction have been covered, so that a very valuable technical toolbox can be found for the modern author of virtual worlds. At the start of the stan-

dardization process back in 1994 some bright minds gathered at various companies inspired by the novel "Snowcrash" published in 1992 in order to invent virtual worlds. In this fiction a parallel world with the interaction of computer generated avatars has been described that can be related to the modern virtual worlds of today in use. The idea of a universal standard for virtual worlds and common interactivity emerged and was undertaken soon after in a concerted effort.

After various discussions the Virtual Reality Modeling Language (VRML 1.0) was introduced in 1994 as an extension of the Inventor format. This format was developed by the American company Silicon Graphics Incorporated that was occupied solely with the development of computer graphics and visualization software. In this first version already extensions of the Inventor file format such as Web Links for the Internet as well as viewpoints were present. The second version (VRML 2.0) has become official ISO standard (ISO 14772) in December 1997 and was therefore called VRML97 according to the naming conventions popular at that time. In this specification many kinds of interactivity components were introduced, e.g. scripting using JavaScript (called VRML Script) and the concept of sensors. Sensors are used to scan the 3D virtual world to detect avatars within a specific distance. In this case, an event is fired which triggers, e.g. a door opening. Also the rigid scene graph structure was reworked and augmented with the concept of nodes. Also for the first time the combination of films in the motion picture experts group (MPEG) format was presented. This standardized functionality combined with audio and video was a breakthrough in the computer graphics community at that time.

The development of the standard was continuously followed and updated until today. A more detailed timeline can be found at www.web3d. org/examples/timeline/timeline.html. With the advent of XML and the emerging advantages for server based communication and distribution of 3D worlds the standard was renamed to X3D in

2004. In this new version different profiles have been introduced in order to respect the capabilities of low footprint devices, such as cell phones and PDAs. Also today the development goes on in various working groups of experts; in particular subjects such as Medicine, geographical information systems, and human animation for e.g. avatars.

CURRENT CHALLENGES AND SOLUTION APPROACHES

The lack of standards has been identified as one of the major challenges for today's VW market. Although the number of VW's is growing steadily, the pure quantity of inhomogeneous game, social and business worlds makes it visibly harder for investors to decide for the 'right' VW. As long as new VW's are emerging frequently, experience their short-term hype, bob up and down with numbers of concurrent users and actual usage, and finally perish unnoticed again, it is still a financial risk for companies to invest too much and too early into experiments with VW's. This is especially true in times of global recession, although VW's could save costs for travel, training, and collaboration for affected companies.

By contrast, the international ISO/IEC standard X3D is available already today, designed and maintained by the international Web3D consortium, with origins in the VRML standard, widely used within different application fields and supported by professional 3D tools since many years. With its basis on XML, the description language and the open data format X3D is fully compatible to the Web standards of the World Wide Web Consortium (W3C) and therefore integrates seamlessly into 3D Internet and Web 2.0 / 3.0 approaches. Thus VW's built with X3D are not only interoperable with each other per se, but also with other current and future XML-based applications of the WWW.

The Recommendations of the W3C are highly trusted and are the building blocks of today's Internet and World Wide Web. Besides the many

advantages of seamless integration into Web applications, the basis of XML also allows the deployment of generic tools and concepts to X3D. Therefore the W3C Security Recommendations for XML are also applicable to X3D files. They contain specifications for signature, encryption and key management as well as for canonicalization (C14N) of XML documents. As a result of the joint working group of W3C and IETF the specification of XML digital signatures offers services for integrity, message authentication and signer authentication. In a combination of the specified services, XML-based files can be canonicalized, signed and encrypted, which provides a state-of-the-art security approach in Web-based communication also for X3D.

The appliance of the W3C Security Recommendations to X3D-based VW's is closely interrelated with the binary encoding of X3D files. Besides the human readable text format of X3D as a XML language with the file extension ".x3d" according to ISO/IEC 19776-1, there are two additional data formats available for X3D files. Alternatively X3D files can be encoded in ClassicVRML with the file extension ".x3dv" according to ISO/IEC 19776-2 that provides all of the nodes and functionalities of the X3D specification in the traditional syntax of the X3D predecessor VRML97. Both file formats can be encoded as Binary X3D files with the extension ".x3db" according to ISO/IEC 19776-3.

While the binary encoding of X3D files tends to reduce the file size and thus the load times for VW's as well as prepares them for streaming approaches, it otherwise provides already more security than the X3D files in plain text per se. Binary X3D files that are downloaded from an Internet server by a X3D viewer client can still be rendered indeed, but the source code of the 3D scenery is not visible anymore and can not be simply copied, edited or altered with a text editor. From that point of view the binary encoding of X3D-based VW's offers almost a similar level of security like other non-standardized proprietary

VW implementations. Hence binary encoded X3D files help to guard intellectual property rights, avoiding illegal object duplications and to protect investments for the modeling of elaborated 3D models and interactive VW sceneries.

However, the Security approach of X3D goes far beyond just binary file encoding (Williams 2009). According to ISO/IEC 19776-3 the complete process for binary encoding of X3D files is composed of up to six successive steps, including conversion, canonicalization, encryption, signing, and compression. All of these central steps follow the recommendations of the W3C for the common handling of XML-based data and thus are also applicable to X3D files. Correspondingly also the available XML tools - like XSLT style sheets for transformations from one file format to another - can be used for each of the consecutive X3D processing steps. In detail the following methods can be applied to an original plain text file in order to generate a properly compressed and secured X3D file that fulfills the advanced requirements of the W3C and Web3D consortium for state-of-the-art Security in Internet applications.

1. **Original file:** A 3D scene graph is described in an arbitrary X3D plain text format (e.g.. x3dv,.wrl) other than XML (.x3d).
2. **Conversion:** The scene graph is transformed (e.g. by applying a XSLT stylesheet) to the XML encoded format (.x3d) according to ISO/IEC 19776-1.
3. **Canonicalization:** The XML encoded source code is optimized, and redundancies are eliminated according to the W3C Exclusive XML Canonicalization Recommendation.
4. **Security:** Based on the XML Security approach the XML code is optionally encrypted (according to the W3C XML encryption recommendation), and signed with a digital signature (according to the W3C XML signature recommendation).
5. **XML Compression:** The XML code is compressed with the Fast Infoset algorithm according to ISO/IEC 24824-1 and results into a binary X3D file (.x3db).
6. **GZIP Compression:** The binary X3D file is optionally compressed supplementary with the GZIP algorithm according to IETF RFC 1952 and results into a compressed X3D file (.x3d.gz).

All of the methods named and described above are based on international accepted standards and approaches according to ISO/IEC, W3C Recommendations and IETF RFC. The X3D security page gives detailed examples about the usage of the methods above (X3D Security, 2009).

The institutions behind the W3C are representing the most reliable and reputable instances of today's Internet and Web society and infrastructure. They are providing an outstanding grade of transparency, independency, durability, stability and potential for broadest acceptance that usually cannot be reached by any proprietary platform of privately held operators. The standards are open, generally not owned by companies with individual commercial interests, and can be used without the risk of costs for expensive royalties.

These criteria should be taken into consideration while evaluating the most appropriate platform for a projected 3D application. In the long run standards are the most reliable basement for web applications. And this is exceptionally true with regard to the different aspects of Security in persistent multi-user VW's linked to real-world economic systems. Besides also pure business environments like Intraworlds and Extraworlds with highly confidential content can benefit from applying common and proven Intranet and Extranet methods also to virtual meeting, sales, training or collaboration worlds. Business in 3D will be much easier based on XML encoded files ensuring authenticity, integrity and confidentiality. And it will be much more comfortable to exchange or embed other XML based data within X3D-based VW's without any transformation in proprietary formats back and forth. Finally customers will trust much more into virtual business if it occurs in familiar network environments guarded by firewalls and other established security mechanisms.

It should not be concealed that standardization is more a long-term business than a quick win. The development of a stable and reliable standard takes time, but the applications based on a standard have a much better chance to be supported for many years and from many systems. Sometimes special high-performance features are developed much faster and easier for a dedicated proprietary platform, especially in the very dynamic field of 3D graphics. But if a VW relies on such special features, and the dedicated platform runs off some day for various reasons, probably also the VW has its close-down. If the VW, a virtual region or some complex assets have been modeled with a proprietary in-world tool then, the chance to save and export the complete interactive 3D inventory to another platform will also be low. So in most cases it pays off in the long-run to take the time to first develop a standard and then to build VW's based on it.

X3D is a technically mature and well-engineered standard for 3D applications and VW's for many years now. From its initial development as VRML 1.0 in 1994 it had plenty of time to become optimized and to cover a broad range of requirements for an almost unlimited field of 3D-related applications. The Web3D consortium had to learn its lessons and has finally defined a very stable and at the same time flexible framework that can easily be extended with new features. With its XML encoding X3D has captured additional potential and flexibility that prepares the international ISO/IEC standard greatly for future Web requirements.

PROVIDER-SPECIFIC SOLUTIONS AND RECOMMENDATIONS

In the real-world of current 3D business, companies relying on X3D often ask the question to vendors how to secure their 3D content applications that are produced with a significant budget. What can make a human readable 3D graphics format secure in order to keep IP rights even if used on the Internet? However in the case of secure applications this feature is not wanted. So the human readable format needs to be encrypted either from its binary representation or from ASCII form. An important part of the standardization rules of the Web3D consortium prohibits patents to be taken on procedures and techniques used in the X3D standard. This gives vendors the confidence that their application is not encumbered by patent disputes that might halt or stop the lifetime of a product based on X3D. The following section explains how security is enabled from the perspective of the 3D viewing technology developer Bitmanagement and how secure VWs are delivered already today on the Web, CDROM and single installations.

In order to ensure the interoperability of 3D worlds it is important that the implementations from different vendors of a standard do not differ in the visualization result. This is the main reason why a conformance test program and conformance test suite has been issued by the Web3D consortium. This X3D Conformance test has been successfully completed, enhanced and amended for instance by Bitmanagement with the help of the BS Contact 3D viewer (Bitmanagement 2009). BS Contact is a high performance 3D viewer that has been developed continuously following the X3D standard for more than a decade.

After a new software has been developed there are many company internal tests in order to secure that the quality of the support of the standardized nodes can be met. Companies who develop X3D conforming browser technology have to comply with ISO 19776. The conformance test is divided into 12 components of the interchange profile of the X3D specification. In this profile there is also defined for which level the particular components have to be tested. In total 120 specific tests have to be performed that present a good range of the level capabilities of the components, such as core, time, networking, grouping, rendering, shape, geometry3d, lighting, texturing, interpolation, navigation and environmental effects. In contrast to proprietary solutions of virtual worlds that do not have a rigid testing the standard compliance test suite and program is a big plus for security and reliability. For instance the conformance test was run with the BS Contact 3D viewer for the Interchange Profile of X3D which consists of 12 components constituting 120 tests in total. The compliance test ensures a consistent and reliable implementation of the X3D specification and contains also a distinction between rendering in OpenGL and DirectX. A summary of the test results for the individual components and the accompanying tests for the BS Contact 3D viewer can be found at the link http://www.bitmanagement.de/download/conformance/conformance-submit.pdf.

CLIENT-SIDE SECURITY

3D graphics data using the X3D standard can be transformed with BS Encrypt (the encryption tool from Bitmanagement) into an encrypted binary format, that does no longer reveal the syntax of the 3D geometry data to third parties. Thus 3D models, e.g. CAD drawings, can be presented on the Internet, however third parties cannot apply unwanted changes to these contents. Copying of the encrypted models is still possible by anyone on the Internet, however the display of these data can only be done if the correct license keys are present. This fact is used for instance in the automotive industry in the following way. The process of developing a car is very costly. The data of the parts of the car such as an engine are usually represented in CAD models that can also be expressed in X3D. The car maker relies to a large extend on a supply chain of companies that need to fit their parts into the bigger picture of the engine.

With the encryption and licensing mechanism used in BS Contact for instance the car maker can send an encrypted CAD model of the engine to the supplier with a license valid for a three months evaluation. The supplier can adapt his product during that time in a way that it fits exactly into the engine of the car manufacturer. After three months however the license to view the car manufacturer's engine is no longer valid leaving only the encrypted model on a hard disk of the supplier. This content is useless, if it cannot be displayed or integrated again into other authoring tools. This licensing mechanism literally self destroys the content after the three month time by itself giving the car manufacturer some more assurance that their valuable data of the engine is not used in another way than the intended. An example of a supplier company that uses such kind of encryption for their products in the digital factory area is Tarakos (Tarakos, 2009).

After encryption the geometry data can no longer be imported with success into authoring tools. In addition the encrypted source is no longer human readable and hides therefore all the information about its creation. The encrypted model can only be viewed with the BS Contact 3D renderer, if a valid license key for the encrypted content in its appropriate location is available. The respective license keys can be issued for websites, CD ROM volumes and single computers. Technically speaking BS Encrypt relies on the CryptAPI of Microsoft with 128 bit key length and the well known RC4 (also known as ARC4 or ARCFOUR) algorithm. The embedded RC4 algorithm is also used in SSL-type internet-banking transfers and standards such as SSH_1, HTTPS, WEP and WPA. The fact that the respective encryption algorithms is already present on the Microsoft operating system - thus on most computers without installation - makes the handling of export restrictions easier for the designers and creators of virtual worlds.

Figure 1 shows a simple example of an encrypted X3D scene in XML encoding. The scene consists of a simple blue box in the center

Figure 1.

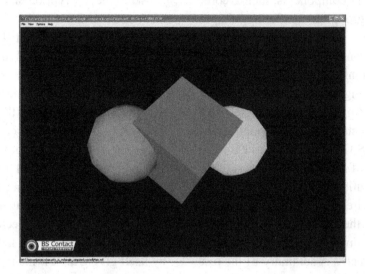

of the screen. Two other spheres are joined by Inline nodes from other files that need to be also encrypted. It is important to note that both inline files have to be encrypted as well in order to ensure security. Otherwise the encryption of the main file could be bypassed.

```
File Main.x3d
<?xml version="1.0"
encoding="UTF-8"?>
<X3D profile="Immersive" ver-
sion="3.0">
<head></head>
<Scene>
  <Viewpoint DEF="_1" fiel-
dOfView='0.844'
    orientation='-0.967 -0.251 -0.033
0.561'
    position='-0.882 3.539 5.814'>
  </Viewpoint>
  <NavigationInfo DEF="_2"
type='"EXAMINE"'/>
  <Transform rotation='0 0 1 0.78'>
    <Shape>
      <Appearance>
        <Material diffuseColor='0.2
0.2 0.5'
```

```
        emissiveColor='0.15 0.15
0.5'>
      </Material>
    </Appearance>
    <Box
containerField="geometry"/>
   </Shape>
  </Transform>
  <Transform DEF="_3" transla-
tion='-1.5 0 0'>
    <Inline DEF="_4" url='"Inline.
wrl"'
      bboxCenter='0 0 0' bboxSize='2
2 2'>
    </Inline>
  </Transform>
  <Transform translation='1.5 0 0'>
    <Inline DEF="_5" url='"Inline2.
wrl"'
      bboxCenter='0 0 0' bboxSize='2
2 2'>
    </Inline>
  </Transform>
</Scene>
  </X3D>
File Inline1.x3d:
<?xml version="1.0"
```

```
encoding="UTF-8"?>
<X3D profile="Immersive" ver-
sion="3.0">
<head></head>
<Scene>
  <Shape DEF="_1">
    <Appearance>
      <Material diffuseColor='0.5
0.25 0.15'
        emissiveColor='0.5 0.25
0.15'>
      </Material>
    </Appearance>
    <Sphere containerField="geometry"
DEF="_2"/>
  </Shape>
</Scene>
 </X3D>
File Inline2.x3d:
<?xml version="1.0"
encoding="UTF-8"?>
<X3D profile="Immersive" ver-
sion="3.0">
<head></head>
<Scene>
  <Shape DEF="_1">
   <Appearance>
     <Material diffuseColor='0.25
0.5 0.15'
       emissiveColor='0.25 0.5
0.15'>
     </Material>
   </Appearance>
   <Sphere containerField="geometry"
DEF="_2"/>
  </Shape>
</Scene>
</X3D>
```

After encryption with the BS Encrypt helper program the resulting main file is represented by an unordered junk of data similar to the following text. This data cannot be reused in authoring tools because parsing of the data is not possible

anymore. With the correct license key however the encrypted X3D content can be viewed and used as intended.

Resulting file Main-crypt.x3d:

BSCRYPT0@   _h _1 ¿1   °^á?_€
g¿#Ï`Y€n0_vHqxÇE   !ª Ìy%Um?_?É
²ÜËí9D¼bÕ‾¦™å_^ý ±ÝÒ86n Co:ë
;^ßœn^Ù©fA¾W_j(,.fÚå_/™"ÅöŒHrŸ_R^0Ð
u_&7"Ï^Bè¹¶_™¾ 77'(ckèÈ„BîÂf¬æçÄ__,6_
ÒeŸ&8_Ì_f¼s_ný_M_¡1">õ_M_ÅÒïÚ¾_
ªLc'³_£"HÜ#9_0Ãµ« Îï"R_1‾v»§&ýùÐæ'1»»¥?
¡M_!‾¿ÿ:{ÛÏ1Èÿî;Efyœ
/ÉlHd½F5þš ª«4
í«Ó__²ªŒzb6ã_‹²ØGìxÇè×âr}_gÒRÁM©µÀþ
ò‹[z¶@ÞD²Ç_{_ÉhkTûyð¥_iR§ëfù.‡-
JXt8ÄÑàÙ_—)01ãa•«2_dé_ÏÍÏ&×*"Â"q_
ÀË¢_°†Uâ\v|‡Š.6ªÄ½¶ûÎÛb•Ï_F_M__&2Tž

qÌMÓÎ^oÕm°$_;ß_Œ1LE,`_Žå|…
SäÖã__¤qd7_~žtM-§^G„:0rœvà[`\^Ì
a×w¹_ò÷M_³ë_´_4²_{ç"ÌÄš,Ú_I5÷
pyJŠ2ü-Ù__]_t_TÑ_»ô©_À\Î°C'_Ô-C®`‡@
u_'Ø_Â8_O_3´½Ó3&‾\]+W²K_¥_Ú*÷ô_Œ74
Vgši›Ñµ_)=ô¬`s©D.—"J<Î^žõnýj„_
Bdå¤ÌŠnb,G¶þ"#1½Ò¢Ït̂êwÀ{K"`_-pÁíÏ`³{_
Êx'_0Ø_1"-FßôÐf_ÑÄ76Œc_Ê†Í*Evjí<^ëìs-
,+"ê6!®Ì6GÝn'øš*²šüfCölL©Å/ŒŒßãÄ?sNy_
ØžrîêÆ\(¬šÞ5'/¤_aûC[¬¹àcçÜ©Åö°

MULTI-USER SERVER SECURITY

It is possible to implement a safe server side protocol on the X3D standard recommendations. The following example of the multi-user server BS Collaborate from Bitmanagement is in line with the networking group of X3D. The system is build up on the X3D proposal for a networking component, called networkSensor node. These nodes allow X3D scenes to connect to arbitrary servers or direct links between two X3D players. With these nodes you are able to manipulate virtual objects collaboratively in real time. The Bitmanagement Software node extension allows you to communicate during these manipulations. Only registered users are able to connect. With the internal login interface there is no hassle of external user management with websites or similar.

These multi-user features are included in BS Contact 7.2 Web 3D browser. This means that on client side only the BS Contact 7.2 must be installed to connect with a multi user environment. BS Collaborate's tasks are to manage the login requests, user avatars and events from the connected clients. In order to store persistent events the server has the ability to connect to different ODBC SQL databases or write the events in a file system as a fall back. An existing user database can be used as the database that stores user accounts. This can be configured in the configuration file. With this file you can customize the server and adjust properties to your needs. You can expand the functionality of the server by writing your own server side script. These scripts can add functionality to the multi-user environment.

On the scene authoring side, the BS Collaborate server implementation is based on a node that specifies the connection parameters for the server connection and a node that handles session based messages to/from the server. These messages inform the scene when a user has joined, when other users move, about chat messages, etc. The scene can then respond to these messages, e.g. by showing a buddy list.

An example scene may look like this:

```
DEF MU BSCollaborate
{
    connection NetConnection
    {
        address "test.bitmanagement.com"
        port 12345
    }
}
ROUTE SomeScript.credentials TO
MU.tryLogin
ROUTE MU.loginResult TO SomeScript.
loggedIn
```

After initialization the BS Collaborate node uses the associated Connection node to connect to the server. It than waits until reception of the user name and password on the tryLogin field. When it receives those, it uses them to authenticate with the server and establish an identity. This way a 3D scene can show a login screen asking for login and password directly in the 3D window. No external HTML form or similar is required. Alternatively a script node could just send some constant values to BS Collaborate.tryLogin if no user identification is required.

Right after a user has logged in, the BS Collaborate node populates its users field with nodes describing all other users currently logged in. For each user in the scene an event is sent over the hasJoined starting with the own user. The BS Collaborate node in other clients will add a record to their users field and send an event over their hasJoined field, so that all clients are informed of our arrival. Similarly, if later during a session a new user joins or leaves the session, this is indicated via hasJoined and hasLeft, and the users are updated by adding a new node or removing the one corresponding to a leaving user. This way a 3D scene can freely query the list of currently connected users and respond to changes in that list, and implementing for instance a buddy list.

To sum up, the Web3D consortium has spent more than 10 years in a concerted effort to provide in X3D a consistent standard for Virtual Worlds that can be used in a comprehensive and secure way. The recommendations of this work can be used to construct a human readable or encrypted virtual world that can be optimized for security by encryption on the client side and the use of common purpose protocols and connection mechanisms on the server side.

FUTURE DEVELOPMENT DIRECTIONS

To achieve the predictions of popular market research institutions about the penetration of Virtual Worlds in the future Web 3.0, 3D-Internet or similar, it is important not to disappoint the expectations. This risk can be reduced from at least two directions: by inspiring realistic expectations and by satisfying the resulting anticipations of potential users, investors, providers and operators. Looking back in the history of online VW's at least two big hypes have been undergone already: VRML in 1994 and Second Life in 2006. The third attempt should definitely hit the mark now. If VW's want to become a serious and natural way of communication – and the technical and infra-structural conditions seem to be mature enough in the meanwhile – it is obvious that they should also match some of the fundamental characteristics of today's extremely successful World Wide Web. The Web is not owned by a single company, not operated on a dedicated platform and does not only support proprietary encoded content. It is an open system, with open standards, reliable and transparent concepts, developed by many independent institutions and competent engineers around the world. Why not try to adopt as much as possible of these success factors also to the field of Virtual Worlds?

X3D already covers most of these criteria and provides them to the field of VW's, and it is prepared to be extended with future requirements of tomorrow's Internet. Instead of reinventing the wheel maybe the best of what is already available today should be simply deployed, while valuable but narrow resources should be invested into the development of truly new and groundbreaking features. Thus the generic challenges in the overall field of VW's could be resolved, resulting in fundamental building blocks of tomorrow's 3D-Internet and new business opportunities for everybody.

Many fundamental questions in the field of VW's are still open. Security is just one of the generic topics, and there are many efforts in the working groups of the W3C and Web3D consortium to develop and provide generic solutions. The resulting Recommendations, RFC's and ISO standards are available to the public, and could be used to build an interoperable, open and stable Metaverse, for social worlds of private communities, entertainment worlds for gamers or intraworlds for companies. It is worth to be part of that intitiative and to support the development of a standard for the 3D-Internet together. There is too much work to do for just one of us.

CONCLUSION

With the appeal to bundle the efforts and resources for defining secure standards for virtual worlds this chapter concludes also with the advice to check out the already available standards as well as the running initiatives online. Please refer to the sections References and online resources for additional sources and initiatives to become part of it. In general the sites of the two main consortiums Web3D for X3D and W3C for the overall Web are both very good starting points to touch-and-go with your own activities. The well-structured working groups make it easy to find your specific topics of interest, like for example the W3C working group for XML Security. All states, results, standards and concepts are available for free and are just waiting to be applied in new and outstanding VW projects.

REFERENCES

W3C. (2009). *HTML 5 - A vocabulary and associated APIs for HTML and XHTML*. Working draft. Retrieved December 1, 2009, from http://www.w3.org/TR/html5/no.html#declarative-3d-scenes

W3C. (2009). *World Wide Web Consortium*. Retrieved October 30, 2009, from http://www.w3.org

W3C. (2009). *XML Encryption Recommendation*. Retrieved October 30, 2009, from http://www.w3.org/TR/xmlenc-core/

W3C. (2009). *XML - Extensible Markup Language Recommendation*. Retrieved October 30, 2009, from http://www.w3.org/TR/xml11/

W3C. (2009). *XML Signature Recommendation.* Retrieved October 30, 2009, from http://www. w3.org/TR/xmlsig-core/

Adobe flash. (2009). Retrieved October 30, 2009, from http://www.adobe.com/products/flashplayer

Behr, P. E., Jung, Y., & Zöllner, M. (2009). X3DOM, A DOM-based HTML5/X3D Integration Model. In *Proceedings of Web3D 2009 conference.* New York: ACM.

Bitmanagement. (2009). *Interactive Web3D Graphics.* Retrieved October 30, 2009, from http://www.bitmanagement.com

Contact, B. S. 7.2. (2009). *A Web3D viewer from Bitmanagement.* Retrieved October 30, 2009, from http://www.bitmanagement.com/en/download

Google. (2009). *O3d, an javascript based scenegraph api.* Retrieved October 30, 2009, from http://code.google.com/apis/o3d/

IBM Emergence of the 3D-Internet. (2009). Retrieved December 1, 2009, from http://www.ibm.com/virtualworlds/index.shtml

IBM Lotus Sametime. (2009). Retrieved December 1, 2009, from http://www-03.ibm.com/press/us/en/pressrelease/27831.wss

Integrated Virtual Networks. (2009). Retrieved December 1, 2009, from http://www.ivn3.com/applications.php

Khronos. (2009). *Khronos details WebGL Initiative to Bring Hardware-Accelerated 3D Graphics to the Internet.* Retrieved October 30, 2009, from http://www.khronos.org/news/press/releases/khronos-webgl-initiative-hardware-accelerated-3d-graphics-internet/

Microsoft. (2009). *Silverlight.* Retrieved October 30, 2009, from http://www.microsoft.com/directx/

MPEG. (2009). *Motion Picture Experts Group.* Retrieved October 30, 2009, from http://www. mpeg.org/

OpenSimulator. (2009). *3D Application Server.* Retrieved October 30, 2009, from http://opensimulator.org/wiki/Main_Page

Project. (2009). *Papervision3d.* Retrieved October 30, 2009, from http://blog.papervison3d.org/

Sun. (2008). *Open Virtual Worlds.* Retrieved December 1, 2009, from http://www.sun.com/service/applicationserversubscriptions/OpenVirtualWorld.pdf

SUN Project Darkstar Roadmap. (n.d.). Retrieved December 1, 2009, from http://projectdarkstar.com/technology-roadmap-may-09.html

Tarakos. (2009). *TaraVR Builder.* Retrieved December 1, 2009, from http://www.taravrbuilder.com/eng/Home.html

Web3D. (2009). *X3D specifications ISO/IEC 19776 (1/2/3).* Retrieved October 30, 2009, from http://www.web3d.org/x3d/specifications/

Web3D Consortium. (2009). Retrieved October 30, 2009, from www.web3d.org

Web3D.org. (2009). *X3D Security.* Retrieved October 30, 2009, from http://www.web3d.org/x3d/content/examples/Basic/Security/X3dSecurityReadMe.html

Wei, S. Stocker. (2009). Function-based haptic collaboration in X3D. In *Proceedings of Web3D 2009 conference.* New York: Association for Computing Machinery.

Williams, J. S., Sr. (2009). *Document-based Message-Centric Security using XML authentication and encryption for coalition and interagency operations.* Master's Thesis, Naval Postgraduate School, Monterey, California, Security classification: unclassified.

Chapter 11
Aspect–Oriented Programming and Aspect.NET as Security and Privacy Tools for Web and 3D Web Programming

Vladimir O. Safonov
St. Petersburg University, Russia

ABSTRACT

This chapter covers the use of aspect-oriented programming (AOP) and Aspect.NET, an AOP toolkit for the .NET platform, to implement Web and 3D Web security and privacy. In this chapter the author shows that AOP is quite suitable as a trustworthy software development tool. AOP and Aspect.NET basics are overviewed using simple examples. Principles of applying Aspect.NET for Web and 3D Web security and privacy implementation are also discussed. The chapter presents a library of sample aspects implementing security and privacy for Web programming.

ASPECT-ORIENTED PROGRAMMING AND ITS USE FOR TRUSTWORTHY COMPUTING

Aspect-oriented programming (AOP) (Safonov, 2008) is a prospective approach to software development and maintenance. It is based on the concept of a *cross-cutting concern*. A *concern* in software design is an idea, consideration, or task. A *cross-cutting concern* is a concern that cannot be implemented as a hierarchy of modules – classes or procedures, and, therefore, whose

implementation requires injection and activation of lots of new fragments of code (statements or definitions) scattered throughout the code of the target application.

Typical examples of cross-cutting concerns are logging, security and privacy (in particular, in Web and 3D Web applications), since the implementation of all of them requires injecting into the target application code of many specific API calls to implement logging (e.g., tracking method calls and returns), security (e.g., permission checks), and privacy (e.g., encoding / decoding of information).

DOI: 10.4018/978-1-61520-891-3.ch011

Currently most of the AOP tools are implemented for the Java platform. The most popular of them is AspectJ (AspectJ, 2001) - an extension of the Java language by AOP constructs and features. As for .NET, most of the existing tools for that platform are at research and experimental stage.

Aspect in AOP is an implementation of a cross-cutting concern. Aspect is considered as a new kind of *module* with specific ways of definition and use. In our terminology (Safonov, 2008), an aspect consists of a set of *actions*, specified in the aspect definition, each of them accompanied by its *weaving condition*. The purpose of the aspect is to reuse its actions in a variety of target applications by *weaving*. *Weaving* the aspect is the process of combining the code of the target application with the code of aspect in such a way that the actions of the aspect be activated in the *join points* of the target program selected by the *weaver* (part of the AOP toolkit) using the aspect's *weaving rules*. For example, a weaving rule in a security aspect can prescribe to weave a call of the security action *PermissionCheck()* before each call of the method *ResourceUpdate()*, wherever the latter call is found in the target application. Weaving is performed automatically by the specific component of the AOP toolkit, referred to as *weaver*.

Another example is related to privacy. Suppose that the method *TransferPrivateData()* of the target application is responsible for the transfer of some private data over the network, and the method *UsePrivateData()* implements the use of the private data by a network client. To protect the data from the attack, it is reasonable to encrypt them before the transfer, and decrypt after the transfer. If this encryption / decryption functionality is not implemented in the original version of target application (which is often the case in software practice), there is no need to change the target application's code manually, which is error-prone. It is possible to use AOP and to develop an aspect with two actions – *Encrypt()* and *Decrypt()*, such that the weaving rules of the aspect prescribe to insert the call of *Encrypt()* before each call of

TransferPrivateData(), and the call of *Decrypt()* – after each call of the *UsePrivateData()*.

Even such simple example leads us to the conclusion that AOP could be a very powerful tool to implement security and privacy. Much more examples of using AOP for the purpose of trustworthy computing are provided in (Safonov, 2008). This chapter discusses how to implement these ideas in practice for Web and 3D Web programming, using our AOP toolkit for the .NET platform – Aspect.NET.

In general, as stated and explained in (Safonov, 2008), AOP methods appear to be generically related to application of *trustworthy computing* (TWC, 2002) – the approach initiated by Microsoft in 2002. Trustworthy computing (TWC) is a set of principles how to make the application code satisfying the *pillars* of TWC – *security, privacy, and reliability*. In software practice, in initial versions of many software products, such issues are often ignored or not paid enough attention to, for a number of reasons, e.g., lack of time, lack of secure code development experience, and so on. As the result, the software product appears to be vulnerable to attacks and unreliable. So, the product development team has to solve TWC problems of the product later, during its maintenance, as part of fixing bugs or implementing requests for enhancement. It takes a lot of time and human resources to examine the existing product code and try to add to it manually some new non-trivial security, privacy, or reliability functionality. So, in practice, the problem of *improvement* (or *modernization*) of the existing product code to make it more secure and reliable appears to be very important. AOP is a quite suitable technique to solve this problem, since it enables a way to define special modules – *aspects*, implementing such new functionality, and a way to safely and automatically apply aspects by *weaving* – injecting the fragments of code defined as parts of the aspect.

Without using AOP, developers or maintainers of software products would have to add cross-cutting functionality to the existing code manually, using the minimal support provided by common use integrated development environments (IDE). This process may lead to introducing bugs into the existing code. To continue the above security example, if the *ResourceUpdate()* method is called, say, 101 times in the application's code, the developer should manually track all those calls, located in different modules of the code, using the editor of the IDE and options like refactoring or navigation to definition, and manually insert necessary calls of the *PermissionCheck()* method before the *ResourceUpdate()* method calls found. This kind of "mundane" engineering activity is likely to cause introducing new bugs into the code. For example, the developer can only modify 100 calls but forget to update the 101-th one, for some reason (e.g., because of being interrupted for a more urgent issue). AOP guarantees that all changes of the target application code are made safely: the weaver cannot "forget" to modify each of the necessary 101 calls of the target method.

The AOP approach causes another issue: *blind weaving*. If the user cannot control the process of weaving, i.e., cannot "explain" to the AOP toolkit that some of the injections according to the aspect's weaving rules would be redundant, the result of weaving can be unclear and non-predictable. Most AOP tools, including our Aspect.NET, provide ways of visualizing the result of weaving. But, as we'll see later, of all the AOP tools known by now, only our Aspect.NET toolkit offers *user-controlled weaving* – an option for the user to deselect some of the redundant join points before the actual weaving. This really makes the process of weaving more reliable, and solves the problem of blind weaving by delegation of the final corrections and approvals of the weaving results to the user.

RELATED WORK

The problem of using AOP for implementing security, in particular, Web security and 3D Web security, has been the focus of attention by many researchers since the very origin of AOP in the 1990s. Most of those research works are done for the Java platform.

The paper (Viega et al., 2001) seems to be one of the earliest devoted to applying AOP to security. The authors are among the first researchers who noticed and justified the suitability of AOP to implement security, as a separate cross-cutting concern, allowing security concerns to be specified modularly and applied to the main program in a uniform way.

The paper (de Win et al., 2006) analyzes AOP and its application from the viewpoint of security and trustworthiness. It discusses the authors' experience of developing and applying secure and non-secure aspects using the Java platform, and the specific AOP tool – AspectJ. The authors notice that some AOP features implemented in AspectJ – "invocation hijacking" by interception of method calls (replacing the calls of some selected methods by calls of the aspect methods); privileged aspects (aspects that have access to private data of the target class), and so on, may appear to be non-secure, and increase the risk of adding vulnerabilities to code. Partial solutions and recipes, such as security policy implementations to avoid dangers of AOP use are proposed. One of the serious security problems related to the use of AspectJ is noticed by the authors: the identity of aspects is lost after weaving, so the resulting code or the runtime system cannot detect whether or not to allow the particular aspects to perform some actions. Our opinion on this issue is as follows. Most of the problems analyzed by the paper are actually the problems of AspectJ and its implementation of AOP. AspectJ uses its own specific compiler from the AOP-extended Java language. So it is not fully integrated to Java technology and its compilation and runtime model. For that reason, aspects, when woven, are "lost" within the resulting code. To enable a better security, the authors offer a solution of extra "instrumentation" of the woven code by specific checks whether or not the particular actions are allowed. This decision leads to inefficiency at runtime. On the contrary, our approach to AOP implementation, as will be shown below, enables full integration to .NET model and doesn't cause efficiency loss as the result of aspect weaving.

In (Mourad et al., 2008), using AOP for security "hardening" of code is considered for some specific tasks such as making sockets secure, using two development platforms: C++, with the AOP tool AspectC++, and Java, with the AOP tool AspectJ. The authors proposed some security hardening code templates, and showed how to implement them using AOP for those two platforms. As the result, the efficiency loss of using AOP is shown to be minimal.

There is a lot of research papers worth mentioning that offer different approached to AOP. Most of them are influenced by AspectJ and its approach of mixing up aspects and classes. In particular, in (Rajan and Sullivan, 2005), the concept of *classpects* is proposed – a kind of mix of aspects and classes. Out viewpoint is quite different: we think that AOP mechanisms and concepts are so generic that they shouldn't depend on the concepts of aspect implementation languages (such as classes), or depend on them in minimal possible way. Otherwise, we think, AOP concepts mixed up with OOP concepts can make it much more difficult for an AOP newbie to understand and use AOP. More details, analysis and justifications can be found in our book (Safonov, 2008, Chapters 3 and 4).

The paper (Mesing and Helmich, 2006), covers using AOP to modify behavior of 3D scenes specified by common use X3D documents. X3D is an extension of VRML widely used as de facto standard to specify 3D scenes and behaviors of their virtual participants. The authors propose to specify aspects applicable to X3D documents by XML files whose syntax is similar to the syntax of aspect definitions in AspectJ. The authors implemented a specific weaver which takes X3D documents and XML aspect specifications defin-

ing necessary updates in the scene and behaviors, and generates the resulting X3D document defining the updated scene. As an example of applying their approach and tool, the authors consider an X3D-based implementation of 3D water polo game. We think this is a very promising research, in view of the popularity of X3D in 3D Web. Please note that the authors had to design and implement their own AOP toolkit applicable for such tasks (probably the first one to apply AOP to X3D documents) which is very time-consuming.

To summarize this brief overview, problems of using AOP to implement security are considered by researchers mostly for the Java platform (due to wide popularity of AspectJ). There are some successful applications of AOP to security for C++, and even for X3D. None of the above papers covers the use AOP to implement security for the .NET platform.

SPECIFICS OF .NET, 3D ENGINES FOR .NET, AND THE PURPOSE OF OUR RESEARCH

Currently AOP for .NET, in particular, the use of AOP to implement .NET security, is at research stage. Nevertheless, .NET is becoming more and more popular, in particular, in the area of Web and 3D Web programming.

The main principles of .NET are using the common intermediate language (CIL), common language runtime (CLR), and common type system (CTS) to enable multi-language interoperability and managed code execution, with full type-checking and exception handling.

The .NET model of Web programming is based on ASP.NET – extension of Active Server Pages (ASP) by Microsoft. ASP.NET allows the users to develop models for dynamic generation of Web pages using any language implemented for .NET, e.g., C#.

The advantage of .NET in the area of security is its enhanced and flexible security model that includes *code access security* (evaluating the set of permissions for an *assembly* - .NET's unit of binary code); *role-based security* (defining the roles of principals and tying sets of security permissions to the roles), and *evidence-based security* (analyzing the *evidences* of an assembly, such as the developer company, digital signature, and Internet zone, and evaluating the set of assembly's permissions based on the collected evidences).

As for the use of .NET for 3D Web, the latest advantage by Microsoft is *Silverlight* (Silverlight, 2009) – an API developed above .NET to develop rich Internet applications with elements of 3D graphics and scenes, to make visualization of Web pages more expressive. Silverlight is fully developed above .NET and uses its own enhanced version of the CLR. The implementation of Silverlight is based on using JavaScript and XAML languages, as well as a specific enhanced .NET virtual machine. XAML is a Microsoft's extension of XML suitable for specifying scenes as well as executable code. The latest version of Silverlight available is Silverlight 3.0. Web sites and images controlled and displayed by Silverlight are very attractive and make great esthetic impression, which is very important for the users. To use Silverlight, it is enough to upload and install a special plug-in for the browser. As for de facto standards of 3D Web – X3D and VRML used by many other companies and projects, the current version of Silverlight is not compatible to them.

To our knowledge, for the .NET platform, there are a number of 3D engines for various domains (mostly game engines), but the use of .NET for 3D Web, in general, is just starting. Most of the existing 3D Web engines use very specific scripting languages that require development of specific AOP tools, like the one proposed in (Mesing and Helmich, 2006) for X3D.

Here is a brief overview of 3D engines for .NET and specifics of their implementation.

The Unity3D engine (Unity3D, 2009) allows the users to develop 3D scripts in C#. However, the code should be compiled by a specific C# compiler supplied as part of the engine, rather than by the commonly used C# compiler from Visual Studio. The latter obstacle makes it problematic to use the resulting binary code in standard .NET environment.

The DX Studio engine (DX Studio, 2009) requires from the users to develop 3D scripts in JavaScript language. The only way of integrating DX Studio into ordinary .NET environment is using it as an ActiveX control in a C# or C++ Web application.

The FlatRedBall engine (FlatRedBall, 2009) is intended for development of games for desktop Web applications. FlatRedBall implementation is based on Silverlight 2.0, so it requires a non-standard Silverlight-specific virtual machine (enhanced CLR) for its use.

There are two open source 3D .NET engines written in C#: Kit3D (Kit3D, 2009) and Balder (Balder, 2009). They are implemented over Silverlight, so they also require a specific enhanced CLR for their use.

The Ogre 3D engine (Ogre, 2009) is a 3D game engine written in C++, as well as many other 3D engines we found. They use standard "unmanaged" version of C++ and don't use .NET environment.

The implementation of Second Life (Second Life, 2009), the most commonly used 3D Virtual World, is written in unmanaged C++ and is not compatible to .NET.

So, as we've found out during our research, the use of .NET for 3D Web is just starting. As for the use of AOP for 3D Web specific tasks (geometry and immersion), it requires developing new AOP tools to support weaving of the code developed in 3D Web specific languages (VRML or X3D), which is a time-consuming task for future research.

Nevertheless, we do think the use of .NET for the 3D Web is very prospective, due to the open nature of .NET, and its rapid evolution, especially in the area of Web programming. Moreover, since 3D Web is based on the same set of basic protocols as ordinary Web (http, ftp, sockets and secure sockets, encryption / decryption, etc.), it seems appropriate to make an initial research on applying AOP for .NET to solve a classical set of Web security and privacy tasks (like authentication, authorization, encryption, etc.), because those solutions are also applicable as a basis for 3D Web implementations for the .NET platform.

The result of our initial research on using AOP and Aspect.NET for Web security and privacy, the library *WebDevelopment_Aspects* of sample aspects to solve Web typical security and privacy tasks, is covered in this chapter. The full source code of the library, in the form of a Visual Studio solution, is available for download at (Aspect. NET, 2008).

Developing support for the use of AOP for specific 3D Web tasks in Aspect.NET is planned as the next step requiring a lot of time.

ASPECT.NET BASICS

Our AOP solution for the .NET platform, Aspect. NET (Safonov, 2008), is based on the following principles:

- Language-agnostic aspects. The aspects for .NET should be actually "CIL-level", applicable to any .NET language, according to the whole idea of multi-language interoperability in .NET. In Aspect.NET, weaving is performed at binary CIL code level.

- The use of custom attributes for implementing aspects. Custom attributes in .NET are user-defined annotations compiled to binary representation and stored with the assembly code. AOP custom attributes predefined in Aspect.NET mark methods as the actions of aspects, and specify the appropriate weaving conditions for those actions. These attributes are understood by our AOP toolkit only, and don't prevent

from the use of common .NET utilities such as debugger or profiler.

- The use of simple AOP meta-language (referred to as to *Aspect.NET*.ML) to specify aspects. In our opinion, mixing up AOP and OOP concepts and entities as in AspectJ language makes it hard to learn and use AOP for a newbie. Instead, we have implemented a meta-language of simple self-evident AOP annotations converted by our tool to custom attributes. The structure of our AOP meta-language doesn't depend on any particular .NET language (e.g., C#), although, in the current release, Aspect. NET currently allows us to use C# and Visual Basic (VB) as aspect implementation languages. Supporting Managed C++ is our task for future releases. Aspect.NET also supports an alternative way of implementing aspects directly in C# or VB with AOP custom attributes, without using the meta-language. Both styles are illustrated in the examples below.

- User-controlled weaving: a new idea and feature, not implemented yet in any other AOP tool except for Aspect.NET, that allows the user to control the process of weaving. Before the actual weaving performs, the user can browse all potential join points in the target application source code, and deselect those of them the user considers redundant. Due to that option, the problem of "blind weaving" is avoided: the user has a tool to examine, understand and control possible outcome of weaving to avoid absurd results.

- Full integration of AOP toolkit with all .NET common use standards, features, and tools. Aspect.NET is implemented as a plug-in to Visual Studio.NET. Due to that fact, software engineers can use AOP with Aspect.NET within the framework of Visual Studio development environment,

Example 1.

```
using System.Net;
public class Utilities
{
    public static void PrintHostIP(string hostName)
    {
        Console.WriteLine
            ("IP address of the host=" +
              Dns.GetHostEntry(hostName).AddressList[0]);
        Console.WriteLine("Press ENTER to exit");
        Console.ReadLine();
    }
    static void Main(string[] args)
    {
        PrintHostIP(Dns.GetHostName());
    }
}
```

with its debugging, profiling, testing, and a variety of other development features. The .NET assembly with woven aspects works the same as any other assembly, and does not contain any extra "instrumentation code", so weaving aspects with Aspect. NET does not make the resulting code less efficient, as compared to the similar code after manual insertion of aspect's actions.

More detailed justification of the above principles and Aspect.NET architecture is provided in our AOP book (Safonov, 2008, Chapters 3 and 4).

Aspect.NET toolkit is available for free download from Microsoft academic Web site. Necessary instructions and references for download and installation of Aspect.NET are provided in (Aspect.NET, 2008).

To introduce the readers into the specifics of AOP with Aspect.NET, let's consider a simple example of implementing Internet security using Aspect.NET.

Let the Internet application needs to print out onto the console the list of all IP addresses of a given host on the network. Here is the code of a .NET application in C# that solves this problem, without taking into account security permissions:

In Example 1, we use the *System.Net* namespace intended for network programming for .NET, and its class named *Dns* (for *DNS – Domain Name Service*).

According to trustworthy computing principles (Safonov, 2008), a secure code should explicitly request and check its security permissions before doing some potentially insecure action, in our case – before requesting the set of IP addresses of the given host.

Imagine that the code of a large network application is already developed, and it contains many calls of *PrintHostIP()* throughout the program. But, in the initial version of the code, no security measures are undertaken - permission checks for requesting IP addresses of a host are not performed. So, our task is to implement security check in this code.

As noted before, using the editor and the IDE of Visual Studio without AOP will require manual search of each call of *PrintHostIP* and insertion

Example 2.

```
%aspect Aspect1
using System;
using System.Net;
using System.Security.Permissions;
class Aspect1
{
    %modules
    private static void DemandDnsPermission() {
        DnsPermission p
            = new DnsPermission(PermissionState.Unrestricted);
        p.Demand();
    }
    %rules
    %before %call *.PrintHostIP(string) && args(..)
    %action
    public static void GetHostAction(string hostname) {
        Console.WriteLine("Hostname="+ hostname);
        Console.WriteLine("Demand DNS permission");
        DemandDnsPermission();
        Console.WriteLine("Demand DNS permission finished");
    } // GetHostAction
} // Aspect1
```

of the security check code before it. That can lead to adding bugs to the code, since it is very easy to forget to modify some of the calls.

Let's solve this problem using our Aspect.NET toolkit. Let's define an aspect to do the necessary work of security checks injection automatically - insert before each call of the method *PrintHostIP* the call of another method (action), *DemandDnsPermission*, that checks for the desirable security permission (see Example 2).

Example 2 is written in C# extended by *AOP annotations* displayed in bold face (special kinds of lines starting with "%") used in Aspect.NET to specify the architecture of the aspect *Aspect1* implemented in C#. Our meta-language of AOP annotations we use in Aspect.NET is referred to *Aspect.NET.ML*. Please note that if we comment

out (or omit) all the AOP annotations, i.e., "forget about AOP", we'll get a correct C# code of a class. This principle was one of our major intents, since it simplifies the users' understanding of AOP and its relation to OOP.

The *%aspect* annotation in Aspect.NET.ML specifies the header of the aspect, including its name – *Aspect1*. The implementation of the aspect is a *class* in C# having the same name.

The *%modules* annotation specifies the *modules* of the aspect – typically, its private methods to be used in aspect's actions below.

The *%rules* annotation specifies the set of the aspect's *weaving rules*. Each rule has the form:

```
Condition %action Action
```

```
%before %call *.PrintHostIP(string)
&& args(..)
```

So the aspect inserts before each call of the method *PrintHostIP* of the target application a call of the method *GetHostAction* defined in the aspect. That method demands from the .NET runtime the permissions necessary to perform the IP address request (by calling the predefined method *Demand* which throws *SecurityException* if the requested permissions are lacking), and outputs to the console the tracing messages to comment the execution of the program.

The first step of the aspect's build in Visual Studio.NET is the call of the Aspect.NET *converter* that converts the AOP annotations written in Aspect.NET.ML to the definitions of *AOP custom attributes* (used in Aspect.NET to annotate each of the aspect's action) in C#. The next step of aspect build is the use of the ordinary Visual Studio's C# compiler to translate the aspect implementation from C# to the binary *assembly*, in the format common for the .NET platform.

To apply the aspect, the weaver uses its weaving rules. The resulting modified binary code of the target application will have all necessary security checks in place.

So, using our toolkit, no one of the *PrintHostIP* method calls (referred to as *join point*, in AOP terms) will be "forgotten", and the work of updating the target application to incorporate the security actions will be performed properly.

With Aspect.NET, updating the target application to strengthen its security can be made even in case the source code of the target application is not available. Only the target assembly (i.e., its binary code) can be used. What the developer of the security aspects needs to know is the target application's API whose behavior needs to be modified. This is possible because Aspect.NET performs weaving at binary assembly code level.

PRINCIPLES AND EXAMPLES OF USING ASPECT.NET FOR WEB SECURITY AND PRIVACY

As explained before, the goal of our research is to develop a library of aspects to apply AOP in Web programming for Microsoft.NET platform. Web programming for .NET is implemented by *ASP. NET*, an enhancement of Microsoft's ASP (Active Server Pages). In this section, we'll consider how to apply AOP with Aspect.NET for solving the following typical kinds of 3D Web and ordinary Web programming tasks:

- logging
- security (authentication, authorization, impersonation)
- cryptography of the query string
- HTML encoding
- extending the user's Web interface
- cryptography of the cookie files
- XML document validation.

Logging Aspects

Logging is chronological recording of events in software system into a *log (journal)*, usually implemented as a file. Logging is a typical example of a cross-cutting concern, so it's a typical task to be solved by AOP. Logging is very closely related to implementation of security, in particular, in Web and 3D Web, since logging in security systems is one of the mostly used method of detecting network attacks, e.g., detecting a "sniffer" application that tries to address hosts in a local network by iterating IP addresses.

Suppose in our Web application there is an execution point that calls the method *ProcessWebData(string arg, int num)*. Now let's develop a logging aspect to be applicable to all such calls under our investigation, referred to as *WebLoggingAspect* (see Example 3).

Example 3.

```
public class WebLoggingAspect: Aspect
{
}
```

Example 4.

```
    {
        get
        {
            return ConfigurationManager.AppSettings["LogFile"];
        }
    }
```

In this aspect (Example 4), we need to define a property that returns the path to the log file, e.g.:

```
private static string LogFile
```

This property retrieves the path to the log file from the *Web.config* configuration file (the *AppSettings* section) of the target Web application.

Now let's add a logging action into our aspect: this action will perform tracing of the start and the finish of a *ProcessWebData ()* method call (see Example 5).

In this example, we annotate the code of aspect's actions by the *AspectAction* attribute to represent the weaving conditions. This is the alternative way of aspect definition in Aspect.NET, in "pure C#" (in attributes), instead of using the "%" style AOP annotation extensions explained above. When using this style of aspect definition, the first step of the aspect build, conversion from AOP annotations to pure C#, is not needed and therefore omitted.

Please note that, when implementing an aspect "in attributes", the developer needs to explicitly inherit the aspect's implementation class from the *Aspect* class, predefined in Aspect.NET.

In the Aspect.NET Framework plug-in for Visual Studio, two kinds of aspect definition projects are supported: *Aspect.NET.ML project* – for developing aspects using Aspect.NET.ML annotations and their further conversion to C# attributes, and *Aspect.NET project* – for developing aspects in pure C#, "in attributes". More details in (Safonov, 2008).

The actions of the above aspect are invoked before and after the call of the *ProcessWebData()* method. They output the following information about the *target method*: what method is called; the type of the method; the type of the target object; the arguments of the method; the type of the returned value. We can apply these actions to any similar kinds of join points. To do that, we only need to change the weaving condition: for example, the condition *%before %call *.** will mean "before call of any method".

The identifiers like *TargetMemberInfo*, not explicitly defined in our aspect, are inherited from the predefined *Aspect* class.

Security Aspects

In Web applications for .NET based on ASP.NET, security is implemented using the following three kinds of operations:

Example 5.

```
[AspectAction("%before %call *.ProcessWebData(..)")]
public static void BeforeLog()
{
    MethodInfo m = (MethodInfo)TargetMemberInfo;
    ParameterInfo[] pars = m.GetParameters();
    Object target = TargetObject;
    TextWriter tw = new StreamWriter(LogFile, true);
    tw.WriteLine(" + [" + DateTime.Now +
                "]: Start call method: " + m.Name +
                ". Number of parameters: " + pars.Length);
    if (TargetObject == null)
    {
        tw.WriteLine("    - Method is static");
    }
    else
    {
        tw.WriteLine("    - Target object: type = " +
                    target.GetType() +
                    ", value = " + target.ToString());
    }
    foreach (ParameterInfo p in pars)
    {
        tw.WriteLine("    - argument: name: " + p.Name +
                    ", type: " + p.ParameterType);
    }
    tw.Close();
}
[AspectAction("%after %call *.ProcessWebData(..)")]
public static void AfterLog()
{
    MethodInfo m = (MethodInfo)TargetMemberInfo;
    TextWriter tw = new StreamWriter(LogFile, true);
    tw.WriteLine(" + [" + DateTime.Now +
                "] – The end of method: " + m.Name);
    tw.WriteLine("    * Returned value type: " + m.ReturnType);
    tw.Close();
}
```

- **Authentication**: the process of identification of the user for the purpose of providing some Web application resource (a section of a Web site, a Web page, a database, etc.) Authentication is based on checking information on the user (e.g., his / her login name and password)

- *Authorization*: the process of checking and providing resource access permissions to the authenticated user
- *Impersonation*: passing to the ASP.NET server process the client's security permissions ("acting on behalf of the user").

Let's consider how to apply AOP and Aspect. NET to the implementation of security for the above kinds of operations.

Authentication and Authorization Aspects

The majority of Web sites provide anonymous access to some of their Web pages, but some others are accessible by registered users only.

If the user would like to get access to some application resource (e.g., to add items to the shopping cart in a Web shop), the Web application checks whether the user is authenticated. At that moment, the user is to present his or her private information, e.g., *username* and *password*. If the user is authenticated, the application allows him (her) to perform the desirable action; if not, refuses and issues the appropriate message. This check should be implemented for all the actions requiring user authentication. So this kind of check can be considered as a cross-cutting concern and

can be implemented in a special module – *aspect*, as shown below.

Another important part of ASP.NET security is *authorization*. On authentication, the application's resources can be accessible for the selected group of users only. Besides, some of the actions of the business logic are not always performed by *all* users, but can be performed by some selected group of users only. So an access permission check of the user is needed before granting access to resources or business logic actions. That kind of check is also a cross-cutting concern, so we'll implement it by an aspect.

Suppose our application performs some kind of business logic implemented by the class *BusinessLogic*. This class implements the actions of the business logic available for authenticated (or some group of selected) users. For example, see Example 6.

In the code of the application, before calling the above methods, it is necessary to authenticate the user and to check his or her authorization, as follows in Example 7.

Here, *User* is an object of a class implementing the interface *System.Security.Principal.IPrincipal*. This object is available as a property of the object describing the Web page *System.Web. UI.Page*. The above kinds of checks can be implemented as actions of an aspect, since they constitute a cross-cutting concern and should be performed with different kinds of business logic and

Example 6.

```
public class BusinessLogic
{
    virtual public void DoSomething()
    {
    }
    virtual public void DoSomethingWithAdminRole()
    {
    }
}
```

Example 7.

```
if (User.Identity.IsAuthenticated)
{
    BusinessLogic.DoSomething();
}
if (User.Identity.IsAuthenticated &&
    User.IsInRole("Administrator"))
{
    BusinessLogic.DoSomethingWithAdminRole();
}
```

in different execution points of the application. Let's call our aspect *WebSecurityAspect*:

```
public class WebSecurityAspect:
Aspect
{
}
```

Let's add to our aspects the following kinds of authentication and authorization actions.

The authentication action of the aspect is shown in Example 8.

The weaving condition %instead %call *.Do-Something() means that, instead of any call of the method *DoSomething()* of any class, the action *AuthenticationAction()* will be called. In that action, we check whether the user is authenticated, using the property *IPrincipal.Identity.IsAuthenticated*. If the user is authenticated, he or she is granted a permission to perform the action of the target object, i.e., to call the method *DoSomething()* of the object of the *BusinessLogic* class. If not, an exception is thrown or some other kind of action is performed.

Example 8.

```
[AspectAction("%instead %call *.DoSomething()")]
public static void AuthenticationAction()
{
    IPrincipal User = HttpContext.Current.User;
    if (User.Identity.IsAuthenticated)
    {
        BusinessLogic BusLog = (BusinessLogic)TargetObject;
        //Perform business action
        BusLog.DoSomething();
    }
    else
    {
        //Throw exception or perform other action
    }
}
```

The authorization action of the aspect is shown in Example 9.

The weaving condition %instead %call *. DoSomethingWithAdminRole() means that, instead of any call of the method *DoSomething-WithAdminRole()* of any class, the aspect's action *AuthorizationAction()* is called. In that action, we check whether the user is authenticated, using the property *IPrincipal.Identity.IsAuthenticated,* and whether the user has administrator's permissions, by checking *User.IsInRole("Administrator").* If both conditions hold, the user is allowed to perform the action of the target object, i.e., to call the method *DoSomethingWithAdminRole()* of the object of the *BusinessLogic* class. If not, an exception is thrown, or some other kind of action is performed.

Impersonation Aspects

Impersonation is a mechanism to grant to the server process of ASP.NET access permissions of an authenticated user. This mechanism works with *Windows authentication* type only. With this kind of authentication, impersonation is performed by the Web server. ASP.NET uses the authenticated IIS user for identification and security checks.

Usually an ASP.NET application code is executed under a user account with limited permissions. In Windows XP, ASP.NET automatically creates a user account named ASPNET. In Windows Server 2003, Windows Vista and Windows Server 2008, ASP.NET uses the *Network Service Account.* That account has its own security permission set which is surely not identical to the permission set of the authenticated user. So the authenticated user cannot use his or her permission set but has to use the permission set of the ASP.NET user account. But in some cases we need to execute the application under the permission set of the authenticated user. The process of executing a code under another user account and with some other's permission set is referred to as *impersonation.*

Impersonation can be considered as a cross-cutting concern, since, each time we need a fragment of code with the authenticated user's permission set, the process of impersonation

Example 9.

```
[AspectAction("%instead %call *.DoSomethingWithAdminRole()")]
public static void AuthorizationAction()
{
    IPrincipal User = HttpContext.Current.User;
    if (User.Identity.IsAuthenticated &&
        User.IsInRole("Administrator"))
    {
        BusinessLogic BusLog = (BusinessLogic)TargetObject;
        //Do business action
        BusLog.DoSomethingWithAdminRole();
    }
    else
    {
        //Throw exception or redirect to Error Page
    }
}
```

Example 10.

```
public class BusinessLogic
{
    virtual public void DoImpersonationTask()
    {
    }
}
```

Example 11.

```
WindowsIdentity windowsID =
    User.Identity as WindowsIdentity;
if (windowsID != null)
{
    WindowsImpersonationContext wiContext =
        windowsID.Impersonate();
    oBusinessLogic.DoImpersonationTask();
    wiContext.Undo();
}
```

should be repeated, and its implementation is represented by a set of tangled execution points of the application. So we think the best way to implement impersonation is an aspect.

Suppose in our application some kind of business logic needs to be performed, implemented by the class *BusinessLogic*. In this class, some action of the business logic is implemented that needs impersonation for its execution. For example, see Example 10.

To impersonate this method, in our Web application we should execute the following code shown in Example 11.

Now let's implement this impersonation mechanism using AOP. Let's add to our *WebSecurityAspect* the action *ImpersonationAction* implemented in Example 12.

The weaving condition %instead %call *Imperson* means that, instead of any call of any method whose name satisfies the *Imperson* wildcard, the aspect's action *ImpersonationAction()* will be called. In that action, we check

whether the current authentication mode is *Windows Authentication*. If so, we impersonate our method. If not, we throw exception or perform another task.

Impersonation under some specific user account. In Web applications, often some actions need to be performed with the permission set of some specific user account. In this case, we should impersonate the actions to be performed under that specific account. Let's consider how to implement this functionality by an aspect.

First, the aspect should import the following system methods (see Example 13).

The method *LogonUser()* is used to register the user on a remote host. The method *CloseHandle()* closes the handle of an open object.

Let's add to our *WebSecurityAspect* the action of impersonation under a specified account (see Example 14).

In this action, the user is registered on a remote host by the *LogonUser()* method. After that, the returned user token is used for impersonation by

Example 12.

```
[AspectAction("%instead %call *Imperson*")]
public static void ImpersonationAction()
{
    WindowsIdentity windowsID =
      HttpContext.Current.User.Identity as WindowsIdentity;
    if (windowsID != null)
    {
        WindowsImpersonationContext wiContext =
          windowsID.Impersonate();
            BusinessLogic BusLog = (BusinessLogic)TargetObject;
        BusLog.DoImpersonationTask();
        wiContext.Undo();
    }
    else
    {
        // The user isn't Windows authenticated:
        // Throw an exception or perform another task
    }
}
```

Example 13.

```
[DllImport(@"advapi32.dll")]
public static extern bool LogonUser
    (string lpszUserName,
     string lpszDomain,
     string lpszPassword,
     int dwLogonType, int dwLogonProvider, out int phToken);
[DllImport("kernel32.dll", CharSet = CharSet.Auto)]
public static extern bool CloseHandle(IntPtr handle);
```

the static method *WindowsIdentity. Impersonate(Token)*.

Cryptography Aspects for the Request String

One of the common ways of passing information between the pages in Web applications is to use *HTTP Query Strings*.

HTTP query string is part of the unified resource locator (URL) that contains some data to be passed to Web applications. For example, if the URL address of the request is:

http://localhost/Recipient.aspx?mydata=asp. net&mytime=27-May-09+14%3a38%3a10,

The value of the request string is:

Example 14.

```
[AspectAction("%instead %call *Imperson*")]
public static void ImpersonationBySpecifedAccountAction()
{
    int returnedToken;
    if (LogonUser(username, machine, password,
        3, 0, out returnedToken))
    {
        IntPtr Token = new IntPtr(returnedToken);
        BusinessLogic BusLogic = (BusinessLogic)TargetObject;
        WindowsImpersonationContext winContext =
          WindowsIdentity.Impersonate(Token);
        if (winContext != null)
        {
            CloseHandle(Token);
        }
        BusLogic.DoImpersonationTask();
        winContext.Undo();
    }
    else
    {
        // Throw an exception or perform another task
    }
}
```

mydata=asp.net&mytime=27-May-09+14%3a38%3a10

In some kinds of URL requests, the request string can be freely viewed or modified by the user. But there are cases when the request string contains a kind of confidential information that should not be viewed by the user. The common ways to solve this problem is to use state management, e.g. *View state*, *Session*, or *Cookies* – but those methods can have other kinds of restrictions. Another alternative is to encrypt the request string. Let's consider how request string encryption can be implemented using AOP and Aspect.NET.

Encryption of the Query String

In (McDonald, 2008), the authors demonstrate an interesting method of request string encryption. In our aspect, we'll use the Hex Encoding method of the referred paper to encrypt a request string (see Example 15).

The *GetString()* method transforms the array of *byte* data into a hexadecimal string, and the method *GetBytes()* performs the inverse action, i.e. transforms the hexadecimal string into a byte array.

Example 16 is an example of request string encryption.

In the above example, the explicit query string *ClearQueryString* is encrypted by a *symmetric encryption* algorithm, also referred to as *SymEn-*

Example 15.

```
// Hexadecimal-based encoding
// that replaces each character with its alpha-numeric code
protected static string GetString(byte[] data)
{
    StringBuilder sb = new StringBuilder();
    foreach (byte b in data)
    {
        sb.Append(b.ToString("X2"));
    }
    return sb.ToString();
}
// Decode hexadecimal-based string
protected static byte[] GetBytes(string data)
{
    //GetString encodes the hex numbers with two digits
    byte[] Results = new byte[data.Length / 2];
    for (int i = 0; i < data.Length; i += 2)
    {
        Results[i / 2] =
            Convert.ToByte(data.Substring(i, 2), 16);
    }
    return Results;
}
```

Example 16.

```
protected void SendCommand_Click(object sender, EventArgs e)
{
    string ClearQueryString =
        "mydata=" + HttpUtility.UrlEncode(MyData.Text)
        + "&mytime=" +
        HttpUtility.UrlEncode(DateTime.Now.ToString());
    byte[] EncryptedData =
        SymEncryption.Encrypt(ClearQueryString);
    string NewQuery =
        "Recipient.aspx?data=" + GetString(EncryptedData);
    Response.Redirect(NewQuery);
}
```

Example 17.

```
byte[] EncryptedData =
   ProtectedData.Protect
      (Encoding.UTF8.GetBytes(ClearQueryString),
   null, DataProtectionScope.LocalMachine);
```

cryption. More detailed description of .NET cryptography is given in (McDonald, 2008).

In our example, besides symmetric encryption, we can use any other encryption methods, such as shown in Example 17.

Here we use *Windows data protection API (DPAPI)* for encryption (McDonald, 2008).

After encryption, the request string needs to be converted to a *string* to be passed to the URL request. One of the possible approaches to do that is to use the static method *Convert.ToBase64String()* which creates a Base64-encoded string. But this string may contain symbols not allowed in a request string. So let's convert it to hexadecimal string using the *GetString()* method. After that, we should redirect the request using *HttpResponse. Redirect()*. Our resulting URL request will look as follows:

http://localhost/Recipient.aspx?data=688558E9 56A2970ECEBB7BA7F7228331DF0AAB5D0 3D8E73A8F00577442BE5921EBEFF51A4B9 79F074175D1772993FD7405B8A1CC1DCF36 7E0F1445FE68CD9C99

Now let's consider the process of decryption of the encrypted query string (see Example 18).

In the above code, the encrypted request string is retrieved from the URL request, then in is passed to the *GetBytes()* method to extract the encrypted data represented as a byte array *byte[] Encrypted-Data = GetBytes(EncryptedQS["data"])*.

After that, the data decryption method is called:

```
string ClearQueryString = SymEncryp-
tion.DecryptToString(EncryptedData);
```

The decrypted string (of the *string* type) is scanned, and its data are passed to the object *DecryptedQS* of the type *System.Collections. Specialized.NameValueCollection*. As the result, we can get the data we need from that object, e.g., *DecryptedQS["mydata"]*.

Encryption and Decryption of Query Strings as a Cross-Cutting Concern

The encryption / decryption mechanism explained above is simple enough, so we can apply it in our Web applications.

The problem occurs when we need to apply the above mechanism in many execution points of the application, i.e., when calling the *HttpResponse. Redirect()* method and when decrypting the query string. While using the application, the customers may realize that it is necessary to encrypt all or some of the request strings. Then, the developers need to update the application code accordingly. By using common OOP methods, the code should be modified "by hand" in many execution points. This problem can be handled by AOP, since it is clear that encryption and decryption is a cross-cutting concern, and it can be implemented as a set of aspect actions to be woven automatically into the target application. All we need to do is to properly define the weaving conditions of the aspect's actions.

Implementation of the Cryptography Aspects

Let's implement the encryption / decryption aspect using the following guidelines.

Example 18.

```
protected void Page_Load(object sender, EventArgs e)
{
    NameValueCollection EncryptedQS = Request.QueryString;
    byte[] EncryptedData = GetBytes(EncryptedQS["data"]);
      // Decode hexadecimal-based string
    string ClearQueryString =
      SymEncryption.DecryptToString(EncryptedData);
    //Split data and add the contents
    int Index;
    string[] SplittedQS =
      ClearQueryString.Split(new char[] { '&' });
    NameValueCollection DecryptedQS =
      new NameValueCollection();
    foreach (string SingleData in SplittedQS)
    {
        Index = SingleData.IndexOf('=');
        DecryptedQS.Add(
            HttpUtility.UrlDecode
              (SingleData.Substring(0, Index)),
            HttpUtility.UrlDecode
              (SingleData.Substring(Index + 1))
          );
    }
    lbMsg.Text = "mydata = " + DecryptedQS["mydata"];
    lbMsg.Text += "<br/>mytime = " + DecryptedQS["mytime"];
}
```

All aspects should inherit from the predefined class *Aspect* of the Aspect.NET platform. Our base class *CryptoAspect* implementing the aspect should contain a static field *SymEncryption* of the type *SymmetricEncryption*. The symmetric encryption algorithm should be implemented by the two static methods *GetString()* and *GetBytes()*, as explained above.

CryptoQueryStringAspect is the main aspect class that inherits from the *CryptoAspect* class. It contains two actions - *RedirectAction()* (the encryption action) and *GetQueryStringAction()* (the decryption action).

The encryption action is shown in Example 19.

In the Example 19's code, the weaving condition:

```
%instead %call HttpResponse.
Redirect(string) && %args(arg[0])
```

In our Web application, the request redirection code will look as shown in Example 20.

The decryption action is shown in Example 21.

The aspect's weaving condition

Example 19.

```
[AspectAction
 ("%instead %call HttpResponse.Redirect(string) && %args(arg[0])")]
    public static void RedirectAction(string Query)
    {
        string[] SplittedQuery = Query.Split(new char[] { '?' });
        string RedirectPage = SplittedQuery[0];
        string ClearQueryString = SplittedQuery[1];
        // Now encrypt the query string
        byte[] EncryptedData =
          SymEncryption.Encrypt(ClearQueryString);
        string NewQuery = RedirectPage + "?data=" +
          GetString(EncryptedData);
        HttpContext.Current.Response.Redirect(NewQuery);
}
```

Example 20.

```
    protected void SendCommand_Click(object sender, EventArgs e)
    {
        string RedirectArg = "Recipient.aspx?mydata=" +
          HttpUtility.UrlEncode(MyData.Text)+
          "&mytime=" +
          HttpUtility.UrlEncode(DateTime.Now.ToString());
        lbMsg.Text = "<b>" + RedirectArg + "</b>";

        Response.Redirect(RedirectArg);
    }
```

```
%instead %call HttpRequest.get_Que-
ryString()
```

means that, instead of any call of *HttpRequest. get_QueryString()* (i.e., when accessing the *QueryString* property of the object of the *System. Web.HttpRequest* class), the aspect's action *GetQueryStringAction()* will be called.

In our Web application, the code to retrieve the data from the request string will look as follows in Example 22.

HTML Encoding Aspects

In Web applications, it is quite common to represent static information by pages not changeable by the users. Examples of such kind of Web ap-

Example 21.

```
[AspectAction("%instead %call HttpRequest.get_QueryString()")]
      public static NameValueCollection GetQueryStringAction()
      {
          HttpRequest Request = (HttpRequest)TargetObject;
          NameValueCollection EncryptedQS = Request.QueryString;
          byte[] EncryptedData = GetBytes(EncryptedQS["data"]);
            // Decode hexadecimal-based string
          string ClearQueryString =
            SymEncryption.DecryptToString(EncryptedData);
          // Split the data and add the content
          int Index;
          string[] SplittedQS =
            ClearQueryString.Split(new char[] { '&' });
          NameValueCollection DecryptedQS =
            new NameValueCollection();
          foreach (string SingleData in SplittedQS)
          {
              Index = SingleData.IndexOf('=');
              DecryptedQS.Add(
                  HttpUtility.UrlDecode
                    (SingleData.Substring(0, Index)),
                  HttpUtility.UrlDecode
                    (SingleData.Substring(Index + 1))
                );
          }
          return DecryptedQS;
          }
```

Example 22.

```
      protected void Page_Load(object sender, EventArgs e)
      {
          NameValueCollection QueryString = Request.QueryString;
          lbMsg.Text = "mydata = " + QueryString["mydata"];
          lbMsg.Text += "<br/>mytime = " + QueryString["mytime"];
      }
```

plications are those to publish news, e.g., http://www.reuters.com.

There is a problem related to this information: it may contain symbols displayed incorrectly by the browser.

For example, if we need to set the following texts for the *Label* control:

```
lbMsg.Text = "if a<b then";
lbMsg.Text = "for bold face one
should use the <b> tag";
```

These texts are displayed in the browser as follows:

```
        if a
        for bold face one should use
the
```

The above texts are surely wrong, since the original texts contain the symbols "<" and ">" which "mislead" the browser.

For this reason, such symbols should be encoded into their *HTML equivalents*, for example, the "<" symbol is encoded into the sequence "<".

The following special symbols have specific encoding equivalents in HTML texts:

- space symbol -
- "<" symbol - &lt
- ">" symbol - &gt
- "&" symbol - &amp
- quote symbol - &quot

Now let's consider how to use AOP for HTML encoding of text.

Hypertext Encoding in ASP.NET

In ASP.NET, we can use the method *System. Web.HttpServerUtility.HtmlEncode()* to encode any text to the text with special HTML-encoded symbols (see Example 23).

Here, *Server* is a property of the class *System. Web.UI.Page* which has the type *System.Web. HtmlServerUtility*.

The encoded texts will be displayed by the browser correctly:

```
if a<b then
for bold face one should use the <b>
tag
```

The HTML encoded texts will look as follows:

```
if a&lt;b then
for bold face one should use the
&lt;b&gt; tag
```

To decode the texts, the method *System.Web. HttpServerUtility.HtmlDecode()* should be used:

```
string text = Server.
HtmlDecode(lbMsg.Text);
```

The method *HtmlEncode()* is often used in case we retrieve a text from a database but we don't know for sure whether it is a legal HTML text.

The problem with the method *HtmlEncode()* is that it does not encode a sequence of spaces into the appropriate sequence of "* *" encodings. So, if our text contains a sequence of spaces, the browser displays one space symbol only. To solve this problem, we can explicitly replace each

Example 23.

```
lbMsg.Text = Server.HtmlEncode("if a<b then ");
lbMsg.Text =
  Server.HtmlEncode("for bold face one should use the <b> tag ");
```

space symbol to "* *" by calling the method *String.Replace()*:

```
    string text = Server.
HtmlEncode(sometext);
text = text.Replace(" ", " ");
```

Besides that, *HtmlEncode()* does not convert line breaks into "*
*", so we also need to explicitly implement this conversion if necessary.

Hypertext Encoding as a Cross-Cutting Concern

As we've seen from the above, each time we need HTML encoding in our application, it can be implemented by an *HttpServerUtility.HtmlEncode()* method call, and each time HTML decoding is needed, it should be implemented by a *HttpServerUtility.HtmlDecode()* method call. So we typically need to make calls of those methods throughout the whole application. Besides that, in many cases, we need to execute some extra code to fix the shortcomings of those predefined methods discussed above - for example, to call *text. Replace(" ", " ")* or to execute some code to convert line breaks to the "*
*" sequences. It may also happen that, on starting to use the application, the customers notice that the textual data retrieved from the database contain special symbols listed above. In those cases, the application developers have to add a new functionality of hypertext encoding and decoding, using the approach discussed above. This functionality has to be added into many tangled pieces of the application code. So hypertext encoding / decoding is a cross-cutting concern, and the most safe and comfortable way to implement it is to use AOP.

Implementation of the HTML Encoding Aspect

Suppose in our application there is an execution point to define the text for the *Label* control:

```
lbMsg.Text = " for bold face one
should use the <b> tag";
```

Let's create an aspect named *HtmlEncodingAspect*, shown in Example 24.

Let's add to this aspect the action *HtmlEncodeAdvice()* whose call should be added to that execution point (see Example 25).

This weaving rule enables injection of the call of *HtmlEncode()* and, after that, the code to convert sequences of spaces into sequences of "* *". After that, the action assigns the encoded version of the text to the control label.

The weaving condition:

```
%instead %call Label.set_Text(string)
&& %args(arg[0])
```

We can also use the same action for the execution points that define the label text for other kinds of controls - *LinkButton, HyperLink, CheckBox, ListItem, RadioButton*, etc. In such case, the weaving condition should be updated to fit to the appropriate execution points. The syntax of weaving conditions in Aspect.NET is covered in (Safonov, 2008). For example, the following version of the weaving condition:

Example 24.

```
    public class HtmlEncodingAspect: Aspect
    {

}
```

```
%instead %call *.set_Text(string) &&
%args(arg[0])
```

Now let's consider the implementation of the aspect's action of decoding. Let in our application there exist execution points to assign the text for the *Label* control, e.g.:

```
string text = lbMsg.Text;
```

Let's add to our aspect *HtmlEncodingAspect* the action shown in Example 27.

The weaving condition:

```
%instead %call Label.get_Text()
```

Example 25.

```
[AspectAction
  ("%instead %call Label.set_Text(string) && %args(arg[0])")]
    public static void HtmlEncodeAdvice(string text)
    {
        Label label = (Label)TargetObject;
        string encodedText =
          HttpContext.Current.Server.HtmlEncode(text);
        encodedText = encodedText.Replace(" ", " ");
        label.Text = encodedText;
    }
```

Example 26.

```
    //We can apply this advice for
    // LinkButton, HyperLink, CheckBox, ListItem, RadioButton
    [AspectAction(
      "%instead %call *.set_Text(string) && %args(arg[0])")]
    public static void HtmlEncodeAdvice(string text)
    {
        string encodedText =
          HttpContext.Current.Server.HtmlEncode(text);
        encodedText = encodedText.Replace(" ", " ");
        if (TargetObject is Label)
        {
            ((Label)TargetObject).Text = encodedText;
        }
        else if (TargetObject is CheckBox)
        {
            ((CheckBox)TargetObject).Text = encodedText;
        ...
        }
    }
```

Aspects for Extending the User's Web Interface

In maintaining Web applications, the developers often come across the problem of extending the user interface of the application, for example, the following ways: to add a Google map into a Web page; to add a reference to some site; to add advertizing Web controls; to add printing a message on some action.

In this section we demonstrate implementation of such new functionality as an aspect, i.e., its implementation as an aspect's action, with the appropriate weaving conditions for necessary join points. The advantage of such solution is its flexibility and reusability. The actions of our aspect will implement this new functionality by dynamic addition of the appropriate controls into the appropriate container defined in the configuration file *Web.config* of our Web application.

Here is a simple example of an aspect that adds to a given Web page a reference to the Web site of our Department of Mathematics and Mechanics of St. Petersburg University.

Suppose in our Web application there exists the *InitPage()* method that initializes the Web page and is called within the event handler *Page_Load()*. Let's define an aspect's weaving rule action to

Example 27.

```
[AspectAction("%instead %call Label.get_Text()")]
    public static string HtmlDecodeAdvice()
    {
        Label label = (Label)TargetObject;
        string encodedText = label.Text;
        encodedText = encodedText.Replace(" ", " ");
        return HttpContext.Current.Server.HtmlDecode(encodedText);
    }
```

Example 28.

```
[AspectAction("%before %call *.InitPage()")]
    public static void AddLinkToMatMexSite()
    {
        Page ThePage = (Page)TargetObject;
        WebControl Container =
          (WebControl)ThePage.FindControl(ContainerID);
        if (Container != null)
        {
            HyperLink hLink = new HyperLink();
            hLink.NavigateUrl = "http://www.math.spbu.ru";
            hLink.Text =
              "<br/> Click here to enter the SPBU math-mech site";
            Container.Controls.Add(hLink);
        }
    }
```

inject a call of the aspect's action before the call of *InitPage()* (see Example 28).

Here, the *HyperLink* control is created dynamically and added to the appropriate *Container* whose identifier is created in the *appSettings* section of the *Web.config* file. Let's retrieve this identifier (*ID*) using the static property *ContainerID* of the aspect:

```
ContainerID = ConfigurationManager.
AppSettings["ContainerID"];
```

Aspects for Cryptography of the Cookie File

One of the common ways to store data on the user side in Web applications is to use *cookie*.

Cookie is a typically small element of data created by the Web server and stored on the user's host machine as a file sent by the Web client (usually browser) to the Web server in any HTTP request to open a page of some Web site. The cookie file contains information about the user collected by the Web server. Application servers can store in cookie files the history of visiting the site, the pages

rendered, the personal settings made by the user when visiting the site, the list of the advertisings displayed by the user, and the user's preferences.

Since cookie files may contain confidential information (e.g., the user name and access conditions), their content should not be accessible to other users. One of the ways to protect cookie from non-authorized access is to encrypt their content.

Let's consider how to encrypt and decrypt cookie using AOP and Aspect.NET.

Cookie Encryption Problem

In ASP.NET, using cookie is very simple. To create a cookie file, Example 29 can be used.

To retrieve information from the cookie file, Example 30 can be used.

Cookie Cryptography

Cookie cryptography is an important task of Web programming. Two approaches to cookie cryptography are known: encryption of every value of the cookie, or encryption of all its content. In the above code, the cookie contains two

Example 29.

```
HttpCookie cookie = new HttpCookie("MyCookie");
cookie["Faculty"] = "Mat-Mex";
cookie["University"] = "SPBU";
cookie.Expires = DateTime.Now.AddDays(1);
Response.Cookies.Add(cookie);
```

Example 30.

```
HttpCookie cookie = Request.Cookies["MyCookie"];
if (cookie != null)
{
    string Faculty = cookie["Faculty"];
    string University = cookie["University"];
        ...
}
```

Example 31.

```
byte[] encryptedFaculty = SymEncryption.Encrypt("Mat-Mex");
byte[] encryptedUniversity = SymEncryption.Encrypt("SPBU");
cookie["Faculty"] = GetString(encryptedFaculty);
cookie["University"] = GetString(encryptedUniversity);
cookie.Expires = DateTime.Now.AddDays(1);
Response.Cookies.Add(cookie);
```

Example 32.

```
Faculty=F469740090506E6E47AFA8FC65CFA18C&University=D3460A53FF90300FBBE6A3A67
CF25731
```

values, "Mat-Mex" and "SPBU", and its content is "Faculty=Mat-Mex&University=SPBU". Let's consider each of the two approaches.

Encrypting each value of the cookie (see Example 31).

In the above code, each value of the cookie is encrypted using symmetric encryption (*SymEncryption*). In principle, instead of the symmetric algorithm, we can use any other kind of encryption, e.g., Windows data protection API (DPAPI). On encrypting a value of cookie, it needs to be converted to a *string* using the method *GetString()*. As the result, the content of the sample cookie will be as follows in Example 32.

Now consider the process of decryption of the encrypted value of the cookie shown in Example 33.

In Example 33's code, the encrypted value of the cookie is retrieved. It is passed to the method *GetBytes()* to get the encrypted data as a byte array:

```
byte[] encryptedFaculty =
GetBytes(cookie["Faculty"])
```

After that, the data decryption method is called:

```
string Faculty = SymEncryption.Decryp
tToString(encryptedFaculty);
```

Cookie content encryption (see Example 34).

The content of the cookie (cookie.Value) is encrypted using the symmetric encryption algorithm.

Example 33.

```
byte[] encryptedFaculty = GetBytes(cookie["Faculty"]);
byte[] encryptedUniversity = GetBytes(cookie["University"]);
string Faculty =
  SymEncryption.DecryptToString(encryptedFaculty);
string University =
  SymEncryption.DecryptToString(encryptedUniversity);
```

Example 34.

```
cookie["Faculty"] = "Mat-Mex";
cookie["University"] = "SPBU";
cookie.Expires = DateTime.Now.AddDays(1);
string value = cookie.Value;
byte[] encryptedValue = SymEncryption.Encrypt(value);
cookie.Value = GetString(encryptedValue);
Response.Cookies.Add(cookie);
```

Example 35.

```
DEEEC43962E19C16C0FA0466D568D2AE5FC79DFB716687C6250BB1137AE1C66C05C7D-
0C9BE8DE299
```

On encryption, it is necessary to convert the encrypted data to a *string* by the method *GetString()*, to pass them to the cookie (HttpSecureCookie, 2009):

```
cookie.Value =
GetString(encryptedValue)
```

As the result, the content of the sample cookie will look as shown in Example 35.

Now let's consider the process of the cookie decryption in Example 36.

This code creates a new cookie with the decrypted content:

```
HttpCookie decryptedCookie = new
HttpCookie("MyCookie", value)
```

After that, we retrieve the necessary value from the cookie:

```
string Faculty =
decryptedCookie["Faculty"]
```

Another way to encrypt cookie is proposed in (HttpSecureCookie, 2009). The author of that paper uses the inner class System.Web.Security. CookieProtectionHelper of ASP.NET to encrypt the cookie content. To access the methods Decode and Encode of that class, the author uses reflection. The following code demonstrates how to use the proposed method in our Web application.

Encryption is shown in Example 37.

As the result, the content of the cookie will look like Example 38.

Example 36.

```
byte[] encryptedValue = GetBytes(cookie.Value);
string value = SymEncryption.DecryptToString(encryptedValue);
HttpCookie decryptedCookie =
  new HttpCookie("MyCookie", value);
string Faculty = decryptedCookie["Faculty"];
string University = decryptedCookie["University"];
```

Example 37.

```
cookie["Faculty"] = "Mat-Mex";
cookie["University"] = "SPBU";
cookie.Expires = DateTime.Now.AddDays(1);
cookie = HttpSecureCookie.Encode(cookie);
Response.Cookies.Add(cookie);
```

Example 38.

idiEWsQ6B_LXOnVosr7EgRYL9Kz0GIV-tX1kQH_ywnuqfH3tTUELMtNqb6Zl4yC-WSgGrEt4y6joK-8bOPhGTAQ2

Example 39.

```
HttpCookie decryptedCookie =
  HttpSecureCookie.Decode(cookie);
string Faculty = decryptedCookie["Faculty"];
string University = decryptedCookie["University"];
```

Decryption is shown in Example 39.

Cookie Encryption as a Cross-Cutting Concern

Our discussion shows that cookie encryption and decryption mechanism is simple enough and can be easily added to our Web applications.

The problem arises when we need to apply this method in many tangled execution points of the application, in each call of the method to assign a cookie value, e.g.:

```
cookie["Faculty"] = "Mat-Mex";
```

In other words, it means that we need to use our mechanism in each call of the method:

```
  HttpCookie.set_Item(string,
string)
```

```
Response.Cookies.Add()
```

So we see that encryption / decryption of cookie is a cross-cutting concern, we can handle this problem with AOP, to avoid adding bugs to the code which is not unlikely using manual code insertions.

Cookie Encryption Aspects

This section explains how to use Aspect.NET to solve the above problem.

Let's implement aspects using the following principles.

All aspects should inherit from the predefined class *Aspect* of Aspect.NET. The base class of our aspect *CryptoAspect* contains a static field *SymEncryption* of the type *SymmetricEncryption* used for symmetric encryption, and two static methods *GetString()* and *GetBytes()* for hexadecimal conversion of strings.

The main aspect class is *CryptoCookieAspect*. It inherits from *CryptoAspect* and contains the

Example 40.

```
[AspectAction
 ("%instead %call HttpCookie.set_Item(string, string) && %args(arg[0],
arg[1])")]
    public static void EncryptAction(string key, string value)
    {
        HttpCookie cookie = (HttpCookie)TargetObject;
        byte[] EncryptedData = SymEncryption.Encrypt(value);
        cookie[key] = GetString(EncryptedData);
    }
```

Example 41.

```
%instead %call HttpCookie.set_Item(string, string)
&& %args(arg[0], arg[1])
```

actions implementing cookie encryption and decryption.

Let our Web application use the above code to create the cookie named *"MyCookie"*.

Let's implement the aspect actions using each of the two approaches to cookie cryptography discussed above in this section.

Cryptography of Every Value of the Cookie
The actions of our aspect will work with the execution points of the Web application where the values of the cookie are assigned:

```
cookie["Faculty"] = "Mat-Mex"
     HttpCookie.set_Item("Faculty",
"Mat-Mex")
     string Faculty =
cookie["Faculty"]
     HttpCookie.get_
Item("Faculty").
```

Let's add to the aspect *CryptoCookieAspect* the actions EncryptAction() and DecryptAction() to encrypt and to decrypt the value of the cookie.

The encryption action is shown in Example 40.

In this action, we define the weaving condition as Example 41.

It means that, instead of any call of the method HttpCookie.set_Item(), the aspect's action EncryptAction() will be called. So Aspect.NET replaces any method call HttpCookie.set_Item() by a call of the aspect's EncryptAction() in all execution points where the method HttpCookie.set_Item() is called. During the replacement, the arguments of the target method are captured and passed as arguments to the aspect's action.

The decryption action is shown in Example 42. This action defines the weaving condition:

```
%instead %call HttpCookie.
get_Item(string) && %args(arg[0])
```

This condition means that, instead of any call of HttpCookie.get_Item(), the aspect's action DecryptAction() will be called. So Aspect.NET replaces any call HttpCookie.get_Item() by the aspect's action call DecryptAction(). During the replacement, the argument of the target method is

Example 42.

```
[AspectAction("%instead %call HttpCookie.get_Item(string) &&
%args(arg[0])")]
    public static string DecryptAction(string key)
    {
        HttpCookie cookie = (HttpCookie)TargetObject;
        string EncryptedValue = cookie[key];
        string value = SymEncryption.DecryptToString(GetBytes(EncryptedVal
ue));
        return value;
    }
```

Example 43.

```
[AspectAction
    ("%before %call HttpCookieCollection.Add(HttpCookie) &&
%args(arg[0])")]
    public static void EncryptCookieAction(HttpCookie cookie)
    {
        string value = cookie.Value;
        cookie.Value = GetString(SymEncryption.Encrypt(value));
    }
```

captured and passed as argument to the aspect's action.

Cryptography of the Cookie Content

To implement this approach, our aspect's actions should be related to the execution points of the application where the cookie is added to the server response:

```
Response.Cookies.Add(cookie)
    cookie = Request.
Cookies["MyCookie"].
```

Let's add to the aspect *CryptoCookieAspect* the actions to encrypt - EncryptCookieAction(), and decrypt - DecryptCookieAction() the cookie content.

The encryption action is shown in Example 43.

This action defines the weaving condition shown in Example 44.

The condition means that, before any call of the method HttpCookieCollection. Add(HttpCookie), the aspect's action Encrypt-CookieAction() is called, and the argument of the target method is captured and passed as argument to the aspect's action.

The decryption action is laid out in Example 45.

Example 44.

```
%before %call HttpCookieCollection.Add(HttpCookie) && %args(arg[0])
```

Example 45.

```
[AspectAction
    ("%instead %call HttpCookieCollection.get_Item(string) &&
%args(arg[0])")]
    public static HttpCookie DecryptCookieAction(string name)
    {
        HttpCookie cookie =
            HttpContext.Current.Request.Cookies[name];
        byte[] EncryptedData = GetBytes(cookie.Value);
        string value =
            SymEncryption.DecryptToString(EncryptedData);
        return new HttpCookie(name, value);
    }
```

This action defines the weaving condition of Example 46.

This condition means that, instead a call of the method HttpCookieCollection.get_Item(string), the aspect's action DecryptCookieAction() will be called. The argument of the target method is captured and passed as argument to the aspect's action.

Next, let's consider how to implement the method of cookie encryption proposed in (HttpSecureCookie, 2009) by our aspect's actions.

Let's add to our aspect the actions EncryptCookieUsingMachineKeyAction() and DecryptCookieUsingMachineKeyAction().

The encryption action is shown in Example 47.

Example 48 is the decryption action.

Aspects for XML Document Validation

XML is now a de facto standard textual formal to represent structured data, to exchange information

Example 46.

```
%instead %call HttpCookieCollection.get_Item(string) && %args(arg[0])
```

Example 47.

```
[AspectAction
    ("%instead %call HttpCookieCollection.Add(HttpCookie) &&
%args(arg[0])")]
    public static void
    EncryptCookieUsingMachineKeyAction(HttpCookie cookie)
    {
        HttpCookie EncryptedCookie =
            HttpSecureCookie.Encode(cookie);
        HttpContext.Current.Response.Cookies.Add(EncryptedCookie);
    }
```

Example 48.

```
[AspectAction
   ("%instead %call HttpCookieCollection.get_Item(string) &&
%args(arg[0])")]
   public static HttpCookie
     DecryptCookieUsingMachineKeyAction(string name)
   {
       HttpCookie cookie =
         HttpContext.Current.Request.Cookies[name];
       HttpCookie DecryptedCookie =
         HttpSecureCookie.Decode(cookie);
       return DecryptedCookie;
   }
```

between the applications, and to create on its basis specialized markup languages (e.g., XHTML), also referred to as dictionaries.

XML defines a class of object data, referred to as XML documents, specific for some problem domain. XML allows the users to define a set of tags, their attributes and the internal structure of the document. In particular, XML plays a special role in VRML and 3D Web.

The following example used throughout this section defines a format to store a product catalog. The document starts with general information on the catalog, followed by the concrete product list (see Example 49).

Example 49.

```
<?xml version="1.0" encoding="utf-8" ?>
<productCatalog>
  <catalogName>Acme Fall 2008 Catalog</catalogName>
  <expiryDate>2008-01-01</expiryDate>
  <products>
    <product id="001">
      <productName>Magic Ring</productName>
      <productPrice>342.10</productPrice>
      <inStock>true</inStock>
    </product>
    <product id="002">
      <productName>Flying Carpet</productName>
      <productPrice>982.99</productPrice>
      <inStock>true</inStock>
    </product>
  </products>
</productCatalog>
```

Due to its flexibility, XML became widely applicable in Web application development. XML is used in Web applications based on ASP.NET when we need:

- To control the data stored in XML files, e.g., to exchange the data with the other applications;
- To store data in XML format and open an opportunity for their future integration. The other third party applications can be designed so as to be able to access those data;
- To use some technology that depends on XML. For example, Web services use a number of standards based on XML – WSDL (Web Service Definition Language), SOAP (Simple Object Access Protocol), and so on.

Since XML is an abstract language, XML dictionaries should be developed for its use. A dictionary allows the developers to agree on a concrete set of tags and attributes to be used. As well known, such dictionaries can be defined using DTD (Document Type Definition) or XML schemas. As compared to DTD, XML schemas are more powerful, more understandable, and more easily modifiable.

The following example of XML schema defines rules for the above XML document describing a product catalog (see Example 50).

An important task of XML document handling is their validation, i.e. checking of their correctness according to some rules defined by DTD or XML schemas. Validation should be done before actual use of an XML document, in the following typical cases:

- Before XML document transformations
- Before processing of XML documents
- Before reading some data from XML documents
- Before XML data binding.

Now let's consider how this typical cross-cutting concern of XML validation can be implemented on .NET platform using Aspect.NET.

XML Validation in .NET

One of the approaches to XML document validation according to its scheme is to use an object of the class *XMLValidatingReader*. To create such an object, the method *XmlReader.Create()* should be used. It should be passed an object of the class *XmlReaderSettings* that defines a XSD schema.

The validation reader throws an exception (or generates an event) to indicate an error in the XML document. Example 51 creates an object of the class *XmlReaderSettings* that defines the schema we need.

Each schema is used for element validation in some *namespace*. If our document contains elements from several namespaces, we can use separate schemas for their validation. The name of the namespace and the path to the schema file are passed to the method:

```
XmlReaderSettings.Schemas.Add(null,
XMLSchemaName).
```

Here, null indicates that the namespace is used which is defined by the attribute targetNamespace in the schema file.

Next, we add an event handler for the validation:

```
settings.ValidationEventHandler +=
XMLValidationHandler.
```

This handler will be used to detect errors in the document. If no event handler specified, an exception will be thrown. For example, the event handler can be implemented as follows in Example 52.

After initializing the validation, we can create a validation reader and implement document validation (see Example 53).

Example 50.

```xml
<?xml version="1.0" encoding="utf-8"?>
<xs:schema id="ProductCatalog"
    xmlns:xs="http://www.w3.org/2001/XMLSchema"
    elementFormDefault="qualified"
    targetNamespace="http://tempuri.org/ProductCatalog.xsd"
    xmlns="http://tempuri.org/ProductCatalog.xsd">
  <xs:element name="productCatalog">
    <xs:complexType>
      <xs:sequence>
        <xs:element name="catalogName" type="xs:string"/>
        <xs:element name="expiryDate" type="xs:date"/>
        <xs:element name="products">
          <xs:complexType>
            <xs:sequence>
              <xs:element name="product"
                  type="productType" maxOccurs="unbounded"/>
            </xs:sequence>
          </xs:complexType>
        </xs:element>
      </xs:sequence>
    </xs:complexType>
  </xs:element>
  <xs:complexType name="productType">
    <xs:sequence>
      <xs:element name="productName" type="xs:string"/>
      <xs:element name="productPrice" type="xs:decimal"/>
      <xs:element name="inStock" type="xs:boolean"/>
    </xs:sequence>
    <xs:attribute name="id" type="xs:integer" use="required"/>
  </xs:complexType>
</xs:schema>
```

Example 51.

```
XmlReaderSettings settings = new XmlReaderSettings();
settings.ValidationType = ValidationType.Schema;
settings.Schemas.Add(null, "ProductCatalog.xsd");
settings.ValidationEventHandler += XMLValidationHandler;
```

Example 52.

```
private static void XMLValidationHandler
   (object sender, ValidationEventArgs e)
{
   Errors.Append
      ("XML Validation Error: <b>" + e.Message + "</b><br/>");
}
```

Example 53.

```
vr = XmlReader.Create(xmlStream, settings);
//Read through the document
while (vr.Read())
{
   if (vr.NodeType == XmlNodeType.Element &&
       !vr.NamespaceURI.Equals(XMLNamSpace))
   {
      Errors.Append
       ("XML Validation Error: <b>The namespace '" +
       vr.NamespaceURI +
       "' of Element '" + vr.Name +
       "' is invalid. It must be '" +
       XMLNamSpace + "'</b><br/>");
   }
}
vr.Close();
```

Here:

```
FileStream xmlStream = new
FileStream(xmlFile, FileMode.Open).
```

In the *while* loop, we check the identity of the namespaces' names. If the names of the namespaces in the document and in the schema are not identical, validation is not performed.

Now let's check the document for possible errors (see Example 54).

If any errors found, an exception of the class XmlSchemaException will be thrown.

Since XML is typically used throughout all the application,, XML document validation should be made whenever an XML document is used, to enable correctness of data processing. So XML validation is a cross-cutting concern and can be implemented using AOP.

Now let's consider how to implement XML validation using Aspect.NET.

XML Validation Aspect

Let in our Web application there exist execution points that call methods of reading and processing data from our sample XML document *Product-Catalog.xml* (see Example 55).

Let's create an aspect named *XMLValidation-Aspect* to be applicable to such execution points.

Example 54.

```
if (Errors.ToString() == String.Empty)
{
    WriteToBrowser("Validation completed successfully<br/>");
}
else
{
    throw new XmlSchemaException(Errors.ToString());
}
```

Example 55.

```
try
{
    string xmlFile = Server.MapPath("ProductCatalog.xml");
    ReadXMLFile(xmlFile);
}
catch (Exception ex)
{
    lbError.Text = ex.Message;
}
```

Example 56.

```
[AspectAction
    ("%before %call *.ReadXMLFile(string, ..) && %args(%arg[0])")]
    public static void ValidateAgaintsXSDSchema(string xmlFile)
    {
        WriteToBrowser
        ("<b>XMLValidationAspect - Action: ValidateAgaintsXSDSchema</b> -
" +
        DateTime.Now +
        "<br/>");
        FileStream fs = new FileStream(xmlFile, FileMode.Open);
        ValidateAgainstXSDSchema(fs, XMLSchemaName);
    }
```

Let's define the following XML validation action in this aspect (see Example 56).

This action contains the following method call:

```
ValidateAgainstXSDSchema(Stream,
string)
```

This method, to be included into our aspect, implements XML document validation. Its first argument contains an XML document represented as a stream; the second argument is a path to the XML schema file. Based on this method, we can create yet another action to be applicable to execution points where XML streams are processed (e.g., when the application receives XML data from the Internet. See Example 57). The method implements the code discussed above.

There exists another way of XML document validation – using the class System.Xml.Linq. XDocument. Now let's create an aspect action to validate XML documents using that class (see Example 58).

Both kinds of the validation actions are woven by Aspect.NET before any call of the method *ReadXMLFile(string, ...)*. To apply the aspect to other kinds of execution points, the weaving conditions should be updated accordingly.

CONCLUSION

Our analysis of 3D Web and ordinary Web programming tasks made in this chapter confirms the applicability of AOP and Aspect.NET for a variety of typical Web security and privacy tasks to be solved, since all of them have essentially cross-cutting nature. AOP is especially valuable when adding a new functionality to the existing application code. As shown above, the advantage of using AOP for making Web applications more secure is the method of code modification supported by AOP: to define an aspect module that implement the new functionality; and to weave the aspect into the target application according to the aspect's weaving rules. The extra advantage of Aspect.NET is its user-controlled weaving option: the user can find and deselect redundant join points prior to actual weaving. This approach allows the Web application developers to avoid a lot of manual error-prone work of updating large code to add cross-cutting security functionality.

The resulting code of the library of Aspect. NET aspects for Web security is available for download at (Aspect.NET, 2008). This library shouldn't be regarded as a complete solution. It is a helpful material for Web developers to learn AOP and practically working examples how to apply AOP for Web security and privacy on the .NET platform.

FUTURE RESEARCH DIRECTIONS

Our research confirms the applicability of AOP with our Aspect.NET toolkit to solve many typical Web application security problems, especially in quite common situation when some new security functionality should be added to the existing Web application code. Our Web aspect library can be a basis for further implementation of 3D Web applications on the .NET platforms, since Web protocols and mechanisms supported are also used in 3D Web.

Surely this research is only a starting point for further research directions in this area. In particular, the following directions of further research look prospective in our opinion:

- Investigating an appropriate way of quantitative assessment of positive effect of applying AOP to productivity of Web application developers. Some results on such assessment of the use of Aspect.NET are provided in (Safonov, 2008, Chapter 4), but not specifically for Web programming;
- Implementing AOP tools applicable to specific 3D Web scripting languages used for specification of schemes and behaviors in most 3D Web engines - for VRML and X3D, for the first turn. In the current state, Aspect.NET is applicable to 3D Web engines implemented in C# in standard .NET environment (CLR, Visual Studio.NET, etc.). But, as we've found during our initial research how to apply Aspect.NET to 3D Web security, there are actually no open source 3D Web engines satisfying .NET

Example 57.

```
private static void ValidateAgaintsXSDSchema
(Stream xmlStream, string xsdFile)
{
    XmlReader vr = null;
    try
    {
        Errors = new StringBuilder();
        XmlReaderSettings settings = new XmlReaderSettings();
        settings.ValidationType = ValidationType.Schema;
        settings.Schemas.Add(null, XMLSchemaName);
        settings.ValidationEventHandler +=
          XMLValidationHandler;
        vr = XmlReader.Create(xmlStream, settings);
        while (vr.Read())
        {
            if (vr.NodeType == XmlNodeType.Element &&
                !vr.NamespaceURI.Equals(XMLNamSpace))
            {
                Errors.Append
                ("XML Validation Error: <b>The namespace '" +
                 vr.NamespaceURI +
                 "' of Element '" + vr.Name +
                 "' is invalid. It must be '" +
                 XMLNamSpace + "'</b><br/>");
            }
        }
        if (Errors.ToString() == String.Empty)
        {
            WriteToBrowser
                ("Validation completed successfully<br/>");
        }
        else
        {
            throw new XmlSchemaException(Errors.ToString());
        }
    }
    finally
    {
        if (vr != null) vr.Close();
        xmlStream.Close();
    }
}
```

Example 58.

```
[AspectAction
  ("%before %call *.ReadXMLFile(string, ..) && %args(%arg[0])")]
public static void
ValidateAgainstXSDSchemaUsingXDocument(string xmlFile)
{
    XDocument doc = XDocument.Load(xmlFile);
    XmlSchemaSet schemas = new XmlSchemaSet();
    schemas.Add(null, XMLSchemaName);
    // Validate the document (with event handling for errors)
    doc.Validate(schemas, XMLValidationHandler);
}
```

standards; all of them use their own enhanced versions of .NET virtual machine. Currently Aspect.NET is not applicable to weaving aspects to the code written in VRML, X3D, Lua, or C++ - those languages are, to our knowledge, mostly used now for the implementation of the existing 3D Web engines. Extending Aspect. NET to "understand" and manipulate code written in those languages, or developing a new AOP toolkit for .NET platform to do that, is a serious research challenge that requires a lot of time-consuming work, but it is surely worth doing to make AOP more helpful to solve typical 3D Web security and privacy tasks.

ACKNOWLEDGMENT

The author is grateful to PhD student Nguyen Van Doan for preparing the Web aspect examples used throughout the chapter and the implementation of the WebAspects library for Aspect.NET.

REFERENCES

Aspect, J. (2001). Retrieved from http://www.aspectj.org.

Aspect.NET. (2008). Retrieved from http://www.aspectdotnet.org.

Balder (2009). Retrieved from http://balder.codeplex.com/.

De Win, B., Piessens, F., & Joosen, W. (2006). How secure is AOP and what can we do about it? In *Proceedings of the 2006 international Workshop on Software Engineering For Secure Systems* (pp. 27-34). New York: ACM.

FlatRedBall. (2009). Retrieved from http://www.flatredball.com/frb/.

HttpSecureCookie. (2009). *A Way to Encrypt Cookies with ASP.NET 2.0*. Retrieved from http://www.codeproject.com/KB/web-security/HttpSecureCookie.aspx.

Kit3D (2009). Retrieved from http://kit3d.codeplex.com/.

MacDonald, M., & Szpuszta, M. (2008). *Pro ASP. NET 3.5 in C# 2008: Includes Silverlight 2*, (3rd ed.). New York: NY, Apress publishers.

Mesing, B., & Hellmich, C. (*18-21 April 2006*). Using aspect-oriented methods to add behaviors to X3D documents. In Web3D 2006 Proceedings, Columbia, Maryland (pp. 97–107). New York: ACM.

Mourad, A., Laverdiere, M., & Debbabi, M. (2007). Towards an aspect-oriented approach for the security hardening of code. In *Proceedings of the 21st international Conference on Advanced information Networking and Applications. Workshops Proceedings. Volume 1* (pp. 595-600). New York: IEEE Computer Society.

Ogre (2009). Retrieved from http://www.ogre3d.org/about/features.

Rajan, H., & Sullivan, K. J. (2005). Classpects: Unifying aspect- and object-oriented language design. In *Proceedings of the 27th international Conference on Software Engineering* (pp. 59-68). New York: ACM.

Safonov, V. O. (2008). *Using aspect-oriented programming for trustworthy software development*. Hoboken, NJ: Wiley Interscience. John Wiley & Sons. doi:10.1002/9780470283110

Second Life. (2009). Retrieved from http://www.secondlife.com.

Silverlight (2009). Retrieved from http://www.silverlight.net

Studio, D. X. (2009). Retrieved from http://www.dxstudio.com/.

Trustworthy Computing. (2008). *Microsoft Trustworthy Computing (TWC) Initiative Web Site*. http://www.microsoft.com/mscorp/twc/default.mspx.

Unity3D (2009). Retrieved from http://unity3d.com/.

Viega, J., Bloch, J. T., & Chandra, P. (2001). Applying aspect-oriented programming to security. *Cutter IT Journal, 14*(2), 31–39.

ADDITIONAL READING

Aspect-oriented software development Web site. http://aosd.net

Safonov, V., Gratchev, M., Grigoriev, D., & Maslennikov, A. (2006). Aspect.NET – aspect-oriented toolkit for Microsoft.NET based on Phoenix and Whidbey. In: J. Knoop, V. Skala (Eds.). *NET Technologies 2006 International Conference. Univ. of West Bohemia Campus Bory, May 29 – June 1, 2006, Pilsen, Czech Republic. Full Paper Proceedings* (pp. 19-29). http://dotnet.zcu.cz/NET_2006/NET_2006.htm

Safonov, V. O. (2003). Aspect.NET – a new approach to aspect-oriented programming. *NET Developers Journal, 1*(4), 36–40.

Safonov, V. O. (2004). Aspect.NET – concepts and architecture. *NET Developers Journal, 2*(9), 44–48.

Safonov, V. O. (2008). *Using aspect-oriented programming for trustworthy software development*. Hoboken, NJ: Wiley Interscience. John Wiley & Sons. doi:10.1002/9780470283110

Safonov, V. O., & Grigoriev, D. A. (2005). Aspect. NET: aspect-oriented programming for Microsoft. NET in practice. *NET Developer's Journal, 3*(7), 28–33.

Chapter 12
Modeling Secure 3D Web Applications

Krzysztof Walczak
Poznań University of Economics, Poland

ABSTRACT

This chapter describes a novel approach to building 3D web applications, called Flex-VR, which can be used a basis for implementing security solutions. Two key elements of the approach are described: scene structuralization and content modeling. The scene structuralization enables decomposition of a 3D scene into independent geometrical and behavioral objects, called VR-Beans. Virtual scenes with rich interactivity and behavior can be dynamically created by combining sets of independent VR-Beans. The second element – the content model – is a generalized high-level description of the application content. The model enables efficient manipulation of content elements and dynamic composition of virtual scenes. Flex-VR provides a fine-grained semantically-rich content structure, which can be used as a basis for defining access privileges for users and groups. Five levels of user privileges definition in the Flex-VR approach are described. An application of Flex-VR in the cultural heritage domain is presented that demonstrates how user privileges can be defined at all levels.

INTRODUCTION

For more than a decade experts and standardization bodies have been working on standards, such as VRML/X3D and MPEG-4, which enable publication of three-dimensional (3D) content on the web. These standards – formally approved by ISO/IEC – have now reached the level of maturity

that enables creation of appealing, high-quality, interactive 3D web content. Moreover, through continuous updates these standards incorporate recent advances in computer graphics, animation and interaction techniques.

During the same period we have observed remarkable progress in hardware performance, including cheap but powerful 3D accelerators available in most contemporary graphics cards, and rapid growth in the available network band-

DOI: 10.4018/978-1-61520-891-3.ch012

width, which is now sufficient to deliver the large amounts of data required by network-based 3D interactive multimedia applications. Therefore, technical problems related to the publication of 3D content on the web have now virtually disappeared.

Users are also prepared for this change. Popularity of 3D computer games, on-line communities and movies based on 3D computer graphics results in increasing familiarity of users with 3D graphics and – at the same time – is raising their expectations. E-commerce, education, training, entertainment and cultural heritage are notable examples of application domains that can largely benefit from the use of interactive 3D web technologies. Potentially viable business models accompany commercial exploitation of on-line 3D applications.

Despite these evident technical, social and economical prospects, the actual uptake of 3D applications on the web is still very low. Apparently, the sole ability to publish some pre-designed 3D content is not enough for wider deployment of 3D web applications. Such applications require enormous amounts of meaningful content, which must be highly dynamic, interactive and secure.

Lack of security in 3D web environments is one of important limitations of the current 3D web standards. This limitation is, to a large extent, a result of the currently used 3D data model. Web 3D content is typically stored in files – often textual. One scene usually corresponds to one file. The use of the "inline" feature to include other files is allowed, however, there are limitations on the available functionality. Privileges can be defined at the level of files – there is no way to define more fine-grained privileges to geometrical, functional or semantic elements of the 3D web environments.

A much more sophisticated and flexible security solution is necessary to support creation of complex 3D web applications in practice. The security system should enable definition of privileges, which could be used both at the content creation and at the content consumption phases. At the content creation phase, different users or groups may have different read or write privileges to spatial, temporal or logical parts of the 3D application content. At the content consumption phase, users may be granted privileges to access different parts of the content, to execute different operations within the content and to store results of their interactions.

In this chapter, we describe a generic approach to modeling 3D applications, called Flex-VR, which enables definition of fine-grained content access privileges, which can be used both at the content creation phase and at the content consumption phase. The approach consists of two main elements. The first element required to support creation of flexible secure 3D applications is an appropriate organization of the virtual scene content sent to the client browser. Traditional organization of virtual scenes based on a declarative scene graph with additional separate dataflow graph is not suitable for flexible modeling of application content, building highly dynamic systems and implementing security. Therefore a shift of paradigm towards a component based approach is required.

The second element is a high-level data model of the 3D application content. Such model is critical to enable efficient organization, manipulation and exchange of content between applications and to enable application of different access privileges to different parts of the content. Based on the generic model, particular virtual scenes are created dynamically as specific projections of the model based on the user's privileges, preferences and interaction history.

BACKGROUND

3D Web Applications

3D web applications are based on a similar paradigm as recently flourishing *Rich Internet Applications* (RIA), which can be used instead of typical desktop applications. Unlike 3D games or stationary VR installations, 3D web applications are fully described by content downloaded from the web. The content contains all the elements that constitute an application – the media objects (3D geometry, sounds, video clips, etc.) and the specification of their behavior (interaction, scenarios, physics, etc.). To be executed, a 3D web application – similarly as other RIAs – requires a *runtime environment*, which interprets the content and provides a bi-directional interface to a user. This function is performed by 3D browsers, which are responsible for multimodal rendering of the content and for providing means of navigation and user interaction. 3D browsers are usually implemented as plug-ins to standard web browsers such as Internet Explorer or Firefox, although standalone 3D browsers also exist.

3D Web Content Standards

The most important standards enabling publication of 3D content on the web are VRML, X3D and MPEG-4. VRML – the *Virtual Reality Modeling Language* – is a textual file format for describing and publishing interactive, animated 3D multimedia content. The standard has been developed by the *Web3D Consortium* (VRML, 1997, 2002) and standardized by ISO/IEC. Application areas of VRML include scientific visualization, engineering, architecture, education, entertainment and e-commerce.

VRML browsers, as well as authoring tools enabling creation of VRML files, are available for various platforms. Currently, the most popular browsers include *ParallelGraphics Cortona* (ParallelGraphics, 2007), *Bitmanagement BS Contact* (Bitmanagement, 2009), *Octaga Player* (Octaga, 2009) open-source *Xj3D* (Xj3D, 2007) and *InstantReality* (Fraunhofer, 2009).

X3D – *Extensible 3D* – is the successor to VRML, also developed by the Web3D Consortium and standardized by ISO/IEC (Web3D, 2008). X3D has been designed to keep backward compatibility with VRML, while providing more

advanced functionality, enabling integration with XML, componentization and extensibility.

MPEG-4 is a standard developed by the *Moving Picture Experts Group* (MPEG) (MPEG, 2009) – a working group of the subcommittee *SC29 Coding of audio, picture, multimedia and hypermedia information* of the *Joint Technical Committee 1* of ISO (ISO, 2009) and IEC (IEC, 2009). MPEG-4 is a complex standard enabling representation of both natural and synthetic content. The scene structure of MPEG-4 is based on VRML and extended to support more advanced functionality, representation of 2D content and integration with streaming media (Koenen, 2002).

Proprietary solutions for visualization of 3D models on the web include *Cult3D* by *Cycore Systems* (Cycore, 2009), *Shockwave3D* by *Adobe Systems* (Adobe, 2009), *Blaze3D* by *Holomatix* (Holomatix, 2009) and *vSpace* by *Kaon Interactive* (Kaon, 2009).

Creation of 3D Content

Preparation of interactive 3D content is a complex process, which involves three main steps: creation of 3D models and animations, assembling the models into virtual scenes and programming scenes' behavior. Increasing availability of automatic or semi-automatic 3D scanning tools helps in acquisition of accurate 3D models of real objects or interiors. Most popular techniques include laser scanning, photogrammetry with structured light and video-based acquisition. Progress is still needed to make the process fully automatic, enable scanning of objects with arbitrary shapes and acquisition of advanced surface properties such as transparency or reflections. Scanning animated objects is still challenging, but the progress in this field is very fast. 3D design packages such as Autodesk's *3ds max*, *Maya*, Softimage's *XSI* or open source *Blender* can be used to refine or enhance the scanned models and to create imaginary objects. The same tools can be used to assemble the 3D objects into complex virtual scenes.

Programming of behavior in VRML/X3D/MPEG-4 scenes is based on the *dataflow* paradigm. Dataflow programming is a powerful concept, which enables efficient implementation of interactive 3D graphics, in particular providing smooth animations, inherently supporting concurrent execution and enabling various kinds of optimization. However, this approach has several important disadvantages, which become more and more apparent with the shift from the static 3D web content model to the rich 3D web applications model (Bues et al., 2008).

Related Works

The basic content organization and programming mechanisms provided in VRML/X3D and MPEG-4 as described above may be successfully used to create simple 3D scenes, however, designing complex scenes with non-trivial behavior at this level is a burdensome task. Therefore, significant research effort has been invested in the design of methods, languages and tools for specifying behavior of virtual objects and scenes at a higher level of abstraction. The solutions can be broadly classified into four groups.

The first group constitute scripting languages for describing behavior of virtual scenes. An early example of a scripting language designed for creating VR interaction scenarios is MPML-VR (Multimodal Presentation Markup Language for VR) (Okazaki et al., 2002). This language is a 3D adaptation of the MPML language originally targeted at creating multimodal web content, in particular to enable content authors to script rich web-based interaction scenarios featuring life-like characters. Similar solutions, also developed for controlling life-like characters, are VHML (Virtual Human Markup Language) (Marriott et al., 2001) for scripting virtual characters' animation and APML (Affective Presentation Markup Language) (De Carolis et al., 2002) focusing on presenting personality and emotions in agents. Recent developments in the field of programming

high-level behavior of human characters focus on specification of the BML (Behaviour Markup Language), which can be then translated into low level animation commands such as BAP/FAP in MPEG-4 (Vilhjálmsson et al., 2007).

General-purpose virtual scene behavior programming solutions include VEML (Virtual Environment Markup Language) based on the concept of atomic simulations (Boukerche et al., 2005). An extension to the VRML/X3D standards enabling definition of behavior of objects, called BDL, has been described in (Burrows, England, 2005). Another approach, based on the concept of aspect oriented programming, has been proposed in (Mesing, Hellmich, 2006).

The second group of solutions are integrated application design frameworks. Such frameworks usually include some complex languages and tools that extend existing standards to provide additional functionality, in particular, enabling specification of virtual scene behavior. Interesting works include Contigra (Dachselt et al., 2002) and Behavior3D (Dachselt, Rukzio, 2003), which are based on distributed standardized components that can be assembled into 3D scenes during the design phase. However, this approach is still based on the dataflow paradigm and standard event processing, making it difficult to specify more complex behaviors. Another solution, based on the use of distributed components accessible through web services has been proposed in (Zhang, Gračanin, 2007).

The third group of solutions aim at simplifying the process of designing complex virtual scenes by using special graphical applications for designing scenes' behavior. Recent research works in this field include (Arjomandy, Smedley, 2004), (Vitzthum, 2006) and (Pellens, 2006, 2008). An advanced commercial product in this category is Virtools (Dassault, 2008).

Finally, in the fourth group of solutions, a 3D scene contains only specification of the geometrical and aural representation, and sensors, while the behavior of the scene is controlled from an external program. Animations may be either contained in the scene – and only triggered from the external program – or may be entirely driven by the external program. A typical example of this approach is *Ajax3D* – a recently developed method of programming interactive web 3D applications based on a combination of JavaScript and the external SAI interface (Parisi, 2006).

The content creation methods described above, although designed to make the process of content preparation more efficient, are still conceptually complex and time-consuming, require significant technical expertise and sophisticated tools. Even if low-level programming can be in some cases replaced by higher level languages or graphical design tools, still graphical and functional complexity of the resulting 3D applications requires complex scenarios and complex diagrams, which are usually beyond the capabilities of non-technical users.

Practical 3D web applications require enormous amounts of complex, interactive and secure content, which – in most cases – must be created by *domain experts*, such as museum curators, teachers and salesmen – who cannot be expected to be proficient in 3D graphics design and computer programming. Therefore, there is a clear need for a simple to use method of creating interactive 3D web content. One of the key requirements for such a method is the availability of a flexible mechanism for defining users' access privileges to different parts of the content, which would be applicable both at the content creation phase and at the content consumption phase.

THE FLEX-VR SCENE STRUCTURALIZATION

Increasing complexity, dynamism and the central role of behavior in 3D applications renders the current model of virtual scenes based on a scene graph with additional independent behavior graph impractical. This is particularly evident when a 3D application must incorporate some non-trivial

security constraints. Efficient creation and manipulation of highly-interactive and secure 3D applications requires a new paradigm.

First, we need to take into account the fact that an interactive 3D application is much more than just the presented 3D content, in the same way as, for example, a text editor is much more than the set of graphical widgets it is currently displaying. Second, the 3D content (geometry, audio and possibly also other modalities in the near future) is just a way of communicating the state of the application to a user. 3D objects may appear, disappear, and be replaced by other objects as the application state changes. Third, in the case of an interactive 3D application, it is much more likely that the presented content will change than that the application logic will change. Finally, users may not have uniform access privileges to all 3D application content and the types of operations allowed on the content may be different for different users.

These observations are known to programmers creating 3D applications based on a scene graph APIs, such as *OpenInventor* (SGI, 2006), *OpenSG* (OpenSG, 2009), *OpenSceneGraph* (OSG, 2009) or *Java3D* (Sun, 2009). In such applications, the scene graph represents the current state of the application 3D interface, while a separate application layer is responsible for manipulating the scene graph and handling events. With VRML/X3D, a similar functionality can be achieved using the *EAI/SAI* (*External Authoring Interface/Scene Access Interface*) interfaces respectively. In X3D, external SAI interface enables other applications (e.g., applets or other components on a web page) to communicate with a 3D scene. Internal SAI interface enables similar communication from within the 3D scene – using a Script node. A Script node may contain a program (or script) in any programming language supported by the browser (typically *Java* or *ECMAScript*). A script may communicate with other scene nodes by receiving and sending events through standard routes.

In VRML/X3D/MPEG-4 virtual scenes, scripts are often used to perform some specific, simple tasks (e.g., open door if some condition is satisfied). However, a program contained in a *Script* node can be arbitrarily complex. In an extreme case, a single *Script* node can create and manipulate the whole 3D scene. In such a case, the SAI acts as the scene graph API, while the script is equivalent to the application layer. This solution is powerful in that it enables flexible manipulation of the scene from within the script. However, creation of such content is complex and it does not support dynamic composition of content based on user interactions, preferences and privileges, which is necessary in majority of complex 3D applications.

To provide a sufficient level of flexibility in configuration of complex interactive 3D applications that would support implementation of access privileges, some specific organization of the content is required. In Flex-VR, virtual scenes are specifically organized according to a novel structuralization model called *Beh-VR*. The Beh-VR model is based on decomposition of 3D application content into independent geometrical and behavioral objects, called VR-Beans (Walczak, 2006). Virtual scenes with rich interactivity and behavior can be dynamically created by selecting and combining sets of VR-Beans.

VR-Bean Objects

In the Beh-VR model, a virtual scene is built of software elements called VR-Beans. Technically, VR-Beans are objects, implemented as standard script nodes, but conforming to a specific convention. Conformance to this convention enables combining arbitrary sets of VR-Beans into technically correct 3D scenes and provides means of inter-object discovery and communication. Beh-VR applications are fully compliant with existing 3D content standards and therefore can run in standard 3D browsers.

Figure 1. The structure of a VR-Bean object

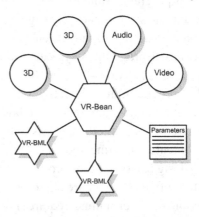

Each VR-Bean consists of at least one *scenario script*, an optional set of *media components* and an optional set of *parameters* (Figure 1). The scenario script is the main element controlling each VR-Bean. Scenario scripts are programmed in a novel, high-level, XML-based programming language called *VR-BML* (*Virtual Reality Behavior Modeling Language*) (Walczak, 2008a). Each script contains specification of the appearance and the behavior of a single VR-Bean object. Scenarios describe what happens when the object is initialized, what actions are performed by the object and what are the responses of the object to external stimuli. In some cases, there may be several different scenarios controlling a VR-Bean depending on the presentation context.

VR-BML uses a hybrid approach based on both declarative programming for high-level elements (e.g., event actions) and imperative programming for low-level elements (e.g., algorithm details). This hybrid approach enables VR-BML to take the best of the two worlds enabling the programmer to concentrate on important elements and leave the common elements to the Beh-VR framework.

Each behavior script may create any number of *scene components*, which are geometrical or aural manifestation of the VR-Bean in a virtual scene, but there may be also VR-Beans that do not directly manifest themselves. A VR-Bean may contain a number of media components, which are used for creating the scene components. Examples of media components are *3D models* (X3D/VRML/MPEG-4), *images, audio* and *video* sequences, and *texts*. A VR-Bean can be also associated with a set of *parameters*. Parameters are characterized by a name, a type (integer, string, Boolean, etc.) and a value. Parameters can be read by scenario scripts and can be used in determining appearance and behavior of objects.

Structure of Beh-VR Scenes

A Beh-VR scene is created dynamically by combining independent VR-Bean objects. Each VR-Bean object is controlled by a VR-BML behavior script (Figure 2).

A behavior script may load any number of media components into the virtual scene, thus creating geometrical, aural or behavioral manifestation of the VR-Bean – scene components. The scene components may be created during the object initialization phase or later during the object lifetime. Objects may also freely change their representations at any time. A scenario can create and destroy scene components and can communicate with the scene components within a single VR-Bean by sending and receiving events

to/from the components. Each script can control all scene components it has created, but has no direct influence on other scene components.

Since the contents of a Beh-VR scene is composed ad-hoc, communication between objects becomes a critical element. Meaningful communication requires identification of objects present in the scene, well-defined roles of objects and existence of technical means of communication.

Identification of objects is possible due to a hierarchical system of *categories* and a process of *registration* and *discovery*. Each object may be registered in an arbitrary number of categories. The categories also define roles of objects in the scene. An object assigned to more than one category plays several different roles in a scene.

Communication between objects is realized using two mechanisms: *public values* and *method invocation*. Public values are named public expressions that can use variables and events from a single VR-Bean. Each VR-Bean can explicitly read public values, can be notified when such a value changes, and public values can be directly assigned to input events of scene components.

Method invocation can be performed on single objects, lists of objects and the whole categories. A method consists of a sequence of VR-BML commands, which may change the state of a VR-

Figure 2. A Beh-VR structure and the resulting 3D scene

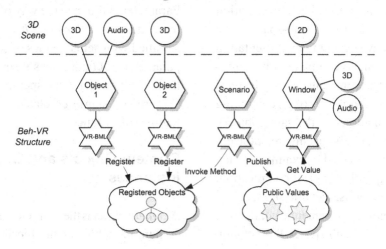

Bean, alter its representation in the virtual scene, invoke other methods, etc. Each method may have any number of parameters. Formal specification of parameters is provided in the method definition, while actual parameter values are set in a method call.

The Flex-VR Content Model

To enable flexible organization, management and exchange of 3D application content as well as definition of fine-grained access privileges to the content, a versatile content model is required. In this section we describe the Flex-VR content model (Walczak, 2008b). On the one hand, the Flex-VR content model describes a 3D application on a much higher level of abstraction than a typical content representation standard, such as VRML or X3D, making it easier to manipulate content elements and dynamically compose virtual scenes. On the other hand, it provides a detailed content structure that can be used for defining fine-grained user access privileges. The Flex-VR content model may be stored in a content database to provide persistence, high-performance data manipulation, multi-user access and transactional processing.

Presentation Spaces

In the Flex-VR approach, the 3D application content is organized hierarchically. The hierarchy is built of *presentation spaces*. Each presentation space may have any number of sub-spaces. The depth of the hierarchy is not limited. Presentation spaces may correspond to complete virtual environments, parts of environments, or may be used merely as containers for objects (e.g., containing alternative representations of the same object). The semantics of the sub-spacing relationship depends on the super-space. For example, it may denote spatial, temporal or logical composition, alternative representations, scenario steps, etc. In some cases there may be no semantic connection of the super-space and the sub-spaces. Presentation spaces are containers that may generally hold three types of elements: *instances of content templates*, *instances of behavior templates* and *instances of content objects*.

Templates and Template Instances

A *template* is a parameterized program used to generate representations of presentation spaces. There are two types of templates: *content templates* and *behavior templates*. Content templates are used to generate representations of the space and to select content objects that should be included in this representation. Simplest templates generate scenes merely by combining content objects. More complex templates may additionally include background elements such as a model of a room, environmental properties (e.g. a fog), etc.

Each of the content objects may contain its own behavior script. In some cases, however, it is useful to have the same (or similar) behavior shared by a number of objects. To achieve this, an instance of a behavior template, used to generate scripts implementing common object behavior, may be also included in the presentation space.

Templates may be encoded in any scripting language that is suitable for content generation (X-VRML, PHP, JSP, etc.) (Walczak & Cellary, 2003). A template consists of a template implementation and a set of template parameters, each of which has a name, a type and a default value. Parameters influence the way of execution of the template code. A *template instance* is a template supplied with actual values of some of its formal parameters. Default values are used for parameters that do not have a value specified in the instance (Figure 3). A single template can have an arbitrary number of instances.

Content Objects and Object Instances

A *content object* is the basic element of the Flex-VR content model. Content objects may correspond

Figure 3. A template and a template instance

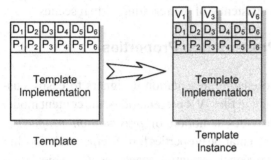

P – Parameter, D – default value, V – actual value

to simple 3D objects, complex objects gathering several components – 3D models and other media, or VR-Bean objects with their own behavior specification.

A content object consists of a number (zero or more) of *media components* and *content object metadata* (Figure 4). Media components are representations of the content object in various media. Examples are 3D model, image, video sequence, audio sequence, and text. More than one media component of the same type may be associated with a content object. Media components are used to represent the content object in a virtual scene. Media components may be shared by content objects. Media components are associated with *media component metadata* providing component description.

A *content object instance* is a content object assigned to a presentation space, optionally with a set of presentation properties. Similarly as in the case of templates, content objects can have multiple instances in the same or different presentation spaces.

Presentation Domains

A common problem in the design of 3D applications is caused by different hardware and software environments, in which the applications must run (e.g., an immersive system versus a laboratory equipped in PC computers). Also, often the applications must be targeted at different groups of users (e.g., a group of school children playing with a system while visiting a museum versus an archaeologist trying to find some details about a specific cultural object). To enable reuse of the same generic content model on different target platforms and with different presentation methods, while keeping consistency of the designed presentation structure and the content, the notion of *presentation domains* has been introduced. A presentation domain corresponds to a target environment or a usage scenario for the 3D application.

An example of a presentation domain hierarchy is presented in Figure 5. For the "WEB.LOCAL" domain, "WEB" is the name of the parent domain,

Figure 4. The structure of a content object

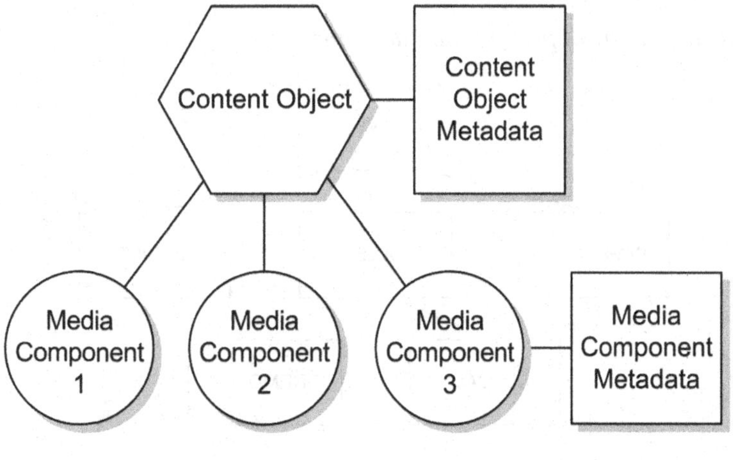

while "LOCAL" is the name of the sub-domain. "ANY" is an abstract super-domain of all domains, and has no practical implementations.

In the Flex-VR content model, in each presentation space there may be a separate template for each presentation domain. For example, a space with a virtual museum exhibition may contain three sets of content templates and behavior templates, which enable presentation of the system (1) on a high-end immersive installation in the museum, (2) remotely over the Internet on a standard PC computer, and (3) locally in the museum on small portable computers in form of an interactive guide. The templates may differ in the selection of the content objects, quality of the 3D models, interaction methods, etc.

To make the process of designing large virtual reality applications more efficient, the notion of template instance inheritance has been introduced. If a presentation space does not contain a template instance in a particular presentation domain, first a template instance in a super-domain is used – if it exists in the presentation space. If not, a template instance from a higher-level presentation space is used – in the same domain or a super-domain. Since inheritance concerns template instances and not only templates, all values of template parameters set in the upper-level presentation domain or the upper-level presentation space are preserved in the sub-domain or sub-space. This significantly speeds-up the design of large content models and

enables to easily maintain visual and behavioral consistency of the resulting virtual scenes.

Presentation Properties

To enable presentation designers to easily customize Flex-VR presentations, the content model provides a notion of *presentation properties*. Presentation properties form a ternary relationship between presentation spaces, content objects and media components. Each presentation property is assigned to a presentation space, and it may be also optionally assigned to a content object or to a content object and a media component. If a presentation property is assigned to a presentation space only, it describes the presentation space. Such a value can be used by a template to create representation of the presentation space. An example of space-level presentation property can be a description of a presentation space.

If a presentation property is assigned to a presentation space and a content object, it describes the presentation of this content object within the presentation space. A textual label describing an object is a good example of a content object-level presentation property.

If a presentation property is assigned to a presentation space, a content object and a media component, then it describes the presentation of this particular media component, within the content object within the presentation space.

Figure 5. An example hierarchy of presentation domains

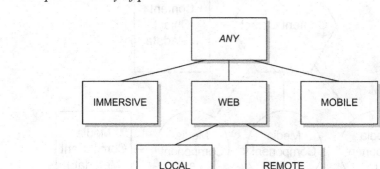

Scale of a 3D model is an example of a media component-level presentation property.

Presentations

The overall structure of a Flex-VR presentation is shown in Figure 6. A presentation designer builds Flex-VR presentations by forming a hierarchy of presentation spaces and creating – in the presentation spaces – instances of content templates, instances of behavior templates and instances of content objects, and by setting values of presentation properties.

Different presentations can be achieved by the creation of template instances and content object instances derived from the same template or content object but supplied with different sets of parameter values or properties. In some presentations, template parameters and content object properties that are not fixed by a content designer can be changed by end-users.

ARCO: AN APPLICATION OF FLEX-VR

The Flex-VR approach has been exploited in several practical 3D/VR applications in the domains

Figure 6. The structure of a Flex-VR presentation space

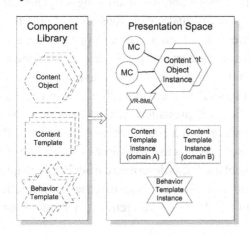

of cultural heritage, entertainment and interactive television production. An example of a Flex-VR application is *ARCO – Augmented Representation of Cultural Objects*. ARCO is a system enabling museums and other cultural heritage institutions to create, manage and display virtual exhibitions of cultural objects. These exhibitions – in form of dynamically generated 3D interactive multimedia presentations – can be accessed locally, on computers installed inside the museums, or remotely over the Internet (Walczak, Cellary & White, 2006).

The use of Flex-VR enables configuration of virtual exhibitions from components – digitized objects, virtual room templates and behavior templates. As a result, the process of creating an exhibition can be easily performed by museum staff without advanced knowledge in computer programming and 3D design.

All kinds of data generated and used in the process of designing virtual exhibitions is stored in the ARCO database, designed according to the Flex-VR approach. The whole ARCO process can be divided into three main phases: content creation, content management and content presentation. Content creation involves different methods of digitization of cultural objects, such as scanning, photographing and recording. Content management is performed by the use of a user-friendly content management application connected to the ARCO database (Figure 7 left). Content presentation involves dynamic composition of 3D virtual scenes based on the Flex-VR content model stored in the database. The scenes are created in accordance with the Flex-VR scene structuralization model (Beh-VR). An example of a virtual exhibition is presented in the Figure 7 on the right.

Support for a flexible system of user privileges and security were important factors in the design of the ARCO system for several reasons. First, preparation of complex virtual exhibitions requires involvement of diverse groups of specialists responsible for different aspects of the design

Figure 7. ARCO System: the content management application (left) and an example virtual exhibition (right)

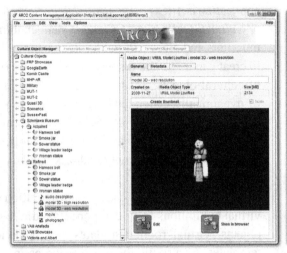

process, such as digitizing and describing objects, designing graphical templates, programming behavior and, finally, composition and publishing of the virtual galleries. These groups should have different privileges to different functional and logical parts of the system. Second, usually different teams of people are responsible for the creation of different exhibitions (i.e., the Flex-VR presentations). Some of the content (e.g., templates or graphical objects) may be shared by the teams, while access to other content (e.g., presentations) should be restricted. Third, the same database (ARCO server) may be shared by a number of small museums to reduce the software and infrastructure costs. Each museum should be able to access only content belonging to this museum. Access to other museums' content should be strictly forbidden. Finally, different types of presentations may be allowed for different groups of users. Typically, better content and more interaction is offered to users accessing the presentations from inside the museum, while only a limited version is available over the Internet. Also, staff members may have access to web interfaces providing editing and annotation functions, while

common users usually have access to simple read-only interfaces.

User Privileges in Flex-VR

The Flex-VR approach enables flexible implementation of a user privilege system within the 3D application content. The Flex-VR content model offers necessary logical structures that enable definition of fine-grained access privileges. Dynamic composition of virtual scenes based on the model provides a secure mechanism for limiting user access to different elements and parts of the 3D content. The Flex-VR scene structuralization method enables proper functioning of dynamically composed virtual scenes consisting of only those elements to which a user has appropriate access rights – including both passive and active elements.

In Figure 8, a functional diagram of the overall Flex-VR framework with a system of access privileges is presented. The framework consists of a server and a client. On the server side, a database system is used to implement the Flex-VR content model, as described earlier in this chapter. A template instance is used to retrieve information from the database and generate a virtual scene, which is sent to the client. The scene is structured according to the Beh-VR scene structuralization, also described earlier in this chapter. The Beh-VR scene structure generates and controls a 3D virtual scene, which is presented to a user.

In Flex-VR, privileges can be defined *declaratively* at the levels of *presentation spaces*, *content object folders*, single *content objects* and *media components*, and *presentation domains* (Figure 8 – lower left part). Privileges can be also defined *imperatively* within the content templates and behavior templates (Figure 8 – upper left part).

Privileges defined declaratively are static. They can be used both at the content creation and at the content consumption phases. An important characteristics of the privileges defined declaratively is that they can be implemented at the level of the database management system by the use of user accounts, roles, privileges, views, etc. This offers a very high level of security and simplifies the design of the application server and client applications. Users cannot perform illegal actions or access restricted data regardless of the tool and the access method they use.

Privileges declared imperatively in the templates provide dynamism and more flexibility than privileges defined declaratively, but they can be used only at the content consumption phase. Furthermore, these privileges are verified in the application server (which interprets templates) and not within the database management system and, therefore, provide lower level of security. Consequently, this type of privileges is more suitable for limiting user's access for presentation purposes and not really for implementing a security policy.

The five levels of privilege definition in Flex-VR are described in more details in the following subsections.

Privileges to Presentation Domains

Definition of access privileges to presentation domains is the most coarse-grained, but at the same time the most frequently used, method of defining access privileges in Flex-VR. Presentation domains correspond to different target environments or categories of users of the 3D content. Therefore application of access privileges at this level is conceptually simple and natural.

Figure 8. Functional diagram of the overall Flex-VR framework with access privileges

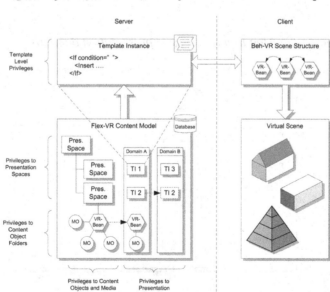

Application of privileges to presentation domains affects users' ability to access or modify content presented in a particular domain. At the content consumption phase a user or group may have access to a particular presentation domain, but not to other presentation domains. For example, in an on-line virtual museum exhibition, standard-quality content may be available for everyone for free, while high-quality content may be available for registered users only. In such a case, a casual user accessing the exhibition will be able to see the exhibition in standard quality domain, but not the high-quality domain. A registered user will be able to see the same exhibition in both domains – the standard domain and the high-quality domain.

Application of user access privileges at the level of presentation domains can be also useful at the content creation phase. Users may or may not be allowed to modify content, which is presented using a particular domain. For example, in a virtual museum exhibition a designer may be allowed to create a new exhibition for a specific purpose, but he or she may not be allowed to modify the main Internet exhibition available on-line. To impose this restriction, as a rule, a user is not able to access or to modify (depending on the type of the privilege) content of any presentation space that

contains a presentation template in a domain, to which the user has no appropriate privilege.

In Figure 9, the process of assigning user's access privileges to presentation domains in the ARCO system is presented. The list on the right contains domains to which the user has write access, while the list on the left contains the domains to which the user does not have write access. Domains can be moved between these two lists by pressing appropriate arrow buttons. To simplify the interface, hierarchical domains are presented in a form of a flat list.

Privileges to Presentation Spaces

Application of access privileges to presentation spaces affects users' ability to read or modify content and properties of particular spaces. Access privileges defined at this level can be used both at the content creation phase and at the content consumption phase. At the content creation phase, read and write privileges can be used to restrict users' ability to access or to modify content and properties of the spaces. At the content consumption phase, the read privilege enables users to access content of the space, while the write privilege enables them to store results of their interactions within the 3D content. Such results

Figure 9. ARCO System: configuring user's access to presentation domains

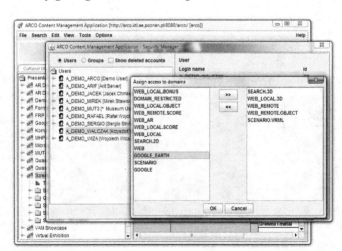

Figure 10. ARCO System: configuring user's access to presentation spaces

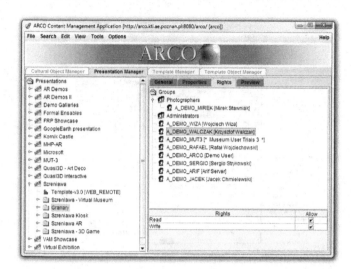

are stored as values of properties of the spaces and the contained elements.

Access privileges to presentation spaces may be combined with the access privileges to presentation domains. In such a case, to access a presentation space, at the content consumption phase, a user must have privileges (read or write) to both the presentation space and the presentation domain, through which the access is performed. To access a presentation space at the content creation phase, a user must have privileges to both the presentation space and all presentation domains that can be used to access this presentation space.

In Figure 10, the ARCO Presentation Manager tool is presented. By the use of the Presentation Manager museum users can design virtual exhibitions by combining digitized cultural objects with content templates and behavior templates. Privileged users can assign other user's read and write privileges to particular spaces (Figure 10 on the right).

Privileges to Content Object Folders

One of the basic types of access privileges in Flex-VR are privileges to content object folders. In Flex-VR, media components are assigned to content objects, which are assigned to folders. Folders can form hierarchical structures. Therefore, the ability to associate access privileges with the content object folders provides an efficient tool to limit user's access to the available collection of content elements. Privileges at this level are used only at the content design phase.

In Figure 11, the ARCO Cultural Object Manager, which enables management of content objects and media components, is presented. A privileged user can set access privileges of users to particular content object folders. The *read* privilege means that the user will be able to browse the folder and examine the contained objects, while the *write* privilege means that the user will be able to add, modify and remove objects from this folder.

Privileges to Content Objects and Media Components

Access privileges can be also defined at the level of particular content objects and media components. Such privileges affect user's ability to read and modify the object. In contrast to privileges defined at the level of content object folders, privileges defined at the level of particular objects or com-

Figure 11. ARCO System: configuring user's access to content object folders

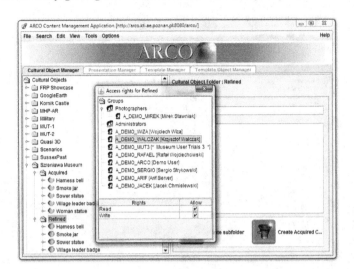

ponents can be used both at the content creation and at the content consumption phase.

If a user has no read privilege to an object, he or she will not be able to access the object in the authoring interface during the content creation phase and virtual scenes created by the user at the content consumption phase will not contain this object. Due to dynamic binding, the Beh-VR approach guarantees that virtual scenes containing a subset of objects will still be technically correct. The write privilege is necessary to modify an object during the content creation phase or to update object properties during the content consumption phase.

To avoid setting access privileges to particular media components, which in real application cases would be a time-consuming task, access privileges can be grouped and applied at the level of media component types. For example, a user may have access to all components of the type *Low-quality 3D object*, but not to components of the type *High-quality 3D object*. This approach can be used to efficiently limit users' access to content of the particular type.

For limiting users' access to objects and components during the content consumption phase, instead of defining privileges for every user or group, it may be more efficient to define visibility of objects or components in particular presentation domains. In connection with privileges defined at the level of presentation domains, this mechanism limits visibility of objects and components depending on user's access to presentation domains. In Figure 12, the process of setting visibility of a content object and a media component in different presentation domains in the ARCO system is shown.

Access Rules in Presentation Templates

In addition to the privileges defined declaratively at the level of presentation domains, presentation spaces, content object folders, content objects and media components, which are structurally fixed, and which can be verified by the Flex-VR content management system, content access rules in Flex-VR can be also defined in an imperative form in presentation templates – both content templates and behavior templates. Access rules defined in templates are implemented within the template code.

Access rules defined in the template code can be used only during the content consumption

Figure 12. ARCO System: setting visibility of objects and components in presentation domains

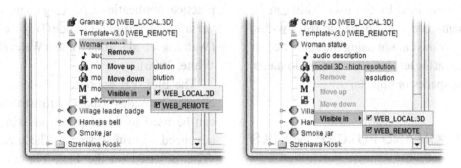

phase, because only at this phase templates are interpreted. These rules can filter elements of the presentation spaces – content objects, media components and sub-spaces.

A simplified fragment of a Flex-VR content template implemented in X-VRML is presented in Figure 13. First, a list of content objects is retrieved for a particular presentation space (line 02). Then (lines 04-07), depending on the value of the HQ variable, the media type to be displayed is set to either high resolution models or web resolution models (cf. Figure 7 left). For each content object in the presentation space, the

list of media components of the particular media type is extracted (line 14) and inserted into the resulting virtual scene code (line 21).

Access rules defined in templates are flexible and dynamic – in the sense that they can change during the 3D application lifetime. Moreover, rules of access defined in templates can be arbitrarily complex and take into account properties of the content, history of interaction and other factors. For example, while interacting with a virtual scene, a user can provide an authorization code by pressing virtual buttons. Then, after entering another room (implemented as another pre-

Figure 13. ARCO System: access rules in presentation templates

```
01   ...
02   <ARCO_PF_Props spId="{@spaceId}" propName="CHILD_CO_IDS" varName="coList"/>
03
04   <If condition="{@HQ}">
05       <Then> <Set name="3DmediaType" value="model 3D - high resolution"/> </Then>
06       <Else> <Set name="3DmediaType" value="model 3D - low resolution"/> </Else>
07   </If>
08   ...
09   <For name="COidx" from="0" to="{sizeOf(@coList)}">
10       ...
11       Transform {
12           translation <Insert value="{@objectPosition}"/>
13           children [
14               <ARCO_CO_Props coId="{@coList[$COidx]}"
15                               propName="CHILD_MO_IDS:{@3DmediaType}" varName="moList"/>
16               <For name="i" from="0" to="{sizeOf(@moList)-1}">
17                   <Set name="currentMO" value="{@moList[$i]}"/>
18                   Transform {
19                       scale <Insert value="{$scaleFactor $scaleFactor $scaleFactor}"/>
20                       children [
21                           Inline { url "<Insert value="{@moPath+$currentMO}"/>" }
22                       ]
23                   }
24               </For>
25               ...
26           ]
27       }
28   </For>
```

sentation space), the presented content may depend on the code provided by the user. This can be easily implemented using dynamic rules within the template code, but not using the static access rights defined at the level of presentation domains, presentation spaces or objects.

CONCLUSION AND FUTURE WORKS

In this chapter, we have presented a new approach to modeling 3D application content, which is suitable for implementation of access rights at different levels. This approach, called Flex-VR, provides a more practical alternative to the standard content modeling techniques, while at the same time keeping full compatibility with the 3D content standards such as VRML, X3D and MPEG-4.

The Flex-VR approach provides features that are critical to enable implementation of advanced secure 3D web applications. First of all, it defines a new level of virtual scene content structures on top of the classical scene graph and dataflow level. This new level, called Beh-VR, enables efficient composition and manipulation of the virtual scene content, especially in the case of virtual scenes rich in interactions, dynamism and behavior, which are the most challenging for implementing security.

Secondly, Flex-VR provides data structures (the Flex-VR content model), which can be used to efficiently manage 3D application content. It provides fine-grained elements such as presentation spaces, presentation domains, content objects and media components, which can be conveniently used by designers to define access rights of users or groups to content.

Finally, the Flex-VR is based on dynamic generation of virtual scenes with the use of templates. Dynamic generation offers a potentially high level of security, since the objects that are not accessible to a user will not be included in the generated scene. Furthermore, the dynamic generation can be used to implement more complex – application dependent – access privileges to content.

The Flex-VR approach has been used in several practical applications, proving its usefulness and versatility. Examples include (Boyle et al., 2002), (Walczak et al., 2004) and (Walczak, Cellary, White, 2006).

The Flex-VR approach, as described in this chapter, provides a basic infrastructure, which can be used to develop various kinds of more advanced security systems. These can be static systems based on the Flex-VR content model or dynamic systems based on the Beh-VR scene structuralization level. The latter systems may take into account numerous properties of objects and dependencies between objects, which are impossible or hard to implement when unstructured 3D scenes are used.

REFERENCES

Arjomandy, S., & Smedley, T. J. (2004). Visual specification of behaviours in VRML worlds. In *Proc. of the 9th International Conference on 3D Web Technology*, Monterey, CA, (pp. 127-133). New York: ACM.

Boukerche, A., Zarrad, A., Duarte, D., Araujo, R., & Andrade, L. (2005). A Novel Solution for the Development of Collaborative Virtual Environment Simulations in Large Scale. In *9th IEEE International Symposium on Distributed Simulation and Real-Time Applications*, (pp. 86-96).

Boyle, E., Cellary, W., Huminiecki, O., Picard, W., Stawniak, M., Walczak, K., & Wojciechowski, R. (2002). Dynamic Creation of MPEG-4 Content with X-VRML, In *Proc. of the 5th Int. Conf. on Business Information Systems BIS 2002*, Poznan, Poland, (pp. 358-366).

Bues, M., Gleue, T., & Blach, R. (2008). Lightning. Dataflow in Motion. In *Proc. of the IEEE VR 2008 Workshop SEARIS - Software Engineering and Architectures for Interactive Systems*, Reno, NV, USA. Aachen, Germany: Shaker Verlag

Burrows, T., & England, D. (2005). YABLE-yet another behaviour language. *Proc. of the 10ᵗʰ International Conference on 3D Web Technology*, Bangor, UK, (pp. 65-73).

Dachselt, R., Hinz, M., & Meissner, K. (2002). Contigra: an XML-based architecture for component-oriented 3D applications. In *Proc. of the 7ᵗʰ International Conference on 3D Web Technology*, Tempe, AZ, (pp. 155-163).

Dachselt, R., & Rukzio, E. (2003). Behavior3D: an XML-based framework for 3D graphics behavior. In *Proc. of the 8ᵗʰ International Conference on 3DWeb Technologies*, Saint Malo, France, (pp. 101-112).

De Carolis, B., Carofiglio, V., Bilvi, M., & Pelachaud, C. (2002). APML, A Mark-up Language for Believable Behavior Generation. In *Proc. of AAMAS Workshop Embodied, Conversational Agents: Let's Specify and Compare Them!* Bologna, Italy

Koenen, R. (2002). *Overview of the MPEG-4 Standard.* Retrieved from http://www.chiariglione.org/mpeg /standards/mpeg-4/mpeg-4.htm

Marriott, A., Beard, S., Stallo, J., & Huynh, Q. (2001). VHML - Directing a Talking Head. In *Proc. of the Sixth International Computer Science Conference Active Media Technology*, (LNCS Vol. 2252, pp. 18-20). Hong Kong. Berlin: Springer.

Mesing, B., & Hellmich, C. (2006). Using aspect oriented methods to add behaviour to X3D documents. In *Proc. of the 11ᵗʰ International Conference on 3D Web Technology*, Columbia, MD, (pp. 97-107).

Okazaki, N., Aya, S., Saeyor, S., & Ishizuka, M. (2002). A Multimodal Presentation Markup Language MPML-VR for a 3D Virtual Space. In *Proc. of the Workshop on Virtual Conversational Characters: Applications, Methods, and Research Challenges*, Melbourne, Australia.

Parisi, T. (2006). *Ajax3D: The Open Platform for Rich 3D Web Applications.* White Paper, Media Machines, Inc., Aug, 2006. Retrieved from http://www.ajax3d.org/whitepaper/

Pellens, B., De Troyer, O., & Kleinermann, F. (2008). CoDePA: a conceptual design pattern approach to model behavior for X3D worlds. In *Proc. of the 13ᵗʰ International Symposium on 3D Web Technology*, Los Angeles, CA, August 09 – 10, (pp. 91-99). New York: ACM.

Pellens, B., Kleinermann, F., De Troyer, O., & Bille, W. (2006). Model-Based Design of Virtual Environment Behavior. In H. Zha, Z. Pan, H. Thwaites, A. C. Addison, M. Forte (Eds.), *Interactive Technologies and Sociotechnical Systems, 12ᵗʰ International Conference, VSMM2006, Xi'an, China, October 18-20, 2006, Proceedings* (LNCS 4270, pp. 29-39). Berlin: Springer.

Vilhjálmsson, H., Cantelmo, N., Cassell, J., Chafai, N. E., Kipp, M., Kopp, S., et al. (2007). The Behavior Markup Language: Recent Developments and Challenges. In *Intelligent Virtual Agents*, (LNCS 4722, pp. 99-111). Berlin: Springer.

Vitzthum, A. (2006). SSIML/Components: a visual language for the abstract specification of 3D components. In *Proceedings of the 11ᵗʰ International Conference on 3D Web Technologies*, Columbia, MD, Apr. 18-21, (pp. 143-151).

Walczak, K. (2008b). Structured Design of Interactive VR Applications, In *Proc. of the 13ᵗʰ International Symposium on 3D Web Technology Web3D 2008*, Los Angeles, CA, (pp. 105-113). New York: ACM Press.

Walczak, K., & Cellary, W. (2003). X-VRML for Advanced Virtual Reality Applications. *Computer, 36*(3), 89–92. doi:10.1109/MC.2003.1185226

Walczak, K., Cellary, W., Chmielewski, J., Stawniak, M., Strykowski, S., Wiza, W., et al. (2004). An Architecture for Parameterised Production of Interactive TV Contents, 11th International Workshop on Systems, Signals And Image Processing. In *Proc. of the International Conf. on Signals And Electronic Systems IWSSIP 2004*, Poznan, Poland, (pp. 465-468).

Walczak, K., Cellary, W., & White, M. (2006). Virtual Museum Exhibitions. *Computer, 39*(3), 93–95. doi:10.1109/MC.2006.108

Walczak. (2006). Beh-VR: Modeling Behavior of Dynamic Virtual Reality Contents. In H. Zha et al. (Eds.), *The 12th International Conference on Virtual Systems and Multimedia VSMM 2006*, (LNCS 4270, pp. 40-51). Berlin: Springer Verlag.

Walczak. (2008a). VR-BML: Behaviour Modelling Language for Configurable VR Applications. In M. Ioannides, A. Addison, A. Georgopoulos, L. Kalisperis (Eds.), *Digital Heritage, The 14th International Conference on Virtual Systems and MultiMedia VSMM'08*, Archaeolingua, (pp. 295-302).

Zhang, X., & Gračanin, D. (2007). From coarse-grained components to DVE applications: a service- and component-based framework. In *Proceedings of the 12th International Conference on 3D Web Technology*, Perugia, Italy, April 15-18, (pp. 113-121).

ADDITIONAL READING

Adobe (2009). *Adobe Shockwave Player*. http://www.adobe.com/products/shockwaveplayer/

Bitmanagement (2009). *BS Contact VRML/X3D*. Bitmanagement Software GmbH. http://www.bitmanagement.de/products/bs_contact_vrml.en.html

Cycore (2009), *Cult3D*. Cycore Systems AB. http://www.cult3d.com/

Dassault Systèmes. (2008), *Virtools 4*, http://www.3ds.com/products/3dvia/3dvia-virtools/

Flex-VR and the ARCO System

Fraunhofer (2009). *Instant Reality Player*. Fraunhofer IGD. http://instantreality.de/home/

Holomatix (2009). *Blaze 3D*. http://www.holomatix.com/

IEC. (2009). *International Electrotechnical Commission*. http://www.iec.ch/

ISO. (2009). *International Organization for Standardization*. http://www.iso.org/

Kaon (2009). *Kaon's vSpace*. Kaon Interactive. http://www.kaon.com/software/

MPEG. (2009). *Moving Picture Experts Group home page*. http://www.chiariglione.org/mpeg/

Octaga (2009). *Octaga Player*. Octaga AS. http://www.octaga.com/

Open, S. G. (2009). *OpenSG website*. http://www.opensg.org/

OSG. (2009). *Open Scene Graph website*. http://www.openscenegraph.org/

ParallelGraphics. (2007). *Cortona VRML Client*. http://www.parallelgraphics.com/products /cortona/

Patel, M., White, M., Mourkoussis, N., Walczak, K., Wojciechowski, R., & Chmielewski, J. Metadata Requirements for Digital Museum Environments, *International Journal on Digital Libraries, Special Issue on Digital Museum*, Volume 5, Number 3, May/2005, Springer-Verlag, pp. 179-192, ISBN: r: ISSN: 1432-5012, 05/2005

SGI. (2006). *Developer Central Open Source – Open Inventor*. http://oss.sgi.com/projects /inventor/

Stawniak, M., & Walczak, K. Geographical Presentation of Virtual Museum Exhibitions, *The 7th International Symposium on Virtual Reality, Archaeology and Intelligent Cultural Heritage VAST 2006*, October 30 - November 4, 2006, Nicosia (Cyprus), ed. M. Ioannides, D. Arnold, F. Niccolicci, K. Mania, Eurographics Association, Switzerland, pp. 101-108, ISBN: 1-56881-358-9

Sun (2009). *Java 3D*. Sun Developer Network. http://java.sun.com/javase/technologies/desktop /java3d/

VRML. (1997). *The Virtual Reality Modeling Language*. International Standard ISO/IEC 14772-1:1997. Web3D Consortium. http://www. web3d.org/

VRML. (2002). *The Virtual Reality Modeling Language*, ISO/IEC14772-1:1997/Amd. 1:2002 — VRML97 Amendment 1. Web3D Consortium. http://www.web3d.org/

Walczak, K. Dynamic Composition of Behavior-rich VR Content, *The 1st International IEEE Conference on Information Technology*, Gdansk, May 18 – 21, 2008, ed. Andrzej Stepnowski, Marek Moszyński, Thaddeus Kochański, Jacek Dąbrowski, Gdansk University of Technology, pp. 333-336, ISBN: 978-1-4244-2244-9

Walczak, K. Flex-VR: Configurable 3D Web Applications, *The International Conference on Human System Interaction HSI 2008*, May 25-27, 2008, Kraków, CD, IEEE, pp. 135-140, ISBN: 1-4244-1543-8

Walczak, K. (2009). *Configurable Virtual Reality Applications* (p. 240). Wydawnictwa Uniwersytetu Ekonomicznego w Poznaniu.

Walczak, K., Modelling Behaviour of Configurable VR Applications, *International Journal of Architectural Computing*, Vol. 01, Issue 07, Multi-Science Publishing Co Ltd (UK), pp. 77-103, ISSN: 1478 0771, 2009

Walczak, K., & Wiza, W. Designing Behaviour-rich Interactive Virtual Museum Exhibitions, *The 8th International Symposium on Virtual Reality, Archaeology and Cultural Heritage VAST 2007*, Brighton (UK), November 26-30, 2007, pp. 101-108

Web3D (2008). *Web3D Consortium*. http://www. web3d.org/

Wojciechowski, R., Walczak, K., & Cellary, W. Mixed Reality for Interactive Learning of Cultural Heritage, *First International VR-Learning Seminar, in conjunction with the 7th International Conference on Virtual Reality*, VRIC - Laval Virtual 2005, 20-22 April 2005, Laval (France), pp. 95-99, ISBN: 2-9515730-4-9

Wojciechowski, R., Walczak, K., White, M., & Cellary, W. *Building Virtual and Augmented Reality Museum Exhibitions*, Web3D 2004 Symposium - the 9th International Conference on 3D Web Technology, Monterey, California (USA), ACM SIGGRAPH, pp. 135-144

Xj3D (2007). *Xj3D Project*. Web3D Consortium. http://www.xj3d.org/

Chapter 13
An Access Control Model for Dynamic VR Applications

Adam Wójtowicz
Poznań University of Economics, Poland

Wojciech Cellary
Poznań University of Economics, Poland

ABSTRACT

There is a need for refining data security and privacy protection in virtual reality systems which are interactive, creative and dynamic, i.e. where at run-time mutually interactive objects can be added or removed in different contexts while their behavior can be modified. In virtual worlds of this kind, operations on particular objects either should or shouldn't be allowed to users playing different roles with respect to inter-object interactions. In the VR-PR method presented in this chapter, where VR-PR stands for "Virtual Reality–Privilege Representation", privileges are represented by pairs, each comprising an object and a meta-operation. Meta-operations are induced automatically from possible object interactions, i.e. generated using automatic analysis of the object method call graphs. Meta-operations reflect the method call scope admitted and are used in the process of creating and modifying privileges, which in turn is controlled by a validation mechanism. Expressive and flexible, privileges based on meta-operations are consistent with a set of objects composing a virtual world, as well as with the interactions between those objects, both interactions and objects permanently evolving. In this chapter it is shown in a series of use cases how the VR-PR approach can be applied to various types of object-oriented virtual worlds. The examples are followed by a broader discussion of the privilege lifecycle in the same virtual environment.

INTRODUCTION

Modern virtual worlds constitute interactive environments where interactions take place not only between a user and multiple virtual objects but also among the objects themselves, calling methods in reaction to internal and external events. Virtual worlds are also dynamic and creative – users create new objects at run-time, modify them, assemble them into more complex objects,

DOI: 10.4018/978-1-61520-891-3.ch013

extend their functionality, etc. Multi-access virtual worlds promoting user creativity and sociability cannot impose too many restrictions in the phase of creation of users' objects. One way of doing this is providing effective but unobtrusive data privacy protection, for example flexible access control using privileges based on interactions between objects in a persistently running virtual world. Possible interactions could be thoroughly analyzed by taking into account the call range of object methods, whereas the privilege system should automatically encompass newly created objects. It should also be expressive enough to handle various dependencies, as objects are created not only from scratch by a user playing the content creator role but also as compositions of preexisting objects coming from different sources.

Here it must be stressed that methods of privilege modeling developed so far are not sufficient for highly dynamic, creative virtual worlds. They are either geometry-centric with no advanced interaction support or coarse-grained with flexible privilege modeling capabilities.

In this chapter a new method called VR-PR (Virtual Reality–Privilege Representation) is proposed of flexible user privilege representation for virtual world objects, maintaining compatibility with access control standards and the data model. The VR-PR method consists of automatic analysis of relationships and interactions between objects of a dynamic virtual world constructed according to an object-oriented data model, like the one presented by Walczak (2008; 2006). To achieve this, a meta-operation layer is inserted between the extended access control mechanism and the object-oriented virtual world data model. The layer reflects real interactions between objects, where the interactions are represented by a set of meta-operations aggregating similar call graphs. A set of meta-operations may evolve over time–however, its evolution is typically much slower than transformations of virtual world objects, interactions and structure changes. The VR-PR method is composed of two main steps

that are alternately performed during virtual world run-time: the first one is automatic generation of meta-operations and the other one is privilege creation and modification. To guarantee consistency of meta-operations used during the second step, meta-operations created in the first step are based on automatic analysis of call graph of methods implementing interactions between objects.

This chapter is organized as follows. In Section 2 the state of the art in the field of access control models which can be applied to multiuser virtual worlds is presented, followed by critical remarks and an exemplary data model for the VR-PR approach, i.e. the object-oriented Beh-VR approach to constructing dynamic virtual worlds. In Section 3 the VR-PR approach to privilege modeling and validation is proposed, based on the induction of meta-operations used to express privileges. To illustrate this it is described in a set of use cases how the approach can be applied to various types of object-oriented virtual worlds. The last part of Section 3 is a discussion providing context of the approach. In Section 4 it is shown how the VR-PR method of representing user privileges is applied to object-oriented virtual worlds designed according to the Beh-VR method. In Section 5 future research directions related to the VR-PR approach are discussed. Section 6 concludes the chapter.

BACKGROUND

Background Overview

Constantly increasing processing power of computers and throughput of telecommunication networks, as well as progress of virtualization techniques permit servers and clients to handle more and more advanced virtual reality (VR) systems. Proliferation of VR systems in various domains increases competition between them. Only those VR systems outlast which attract and keep alive communities of their users. Nowadays, fancy 3D interfaces are not enough to attract and keep long-term users. The key factor is content that has to constantly evolve to remain attractive. However, the cost of content creation, maintenance and development for a large population of users is very high. A solution to this problem is to provide systems with content that is generated by user communities in a truly social way. User-generated content is not only cheaper to develop and maintain, but also more authentic and closer to users who invest their time and emotions.

The growth of the VR systems supporting user-generated content meets a natural barrier if the users cannot be sure whether they are able to control the access to their content. To encourage users to actively participate in content development, it is necessary to assure that: (1) the user content will not be misused in any part (2) interacting with content populating environment is always safe for user and his or her content (3) author rights to the content will be preserved. Approach to flexible access control of VR content in multiuser environment that is described in next section of this chapter responds to the above requirements.

Literature Review

Access Control Models

When designing virtual worlds, to control access to objects both Role-Based Access Control (RBAC) model (Sandhu, Ferraiolo & Kuhn, 2000) and Attribute-Based Access Control (ABAC) (Priebe, Dobmeier, Schläger & Kamprath, 2007) may be applied. In the RBAC model privileges are assigned to roles instead of every single user, which makes privilege management less error-prone and more consistent. RBAC can simulate older access control concepts like Mandatory Access Control or Discretionary Access Control and it can be extended to support role hierarchies, constraints, profiling, sessions, context or authorization rules. However, RBAC has limitations related to access control in federated systems with different role semantics in different systems. Also, when users

are too diversified, they cannot be easily categorized, which leads to unwanted proliferation of roles. In such cases ABAC performs better. In the ABAC model authorization is based not on user roles but on arbitrarily selected set of user attributes, which may be object metadata or digital credentials. However, ABAC and RBAC (even including extensions) are just general purpose access control models. They are useful in the virtual worlds domain at various levels–the roles, the users, their credentials–but they do not solve the problem of privilege granting in highly dynamic virtual worlds.

Access Control in CAD Systems

Research on data privacy protection in virtual environments is derived from the output of either CAD or VR communities. The majority of research effort on advanced privileges modeling in virtual environments is based on the CAD achievements because there is a need in the industry for CAD systems providing data privacy protection while enabling safe collaboration. Thus, the CAD area is a source of many interesting ideas adopted to virtual environments.

Qiu, Kok, Wong and Fuh (2007) propose a role-depended access model to 3D environments. In CAD applications, modeling is realized as a sequence of design features i.e. geometry transformations. In this approach each design feature of an object is assigned to one of predefined access levels representing modes of detail reduction. A role is defined by selecting an access level for each object. It protects object geometry only–the protection does not concern interactions or behaviors. Users update objects independently, then objects are synchronized by the central system. Such asynchronous approach is justified in some CAD collaborative applications but it is not useful in virtual world practice.

Wang, Ajoku, Brustoloni and Nnaji (2006) propose an access control model for distributed 3D collaborative engineering systems. In this model RBAC extension is used, called Scheduled Role-Based Distributed Data Access Control (S-RBDDAC), which consists of partial data sharing mechanism and fine grained access control. Access granularity is supported on different levels–assembly, component, feature and surface–which form a hierarchy. Access control is schedule-aware, which means permissions depend on function that a user performs in a given project within a particular period. Dynamic geometric and non-geometric constraints can be modeled, but inter-object interactions and their different semantics are not supported as an element of the privilege system. Only basic operations such as read, write and modify are used to form privileges.

Cera, Kim, Han & Regli (2004) propose a system called FACADE, which is synchronous collaborative 3D virtual environment enabling selective sharing of 3D objects. FACADE authors classify their work as both data–and interaction-centric, however, interaction is regarded here only as inter-user design-time interaction and not inter-object dynamic behavior. There are cross-hierarchy relations between objects called "need-to-know requirements", but their nature is static and they are explicitly defined by designers. This concept provides role-based views on modeled data with read/write privileges granularity. Read privilege is extended to continuous scale of mesh resolution, but since only geometry is considered there is no support for whole spectrum of high level operations that could form privileges.

Access Control in Multimedia Systems

From among not CAD-based approaches, the most distinguished are rule-based access control models developed for the multimedia domain as the whole. Such models have been even a subject of standardization as a part of MPEG-21–Right Expression Language (REL) (Wang, Demartini, Wragg, Paramasivam, & Barlas, 2005). Unfortunately, Digital Item (DI) representation which sets a base for this model is not expressive enough

to support complex behavior-rich 3D objects. Other access control standards in the multimedia context like Extensible Access Control Modeling Language (XACML) (Moses, 2005) are even more general.

An interesting rule-based access control model has been developed for and implemented in the DEVA system (Pettifer & Marsh, 2001). In the DEVA approach, execution of a given operation is controlled by access rules expressed by source code defined in so called keys. However, both operations and keys have to be explicitly defined by users. There is no automatic induction of operation dependencies, so users are responsible for maintaining access rules consistency. It is not clear how DEVA approach is integrated with standard access control and how privileges are represented.

Protecting Virtual World Data

In the area of modeling virtual worlds, a number of works are devoted to methods of modeling virtual worlds not only as sets of geometrical objects but semantically (Latoschik, Biermann & Wachsmuth, 2005; Lugrin & Cavazza, 2007; Pittarello & De Faveri, 2006; Gutierrez, Vexo & Thalmann, 2005). Such approaches enable application of algorithms automatically exploring content of the virtual world, reusing objects in different contexts and taking advantage of domain knowledge stored in external ontologies. However, there has been no effort to integrate semantic virtual world models with user privileges control to protect data privacy.

Access control model of the commercial virtual worlds is usually very simple: only few operations from predefined list can be used to form user privileges and access control for objects is based on two role states only (owner/non-owner).

In the most popular Second Life (2009) virtual world access control model is a bit more complicated. Owner/non-owner simple access control model for objects has been extended to support group privileges used for collaboration of two or more persons in a shared parcel of land. One can use some of three predefined roles (Everyone, Officer, Owner) or can define new roles for different users who work on a common project. Roles are defined by assigning so called "capabilities" to a given role, such as "Always allow create objects" or "Send Notices". But still the list of "capabilities" is predefined, fixed and coarse-grained. Moreover, "capabilities" cannot be assigned to selected resources.

In Second Life some elements of the access control for the objects owned by a given user can be defined by him or her in scripts written in the virtual world's scripting language. However, business logic coded in the scripts is orthogonal to the Second Life's access control model and its consistency with the virtual world data model cannot be validated nor automatically analyzed.

In the virtual world competitive to Second Life, Active Worlds (2009), possibilities of collaboration are even more simplified. The right to work on someone else object can be granted by the owner of that object only, using a so-called "privilege password" mechanism.

Besides the aforementioned limitations, in virtual worlds such as Second Life or Active Worlds there is a problem with access control related to the fact that it is proprietary and vendor-dependent. As such, the access control can always be subject of change.

Beh-VR: Structured Design of Virtual Worlds

The next research field related to this chapter is structured design of virtual worlds. It focuses on methods of building VR applications in which content is dynamically configured from high-level elements, thus it can be relatively easily created and modified by domain experts and common users. However, those reusable elements lack integrated user privilege support. An approach to VR structured design which inherently supports interactive behavior-rich scenes is Beh-VR (Walczak, 2008; Walczak 2006). In the Beh-VR

approach, 3D scene-specific elements such as geometry, virtual object attributes and behavior definition are seamlessly modeled using concepts of an object or a bean (Walczak, 2008b). As a consequence, imperative approach (control-flow) is used, which wraps declaratively represented models (data-flow). A Beh-VR application is built of software components called VR-Beans. Technically, VR-Beans are objects, controlled by standard script nodes conforming to a specific convention. Conformance to this convention enables combining arbitrary sets of VR-Beans into technically correct 3D scenes and provides means of inter-object communication. Each VR-Bean consists of at least one scenario script, an optional set of media objects and an optional set of properties. The scenario script is the main element controlling each VR-Bean. Scenarios are programmed in a high-level XML-based programming language. They describe what happens when the object is initialized, what actions are performed by the object and what are the responses of the object to external stimuli. In some cases there may be several different scenarios controlling a VR-Bean, depending on the presentation context. Scenario scripts can inherit methods and actions from scenario classes that form inheritance hierarchies.

A scene is created dynamically by combining independent VR-Bean objects. Since the content of a scene is generally not known at the design time, communication between objects becomes a critical element. It is realized using mechanisms of public values and method invocation.

A Beh-VR application consists of a hierarchy of presentation spaces. Each presentation space may contain a set of VR-Bean objects and one or more content or behavior templates. To simplify creation of complex VR presentations, each presentation space may be associated with a content pattern, which defines a tree of categories together with default scenarios for objects in the categories and a tree of subspaces. Objects assigned to a category inherit methods and actions from the pattern scenarios, but can also override the default implementation with some object-specific implementation. Categories defined in a content pattern act as software component interfaces.

Designing a Beh-VR application consists of three steps: creating presentation spaces, assigning content patterns to the spaces and assigning objects to specific categories in the patterns. A content designer can also set properties of the spaces and the objects (appearance, size, location, state etc.). While a pattern defines the overall structure of the presentation, the objects assigned to categories by a content designer provide the actual implementation of particular methods and actions. The assigned objects also contain specific media components such as 3D models and sounds. Therefore, entirely different presentations can be created by assigning different sets of objects to presentation spaces with the same content pattern. Beh-VR approach has been described in details by Walczak (2008; 2006; 2008a; 2008b).

VR-PR APPROACH

The Concept of VR-PR

Interactive virtual worlds permit inclusion of content dynamically generated by users. Consequently, in such virtual worlds the structure of the data model evolves which entails specific requirements for the access control model. In standard access control models such as RBAC and its extensions, privileges are formed as a pair: operation-resource. Typical operations are "read", "write", "execute", "modify". However, in dynamic virtual worlds based on the object-oriented paradigm a question arises: how to build an access control model appropriate to a very large number of dynamic classes, objects and methods that would be both flexible enough to encompass a large variety of possible operations and understandable and manageable for users? In such virtual worlds objects are the resources but operations may be defined differently. If an operation is an

object method, privileges are too dependent on the data model. When a method changes or a new class is added, the operation set used to define privileges has to be changed accordingly. If an operation represents all the object's methods, i.e., privileges are defined with the object granularity, another problem arises: different methods of an object usually have different semantics and they call different methods (i.e. have different call graphs), so their range of penetration of a virtual world is different, which is not reflected by such a privilege system. Moreover, it is also very dependent on data model changes. If an operation is a primitive one, for example "read" or "write", privilege system is independent of the data model changes, but it does not follow evolution of the virtual world, so it is useless in case of dynamic virtual worlds that constantly evolve. If the set of operations is not fixed but is updated by human operators according to data model changes, the risk of inconsistencies grows drastically.

To solve this problem in the VR-PR approach the concept of meta-operations is used. A meta-operation is a conceptual extension of an operation from standard access control models. Similarly to a regular operation, it is used to define privileges in conjunction with objects. However, unlike standard access controls models, meta-operations can represent arbitrary operations performed by objects, not only "read", "write" or "execute", which are useful in a file system or a database but are far from being sufficient in a complex virtual reality environment.

Since operations performed by an object are not known a priori, interaction functionality scope must be automatically induced from the object-oriented virtual world data model. In other words, a meta-operation is a set of bindings to similar object methods induced from method call graphs. Each meta-operation has a type assigned to it. Meta-operations form a hierarchy reflecting call graphs inclusion. Meta-operations reflect all the method calls i.e. all in-world interactions among the objects, which may be complex, diverse and dynamic. The set of all meta-operations is generated in a way assuring each method call to be bound to at least one induced meta-operation. Meta-operations are intuitively understandable to virtual content authors, publishers, administrators or other users authorized to create new privileges or to modify existing ones.

In the VR-PR approach the privileges are processed in two phases. The Meta-Operations Generation Phase (MOGP) follows the virtual world data model evolution by regenerating meta-operation set on each change. It is performed by the induction process based on the analysis of similarity of virtual object's method call graphs, as well as on the analysis of relationships between elements of the data model. A set of available meta-operations is generated from potential method calls (inter-object relationship: uses-a), known both before and at the run-time, and from the class hierarchy and object set structure (relationships: is-a, instance-of, part-of). It is during the MOGP phase that meta-operation type categorization and generalization hierarchies are built.

Meta-operations are induced by logical unification of different methods. This means that methods having similar call graphs are logically bound to a common meta-operation in the privilege system. In turn, in the virtual world these methods are still recognized as separate ones.

Meta-operation generation is based on methods call graphs. Call graphs are usually constructed by compilers for compilation optimization or by software engineering tools to give programmers better understanding of the code through its visualization. Here a call graph is a basic data structure used to induce meta-operations by method's call graphs similarity analysis. From the data security and privacy point of view, measuring the level of similarity of the methods by measuring the level of similarity of their call graphs is justified. A meta-operation which groups methods with similar call graphs describes well the range of penetration of the virtual world by a set of calls. In the VR-PR approach, the allowed method call penetration range of a given world is controlled by the privilege system. It makes the function of a privilege to protect objects really fulfilled, by protecting the system against non-authorized deep method calls in the dense net of variable behavioral dependencies.

The second phase of the approach is the Privilege Creation and Modification Phase (PCMP). Meta-operations induced during the first phase are used to form privileges by assigning them to objects. This process is controlled by an access control mechanism which forces its consistency with the data model.

In Figure 1 a sequence diagram is presented, which includes actors (User1 playing the content

Figure 1. Sequence diagram of the VR-PR approach

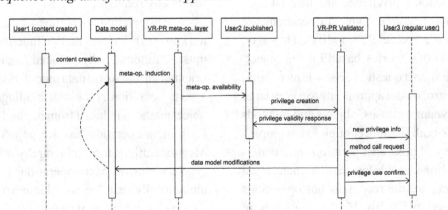

creator role, User2 playing the publisher role and User3 who is a regular user interacting with the virtual world content), software modules of the VR-PR approach and their time-dependent interactions. Highly variable and interactive part of the approach, i.e. virtual world objects, is represented by single aggregating element "data model" on the diagram. Users having content creator roles influence this data model by adding and changing objects and classes. Such actions cause (re) generation of meta-operations, which become available for a publisher user (User2). He or she creates privileges, which are then validated by the VR-PR Validator module. Next, the validation result is sent back to the publisher (User2), he or she assigns the privilege to a selected role and new privilege information is sent to all users having this role. Such user is denoted on the diagram as User3. User3 can use the privilege by sending method call request via the VR-PR Validator checking whether request conforms to

the privilege or not. Then the method is executed, which may cause data model modifications. It triggers a meta-operation regeneration process, which is followed by all the steps described above.

The same scenario is depicted in Figure 2 focusing on the way in which the meta-operation mechanism protects the allowed range of calls in a virtual world. To promote creativity, content creators can add and modify their objects and classes in an unsupervised manner. Thus, it cannot be guaranteed that the designed methods call only methods considered as permitted in a given context. Meta-operations reflect the range of calls as it is depicted by the dotted area in Figure 2. After the insertion of new objects into the virtual world by a content creator (1), meta-operations are induced from the method call graph (2). Next, when a meta-operation becomes available to the publisher (3), he or she can create privileges (4), which are verified by the VR-PR Validator (5).

Figure 2. Virtual world actors in the VR-PR approach

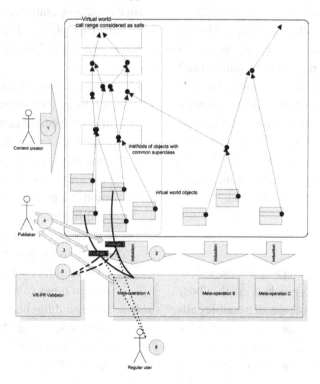

Finally, a regular user can use them and call appropriate methods (6).

It is possible to automate not only the induction of meta-operations used in privileges but also the detection of an attack on some objects in the VR system (malicious method calls and the detection of a security hole in the VR system (potential method call combination). Given calls can be compared with known dangerous call patterns (the simplest pattern case: data harvesting) by the call graph matching algorithm which is originally used in the VR-PR approach to induce meta-operations–artificial "bad" meta-operations may be constructed (which will not form any privileges or will form special privileges for security audit purposes only) and compared with existing call graphs. Other virtual world security threats (described by ENISA (2008) in the virtual worlds context) such as automation attacks (massively obtaining free objects), harassment (ganking in virtual world), risks to intellectual property (using copyrighted material), spam in virtual world or attempts of a virtual world service denial can be detected by automated analysis of call graphs as well.

Moreover, once the attack on some objects (malicious method calls) or the presence of a security hole (potential method call combination) is detected in the VR system, it is easy to neutralize it. The identification of a meta-operation corresponding to dangerous method call graphs and global deactivation of all privileges which use this meta-operation is fast and in-depth. There is no risk that some privileges enabling malicious method calls will be accidently omitted.

The MOGP Phase

In the VR-PR approach, meta-operation induction is based on static call graph–a graph whose nodes are methods and edges are all possible calls of other methods. A node represents a method in the context of a given object, which means that if a given class has many instances, then for each method of this class there are as many nodes as instances. The call graph is created from the source code of virtual world objects. Global and local call graphs are distinguished. The global call graph contains all the methods and all the potential calls of other methods included in the source code of all the objects composing a virtual world at a given moment. It is updated incrementally when the data model changes. A local call graph is developed for each method. It is a subgraph of the global call graph built starting from a given method and containing all the methods that are called by this method and all their callees. Despite the regeneration of a call graph at run-time in the VR-PR approach, it is not a dynamic call graph, i.e. it is not a result of the analysis of run-time calls but the method call dependencies in the source code.

Meta-operations have types assigned. Types reflect the way meta-operations have been induced. When a given meta-operation is based on the methods with identical local call graphs, its type is called fully-matching. When call graphs of two unified methods span on methods belonging to the same classes (but based on different objects sets), such a meta-operation is called class-matching.

The first phase of the VR-PR approach is composed of the following five steps (Figure 3):

1. Construct the global call graph. This graph is a basic data structure for the meta-operation automatic generation process.
2. Induce meta-operations. The induction of each meta-operation is preceded by a local call graph pre-selection. Each meta-operation is generated by a logical unification of different methods, based on similarity analysis of method's local call graphs and on the analysis of the static class hierarchy and the object set structure.
3. Assign types to meta-operations.
4. Store bindings between each meta-operation and the set of methods which have been a base of its induction for further use during the PCMP phase.

Figure 3. MOGP: meta-operations generation

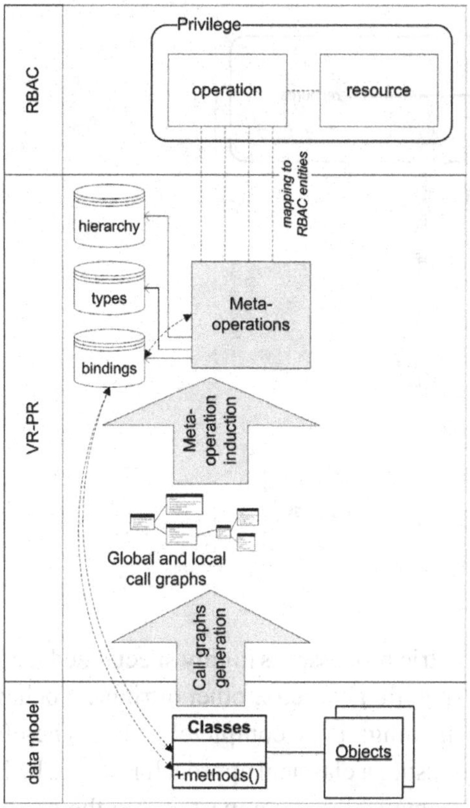

5. Build meta-operations hierarchy according to the composability criterion. It is orthogonal both to the role hierarchy and the class inheritance hierarchy.

Potentially, the logical unification can be performed on two methods, which in turn may be:

- Different methods of different classes (but having similar calls); or
- The same method, but in different object context (parameterized or using non-static field values); or
- Different methods of the same class.

The induction of each meta-operation is based on the analysis of the calls from methods match-

ing these cases. The aforementioned cases are distinguished during the selection of methods to be logically unified, as well as during the call similarity analysis.

The PCMP Phase

In the PCMP phase of the VR-PR approach the induced meta-operations are used to create privileges by assigning meta-operations to objects and binding the privileges created in this way to roles (Figure 4). Whether a given meta-operation may be assigned to a given object or not, depends on the privilege validation mechanism. Privilege validation can work in two modes: strict privileges and potential privileges. In the strict privileges mode a privilege may be created only if a given meta-operation has been induced from the requested object. In the potential privileges mode a given meta-operation can be assigned to an object even if the operation has not been induced from any of the object's methods. Such privileges are used when it can be anticipated that taking into account data model dynamism some objects will gain new competences. However, in the moment of the creation of such privileges they do not make any new method calls allowed because those methods are at this moment inexistent.

Since all the calls which are triggered by a given operation, including all the call dependences (represented by a call graph), are known before each iteration of the privilege creation phase, during privilege assignment this knowledge can influence final decision whether a given privilege can be assigned or not. Thus, after privilege assignment, it is guaranteed during runtime that no access error will arise related to the lack of privileges to any of dependent methods called. This follows from the fact that each meta-operation stores all the bindings to the methods which were the basis of its induction.

Figure 4. PCMP: privilege creation/modification

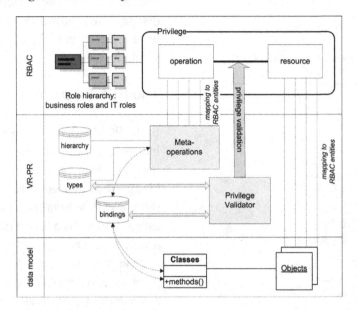

VR-PR Use Cases

Use Case: Security System of a Building—Co-Designing a Replacement Object

As the first use case, consider a security system of an office building, which is co-designed using 3D modeling and simulation environment. The designed building contains a number of rooms, corridors, elevators etc. Inside the building there are move sensors, RFID markers, automatic door locks, keypads for security codes, biometric processors etc. There is a user playing the Designer role, a user playing the Tester role and a user playing the Project Manager role. A remote Designer creates a new biometric processor that is an interactive part of the building security system. Assume that interactions of the biometric processor with other parts of the designed building security system are identical to interactions of a number of other biometric processors. The new biometric processor is more efficient and therefore has to replace some of the existing biometric processors. However, the considered

biometric processor is highly specialized itself, it has specific geometry, other attributes, behavior and naming: it is completely new. Therefore, when using a classical approach it would be hard to automatically encompass it into the privilege system governed by the access control system: the procedure of identifying and analyzing its methods would have to be performed manually by an IT skilled person – an access control administrator.

In the VR-PR approach all the method calls of the new "biometric processor" object are analyzed automatically and meta-operations are generated and regenerated automatically as well. In the case considered, methods of the new object "biometric processor" are automatically bound with existing meta-operations. This is possible because interactions of the new "biometric processor" object and the other parts of the designed building security system are identical, so the meta-operations generated are already valid for the new object. Thus, the VR-PR engine notifies the Project Manager about the meta-operation update. The Project Manager can see the new changes on his or her console. The meta-operation has its place in the meta-operations hierarchy. The meta-operation hierarchy is well known to the Project Manager, because it contains other meta-operations frequently used by him or her so each a new change or binding can be perceived in the correct context.

A meta-operation is described by general metadata and it is much more understandable for the Project Manager than the technical names of the methods of a new object. He or she can seamlessly create some new privileges using updated meta-operations (as an RBAC operation) and the new object (as an RBAC resource). In this scenario he or she creates privileges enabling the Tester user to execute methods of the "biometric processor" object and to test it while cooperating with other objects composing the system.

Use Case: Security System of a Building—Co-Designing a New Object

The second use case is an extension of the previous one. Now assume that the Designer who is an external collaborator has created a new part of the system: a monitoring camera that has not only a new geometry and other attributes, but also a completely new role in the system. Thus, its interaction pattern, which is a method call graph, is unique and therefore cannot be bound to any existing meta-operation (the direction and focus of the camera is controlled by the operator, camera detects suspicious move patterns and reports it to the right departments and security offices). Instead, new meta-operations are created and inserted into the meta-operation hierarchy. The Project Manager is notified about these changes and becomes conscious of what real actions are hidden behind these method calls and how deep are the consequences of the execution of the methods of the new object (call graph visualization is a supporting technique here). This audit is especially significant in the case considered because of a lower level of trust to external collaborators. The Project Manager can use a new meta-operation in conjunction with one or more new object to create privileges for those users who are entitled to use a

new monitoring camera object and all dependent (called) methods of other parts at the same time.

Use Case: Interactive Multi-Role Learning

In the third use case, the VR-PR approach can be applied to a multiuser interactive virtual museum implemented in the ARCO system (Walczak, 2008b). Such a virtual museum not only serves as a digital representation of cultural objects but also plays the role of an environment enabling visitors to educate themselves (often as a part of formal education) by manipulating various objects (simulating historical events, constructing machines, modeling interactive characters) and interacting with other visitors. In such creative learning space students create new objects or modify existing ones following a museum guide's requirements specified according to the historical background of a given museum. The key aspect of the learning process is that behavioral functionality of objects defined by a single student has to be partially shared with team-members, partially shared with all other students, while the whole functionality should be accessible to the museum guides. Partial knowledge about the environment functionality stimulates participants to carry out game-like experiments and enables deep understanding of the simulated historical circumstances. For instance in a nineteenth century battlefield scenario some students can impersonate army commanders of different ranks with different levels of commandment competences while other students may be responsible for modeling those commanders and the behavior of their armies according to the historical guidelines. Since modeling process is based on software tools implemented according to the VR-PR approach, a museum guide can selectively assign privileges to roles with fine-grained precision of object methods, as soon as a given historical object is modeled and added or uploaded at run-time to the VR environment. During multiuser simulation new interactive historical objects are added. Following data model changes, the meta-operations hierarchy is being built at the same time. A museum guide can track the meta-operation hierarchy and basing on that can assess on-line whether the student groups correctly modeled the composed behaviors of the military units.

VR-PR Approach Discussion

The MOGP and PCMP phases described in Section 4 are following each other at run-time. Creating privileges is not a static task performed only during the creation of a virtual world, but a dynamic process following virtual world evolution. Users, roles and the virtual world data model evolve naturally, while core structures of the access control model as meta-operations hierarchy remain persistent. In earlier approaches the operation set was static, though operations allowed on resources were defined with different semantics and complexity, i.e. read/write, execute/modify/insert/ append or activate/play/reorganize. In some cases, the operation set could evolve via non-automated changes following data model modifications, which does not assure privileges consistency. In the VR-PR approach, dynamism of the virtual world is inherently taken into account. Defining privileges using automatically regenerated high-level meta-operations makes the process of role creation and management consistent, because of the internal consistency of the meta-operation set and the consistency of meta-operations with the data model currently used. In the VR-PR approach the meta-operations layer stabilizes the process of privilege management. It is updated on-change (i.e. when new objects or new interactions appear), but the updates do not change the meta-operations set significantly–especially when meta-operations are induced hierarchically and form a tree structure. Thus, access to meta-operations provides a role manager or any user eligible to create or modify a privilege, who is not a 3D modeling expert, nor a programmer, with a safe tool.

In the VR-PR approach, a privilege is composed of an object and an operation allowed on this object. Any access control model that is compliant with this representation, can be used in conjunction with the VR-PR approach. Therefore any RBAC-based access control model can be applied with all the benefits of using the concept of roles or any other extended mechanisms mentioned in Section 2. Similarly, ABAC access control model representing privilege is a pair "objects descriptors–operation" can be applied as well.

The VR-PR approach makes it possible to avoid unwanted frequent redefining and proliferation of roles. Unwanted proliferation of roles takes place when privilege changes do not follow and reflect real business requirements which are redefined for a given role (e.g. a virtual world user gains new duties), but are forced by a data model activity modification on a low level (e.g. competences of the object to which privileges have been already granted are changed). The advantage of the VR-PR approach is that meta-operations can be regenerated without modifying privileges which are assigned to them, as well as without role-privilege and user-role assignment modifications.

The two phases of the VR-PR approach can be perceived as a part of a more general process of virtual world privileges lifecycle. In this process four phases are cyclically following each other (Figure 5). The MOGP phase precedes the PCMP phase as it has been described above. After privilege creation performed in the PCMP phase, virtual world content (scenes) is pre-generated according to defined privileges. This is the content preparation phase. Different versions of the 3D data have to be stored to be efficiently served on-demand as a response for roaming virtual world user's requests. Next, when 3D content is already served to the user, he or she can interact with it and–in consequence–modify the data. In modern virtual worlds, changes can be minor (as object parameter update), but also major as class interactivity (methods) redefinition. In the latter case access control model has to reorganize

Figure 5. Virtual world privileges lifecycle

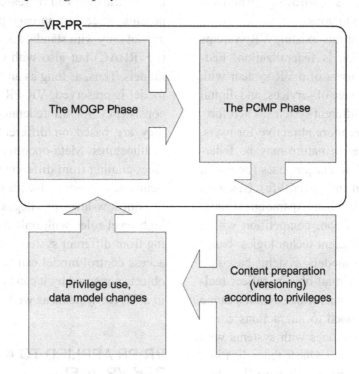

its privilege-related data to reflect data model changes. This is performed by the MOGP phase which closes the cycle.

To improve the quality of meta-operations induction and therefore privilege creation, in the extended version of the approach extra factors are taken into account apart from call graphs, uses-a, part-of, is-a, and instance-of relations analysis. One of them, appropriate for multimedia 3D objects, are metadata represented in the MPEG-7 format. All metadata levels can be used: syntactic metadata, structural metadata, semantic metadata, as well as ontologies. Fundamental is the method of automatic generation of metadata, and what is significant in dynamic virtual worlds domain, because of frequent object redesign and transformations, metadata regeneration and adaptation to modifications. Since automatically generated metadata set for a single object describing the object on the syntactic, structural and semantic levels, containing a lot of technical metadata, often is very large, metadata pre-selec-

tion has to be performed. It is both quantitative and qualitative filtering process. Moreover, in decentralized virtual worlds, metadata come from different sources and new objects are compositions of preexisting objects, there is a problem of metadata integration and preserving consistency of relevant metadata.

However, both user-generated and automatically-generated metadata in large, diversified and dynamic datasets have limited application for security related purposed. User-generated metadata cannot be perceived as reliable, since world can be freely accessible for content and metadata creators, and automatically-generated metadata are biased: they are highly dependent on the generating algorithm. Call graphs are a more objective base of reasoning, they are related to what actually object does in the world and what are its interactions. Metadata analysis is considered here as a supportive technique. Finally, meta-operations induction can be interactively parameterized by human supervisor or external ontologies in specific cases, when logical unification decisions are ambiguous.

New trend that permits existing VR systems to survive competition is federalization. Federalization provides users of a VR system with access to a broader range of services, and digital assets coming from different systems. Therefore, federated systems are more attractive for users. VR systems of different nature may be federated: designed for different purposes (business, co-design, entertainment, social life), based on different inter-user relationships paradigms (mass, niche, groups competition, competition within groups), based on different technologies, based on different business models, systems based on the assumption that virtual objects reflect real-world objects with systems which do not assume that, systems constrained to interactions corresponding to real-world ones with systems with unconstrained interactions. Due to federalization, a border between all aforementioned VR system can be blurred. As a result of federalization of different systems, a significant synergy effect can be achieved.

Technically, federalization enhances scalability, extensibility, capability of specialization of the system and a level of data and code reuse. The number of papers devoted to this challenge has been published, but the problem of user privilege representation in federated 3D virtual environments is scarce.

In a federated VR system not only new content is continuously added to the system by distributed content creators, but also whole sub-spaces may by dynamically added or removed. These circumstances intensify the need of automation and machine-aided management of the user privileges across federated systems. Hubs grouping distributed systems can be responsible not only for bridging data and events, and synchronization tasks, but also for security interoperability and access control management. Therefore, most of the VR-PR approach functionality: call graph similarity analysis, meta-operation induction

and notification can be realized in hubs. This is possible since the approach presented is compliant not only with standard access control models (i.e. RBAC) but also with object-oriented data models. Thus, as long as an object-oriented data model is preserved, VR-PR can force privilege consistency for all federated systems, even if they are based on different technologies and architectures. Meta-operations and their hierarchies coming from different sub-systems can be seamlessly integrated with each other contrary to both low-level privileges and resources and high-level roles with unknown semantics coming from different systems. Moreover, since the access control model can be easily unified, the objects governed by it can be more easily reused in different systems as well.

VR-PR APPLIED TO A BEH-VR SCENE

Assumptions

The Beh-VR approach significantly reduces the effort put into designing and creating complex VR scenes as it has been described in Section 2. However, the structured design approach lacks user privilege support. Thus, the VR-PR approach can be applied to it as a natural extension of the Beh-VR concept. The VR-PR approach does not impose any requirements on a Beh-VR-compliant scene. All concepts of role-based access control become available for the virtual world designed with the Beh-VR approach. A VR-PR layer provides a knowledge base about available operations in the Beh-VR scenes in the context of privileges expression.

Standard access control models deal with operations applied to passive resources which have no behavior. In turn, in the Beh-VR approach, which is object-oriented, data model objects are active, i.e. their behavior is implemented by object methods. Since there is a need to use both approaches, based on active and passive object assumptions, it can be noticed that the operation set which is a part of the access control model cannot disregard interactions of the objects implemented in its methods. The selection of an applicable operation depends on the call range of object methods. Meta-operations induced from Beh-VR data preserve the encapsulation of the object-oriented model (they are a selection of the original methods) and can be used in the access control model. They fill the gap between the two models mentioned above.

In the simplest case the VR-PR approach can be applied to a Beh-VR scene under the following assumptions:

- A scenario script (the active one for its VR-Bean, depending on the presentation context) is considered to be a VR-PR object,
- A scenario class is considered to be a VR-PR class.

In the Beh-VR approach method invocation is one of the main means of communication (the approach is based on a control-flow paradigm, unlike most of other methods of structured VR design). Thus, call graph construction followed by meta-operations induction (the MOGP phase) can be applied. Any other means of communications, such as communication via public values, can be mapped on artificial method calls and analyzed as well. Next, regular privilege creation (the PCMP phase) can be performed as described in Section 3. Meta-operations induced in this way can be useful in the automatic or semi-automatic generation of Beh-VR content pattern categories.

In a more advanced case of the VR-PR application, meta-operation induction is based not directly on VR-Bean's scenario scripts, but on default scenarios of the content pattern category. In this situation, the meta-operations induced should be considered on a higher level of abstraction—on a level of software components which are modeled by content pattern categories. High level

privileges can be created and used. They base on the results of the analysis of the interactions not between particular objects but between whole software components.

In applications based on object data model designed according to the classical approach, access to methods on the class level is verified at compile-time and on the object level–at runtime. However, in the Beh-VR approach objects (scenarios) and classes (scenario classes) are interpreted in the same phase. Thus, classical phase separation can be replaced by a more flexible and access-control-consistent one. With the VR-PR approach the same access control mechanism and privilege representation is used on both levels, but class abstraction layer is still preserved.

Beh-VR does not support reflection. This mechanism is known as particularly challenging for call graph algorithms. The lack of this mechanism makes global call graph creation and local call graph comparison in the VR-PR approach much faster. The speed of generation, regeneration and comparison of call graphs is crucial in the VR-PR approach, because of its on-change launching procedure described in Section 3.

Generally, not only in Beh-VR approach, but in all object-oriented applications during their lifetime there is drift towards decreasing the size of the methods and increasing the number of calls. Along with increasing the number of calls, inter-object dependencies become more complex. Thus, a need for an automatic analysis for security purposes becomes critical. This is yet another motivation for applying the VR-PR approach to the Beh-VR worlds.

Illustrative Example

The following example is loosely inspired by the virtual studio data objects (Walczak, Wojciechowski, Wójtowicz, 2005), modeled with the Beh-VR approach. There are two complex objects called *MainStudio* and *BackStudio* corresponding to the areas of a virtual television studio.

The *MainStudio* has been prepared to present general news with background video sequences being displayed simultaneously. Thus, it has *presentBackgroundStory* method implemented. This method calls *displayAsVideo* method of the *Document1* object. *Document1* object is responsible for storing and managing the data presented during a news show and its *displayAsVideo* method is responsible for displaying it in the form of a video sequence. In turn, this method uses *Panel* object and its method play to play this video sequence on a special presentation panel. All these method calls are denoted in Figure 6 by lines.

BackStudio has been prepared for the presentation of the weather forecast by an avatar. Thus, it has *presentWeatherForecast* method implemented. This method calls *displayAsAnimation* method of the *Document2* object. *Document2* object is responsible for storing and managing the data presented during the weather forecast and its *displayAsAnimation* method is responsible for representing the weather forecast data in the form of an avatar animation. In turn, this method uses *Avatar* object and its method animate to animate these data.

The two methods, with the studios objects responsible for initiating the whole procedure of presenting news (*presentBackgroundStory* and *presentWeatherForecast*), call different methods of different objects. Nevertheless, their call graphs are similar (and de facto their semantics is analogous). They both call method of two document objects, possibly belonging to classes with a common superclass. Subsequent calls are analogous as well. Thus, during the MOGP phase they are logically unified to form a new meta-operation: "presentNews". The induction is denoted in Figure 6 by dashed lines. The same procedure is performed to induce "displayDocument" meta-operation on the lower level.

Hypothetically, if *displayAsAnimation* method implementation had been extended to include a call to some other method of different objects (dotted-and-dashed line in Figure 6), graph similarity comparison would fail. The range of penetration of the virtual world objects would be

Figure 6. Meta-operation induction example in a virtual studio

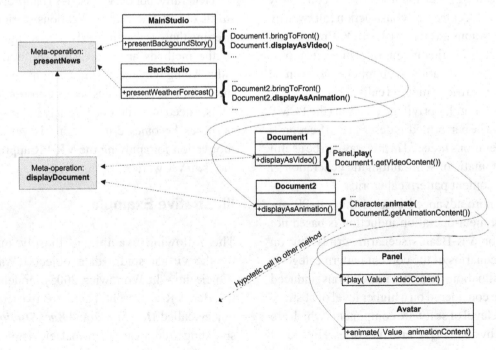

broader for one call graph than for the other, thus *presentWeatherForecast* method would not be of the basis for "presentNews" meta-operation.

The two meta-operations induced in this example form a hierarchy in which "presentNews" operation is the parent of the "displayDocument". This is caused by the fact that the "display Document" operation's methods have call graphs which are subgraphs of "presentNews" operation's method call graphs.

Creating a new privilege by applying "presentNews" meta-operation to the *BackStudio* object (Figure 7, privilege #1) will make the privilege holder (a user assigned to a role with this privilege) eligible to execute the method *presentWeatherForecast* of this object. Similarly, "displayDocument" meta-operation applied to the Document2 object will make *displayAsAnimation* method executable for a given role (Figure 7, privilege #2).

The meta-operations such as those used to construct privilege #1 and privilege #2 are useful especially when scenes contain large number of VR classes, objects and methods, since they aggregate them in an automatic manner. Using meta-operations such as "displayDocument" or "presentNews" is more understandable for the virtual studio administrator than performing manual search and selecting proper object methods. The privileges created strictly control the allowed range of virtual world penetration by method calls.

In the presented sample scenario, privilege #1 and privilege #2 can be used by the virtual studio administrator to create privileges for the virtual studio operator role. For the security and production stability purposes, the operator can execute only methods with calls spanning a well-tested method call range. Later in this scenario, when implementation of the class methods are extended, bindings between meta-operations and methods will be automatically updated, which assures privileges consistency with the data model, and its integrity. The implementation extension will not require modifying privileges which have been already assigned to the operator role, as well as role-privilege and user-role assignment modifications.

Nevertheless, in many cases creating privilege with a given meta-operation and an object will not be allowed and will be blocked by the VR-PR Validator. For instance, applying "presentNews" to the *Document2* object (Figure 7, privilege #3) cannot make *displayAsAnimation* method call legal, because *displayAsAnimation* call graph covers merely a subset of "presentNews" meta-operation call graph. Thus, it cannot be guaranteed that all "presentNews" meta-operation's desired functionality would be executed. Another case is depicted in Figure 7 as privilege #4. Here the meta-operation "displayDocument" is to be applied to the *BackStudio* object. The *presentWeatherForecast* method cannot be executed with this meta-operation, since "displayDocument" range

Figure 7. Privilege creation example cases

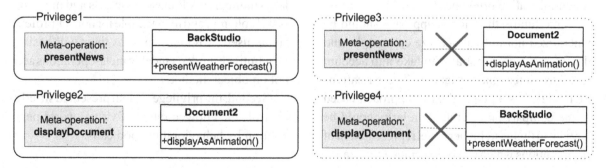

is insufficient to express all the functionality of the *this* method. As it can be seen in the aforementioned cases, a meta-operation can be applied to objects which have a method at the top of the call graph serving as the basis for the induction of the considered meta-operation.

FUTURE RESEARCH DIRECTIONS

Descriptive possibilities of meta-operations may be used in the role-mining process which is performed for security auditing purposes. In the VR-PR approach, each meta-operation forming a privilege assigned to a role expresses meaningful information about the privilege semantics with an explicit representation. Meta-operations used in privileges can be treated as metadata unambiguously describing the role to which those privileges have been assigned. Having such metadata, role-mining process is much more straightforward.

Another challenge which can be solved with the presented approach is the problem of how to prevent a user who is eligible to create limited privileges from browsing the whole meta-operations set. Some meta-operations can reveal object interactions which should be hidden to given groups of users, even those having partial administrative competences. The meta-operations should be visible selectively, based on the role's privileges. In the VR-PR approach using the same algorithm as in the regular case, special meta-meta-operations are induced and used to construct meta-privileges, i.e. privileges used to control the access to privileges creation and modification process, known as administrative privileges.

In the future, the VR-PR approach should be generalized not only to analyze call graphs and class dependencies but also to take into account geometric inter-object relations. These relations are modeled as a graph, thus an approach based on the comparison of graph similarity could be applied. In this case, higher-level representation of the operations which can be executed for instance on objects placed in a given area of the scene can be used to form geometry-centric privileges useful in 3D virtual worlds.

In the VR-PR approach when a source code of an object or a class changes, meta-operations are regenerated accordingly, as in the case of the Beh-VR script being dynamically loaded by a user. However, when this script is not interpreted by the standard Beh-VR engine but by a user-generated code, its analysis is not supported by the VR-PR approach at the current stage of its development. As a part of future research, a mechanism supporting the control over all method calls, including those interpreted by a dynamic code, should be developed.

CONCLUSION

In the VR-PR approach presented in this chapter a new security mechanism based on the concept of meta-operations is proposed to provide data security and privacy. Meta-operations are derived at run-time from the virtual world's current data model and are applicable to the access control model as a part of a privilege, while semantic consistency of the security policies is forced by a two-phase regeneration and validation mechanism so that user rights can still be expressed in a precise, accurate and flexible way.

There are four main advantages of the VR-PR approach which make it innovative in the area of virtual world security.

First, the access control model proposed which is appropriate to a virtual world containing a very large number of VR classes, objects and methods is still coherent and manageable for non-IT professional users, who may express their will basing on intuitively understandable meta-operations and not on object methods.

Second, the privilege system presented strictly controls the allowed range of virtual world penetration by behavioral method calls.

Third, the algorithm for automatic regeneration of meta-operations used in privileges assures privileges consistency with the data model and its integrity, as well as increases the security level of the security policies defined using privileges containing meta-operations.

Finally, the two-phase induce-and-use approach makes the process of privilege management stable: operation set is updated on-change but updates do not transform the operation set as fast as the data model evolves. Consequently, meta-operations can be regenerated without modifying not only privileges which are assigned to them but also role-privilege and user-role assignment.

The VR-PR approach also bridges the semantic gap between low-level operations executed on virtual world objects and abstract roles of virtual world users, both business and IT ones. Development of an abstract layer of meta-operations reduces the risk of inconsistent privilege modifications. It does not violate the RBAC access control model nor object-oriented data model, - it constitutes a middle layer placed between these two models developed for distinct purposes and it is designed with respect to 3D virtual worlds specificity.

REFERENCES

Active Worlds. (2009). Retrieved from http://www.activeworlds.com

Cera, D. D., Kim, T., Han, J., & Regli, W. C. (2004). Role-based viewing envelopes for information protection in collaborative modeling. *Computer Aided Design*, *36*(1), 873–886. doi:10.1016/j.cad.2003.09.014

ENISA. (2008). *Virtual World, Real Money: Security and Privacy in Massively-Multiplayer Online Games and Social and Corporate Virtual Worlds*. Position Paper of European Network and Information Security Agency. Retrieved from http://www.enisa.europa.eu/doc/pdf/deliverables/enisa_pp_security_privacy_virtualworlds.pdf

Gutierrez, M., Vexo, F., & Thalmann, D. (2005). Semantics-based representation of virtual environments. *International Journal of Computer Applications in Technology*, *23*, 229–238. doi:10.1504/IJCAT.2005.006484

Latoschik, M. E., Biermann, P., & Wachsmuth, I. (2005). Knowledge in the Loop: Semantics Representation for Multimodal Simulative Environments. In *Proceedings of the 5th International Symposium on Smart Graphics*, Frauenwoerth Cloister, Germany, (pp. 25-39).

Lugrin, J., & Cavazza, M. (2007). Making sense of virtual environments: action representation, grounding and common sense. In *Proceedings of the 12th international Conference on intelligent User interfaces, IUI '07*, (pp. 225-234). New York: ACM.

Moses, T. (Ed.). (2005). *eXtensible Access Control Markup Language (XACML) Version 2.0*. Retrieved August 1, 2009 http://docs.oasis-open.org/xacml/2.0/access_control-xacml-2.0-core-spec-os.pdf

Pettifer, S., & Marsh, J. (2001). A Collaborative Access Model for Shared Virtual Environments. In *Proceedings of the 10th IEEE international Workshops on Enabling Technologies: infrastructure For Collaborative Enterprises*. WETICE, (pp. 257-262). Washington, DC: IEEE Computer Society.

Pittarello, F., & De Faveri, A. (2006). Semantic description of 3D environments: a proposal based on web standards. In *Proceedings of the Eleventh international Conference on 3D Web Technology*, (Web3D '06), (pp. 85-95). New York: ACM.

Priebe, T., Dobmeier, W., Schläger, C., & Kamprath, N. (2007). Supporting Attribute-based Access Control in Authentication and Authorization Infrastructures with Ontologies. *Journal of software. JSW*, *2*(1), 27–38. doi:10.4304/jsw.2.1.27-38

Qiu, Z. M., Kok, K. F., Wong, Y. S., & Fuh, J. Y. (2007). Role-based 3D visualisation for asynchronous PLM collaboration. *Computers in Industry, 58*(8-9), 747–755. doi:10.1016/j.compind.2007.02.006

Sandhu, R., Ferraiolo, D., & Kuhn, R. (2000). The NIST model for role-based access control: towards a unified standard. In *Proceedings of the Fifth ACM Workshop on Role-Based Access Control*, (RBAC '00), (pp. 47-63). New York: ACM.

Second Life. (2009). Retrieved in from http://secondlife.com

Walczak, K. (2006). Beh-VR: Modeling Behavior of Dynamic Virtual Reality Contents. In H. Zha et al. (Eds.), *The 12th International Conference on Virtual Systems and Multimedia VSMM 2006, Interactive Technologies and Sociotechnical Systems,* (LNCS 4270, pp. 40-51). Berlin: Springer Verlag.

Walczak, K. (2008). Structured Design of Interactive VR Applications. In *The 13th International Symposium on 3D Web Technology Web3D*, Los Angeles, California, USA, (pp. 105-113). New York: ACM Press.

Walczak, K. (2008a). Flex-VR: Configurable 3D Web Applications. In *the IEEE International Conference on Human System Interaction HSI 2008*, Kraków, (pp. 135-140). Washington, DC: IEEE.

Walczak, K. (2008b). VR-BML: Behaviour Modelling Language for Configurable VR Applications, in Digital Heritage. In M. Ioannides, A. Addison, A. Georgopoulos, L. Kalisperis, (Eds.), *The 14th International Conference on Virtual Systems and MultiMedia VSMM'08*, Limassol (Cyprus), Archaeolingua, (pp. 295-302).

Walczak, K., Wojciechowski, R., & Wójtowicz, A. (2005). Interactive Production of Dynamic 3D Sceneries for Virtual Television Studio. In *7th Virtual Reality International Conference VRIC - Laval Virtual 2005*, Laval (France), (pp. 167-177).

Wang, X., Demartini, T., Wragg, B., Paramasivam, M., & Barlas, C. (2005). The mpeg-21 rights expression language and rights data dictionary. *Multimedia. IEEE Transactions on, 7*(3), 408–417.

Wang, Y., Ajoku, P., Brustoloni, J., & Nnaji, B., J. (2006). Intellectual Property Protection in Collaborative Design through Lean Information Modeling and Sharing. *Journal of Computing and Information Science in Engineering, 6*, 149. doi:10.1115/1.2190235

ADDITIONAL READING

Alpcan, T., Bauckhage, C., & Kotsovinos, E. (2007). Towards 3D Internet: Why, What, and How? In *Proceedings of the 2007 international Conference on Cyberworlds*. International Conference on Cyberworlds. IEEE Computer Society, Washington, DC, 95-99.

Bullock, A., & Benford, S. (1999). An access control framework for multi-user collaborative environments. *In Proceedings of the international ACM SIGGROUP Conference on Supporting Group Work. GROUP '99*. ACM, NY, 140-149.

Fang, C., Peng, W., Ye, X., & Zhang, S. (2005). Multi-level access control for collaborative CAD, *Computer Supported Cooperative Work in Design, Proceedings of the Ninth International Conference on, vol.1*, pp. 643-648.

Izaki, K. Tanaka, K. Takizawa, M. (2001). Authorization model based on object-oriented concept, *In Proceedings of the the 15th international Conference on information Networking. ICOIN*. IEEE Computer Society, Washington, DC, 72.

Oliveira, M., Crowcroft, J., & Slater, M. (2003). An innovative design approach to build virtual environment systems., *In Proceedings of the Workshop on Virtual Environments 2003*. EGVE '03, vol. 39. ACM, New York, NY, 143-151

Sallés, E. J., Michael, J. B., Capps, M., McGregor, D., & Kapolka, A. (2002). Security of runtime extensible virtual environments. *In Proceedings of the 4th international Conference on Collaborative Virtual Environments*. CVE '02. ACM, NY, 97-104

Tolone, W., Ahn, G., Pai, T., & Hong, S. (2005). Access control in collaborative systems. *ACM Computing Surveys*, *37*(1), 29–41. doi:10.1145/1057977.1057979

Wong, R. K. (1997). RBAC support in object-oriented role databases. *In Proceedings of the Second ACM Workshop on Role-Based Access Control*, Fairfax, Virginia, United States, RBAC '97. ACM, New York, NY, 109-120

Compilation of References

Abdellatif, A. (2003, May). *Good governance and its relationship to democracy and economic development.* Global Forum III on Fighting Corruption and Safeguarding Integrity, Seoul, Korea. Retrieved April 23, 2009 from http://www.pogar.org/publications/governance/

Abell, J. C. (2009). Wired.com Image Viewer Hacked to Create Phony Steve Jobs Health Story. *Wired Magazine.* Retrieved from January 22, 2009, Retrieved February 20, 2009 from http://www.wired.com/epicenter/2009/01/wiredcom-imagev/

Active Worlds. (2009). Retrieved from http://www.activeworlds.com

Adams, A. (2000). Multimedia information changes the whole privacy ballgame. In *Proc. of Computers, Freedom & Privacy '00*, (pp. 25-32).

Adobe Corporation. (n.d.). *Adobe photoshop CS4 * adding and viewing digimarc copyright protection.* Retrieved from: http://help.adobe.com/en_US/Photoshop/11.0/WSfd1234e1c4b69f30ea53e41001031ab64-7728a.html

Adobe flash. (2009). Retrieved October 30, 2009, from http://www.adobe.com/products/flashplayer

Aghatise, E. J. (2006). Cybercrime definition. *Computer Crime Research Center.* Retrieved January 20, 2009, from http://www.crime-research.org/articles/joseph06/

Ahn, D. H. (2007). Korean policy on treatment and rehabilitation for adolescents' Internet addiction. In 2007 *International Symposium on the Counseling and Treatment of Youth Internet Addiction*, (pp. 49), Seoul, Korea, National Youth Commission

Alexander, R. (2003). *Massively multiplayer game development.* Hingham, MA: Charles River Media, Inc.

Alexander, R. (2005). *Massively multiplayer game development 2.* Hingham, MA: Charles River Media, Inc.

American Cancer Society. (2009). *Relay For Life of Second Life team totals.* Retrieved October 3, 2009 from http://main.acsevents.org/site/TR/RelayForLife/RFLFY09RFLorg?sid=70525&type=fr_informational&pg=informational&fr_id=19490

Andrejevic, M. (2007). *iSpy: Surveillance and Power in the Interactive Era.* Lawrence, KS: University Press of Kansas.

Arakji, R. Y., & Lang, K. R. (2007). The Virtual Cathedral and the Virtual Bazaar. *The Data Base for Advances in Information Systems, 38*(4), 33–39.

Arcos, J. L., Esteva, M., Noriega, P., Rodrguez-Aguilar, J. A., & Sierra, C. (2005). An Integrated Developing Environment for Electronic Institutions. In Unland, R., Klusch, M., & Calisti, M. (Eds.), *Agent related platforms, frameworks, systems, applications, and tools* (pp. 121–142). Birkhaeuser Basel.

Arjomandy, S., & Smedley, T. J. (2004). Visual specification of behaviours in VRML worlds. In *Proc. of the 9th International Conference on 3D Web Technology*, Monterey, CA, (pp. 127-133). New York: ACM.

Arrow, K. J. (1965). *Aspects of the Theory of Risk Bearing.* Helsinki: Yijo Jahnssonis Saatio.

Ascertain (2009). Retrieved from https://www.ascertainsi.com/secondlife/bgConsent.asp. (Accessed 29-May-2009 14:58).

Aspect, J. (2001). Retrieved from http://www.aspectj.org.

Aspect.NET. (2008). Retrieved from http://www.aspect-dotnet.org.

Au, W. J. (2008). *The making of Second Life: notes from the new world*. New York: HarperCollins.

Badler, N., Bindiganavale, R., Bourne, J., Palmer, M., Shi, J., & Schuler, W. (2000). *A parametrized action representation for virtual human agents* (pp. 256–284). Cambridge, MA: MIT press.

Badler, N., Philips, C., & Webber, B. (1993). *Simulating Humans: Computer Graphics, Animation and Control*. Oxford, UK: Oxford University Press.

Balder (2009). Retrieved from http://balder.codeplex.com/.

Balkin, J. M. (2004). Law and liberty in virtual worlds. [Retrieved from Business Source Complete, EBSCO.]. *New York Law School Law Review. New York Law School*, *49*(1), 63–80.

Bamford, J. (2008). *The Shadow Factory: The Ultra-Secret NSA from 9/11 to the Eavesdropping on America*. New York: Random House.

Bargh, J. A., & McKenna, K. Y. M. (2004). The Internet and Social Life. *Annual Review of Psychology*, *55*(February), 573–590. doi:10.1146/annurev.psych.55.090902.141922

Bartle, A. (2004). *Designing Virtual Worlds*. Berkeley, CA: New Riders Publishing.

Bartle, R. A. (1996). *Hearts, clubs, diamonds, spades: players who suit MUDs*. Retrieved April 2, 2009 from http://www.mud.co.uk/richard/hcds.htm

Bartle, R. A. (2006, September 4). Why governments aren't gods and gods aren't governments. *First Monday* [Online], *0*(0). Retrieved April 21, 2009 from http://firstmonday.org/htbin/cgiwrap/bin/ojs/index.php/fm/article/view/1612/1527

Behr, P. E., Jung, Y., & Zöllner, M. (2009). X3DOM, A DOM-based HTML5/X3D Integration Model. In *Proceedings of Web3D 2009 conference*. New York: ACM.

Bers, M. U. (2001). Identity construction environments: Developing personal and moral values through the design of a virtual city. *Journal of the Learning Sciences*, *10*(4), 365–415. doi:10.1207/S15327809JLS1004new_1

Bessière, K., Ellis, J., & Kellogg, W. A. (2009). Acquiring a Professional "Second Life: Problems and Prospects for the Use of Virtual Worlds in Business. In *Proc. of ACM Conference on Human Factors in Computing Systems CHI*, (pp. 2883-2898).

Bimber, O., & Raskar, R. (2005). *Spatial augmented reality: Merging real and virtual worlds*. Wellesley, MA: A K Peters.

Birch, D. (2007). *Digital Identity Management*. Surrey, UK: Gower.

Bitmanagement. (2009). *Interactive Web3D Graphics*. Retrieved October 30, 2009, from http://www.bitmanagement.com

Blizzard Entertainment. *World of warcraft*. (2009). Retrieved February 2009 from http://www.worldofwarcraft.com.

Block, J. J. (2007). Pathological computer use in the USA. In *International Symposium on the Counseling and Treatment of Youth Internet Addiction*, (pp. 433), Seoul, Korea, National Youth Commission.

Bloom, B. S., & Krathwohl, D. R. (1956). Taxonomy of educational objectives: The Classification of Educational Goals, by a Committee of College and University Examiners. In *Handbook 1: Cognitive domain*. New York: Longmans.

Boella, G., van der Torre, L., & Verhagen, H. (2007). Introduction to normative multiagent systems. *Normative multi-agent systems* (pp. 71–79). Internationales Begegnungs- und Forschungszentrum fuer Informatik (IBFI), Schloss Dagstuhl, Germany.

Boellstorff, T. (2008). *Coming of age in Second Life: an anthropologist explores the virtually human*. Princeton, NJ: Princeton University Press.

Boellstorff, T. (2009). Virtual worlds and futures of anthropology. *AnthroNotes, the Museum of Natural History Publication for Educators*. Retrieved September 21, 2009 from http://www.anthro.uci.edu/faculty_bios/boellstorff/boellstorff.php

Bogdanovych, A. (2007). *Virtual institutions*. Doctoral dissertation, University of Technology, Sydney, Australia.

Bogdanovych, A., Berger, H., Sierra, C., & Simoff, S. (2005). Narrowing the Gap between Humans and Agents in E-commerce: 3D Electronic Institutions. In *Proceedings of the 6th International Conference on Electronic Commerce and Web Technologies (EC-Web'05)* (pp. 128–137). Berlin: Springer- Verlag.

Bogdanovych, A., Rodriguez, J. A., Simoff, S., Cohen, A., & Sierra, C. (2009). Developing Virtual Heritage Applications as Normative Multiagent Systems. In *proceedings of Agent Oriented Software Engineering Workshop (AOSE 2009)* organized by AAMAS 2009 (pp. 121–132). Berlin: Springer.

Bogdanovych, A., Simoff, S., & Esteva, M. (2008). Training Believable Agents in 3D Electronic Business Environments Using Recursive-Arc Graphs. In *Third international conference on Software and Data Technologies* (ICSoft 2008) (pp. 339–345). INSTICC.

Bordini, R. H., Hübner, J. F., & Wooldrige, M. (2007). *Programming Multi-Agent Systems in AgentSpeak using Jason*. Chichester, UK: Wiley. doi:10.1002/9780470061848

Bostan, B. (2009). Player Motivations: A Psychological Perspective. *ACM Computers in Entertainment, 7*(2), 22, 1-25.

Boukerche, A., Zarrad, A., Duarte, D., Araujo, R., & Andrade, L. (2005). A Novel Solution for the Development of Collaborative Virtual Environment Simulations in Large Scale. In *9th IEEE International Symposium on Distributed Simulation and Real-Time Applications*, (pp. 86-96).

Bowman, D. A., Kruijff, E., LaViola, J. J., & Poupyrev, I. (2001). An Introduction to 3-D User Interface Design. *Presence (Cambridge, Mass.), 10*(1), 75–95. doi:10.1162/105474601750182333

Boyle, E., Cellary, W., Huminiecki, O., Picard, W., Stawniak, M., Walczak, K., & Wojciechowski, R. (2002). Dynamic Creation of MPEG-4 Content with X-VRML, In *Proc. of the 5th Int. Conf. on Business Information Systems BIS 2002*, Poznan, Poland, (pp. 358-366).

Bragg, M. (2006). *Marc Bragg v. 1. Linden Research, Inc., case no. 06-4925*. US District Court for the Eastern District of Pennsylvania.

Brainyquote (2009). Retrieved from http://www.brainyquote.com/quotes/quotes/f/fernandofl285659.html(Accessed 27-Feb-2009 12:58).

Brandon, P. D., & Hollingshead, A. B. (2007). Characterizing online groups. In Joinson, A. N., McKenna, K. Y. N., Postmes, T., & Reips, U. D. (Eds.), *Oxford Handbook of Internet Psychology* (pp. 105–119). Oxford, UK: Oxford University Press.

Brenner, S. W. (2008). Fantasy crime. *Vanderbilt Journal of Technology and Entertainment Law, 11*(1). Retrieved April 13 2009 from http://works.bepress.com/susan_brenner/

Bruckman, A. (1996) Finding one's own in cyberspace. *Technology Review Magazine*. Retrieved September 24, 2009 from http://www.cc.gatech.edu/~asb/papers/old-papers.html

Bues, M., Gleue, T., & Blach, R. (2008). Lightning. Dataflow in Motion. In *Proc. of the IEEE VR 2008 Workshop SEARIS - Software Engineering and Architectures for Interactive Systems*, Reno, NV, USA. Aachen, Germany: Shaker Verlag

Bugeja, M. J. (2008). Second Life, revisited. Which should take precedence in a virtual-reality campus: Corporate terms of service or public-disclosure laws. *The Chronicle of Higher Education*, 23–27.

Burdea, G., & Coiffet, P. (2003). *Virtual reality technology*. Hoboken, NJ: John Wiley & Sons.

Burmester, M., Henry, P. & Kermes, L.S. (2005). Tracking cyberstalkers: A cryptographic approach. *ACM SIGCAS Computers and Society, 35*(3).

Burrows, T., & England, D. (2005). YABLE-yet another behaviour language. *Proc. of the 10th International Conference on 3D Web Technology*, Bangor, UK, (pp. 65-73).

Cadwallader, B. (2007). Feds take over municipal court Web-hacking probe. *The Columbus Dispatch*, December 22. Retrieved October 26, 2008 from http://www.dispatch.com/live/content/local_news/stories/2007/12/20/clerkh.html

Calongne, C., Endorf, S., Frankovich, D., & Sandaire, J. (2008). A virtual environment for designing user interface prototypes. Consortium for Computing Sciences in Colleges. Rocky Mountain Conference. *JCSC, 24*(1), 188 – 195.

Cannataci, J. A., & Mifsud-Bonnici, J. P. (2007). Weaving the mesh: finding remedies in cyberspace. [Retrieved from Business Source Complete, EBSCO.]. *International Review of Law Computers & Technology, 21*(1), 59–78.. doi:10.1080/13600860701281705

Carnegie-Mellon. (2005). *Insider Threat Study: Computer System Sabotage in Critical Infrastructure Sectors*. Pittsburgh, PA: Software Engineering Institute, Carnegie Mellon University.

Castronova, E. (2006). *Synthetic worlds: the business and culture of online games*. Chicago: Chicago University Press.

Center for Democracy & Technology (CDT). (2007). *Privacy principles for identity in the digital age (draft for comment, version 1.2)*. http://www.cdt.org/security/20070327idprinciples.pdf.

Cera, D. D., Kim, T., Han, J., & Regli, W. C. (2004). Role-based viewing envelopes for information protection in collaborative modeling. *Computer Aided Design, 36*(1), 873–886. doi:10.1016/j.cad.2003.09.014

Chellappa, R., & Sin, R. (2002). Personalization versus privacy: New exchange relationships on the Web. http://www.zibs.com/techreports/Personalization%20versus%20Privacy.pdf. (Accessed 30-May-2009 10:45).

Chevaleyre, Y., Dunne, P. E., Endriss, U., Lang, J., Lemaitre, M., & Maudet, N. (2006). Issues in multiagent resource allocation. *Informatica, 30*, 3–31.

Cikic, S., Grottke, S., Lehmann-Grube, F., & Sablatnig, J. (2008). *Cheat-prevention and analysis in online virtual worlds*. Adelaide, Australia: E-Forensics.

Clarke, R. A., & Knake, R. K. (2010). *Cyber war: The next threat to national security and what to do about it*. New York: HarperCollins.

Clemen, R. T., & Reilly, T. (2001). *Making Hard Decisions*. MA: Duxbury.

COBIT. (2008). *Control Objectives for Information and related Technology, Information Systems Audit and Control Association*. ISACA.

Colella, V. (2000). Participatory simulations: Building collaborative understanding through immersive dynamic modeling. *Journal of the Learning Sciences, 9*(4), 471–500. doi:10.1207/S15327809JLS0904_4

Consalvo, M. (2009) There is no magic circle. *Games and Culture*. DOI: 10.1177/1555412009343575 Retrieved September 21, 2009 from http://gac.sagepub.com/cgi/content/abstract/1555412009343575v1

Contact, B. S. 7.2. (2009). *A Web3D viewer from Bitmanagement*. Retrieved October 30, 2009, from http://www.bitmanagement.com/en/download

Conte, R., & Castelfranchi, C. (1995). *Cognitive and Social Action*. London: UCL Press.

COSO. (2004). *Enterprise Risk Management-Integrated Framework*. The Committee of Sponsoring organizations of the Treadway Commission.

Dachselt, R., & Rukzio, E. (2003). Behavior3D: an XML-based framework for 3D graphics behavior. In *Proc. of the 8th International Conference on 3D Web Technologies*, Saint Malo, France, (pp. 101-112).

Dachselt, R., Hinz, M., & Meissner, K. (2002). Contigra: an XML-based architecture for component-oriented 3D applications. In *Proc. of the 7ᵗʰ International Conference on 3D Web Technology*, Tempe, AZ, (pp. 155-163).

Darken, R. P., & Sibert, J. L. (1996). Wayfinding strategies and behaviors in large virtual worlds. In *Chi '96: Proceedings of the SIGCHI conference on human factors in computing systems* (pp. 142–149). New York: ACM Press.

Davis, J.P., Eisenhardt, K.M. & Bingham, C.B. (2009). Optimal structure, market dynamism, and the strategy of simple rules. *Administrative Science Quarterly, 54*(3), 413-452. Retrieved October 4, 2009 from Business Source Premier. EBSCO.

Dawes, S. S., Bloniarz, P. A., Kelly, K. L., & Fletcher, P. D. (1999). Some assembly required: Building a digital government for the 21ˢᵗ century. *1999 Center for Technology in Government*, (pp. 18).

De Carolis, B., Carofiglio, V., Bilvi, M., & Pelachaud, C. (2002). APML, A Mark-up Language for Believable Behavior Generation. In *Proc. of AAMAS Workshop Embodied, Conversational Agents: Let's Specify and Compare Them!* Bologna, Italy

De Win, B., Piessens, F., & Joosen, W. (2006). How secure is AOP and what can we do about it? In *Proceedings of the 2006 international Workshop on Software Engineering For Secure Systems* (pp. 27-34). New York: ACM.

Decker, K. S. (1998). Task environment centered simulation. In *Simulating Organizations: Computational Models of Institutions and Groups* (pp. 105–128). Menlo Park, CA: AAAI Press / MIT Press.

Delgado-Mata, C., & Aylett, R. (2004). *Emotion and action selection: Regulating the collective behaviour of agents in virtual environments* (pp. 1304–1305). AAMAS.

DeSensi, G., Longo, F., & Mirabella, G. (2007). *Ergonomic and work methods optimization in a three dimensional virtual environment* (pp. 1187–1192). SCSC.

Despain, W., & Kumar, M. (2008, May 15). ION: online worlds and real legal disputes. *Gamasutra*. Retrieved from: http://www.gamasutra.com/php-bin/news_index.php?story=18648

Dibble, J. (1993) *A rape in cyberspace*. Retrieved April 22, 2009 from http://www.juliandibbell.com/texts/bungle_vv.html

Dignum, V., & Dignum, F. (2001). Modelling agent societies: Co-ordination frameworks and institutions. In P. Brazdil & A. Jorge, (Eds.), *Procs. of the 10th Portuguese Conference on Artficial Intelligence (EPIA'01)*, (LNAI 2258, pp. 191-204). Berlin: Springer.

DiPaola, S., & Turner, J. (2008). Authoring the intimate self: identity, expression and role-playing within a pioneering virtual community. *Loading.* Retrieved September 21, 2009 from http://journals.sfu.ca/loading/index.php/loading/issue/view/4/showToc

Douglas, K. M. (2007). Psychology, discrimination and hate groups online. In Joinson, A. N., McKenna, K. Y. N., Postmes, T., & Reips, U. D. (Eds.), *Oxford Handbook of Internet Psychology* (pp. 155–163). Oxford, UK: Oxford University Press, Oxford.

Drago, S., Bogdanovych, A., Ancona, M., Simoff, S., & Sierra, C. (2007). From Graphs to Euclidean Virtual Worlds: Visualization of 3D Electronic Institutions. In G. Dobbie (Ed.), *Australasian Computer Science Conference (ACSC2007)* (Vol. 62, pp. 25–33). Ballarat Australia: ACS.

EC. (2001). The Convention on Cyber Crime. *Council of Europe - Treaty Office CETS No. 185.* Retrieved April 12, 2006 from http://conventions.coe.int/Treaty/en/Treaties/Html/185.htm

Edelman, B. (2006). *Adverse selection in online "trust" certifications*. Working paper retrieved from: http://www.benedelman.org/publications/advsel-trust-draft.pdf

Electronic Privacy Information Center. (2009, August 28). Following Canadian investigation, facebook upgrades privacy. *Epic.org: Social Networking Privacy*. Retrieved from: http://epic.org/privacy/socialnet/default.html

ElfCircle. (2009). Retrieved October 15, 2009 from http://www.slhighfantasy.com/site/

Ellis, J. B., Luther, K., Bessiere, K., & Kellogg, W. A. (2008). *Games for virtual team building. DIS 2008, Cape Town, South Africa* (p. 295). New York: ACM.

ENISA. (2008). Retrieved from http://www.finextra.com/finextradownloads/newsdocs/enisa_pp_security_privacy_virtualworlds.pdf

ENISA. (2008). *Virtual World, Real Money: Security and Privacy in Massively-Multiplayer Online Games and Social and Corporate Virtual Worlds*. Position Paper of European Network and Information Security Agency. Retrieved from http://www.enisa.europa.eu/doc/pdf/deliverables/enisa_pp_security_privacy_virtualworlds.pdf

Entertainment, B. (n.d.) *Blizzard Authenticator*. Retrieved from: http://eu.blizzard.com/support/article.xml?locale=en_GB&articleId=28152

Esteva, M. (2003). *Electronic institutions: From specification to development.* Doctoral dissertation, Institut d'Investigaci'o en Intellig`encia Artificial (IIIA), Spain.

Esteva, M., de la Cruz, D., & Sierra, C. (2002). ISLANDER: an Electronic Institutions editor. In *First international conference on Autonomous Agents and Multiagent Systems (AAMAS 2002)*, (pp. 1045–1052). Bologna: ACM Press.

Falcone, R., Pezzulo, G., Castelfranchi, C., & Calvi, G. (2004). Why a cognitive trustier performs better: Simulating trust-based contract nets. In *Proc. of AAMAS'04: Autonomous Agents and Multi-Agent Systems*, (pp. 1392–1393). New York: ACM.

Farahmand, F., Navathe, S. B., Sharp, G. P., & Enslow, P. H. (2005). A Management Perspective on Risk of Security Threats to Information Systems. *Journal of Information Technology Management*, *6*, 203–225. doi:10.1007/s10799-005-5880-5

Farahmand, F., & Spafford, E. H. (2009). Insider Behavior: An Analysis of Decision under Risk. In *First International Workshop on Managing Insider Security Threats, International Federation for Information Processing (IFIP) International Conference on Trust Management*, Purdue University.

Farahmand, F., Atallah, M., & Konsynski, B. (2008). Incentives and Perceptions of Information Security Risks. In *Proceedings of the Twenty Ninth International Conference on Information Systems (ICIS)*.

Farenc, N., Boulic, R., & Thalmann, D. (1999). An informed environment dedicated to the simulation of virtual humans in urban context. In P. Brunet & R. Scopigno, (Eds.), *Proc. of EUROGRAPHICS"99, 18*(3), 309–318. London: The Eurographics Association and Blackwell Publishers.

Fehr, E., & Fischbacher, U. (2004). Social Norms and Human Cooperation. *Trends in Cognitive Sciences*, *8*(4), 185–190. Available at http://dx.doi.org/10.1016/j.tics.2004.02.007. doi:10.1016/j.tics.2004.02.007

Ferber, J., & Gutknecht, O. (1998). A meta-model for the analysis and design of organizations in multi-agents systems. In *Proc. of the 3rd International Conference on Multi-Agent Systems (ICMAS'98)*, (pp. 128–135). Washington, DC: IEEE Press.

Ferris, J. R. (1997). *Internet Addiction Disorder: Causes, Symptoms and Consequences*, Retrieved September 26, 2001, http://www.files.chem.vt.edu/chem-dept/dessy/honors/papers/ferris.html

Fischhoff, B., Lichtenstein, S., Slovic, P., Derby, S. L., & Keeney, R. L. (1981). *Acceptable Risk*. Cambridge, UK: Cambridge University Press.

Fischoff, B. (1978). How Safe Is Safe Enough? A Psychometric Study of Attitudes Towards Technological Risks and Benefits? *Policy Sciences*, *9*(2), 127–152. doi:10.1007/BF00143739

FlatRedBall. (2009). Retrieved from http://www.flatredball.com/frb/.

Foo, C. Y. (2004). *Redefining grief play*. Other Players conference on multiplayer phenomena, Copenhagen, December 6-8, 2004. Retrieved April 23, 2009 from http://www.tu-chemnitz.de/phil/medkom/mn/spive/index.php?option=com_docman&task=cat_view&gid=18&Itemid=33

Foo, C. Y., & Koivisto, E. M. (2004). *Grief player motivations*. Other Players conference on multiplayer phenomena, Copenhagen, December 6-8, 2004. Retrieved April 23, 2009 from http://www.tu-chemnitz.de/phil/medkom/mn/spive/index.php?option=com_docman&task=cat_view&gid=25&Itemid=33

Food and Drug Administration (U.S.). (2009). Retrieved from http://www.fda.gov/oc/opacom/hottopics/salmonellatyph.html. (Accessed 29-May-2009 14:55).

Fox, M. S., Barbuceanu, M., Gruninger, M., & Lon, J. (1998). An organizational ontology for enterprise modelling. In *Simulating Organizations: Computational Models of Institutions and Groups* (pp. 131–152). Menlo Park, CA: AAAI Press / MIT Press.

Fritsch (2007). *State of the art of privacy-enhancing technology (PET)*. Retrieved from: http://publ.nr.no/4589

Funge, J., Tu, X., & Terzopoulos, D. (1999). Cognitive modeling: knowledge, reasoning and planning for intelligent characters. In *Proc. of SIGGRAPH '99*, (pp. 29–38). New York: ACM.

Garau, M., Slater, M., Vinayagamoorthy, V., Brogni, A., Steed, A., & Sasse, M. A. (2003). The impact of avatar realism and eye gaze control on perceived quality of communication in a shared immersive virtual environment, CHI 2003, Ft. Lauderdale, FL. *CHI Letters*, *5*(1), 529–536.

Gartner (2007). Retrieved from http://www.businessweek.com/globalbiz/content/aug2007/gb2007089_070863.htm?chan=globalbiz_europe+index+page_top+stories

Gartner. (2009). Retrieved from http://www.gartner.com/it/page.jsp?id=503861

Gebhard, P., Kipp, M., Klesen, M., & Rist, T. (2003). Authoring scenes for adaptive, interactive performances. In *AAMAS '03*, Melbourne, Australia, (pp. 725). New York: ACM.

Gee, J. P. (2008). Video games and embodiment. *Games and Culture*. DOI: 10.1177/1555412008317309 Retrieved September 21, 2009 from http://gac.sagepub.com/cgi/content/abstract/3/3-4/253

Global Network Initiative. (2008). *Principles*. Retrieved from: http://www.globalnetworkinitiative.org/principles/index.php

Glover, S. (2008). Alleged myspace 'cyber-bully' indicted in teen's suicide. *Los Angeles Times*, 16 May 2008 (http://www.latimes.com/news/local/la-me-myspace16-2008may16,0,3642392.story).

Goldberg, I. (1995). *Internet Addiction Disorder (IAD) at PsyCom.Net*. Retrieved January 7, 2001 from http://web.urz.uni-heidelberg.de/Netzdienste/anleitung/wwwtips/8/addict.html

Goldin, R. (2006). Hyping Internet Addiction. *Stats Articles*. Retrived August 17, 2009, from http://stats.org/stories/2006/hype_web_addiction_nov16_06.htm

Google. (2009). *O3d, an javascript based scene-graph api*. Retrieved October 30, 2009, from http://code.google.com/apis/o3d/

Gordon, L. A., & Loeb, M. P. (2006). *Managing Cyber-Security Resources, A Cost-Benefit Analysis*. New York: McGraw-Hill.

Grimaldo, F., Lozano, M., Barber, F., & Vigueras, G. (2008). Simulating socially intelligent agents in semantic virtual environments. *The Knowledge Engineering Review*, *23*(4), 369–388. doi:10.1017/S026988890800009X

Grimaldo, F., Lozano, M., & Barber, F. (2008). MADeM: a multi-modal decision making for social MAS. In *Proc. of AAMAS'08: Autonomous Agents and Multi-Agent Systems*, (pp. 183–190). New York: ACM.

Grivna, T., & Polcak, R. (2008). *Kyberkriminalita a pravo (Cybercrime and Law)*. Prague, Czech Republic: Auditorium.

Guo, Y., & Barnes, S. (2007). Why people Buy Virtual items in Virtual Worlds with Real Money. *The Data Base for Advances in Information Systems*, *38*(4), 69–76.

Gutierrez, M., Vexo, F., & Thalmann, D. (2005). Semantics-based representation of virtual environments. *International Journal of Computer Applications in Technology*, *23*, 229–238. doi:10.1504/IJCAT.2005.006484

Hai-Jew, S. (2007). The trust factor in online instructor-led college courses. *Journal of Interactive Instruction Development, 19*(3).

Hai-Jew, S. (2009). Exploring the immersive parasocial: Is it *you* or the thought of you? *MERLOT Journal of Online Learning and Teaching, 5*(2).

Helbing, D., & Molnar, P. (1995). Social force model for pedestrian dynamics. *Physical Review E: Statistical Physics, Plasmas, Fluids, and Related Interdisciplinary Topics, 51*, 4282. doi:10.1103/PhysRevE.51.4282

Heslop, H. (2008). Stroker serpentine wins moral victory. *SLNN.com*, 25 March 2008. (The article is no longer available at the original URL, but it can be viewed in Google's cache at http://74.125.77.132/search?q=cache:LtEIrPPlM38J:www.slnn.com/article/serpentine-wins-moral-victory/).

Hexmoor, H. (2001). From inter-agents to groups. In *Proc. of ISAI'01: International Symposium on Artificial Intelligence.*

Hogben, G. (2007) *Security issues and recommendations for online social networks.* ENISA Position Paper No. 1. Retrieved from: http://www.enisa.europa.eu/doc/pdf/deliverables/enisa_pp_social_networks.pdf

Hogg, L. M., & Jennings, N. (2001). Socially intelligent reasoning for autonomous agents. *IEEE Transactions on Systems, Man, and Cybernetics, 31*(5), 381–393. doi:10.1109/3468.952713

Howard, R. A. (1988). Decision Analysis: Practice and promise. *Management Science, 34*, 679–695. doi:10.1287/mnsc.34.6.679

HttpSecureCookie. (2009). *A Way to Encrypt Cookies with ASP.NET 2.0.* Retrieved from http://www.codeproject.com/KB/web-security/HttpSecureCookie.aspx.

Hu, J. (2000). Outage a deliberate attack, Yahoo says. *CNET News*, February 7, 2000. Retrieved August 5, 2005 from http://news.cnet.com/2100-1023-236594.html

Hübner, J. F., Sichman, J. S., & Boissier, O. (2007). Developing organised multi-agent systems using the Moise+ model: Programming issues at the system and agent levels. *International Journal of Agent-Oriented Software Engineering, 1*(3/4), 370–395. doi:10.1504/IJAOSE.2007.016266

Hübner, J. F., Sichman, J., & Boissier, O. (2002). A model for the structural, functional, and deontic specification of organizations in multiagent systems. In G. Bittencourt & G. L. Ramalho, (Eds.), *Procs. of the 16th Brazilian Symposium on Artifical Intelligence (SBIA'02)*, (LNAI Vol. 2507, pp. 118-128). Berlin: Springer-Verlag.

Hučín, J. (2000). Droga jménem Internet. *Chip CZ, 7/2000*, 7–9.

Hughes, D. M. (2001). The "Natasha" Trade: Transnational Sex Trafficking. *National Institute of Justice Journal January.* Retrieved February 22, 2009 from http://www.ncjrs.gov/pdffiles1/jr000246c.pdf

IBM Emergence of the 3D-Internet. (2009). Retrieved December 1, 2009, from http://www.ibm.com/virtual-worlds/index.shtml

IBM Lotus Sametime. (2009). Retrieved December 1, 2009, from http://www-03.ibm.com/press/us/en/press-release/27831.wss

Integrated Virtual Networks. (2009). Retrieved December 1, 2009, from http://www.ivn3.com/applications.php

International Working Group on Data Protection in Telecommunications. (2008). *The rome memorandum.* Retrieved from: http://blog.stefanweiss.net/2008/04/26/rome-memorandum/

Jason. (2009). Retrieved 2009 from http://jason.sourceforge.net/.

Jirovska, A. (2009). *Negativni vlivy televize na rozvoj ditete.* Unpublished master thesis, Faculty of Pedagogy, Charles University, Prague, Czech Republic.

Jirovsky, V. (2004). *Kybernalita. Presented at regular student lectures at Faculty of Mathematics and Physics.* Prague: Charles University.

Jirovsky, V. (2007). *Kybernalita – kybernetická kriminalita*. Prague: Grada Publishing.

Jirovsky, V. (2007a). *Virtual communities and cyber terrorism*, Paper presented at Security and Protection of Information Conference, Brno 2007, Czech Republic

Jirovsky, V. (2008). *Kyberprostor*. Paper presented at the meeting of the state attorneys and judges on problem of cyber criminality, Kromeriz, Czech Republic

Johnson, E. J., & Tversky, A. (1984). Representations of Perceptions of Risk. *Journal of Experimental Psychology, 113*, 55–70.

Jones, S. (2000). Towards a philosophy of virtual reality: Issues implicit in 'Consciousness Reframed.' [Retrieved from JSTOR.]. *Leonardo, 33*(2), 125–132. doi:10.1162/002409400552388

Kane, S. F. (2009). Virtual Judgment: Legal Implications of Online Gaming. *IEEE Security and Privacy, 7*(3), 23–28. doi:10.1109/MSP.2009.81

Karat, J. (2009). A Policy Framework for Security and Privacy Management. *IBM Journal of Research and Development, 53*(2). doi:10.1147/JRD.2009.5429046

Khronos. (2009). *Khronos details WebGL Initiative to Bring Hardware-Accelerated 3D Graphics to the Internet*. Retrieved October 30, 2009, from http://www.khronos.org/news/press/releases/khronos-webgl-initiative-hardware-accelerated-3d-graphics-internet/

Kim, K., & Prabhakar, P. (2000). Initial Trust, Perceived Risk, and the Adoption of the Internet Banking. *International Conference on Information Systems*, (pp.537-543).

Kirkwood, C. W. (1997). *Strategic Decision Making*. MA: Duxbury.

Kit3D (2009). Retrieved from http://kit3d.codeplex.com/.

Knight, F. H. (1921) *Risk, Uncertainty and Profit*. Gloucester, UK: Dodo press.

Knight, M. M., & Arns, L. L. (2006). The relationship among age and other factors on incidence of cybersickness in immersive environment users. In *APGV*, Boston, Massachusetts, (pp. 162). New York: ACM.

Ko, C., Yen, J., Liu, S., Huang, C., & Yen, C. (2009). *The Associations Between Aggressive Behaviors and Internet Addiction and Online Activities* in Adolescents. *The Journal of Adolescent Health, 44*(6), 598–605. doi:10.1016/j.jadohealth.2008.11.011

Koenen, R. (2002). *Overview of the MPEG-4 Standard*. Retrieved from http://www.chiariglione.org/mpeg /standards/mpeg-4/mpeg-4.htm

Koster, R. (2000). *Declaring the rights of players*. Retrieved April 22, 2009 from http://www.raphkoster.com/gaming/playerrights.shtml

Kottasová, I., & Kubita, J. (2008). Čestí politici vnikli na Facebook. Zatím dva. *Hospodarske noviny,* May 12, 2008. Retrieved September 7, 2008 from http://hn.ihned.cz/2-24682660-500000_d-e4

Kovar, J. F. (2009, August 20). 'Skanks' case could increase online privacy awareness, security sales. *ChannelWeb*. Retrieved from: http://www.crn.com/security/2 19400947;jsessionid=ONRGZFL5M1DKVQE1GHPC KHWATMY32JVN

Krebs, B. (2008). Hackers Hijacked Large E-Bill Payment Site. *The Washington Post*, December 3, 2008. Retrieved January 10, 2009 from http://voices.washingtonpost.com/securityfix/2008/12/hackers_hijacked_large_e-bill.html

Krebs, B. (2009, July 6). Researchers: social security numbers can be guessed. *The Washington Post*. Retrieved from: http://www.washingtonpost.com/wp-dyn/content/article/2009/07/06/AR2009070602955.html?wprss=rss_business

Lab, L. (2009a). *Purchasing land*. 2009. Retrieved October 7th, 2009 from http://secondlife.com/land/purchasing.php

Lab, L. (2009b). *Open Source FAQs*. Retrieved October 6th, 2009 from http://secondlifegrid.net/technology-programs/virtual-world-open-source/faq

Lab, L. (2009c). *Terms of service*. Retrieved October 15, 2009, from http://secondlife.com/corporate/tos.php

Lab, L. (2009d). *Community standards*. Retrieved October 15, 2009, from http://secondlife.com/corporate/cs.php

Lastowka, F. G., & Hunter, D. (2004). The laws of the virtual worlds. [Retrieved from Business Source Complete, EBSCO.]. *California Law Review, 92*(1), 3–73. doi:10.2307/3481444

Lastowka, G. (2009). Rules of play. *Games and Culture.* DOI: 10.1177/1555412009343573 Retrieved September 21, 2009 from http://gac.sagepub.com/cgi/content/abstract/1555412009343573v1

Latoschik, M. E., Biermann, P., & Wachsmuth, I. (2005). Knowledge in the Loop: Semantics Representation for Multimodal Simulative Environments. In *Proceedings of the 5th International Symposium on Smart Graphics,* Frauenwoerth Cloister, Germany, (pp. 25-39).

Lemos, R. (2001). Security sites hit by graffiti gang. *ZDNet. com,* June 14, 2001. Retrieved May 17, 2005 from http://news.zdnet.co.uk/security/0,1000000189,2088969,00.htm

Lessig, L. (2006). *Code and other laws of cyberspace, version 2.0.* New York: Basic Books. PDF version retrieved August 25, 2009 from http://codev2.cc/

Lim, M. Y., & Aylett, R. (2009). An Emergent Emotion Model for An Affective Mobile Guide with Attitude. *Applied Artificial Intelligence Journal, 23,* 835–854. doi:10.1080/08839510903246518

Lin, S. S. J., & Tsai, C. C. (1999). *Internet Addiction among High Schoolers in Taiwan.* Paper presented at the Annual Meeting of the American Psychological Association, Boston August 20-24, 1999. Retrieved July 16, 2008 from http://www.eric.ed.gov/ERICDocs/data/ericdocs2sql/content_storage_01/0000019b/80/29/c4/92.pdf

Lind, E. A., Tyler, T. R., & Huo, Y. J. (1997). Procedural context and culture: variations in the antecedents of procedural justice judgments. [Retrieved from Business Source Complete, EBSCO.]. *Journal of Personality and Social Psychology, 73*(4), 767–780. doi:10.1037/0022-3514.73.4.767

Lind, E. A., & Earley, P. C. (1992) Procedural justice and culture. *International Journal of Psychology, 27*(2), 227. (AN 5777083) Retrieved from Business Source Complete, EBSCO.

Linden Lab. (2009). *SecondLife®.* Retrieved February 2009 from http://secondlife.com/.

Linden Lab. (2009). Terms of Service. (http://secondlife.com/corporate/tos.php). (Accessed 05-Dec-2009 09:49). Actual quote taken from an earlier version 15-Sep-2008.

Linden Lab. (2009). *Upcoming changes for adult content.* https://blogs.secondlife.com/community/community/blog/2009/03/12/upcoming-changes-for-adult-content. (Accessed 20-May-2009 10:53).

Linden Research, Inc. (2009) *How meeting in Second Life transformed IBM's technology elite into virtual world believers,* [case study]. Retrieved April 13, 2009 from http://secondlifegrid.net/casestudies

Linden, A. (2009, March 19). *Three questions for Diane Berry, CEO of TMPA on an event in Second Life.* Blog entry posted to https://blogs.secondlife.com/community/workinginworld/blog/2009/03/19/three-questions-for-diane-berry-ceo-of-tpma-on-an-event-in-second-life

Lo, J. (2008). *Second life: privacy in virtual worlds.* Retrieved from: http://www.priv.gc.ca/information/pub/sl_080411_e.cfm

Lojack (2009). Lojack for laptops. *Lojack.com.* Retrieved from: http://www.lojack.com/pages/laptop.aspx

Ludlow, P., & Wallace, M. (2007). *The Second Life Herald: the virtual tabloid that witnessed the dawn of the metaverse.* Cambridge, MA: The MIT Press.

Lugrin, J., & Cavazza, M. (2007). Making sense of virtual environments: action representation, grounding and common sense. In *Proceedings of the 12th international Conference on intelligent User interfaces, IUI '07,* (pp. 225-234). New York: ACM.

MacDonald, M., & Szpuszta, M. (2008). *Pro ASP.NET 3.5 in C# 2008: Includes Silverlight 2,* (3rd ed.). New York: NY, Apress publishers.

MacGregor, D. G., Slovic, P., Berry, M., & Evensky, H. R. (1999). Perception of Financial Risk: a survey study of advisors and planners. *Journal of Financial Planning, 12*(8), 68–86.

Maher, M. L., Simoff, S., & Mitchell, J. (1997). Formalizing Building Requirements Using an Activity/Space Model. *Automation in Construction, 6,* 77–95. doi:10.1016/S0926-5805(96)00171-9

Malaby, T. M. (2006). Parlaying value: capital in and beyond virtual worlds. *Games and Culture, 1*(2), 141–162.. doi:10.1177/1555412006286688

Malaby, T. M. (2007). Contriving constraints (the gameness of Second Life and the persistence of scarcity). *Innovations, 2*(3), 62–67..doi:10.1162/itgg.2007.2.3.62

Mandal, S., & Lim, E.-P. (2008). Second Life: Limits of creativity or cyber threat? IEEE. 498 – 503.

Manninen, T., & Kujanpää, T. (2007). The Value of Virtual Assets – The Role of Game Characters in MMOGs. *International Journal of Business Science and Applied Management, 2*(1), 21–33.

March, J. G., & Shapira, Z. (1987). Managerial Perspectives on Risk and Risk Taking. *Management Science, 33*(11), 1404–1418. doi:10.1287/mnsc.33.11.1404

Mark, G., & Semaan, B. (2008). Resilience in collaboration: Technology as a resource for new patterns of action. In *CSCW '08,* San Diego, CA, (pp. 137 – 146). New York: ACM.

Marriott, A., Beard, S., Stallo, J., & Huynh, Q. (2001). VHML - Directing a Talking Head. In *Proc. of the Sixth International Computer Science Conference Active Media Technology,* (LNCS Vol. 2252, pp. 18-20). Hong Kong. Berlin: Springer.

Martin, K. (2006). *Google inc., in china* (Case BRI-1004). Business Roundtable Institute for Corporate Ethics, 2006 (http://www.darden.virginia.edu/corporate-ethics/pdf/BRI-1004.pdf).

Mayntz, R. (2003) *From government to governance: Political steering in modern societies.* Paper presented at the IOEW Summer Academy on IPP, Würzburg, Germany, September 7-11, 2003. Retrieved October 16, 2009 from http://www.ioew.de/fileadmin/user_upload/DOKUMENTE/Veranstaltungen/2003/SuA2Mayntz.pdf

McCarthy, M. P., & Flynn, T. P. (2004). *Risk from the CEO and Broad Perspective.* McGraw Hill.

McQuiggan, S. W., Rowe, J. P., & Lester, J. C. (2008). The effects of empathetic virtual characters on presence in narrative-centered learning environments. In *CHI 2008 Proceedings: Character Development,* (pp. 1512), Florence, Italy.

Meadows, M. S. (2008). *I, avatar: the culture and consequences of having a Second Life.* Berkeley, CA: New Riders.

Mentor. (1986). *The Conscience of a Hacker, 1*(7), Phile 3, Phrack Inc. January 8, 1986.

Merrick, K., & Maher, M. L. (2007). Motivated reinforcement learning for adaptive characters in open-ended simulation games. In *ACE '07,* Salzburg, Austria, (pp. 127). New York: ACM.

Mertins, V. (2008). *The effects of procedures on social interaction: a literature review.* Discussion Papers 200806, Institute of Labour Law and Industrial Relations in the European Community (IAAEG). Retrieved April 2, 2009 from http://ideas.repec.org/p/iaa/wpaper/200806.html

Mesing, B., & Hellmich, C. (18-21 April 2006). Using aspect-oriented methods to add behaviors to X3D documents. In Web3D 2006 Proceedings, Columbia, Maryland (pp. 97–107). New York: ACM.

Mesing, B., & Hellmich, C. (2006). Using aspect oriented methods to add behaviour to X3D documents. In *Proc. of the 11th International Conference on 3D Web Technology,* Columbia, MD, (pp. 97-107).

Microsoft. (2009). *Silverlight.* Retrieved October 30, 2009, from http://www.microsoft.com/directx/

Mistral, P. (April 2, 2009) FrizzleFry interview part 2. *The Alphaville Herald/Secondlife Herald.* Retrieved April 22, 2009 from http://foo.secondlifeherald.com/slh/2009/04/frizzlefry-interview-part-2.html#more

Mnookin, J. (2001). Virtual(ly) law: the emergence of law in an on-line community. In Ludlow, P. (Ed.), *Crypto Anarchy, Cyberstates, And Pirate Utopias*. Cambridge, MA: The MIT Press.

Moores, T. T., & Dhillon, G. (2003). Do Privacy Seals in E-Commerce Really Work? *Communications of the ACM, 46*(12), 265–271. doi:10.1145/953460.953510

Moses, T. (Ed.). (2005). *eXtensible Access Control Markup Language (XACML) Version 2.0*. Retrieved August 1, 2009 http://docs.oasis-open.org/xacml/2.0/access_control-xacml-2.0-core-spec-os.pdf

Mourad, A., Laverdiere, M., & Debbabi, M. (2007). Towards an aspect-oriented approach for the security hardening of code. In *Proceedings of the 21st international Conference on Advanced information Networking and Applications. Workshops Proceedings. Volume 1* (pp. 595-600). New York: IEEE Computer Society.

MPEG. (2009). *Motion Picture Experts Group*. Retrieved October 30, 2009, from http://www.mpeg.org/

Murugensan, S. (Ed.). (2008). Finding the real world value in virtual. *Cutter IT Journal for Information Technology Management, 21* (9).

Nath, A. K., & King, R. C. (2009). Customers' perceived security: relative effectiveness of trust transference mechanisms. In *AMCIS 2009 Proceedings*. Retrieved from: http://aisel.aisnet.org/amcis2009/766/

Nechvatal, J. (2001). Towards an immersive intelligence. *Leonardo, 34*(5), 417–422. doi:10.1162/002409401753521539

Nielsen, J. (1998). *2D is Better Than 3D*. Jakob Nielsen's Alertbox.

Noam, E. M. (2007). The dismal economics of virtual worlds. *The Data Base for Advances in Information Systems, 38*(4), 107.

North, D. C. (1990). *Institutions, Institutional Change and Economic Performance*. Cambridge, UK: Cambridge University Press.

Noveck, B. S. (2004/2005). The state of play. [Retrieved from Business Source Complete, EBSCO.]. *New York Law School Law Review. New York Law School, 49*(1), 1–18.

Novosti. (2008). Russian nuclear power websites attacked amid accident rumor. *RIA Novosti*, May 23, 2008, Retrieved February 10, 2009 from http://en.rian.ru/russia/20080523/ 108202288.html

Ogre (2009). Retrieved from http://www.ogre3d.org/about/features.

Okazaki, N., Aya, S., Saeyor, S., & Ishizuka, M. (2002). A Multimodal Presentation Markup Language MPML-VR for a 3D Virtual Space. In *Proc. of the Workshop on Virtual Conversational Characters: Applications, Methods, and Research Challenges*, Melbourne, Australia.

OpenSimulator. (2009). *3D Application Server*. Retrieved October 30, 2009, from http://opensimulator.org/wiki/Main_Page

Parisi, T. (2006). *Ajax3D: The Open Platform for Rich 3D Web Applications*. White Paper, Media Machines, Inc., Aug, 2006. Retrieved from http://www.ajax3d.org/whitepaper/

Pearce, C. (2009). *Communities of play: emergent cultures in multiplayer fames and virtual worlds*. Cambridge, MA: The MIT Press.

Pelechano, N., Allbeck, J., & Badler, N. I. (2008). *Virtual Crowds: Methods, Simulation, and Control*. San Francisco: Morgan & Claypool Publishers.

Pelechano, N., Stocker, C., Allbeck, J., & Badler, N. (2008). Being a part of a crowd: Towards validating VR crowds using presence. In *Proceedings of the 7th International Conference on Autonomous Agents and Multiagent Systems. International Foundation for Autonomous Agents and Multiagent Systems*, (pp. 136–142). New York: ACM.

Pellens, B., De Troyer, O., & Kleinermann, F. (2008). CoDePA: a conceptual design pattern approach to model behavior for X3D worlds. In *Proc. of the 13th International Symposium on 3D Web Technology*, Los Angeles, CA, August 09 – 10, (pp. 91-99). New York: ACM.

Pellens, B., Kleinermann, F., De Troyer, O., & Bille, W. (2006). Model-Based Design of Virtual Environment Behavior. In H. Zha, Z. Pan, H. Thwaites, A. C. Addison, M. Forte (Eds.), *Interactive Technologies and Sociotechnical Systems, 12th International Conference, VSMM 2006, Xi'an, China, October 18-20, 2006, Proceedings* (LNCS 4270, pp. 29-39). Berlin: Springer.

Perez, J. C. (2009, September 11). Twitter: your 'tweets' belong to you. *PC World Business Center*. Retrieved from: http://www.pcworld.com/businesscenter/article/171818/twitter_your_tweets_belong_to_you.html

Perez, S. (2008, February 25). How to manage your online reputation. *ReadWriteWeb*. Retrieved from: http://www.readwriteweb.com/archives/how_to_manage_your_online_reputation.php

Pettifer, S., & Marsh, J. (2001). A Collaborative Access Model for Shared Virtual Environments. In *Proceedings of the 10th IEEE international Workshops on Enabling Technologies: infrastructure For Collaborative Enterprises*. WETICE, (pp. 257-262). Washington, DC: IEEE Computer Society.

Pittarello, F., & De Faveri, A. (2006). Semantic description of 3D environments: a proposal based on web standards. In *Proceedings of the Eleventh international Conference on 3D Web Technology*, (Web3D '06), (pp. 85-95). New York: ACM.

Poulsen, K. (2007). Cyberwar' and Estonia's Panic Attack. *Wired Magazine*, August 22, 2007. Retrieved November 2, 2007 from http://www.wired.com/threatlevel/2007/08/cyber-war-and-e/

Prada, R., & Paiva, A. (2005). Believable groups of synthetic characters. In *Proc. of AAMAS '05: Autonomous Agents and Multi-Agent Systems*, (pp. 37–43). New York: ACM.

Prathivi, P. (2009). The 419. *The SL Revolution*, 3 February 2009 (http://theslrevolution.wordpress.com/2009/02/03/the-419/). (Accessed 29-May-2009 14:58).

Pratt, G. W. (1964). Risk Aversion in the Small and in the Large. *Econometrica, 32*, 122–136. doi:10.2307/1913738

Priebe, T., Dobmeier, W., Schläger, C., & Kamprath, N. (2007). Supporting Attribute-based Access Control in Authentication and Authorization Infrastructures with Ontologies. *Journal of software. JSW, 2*(1), 27–38. doi:10.4304/jsw.2.1.27-38

Prietula, M., Carley, K., & Gasser, L. (1998). *Simulating Organizations: Computational Models of Institutions and Groups*. Menlo Park, CA: AAAI Press / MIT press.

Privacy Rights Clearinghouse. (2009, September 15). *A chronology of data breaches*. Retrieved from: http://www.privacyrights.org/ar/ChronDataBreaches.htm

Project. (2009). *Papervision3d*. Retrieved October 30, 2009, from http://blog.papervison3d.org/

Qiu, Z. M., Kok, K. F., Wong, Y. S., & Fuh, J. Y. (2007). Role-based 3D visualisation for asynchronous PLM collaboration. *Computers in Industry, 58*(8-9), 747–755. doi:10.1016/j.compind.2007.02.006

Rajan, H., & Sullivan, K. J. (2005). Classpects: Unifying aspect- and object-oriented language design. In *Proceedings of the 27th international Conference on Software Engineering* (pp. 59-68). New York: ACM.

Rao, A. S. (1996). AgentSpeak(L): BDI agents speak out in a logical computable language. In S. Verlag, (Ed.), *Proc. of MAAMAW '96*, (LNAI 1038, pp 42–55).

Rao, A. S., & Georgeff, M. P. (1991). Modeling rational agents within a BDI-architecture. In *Proc. of KR'91: The 2nd International Conference on Principles of Knowledge Representation and Reasoning*, (pp. 473–484). San Mateo, CA: Morgan Kaufmann publishers Inc.

Raupp, S., & Thalmann, D. (2001). Hierarchical model for real time simulation of virtual human crowds. *IEEE Transactions on Visualization and Computer Graphics, 7*(2), 152–164. doi:10.1109/2945.928167

Rehm, M., & Rosina, P. (2008). SecondLife® as an Evaluation Platform for Multiagent Systems Featuring Social Interactions. In *Proc. of AAMAS'08: Autonomous Agents and Multi-Agent Systems*, (pp 1663–1664). New York: ACM.

Reilly, W. S. N. (1996). *Believable Social and Emotional Agents*. PhD thesis, School of Computer Science, Carnegie Mellon University, Pittsburgh, PA, USA.

Renaud, C. (2009, January). http://www.christianrenaud.com/weblog/2009/01/the-upside-of-the-lack-of-privacy.html. (Accessed 29-May-2009 14:55).

Reynolds, C. (1987). Flocks, herds and schools: A distributed behavioral model. In *Proc. of SIGGRAPH'87*, (pp 25–34). New York: ACM.

Robertson, J. (2008). Hackers' posts on epilepsy forum cause migraines, seizures. *USA Today*, May 7, 2008. Retrieved September 25, 2008 from http://www.usatoday.com/tech/products/2008-05-07-1007914798_x.htm

Rosedale, P. (2008, April 1). *Prepared statement before the subcommittee on telecommunications and the internet*. Washington, DC: Energy and Commerce Committee of the U.S. House of Representatives. Retrieved from: http://energycommerce.house.gov/images/stories/Documents/Hearings/PDF/110-ti-hrg.040108.Rosedale-testimony.pdf

Rufer-Bach, K. (2009). *The Second Life Grid: The Official Guide to Communication, Collaboration, and Community Engagement*. Indianapolis, IN: Wiley Publishing.

Russo Dos Santos, C., Gros, P., Abel, P., Loisel, D., Trichaud, N., & Paris, J.-P. (2000). Mapping Information onto 3D Virtual Worlds. In *Proceedings of the International Conference on Information Visualization* (pp. 379–386). Washington, DC: IEEE Computer Society.

Safonov, V. O. (2008). *Using aspect-oriented programming for trustworthy software development*. Hoboken, NJ: Wiley Interscience. John Wiley & Sons. doi:10.1002/9780470283110

Sandhu, R., Ferraiolo, D., & Kuhn, R. (2000). The NIST model for role-based access control: towards a unified standard. In *Proceedings of the Fifth ACM Workshop on Role-Based Access Control*, (RBAC '00), (pp. 47-63). New York: ACM.

Schkolne, S. (2002). Drawing with the hand in free space: Creating 3D shapes with gesture in a semi-immersive environment. *Leonardo*, *35*(4), 371–375. doi:10.1162/002409402760181132

Schotter, A. (1981). *The Economic Theory of Social Institutions*. Cambridge, MA: Cambridge University Press.

Second Life. (2009). Retrieved from http://www.secondlife.com.

Security. (2009). *The Web Application Security Consortium (WASC)*. Retrieved anytime from http://www.webappsec.org/

Seidenberg, S. (2008, March 1). Virtual knockoffs. *Inside Counsel*. Retrieved from: http://www.insidecounsel.com/Issues/2008/March%202008/Pages/Virtual-Knockoffs.aspx?k=seidenberg

Sherman, D. K., & Cohen, G. L. (2002). Accepting threatening information: Self-affirmation and the reduction of defensive biases. *Current Directions in Psychological Science, 11*(4), 119 – 123. Retrieved Aug. 29, 2009, from http://www.jstor.org/stable/20182787

Shirky, C. (2003). *A group is its own worst enemy*. Retrieved September 15, 2009 from http://www.shirky.com/writings/group_enemy.html

Sichman, J., & Demazeau, Y. (2001). On social reasoning in multi-agent systems. *Revista Ibero-Americana de Inteligencia Artificial, 13*, 68–84.

Silverlight (2009). Retrieved from http://www.silverlight.net

Silvestrini, E. (2008). Virtual sex toy suit settled. *Tampa Tribune*, 21 March 2008 (http://www2.tbo.com/content/2008/mar/21/virtual-sex-toy-suit-settled).

Siponen, M. T., & Oinas-Kukkonen, H. (2007). A review of information security issues and respective research contributions. *The Data Base for Advances in Information Systems, 38*(1), 62.

Siponen, M. T. (2001). An Analysis of the Recent IS Security Development Approaches. In Dhillon, G. (Ed.), *Information Security Management: Global Challenges in the New Millennium* (pp. 106–107). Hershey, PA: Idea Group, Inc.

Siponen, M. T., & Kajava, J. (1998, 2002). Ontology of organizational IT security awareness—from theoretical foundations to practical framework. In *Enabling Technologies: Infrastructure for Collaborative Enterprises,* 1998. Stanford, CA. 330 – 331. Retrieved May 4, 2009, from http://ieeexplore.ieee.org/xpls/abs_all.jsp?arnumber=725713

Siponen, M.T. (2006). Secure-system design methods: Evolution and future directions. *IT Pro., 40.*

Sivan, Y. (2008a). 3D3C real virtual worlds defined: The immense potential of merging 3D, community, creation, and commerce. *Journal of Virtual Worlds Research, 1*(1).

Sivan, Y. (2008b). "The birth of MPEG-V (MPEG for virtual worlds)." *Metaverse1*, 16 February 2008 (http://www.metaverse1.org/2008/02/birth-of-mpeg-v-mpeg-for-virtual-worlds.html).

Sivan, Y. (2009). Identity 3D3C: Controlling the security and privacy challenges in virtual worlds. *Cutter IT Journal for Information Technology Management, 22* (4).

Slater, M., Sadagic, A., Usoh, M., & Schroeder, R. (2000). Small-group behavior in a virtual and real environment: a comparative study. [Retrieved from Business Source Complete, EBSCO.]. *Presence (Cambridge, Mass.), 9*(1), 37–51..doi:10.1162/105474600566600

Slovic, P. (1987). Perceptions of Risk. *Science, 236,* 280–285. doi:10.1126/science.3563507

SMH. (2008). Soulja Boy at war over MySpace hack attack. *stuff.co.nzNews.* Retrieved November 2, 2008 from http://www.stuff.co.nz/technology/609208

Smith, Anna DuVal. (1998). Problems of conflict management in virtual communities. In P. Kollock and M. Smith (Eds.), *Communities in Cyberspace.* New York: Routledge. Prepublication draft, retrieved March 30, 2009 from http://www.advs.net/cinc.htm.

Solove, D. J. (2004). *The digital person: technology and privacy in the information age.* New York: NYU Press.

Solove, D. J. (2006). A taxonomy of privacy. *University of Pennsylvania Law Review, 154*(3), 477–559. Retrieved from http://papers.ssrn.com/sol3/papers.cfm?abstract_id=667622#. doi:10.2307/40041279

Starodoumov, A. (2005). Real Money Trade Model in Virtual Economies. *Social Science Research Network,* Retrieved June, 2007, from http://papers.ssrn.com/sol3/papers.cfm?abstract_id=958286

Stephenson, N. (1992). *Snow crash.* New York: Bantam Books.

Stone, B. (2009, September 15). Facebook says its finances are looking up. *The New York Times Bits Blog.* Retrieved from: http://bits.blogs.nytimes.com/2009/09/15/facebook-says-its-finances-are-looking-up/?dbk

Stonebruner, G., Gougen, A., & Feringa, A. (2002). *Risk Management Guide for Information Technology Systems,* NIST SP800-30.

Stross, C. (2007). *Halting State.* New York: Ace Books.

Studio, D. X. (2009). Retrieved from http://www.dxstudio.com/.

Suler, J. (1996). *The bad boys of cyberspace: deviant behavior in online multimedia communities and strategies for managing it.* Retrieved April 29, 2009 from http://www-usr.rider.edu/~suler/psycyber/badboys.html

Suler, J. (1996). *The psychology of cyberspace.* Retrieved April 29, 2009 from http://www-usr.rider.edu/~suler/psycyber/badboys.html

Suler, J. (1997). *The Psychology of Cyberspace Homepage* [On-line book]. Retrieved November 12, 2001, from http://www.rider.edu/users/suler/psycyber/psycyber.html

SUN Project Darkstar Roadmap. (n.d.). Retrieved December 1, 2009, from http://projectdarkstar.com/technology-roadmap-may-09.html

Sun. (2008). *Open Virtual Worlds*. Retrieved December 1, 2009, from http://www.sun.com/service/application-serversubscriptions/OpenVirtualWorld.pdf

Sutter, J., & Carroll, J. (2009, Feb. 6). *Fears of imposters increase on Facebook*. Retrieved Feb. 8, 2009, from http://www.cnn.com/2009/TECH/02/05/facebook.impostors/index.html

Taber, J. (2004). Liberal justice can be painful. *The Globe and Mail,* Tuesday, June 15, (pp. A6).

Takashima, K., Omori, Y., Yoshimoto, Y., Itoh, Y., Kitamura, Y., & Kishino, F. (2008). Effects of avatar's blinking animation on person impressions. In *Graphics Interface Conference,* (pp. 169 – 176), Windsor, Ontario, Canada.

Tambe, M. (1997). Towards flexible teamwork. *Journal of Artificial Intelligence Research, 7*, 83–124.

Tang, R. (2001). China-U.S. cyber war escalates. *CNN.COM.* Retrieved June 2, 2005 from http://archives.cnn.com/2001/WORLD/asiapcf/east/04/27/china.hackers/index.html

Tarakos. (2009). *TaraVR Builder*. Retrieved December 1, 2009, from http://www.taravrbuilder.com/eng/Home.html

Taylor, T. (2006). *Play between worlds: Exploring online game culture*. Cambridge, MA: MIT Press.

Taylor, T. L. (2006). The assemblage of play. *Games and Culture*. DOI: 10.1177/1555412009343576. Retrieved September 21, 2009 from http://gac.sagepub.com/cgi/content/abstract/1555412009343576v1

Terdiman, D. (2006, December 20). Newsmaker: virtual magnate shares secrets of success. *CNET News*. Retrieved from: http://news.cnet.com/Virtual-magnate-shares-secrets-of-success/2008-1043_3-6144967.html?tag=item

Thalmann, D., & Monzani, J. (2002). Behavioural animation of virtual humans: What kind of law and rules? In *Proceedings of Computer Animation* (pp. 154–163). Washington, DC: IEEE Computer Society Press.

The Internet Society (ISOC). (2008). *Trust and the future of the internet*. (http://www.isoc.org/isoc/mission/initiative/docs/trust-report-2008.pdf).

Theslrevolution, author unknown (2009). The importance of identity when doing business in virtual worlds. *The SL Revolution*, 4 February 2009 (http://theslrevolution.wordpress.com/2009/02/04/identity-in-virtual-worlds). (Accessed 29-May-2009 15:10).

Thompson, M. (2009). Real banking coming to virtual worlds. *Ars Technica*, 20 March 2009 (http://arstechnica.com/gaming/news/2009/03/real-banking-coming-to-virtual-worlds.ars).

Thorens, G., Khazaal, Y., & Billieux, J., Linden van der M. & Zullino D. (2009). Swiss Psychiatrists' Beliefs and Attitudes About Internet Addiction. *The Psychiatric Quarterly, 80*(2), 117–123. doi:10.1007/s11126-009-9098-2

Totten, I. (2009, Feb. 26). *Second Life Showcase*. Kansas State University Instructional Design Technology Roundtable Presentation.

Trewin, S. M., Laff, M. R., Cavender, A. C., & Hanson, V. L. (2008). *Accessibility in virtual worlds. CHI 2008 Proceedings: Works in Progress. Florence, Italy* (pp. 2728–2729). New York: ACM.

Trustworthy Computing. (2008). *Microsoft Trustworthy Computing (TWC) Initiative Web Site*. http://www.microsoft.com/mscorp/twc/default.mspx.

Tryfonas, T. (2008, April). *IT governance and the role of the information security professional*. Paper presented at Centre for Security, Communications and Network Research University of Plymouth. Retrieved July 7, 2009 from http://www.cisnr.org/presentations/16-04-2008-TheodoreTryfonas.pdf

Tu, X., & Terzopoulos, D. (1994). Artificial fishes: physics, locomotion, perception, behavior. In *Proc. of SIGGRAPH'94*, (pp. 43–50). New York: ACM.

Tversky, A., & Kahneman, D. (1979). Prospect Theory: An Analysis of Decisions under Risk. *Econometrica, 47*(2), 263–291. doi:10.2307/1914185

Tyler, T., & Blader, S. (2003). The group engagement model: procedural justice, social identity, and cooperative behavior. [Retrieved from Business Source Complete, EBSCO.]. *Personality and Social Psychology Review, 7*(4), 349–361. doi:10.1207/S15327957PSPR0704_07

United States Computer Emergency Readiness Team. (2009, May 21). *Cyber security tip st04-002: choosing and protecting passwords*. Retrieved from: http://www.us-cert.gov/cas/tips/ST04-002.html

Unity3D (2009). Retrieved from http://unity3d.com/.

Van den Bos, K., Wilke, H. A. M., & Lind, E. A. (1998). When do we need procedural fairness? The role of trust in authority. [Retrieved from Business Source Complete, EBSCO.]. *Journal of Personality and Social Psychology*, *75*(6), 1449–1458. doi:10.1037/0022-3514.75.6.1449

van Kokswijk, J. (2007). *Digital Ego: Social and Legal Aspects of Virtual Identity*.

Viega, J., Bloch, J. T., & Chandra, P. (2001). Applying aspect-oriented programming to security. *Cutter IT Journal*, *14*(2), 31–39.

Vilhjálmsson, H., Cantelmo, N., Cassell, J., Chafai, N. E., Kipp, M., Kopp, S., et al. (2007). The Behavior Markup Language: Recent Developments and Challenges. In *Intelligent Virtual Agents*, (LNCS 4722, pp. 99-111). Berlin: Springer.

Vinge, V. (1998). True Names. Retrieved from http://www.facstaff.bucknell.edu/rickard/TRUENAMES.pdf

Vitzthum, A. (2006). SSIML/Components: a visual language for the abstract specification of 3D components. In *Proceedings of the 11ᵗʰ International Conference on 3D Web Technologies*, Columbia, MD, Apr. 18-21, (pp. 143-151).

W3C. (2009). *HTML 5 - A vocabulary and associated APIs for HTML and XHTML*. Working draft. Retrieved December 1, 2009, from http://www.w3.org/TR/html5/no.html#declarative-3d-scenes

W3C. (2009). *World Wide Web Consortium*. Retrieved October 30, 2009, from http://www.w3.org

W3C. (2009). *XML - Extensible Markup Language Recommendation*. Retrieved October 30, 2009, from http://www.w3.org/TR/xml11/

W3C. (2009). *XML Encryption Recommendation*. Retrieved October 30, 2009, from http://www.w3.org/TR/xmlenc-core/

W3C. (2009). *XML Signature Recommendation*. Retrieved October 30, 2009, from http://www.w3.org/TR/xmlsig-core/

Walczak, K., & Cellary, W. (2003). X-VRML for Advanced Virtual Reality Applications. *Computer*, *36*(3), 89–92. doi:10.1109/MC.2003.1185226

Walczak, K., Cellary, W., & White, M. (2006). Virtual Museum Exhibitions. *Computer*, *39*(3), 93–95. doi:10.1109/MC.2006.108

Walczak, K. (2006). Beh-VR: Modeling Behavior of Dynamic Virtual Reality Contents. In H. Zha et al. (Eds.), *The 12th International Conference on Virtual Systems and Multimedia VSMM 2006, Interactive Technologies and Sociotechnical Systems*, (LNCS 4270, pp. 40-51). Berlin: Springer Verlag.

Walczak, K. (2008). Structured Design of Interactive VR Applications. In *The 13th International Symposium on 3D Web Technology Web3D*, Los Angeles, California, USA, (pp. 105-113). New York: ACM Press.

Walczak, K. (2008a). Flex-VR: Configurable 3D Web Applications. In *the IEEE International Conference on Human System Interaction HSI 2008*, Kraków, (pp. 135-140). Washington, DC: IEEE.

Walczak, K. (2008b). Structured Design of Interactive VR Applications, In *Proc. of the 13ᵗʰ International Symposium on 3D Web Technology Web3D 2008*, Los Angeles, CA, (pp. 105-113). New York: ACM Press.

Walczak, K. (2008b). VR-BML: Behaviour Modelling Language for Configurable VR Applications, in Digital Heritage. In M. Ioannides, A. Addison, A. Georgopoulos, L. Kalisperis, (Eds.), *The 14th International Conference on Virtual Systems and MultiMedia VSMM '08*, Limassol (Cyprus), Archaeolingua, (pp. 295-302).

Walczak, K., Cellary, W., Chmielewski, J., Stawniak, M., Strykowski, S., Wiza, W., et al. (2004). An Architecture for Parameterised Production of Interactive TV Contents, 11ᵗʰ International Workshop on Systems, Signals And Image Processing. In *Proc. of the International Conf. on Signals And Electronic Systems IWSSIP 2004*, Poznan, Poland, (pp. 465-468).

Walczak, K., Wojciechowski, R., & Wójtowicz, A. (2005). Interactive Production of Dynamic 3D Sceneries for Virtual Television Studio. In *7th Virtual Reality International Conference VRIC - Laval Virtual 2005*, Laval (France), (pp. 167-177).

Walczak. (2006). Beh-VR: Modeling Behavior of Dynamic Virtual Reality Contents. In H. Zha et al. (Eds.), *The 12ᵗʰ International Conference on Virtual Systems and Multimedia VSMM 2006*, (LNCS 4270, pp. 40-51). Berlin: Springer Verlag.

Walczak. (2008a). VR-BML: Behaviour Modelling Language for Configurable VR Applications. In M. Ioannides, A. Addison, A. Georgopoulos, L. Kalisperis (Eds.), *Digital Heritage, The 14ᵗʰ International Conference on Virtual Systems and MultiMedia VSMM'08*, Archaeolingua, (pp. 295-302).

Walther, J. B., Boos, M., & Jonas, K. J. (2002). Misattribution and attributional redirection in distributed virtual groups. In *Proceedings of the 35th Annual Hawaii International Conference on System Sciences, 2002, IEEE Conference Proceedings*. Washington, DC: IEEE Press.

Wang, X., Demartini, T., Wragg, B., Paramasivam, M., & Barlas, C. (2005). The mpeg-21 rights expression language and rights data dictionary. *Multimedia. IEEE Transactions on, 7*(3), 408–417.

Wang, Y., Ajoku, P., Brustoloni, J., & Nnaji, B., J. (2006). Intellectual Property Protection in Collaborative Design through Lean Information Modeling and Sharing. *Journal of Computing and Information Science in Engineering, 6*, 149. doi:10.1115/1.2190235

Web3D Consortium. (2009). Retrieved October 30, 2009, from www.web3d.org

Web3D. (2009). *X3D specifications ISO/IEC 19776 (1/2/3).* Retrieved October 30, 2009, from http://www.web3d.org/x3d/specifications/

Web3D.org. (2009). *X3D Security.* Retrieved October 30, 2009, from http://www.web3d.org/x3d/content/examples/Basic/Security/X3dSecurityReadMe.html

Websense. (2007). *Information Protection and Control: Targeting the Insider Threat* [White paper]. Retrieved September 9, 2008, from www.bitpipe.com

Wei, S. Stocker. (2009). Function-based haptic collaboration in X3D. In *Proceedings of Web3D 2009 conference*. New York: Association for Computing Machinery.

Whang, L., & Chang, G. (2004). Lifestyles of virtual world residents: living in the on-line game "Lineage." [Retrieved from Business Source Complete, EBSCO.]. *Cyberpsychology & Behavior, 7*(5), 592–600. doi:. doi:10.1089/1094931042403091

White, D., & Rea, A. (2008). Just trying to be friendly: A case study in social engineering. *Journal of Information Science and Technology, 4*(2), 59.

Whiz, R. (2009, August 19). Legal impact of the Liskula Cohen court order (the "skank" decision). *Reputation Defender Blog.* Blog entry posted at: http://www.reputationdefenderblog.com/2009/08/19/legal-impact-of-the-liskula-cohen-court-order-the-skank-decision/.

Williams, M. (2000). Virtually criminal: discourse, deviance and anxiety within virtual communities. [Retrieved from Business Source Complete, EBSCO.]. *International Review of Law Computers & Technology, 14*(1), 95–104.. doi:10.1080/13600860054935

Williams, M. (2006). *Virtually Criminal: Crime, Deviance and Regulation Online.* London: Routledge.

Williams, M. (2007). Policing and cybersociety: the maturation of regulation within an online community. *Policing and Society, 17*(1), 59–82.. doi:10.1080/10439460601124858

Williams, D., Ducheneaut, N., Xiong, L., Zhang, Y., Yee, N., & Nickell, E. (2006). From Tree House to Barracks: The Social Life of Guilds in World of Warcraft. *Games and Culture, 1*, 338–361. doi:10.1177/1555412006292616

Williams, J. S., Sr. (2009). *Document-based Message-Centric Security using XML authentication and encryption for coalition and interagency operations*. Master's Thesis, Naval Postgraduate School, Monterey, California, Security classification: unclassified.

Wong, K., & Watt, S. (1990). *Managing Information Security: Management Guide*. New York: Elsevier Advanced Technology.

Wooldridge, M. J., & Jennings, N. R. (1995). Intelligent agents: Theory and practice. *The Knowledge Engineering Review*, *10*(2), 115–152. doi:10.1017/S0269888900008122

Workshop, I. I. (2009, March 1). *Internet identity workshop 9*. Retrieved from: http://www.internetidentityworkshop.com/

Wortham, J., & Kramer, A. E. (2009, August 7). Professor main target of assault on twitter. *The New York Times*. Retrieved from: http://www.nytimes.com/2009/08/08/technology/internet/08twitter.html?_r=2&hpw

Yankelovich, N. (2007). *MPK20: Sun's virtual workplace* [Video]. Retrieved October 15, 2009 from http://research.sun.com/projects/mc/video/MPK20-oct2007.mov

Yee, N. (2006). Motivations of play in online games. [Retrieved from Business Source Complete, EBSCO.]. *Cyberpsychology & Behavior*, *9*(6), 772–775..doi:10.1089/cpb.2006.9.772

Yee, N., Bailenson, J. N., Urbanek, M., Chang, F., & Merget, D. (2007). The Unbearable Likeness of Being Digital: The Persistence of Nonverbal Social Norms in Online Virtual Environments. *Cyberpsychology & Behavior*, *10*(1), 115–121. doi:10.1089/cpb.2006.9984

Yee (n.d.). Avatar and identity. *The Daedalus Gateway*. Retrieved from: http://www.nickyee.com/daedalus/gateway_identity.html

Yee, N. (2001) *Everquest survey*. Retrieved from http://www.nickyee.com/eqt/report.html

Young, K. (1996, August). *Internet Addiction: The Emergence of a New Clinical Disorder*. Paper presented at the 104th annual meeting of the American Psychological Association, Toronto, Canada, August 15, 1996

Young, K. S. (1997) *What Makes the Internet Addictive: Potential Explanation for Pathological Internet Use*. Paper presented at the 105th annual conference of the American Psychological Association, August 15, 1997, Chicago, IL

Zhang, X., & Gračanin, D. (2007). From coarse-grained components to DVE applications: a service- and component-based framework. In *Proceedings of the 12th International Conference on 3D Web Technology*, Perugia, Italy, April 15-18, (pp. 113-121).

About the Contributors

Alan Rea is a Professor of Computer Information Systems at the Haworth College of Business, Western Michigan University in Kalamazoo, MI. At WMU, Alan teaches courses in Information Security, OO and Internet Programming, and e-Business technologies. His primary research involves the intersection between security and virtual realms, and encompasses the development and implementation of technology mechanisms and policies leading towards increased information assurance.

* * *

Fernando Barber Miralles received the MS in Physics from the University of Valencia, Spain, in 1992. He worked at the University Jaume I of Castellon as a lecturer. He has worked as a researcher in several european (EQUATOR, CHIC) and spanish projects. Currently, he is a lecturer in the Department of Informatics, at the University of Valencia, SPAIN, where he is a member of the GREV research group (http://grev.uv.es) and the ACCA team (http://www.acca-group.info). His research is currently supported by the Spanish MEC and the European Commission through several projects. His research currently focuses on Distributed Virtual Environments, planning in virtual environments and Crowd simulations. He has published papers about his research in a number of international journals and conferences.

Anton Bogdanovych has received his PhD in 2008 from the University of Technology Sydney, Australia. Before starting his PhD he spent three years in Germany working in the German Research Center for Artificial Intelligence (DFKI) at the Department of Deduction and Multiagent Systems. From 2007 he is employed as a Postdoctoral Research Fellow in the University of Western Sydney, School of Computing and Mathematics and works on research issues related to Normative Virtual Worlds, Multiagent Systems and Human Computer Interaction. Dr Bogdanovych has developed the concept of Virtual Institutions, including respective formal representations, supporting algorithms and technological solutions. Anton's research interests include Multiagent Systems, general Artificial Intelligence, Virtual Worlds, Virtual Reality, Motion Capturing Virtual Heritage and Data Mining.

Wojciech Cellary is a computer scientist, head of the Department of Information Technology at the Poznan University of Economics. In his professional career he worked at nine universities in Poland, France, and Italy. His research interests are currently focused on internet technologies, multimedia, electronic business and economy, electronic government and information society. He is an author of 10 books and over 150 scientific papers. He gives lectures on electronic business to over 700 students per year. He was a leader of many national and international scientific and industrial projects. He served as a consultant to several Polish ministries, Polish Parliament and Senate, as well as European Commission. He was scientific editor of the report "Poland and the Global Information Society: Logging on" developed under auspices of United Nations Development Programme.

Fariborz Farahmand is a faculty fellow and a research assistant professor at the Center for Education and Research in Information Assurance and Security at Purdue University. Dr. Farahmand has received several awards for scholarship and education, including a fellowship from the Institution for Information Infrastructure Protection (I3P). His research interests are in behavioral economics and its applications in information systems, security and privacy of information systems, vulnerability and risk assessment of information systems, and cost-benefit analysis of information technology investments.

Francisco Grimaldo received a MS in Computer Science from the Universitat de València (Spain) in 2001, a BSc in Telecommunications and Network Engineering from the Universitat de València in 2003 and the PhD in Computer and Information Science from the Universitat de València in 2008. Currently, he is lecturer of Computer Science at the Universitat de València, where he is a member of the GREV research group (http://grev.uv.es). Dr. Grimaldo is also member of the HiPEAC network of excellence (http://www.hipeac.net/) and of the ACCA team (http://www.acca-group.info). His research interests include multi-agent simulation, social engineering, behavioural animation of synthetic characters and crowd simulation. He has published papers on social decision-making applied to autonomous virtual humans and scalability of crowd simulations in a number of international journals and conferences. In 2008, Dr. Grimaldo was awarded the Popularization of Science Prize given by The Joan Lluís Vives University Network (Spain).

Shalin Hai-Jew works for Kansas State University as an instructional designer. She has taught as a college professor in communications and writing for many years. She taught at universities in the People's Republic of China from 1988 – 1990, and 1992 – 1994, with the latter two years as a member of the United Nations Volunteers Programme of the UNDP (United Nations Development Programme). She was a tenured professor at Shoreline Community College in Washington State. She has B.A.s in English and psychology, an MA in English (University of Washington) and an Ed.D. in Educational Leadership with a focus on Public Administration and e-learning (Seattle University). She works on a range of e-learning projects, most recently in biosecurity, mental health, non-profit fund-raising, policies, and public health. She was born in Huntsville, Alabama, in the US.

Vaclav Jirovsky, professor at Czech Technical University in Prague, Czech Republic, dedicate his work to computer security and to interdisciplinary problems of society and technology. Presently, as the Head of Department of Security Technologies and Engineering at Faculty of Transportation Sciences, focus his attention to the field of information technology acceptance and effect of the technology on a society. He and his team are presently active in the research of cyber threats from point of view of security of a society. He is member of many local committees and boards, representative of Czech Republic in Security Program Committee of EU research program FP7 and special court expert.

Nola Johnston is a freelance communication designer and illustrator, and teaches design courses for both the British Columbia Institute of Technology and Emily Carr University of Art and Design. She has been investigating the potential of Second Life since 2006. In 2007 she completed a research document on this virtual world for BCIT and later was hired to construct the BCIT campus in Second Life. In 2009, in a project managed by BCIT and funded by BC Campus, she developed a resource wiki for educators interested in working in Second Life (http://solr.bccampus.ca/wiki/index.php/Main_Page/ Second_Life_for_Educators). A private region owner and active member of Elf Circle, she is fascinated by the ways in which communities develop and thrive in virtual worlds and the opportunities that these new environments offer.

Joerg H. Kloss is one of the early pioneers of interactive 3D graphics on the Internet. He started to build Virtual Worlds already years ago, hold lectures on symposia, and published articles and books about the 3D standards VRML and X3D. He holds a Master's degree in Computational Linguistics, Psychology and Economics, and currently works as a telecommunications professional and consultant in Germany.

Miguel Lozano received the MS in computer engineering from the Technical University of Valencia (Spain) in 1996 and the PhD in computer engineering from the University of Valencia in 2005. Currently, he is an associate professor of Computer Science and Artificial Intelligence within the Computer Science Department of the University of Valencia. He has been involved in a number of scientific and technical projects on real-time 3D graphics and intelligent virtual agents. His current research interests include large scale multiagent systems, social engineering and distributed/parallel architectures. He is a member of the Networks and Virtual Environments Group (http://grev.uv.es) where he supervises different PhD students and participates in research projects carried out within the ACCA Team (http:// www.acca-group.info). He has published papers on intelligent virtual agents and distributed crowd simulations in a number of international journals and conferences.

Juan M. Orduña received the MS in computer engineering from the Technical University of Valencia (Spain) in 1990 and the PhD in computer engineering from the University of Valencia in 1998. His research has been developed inside the ACCA team (http://www.acca-group.info). Currently, he is an associate professor in the Department of Informatics, at the University of Valencia, where he leads the GREV research group (http://grev.uv.es). He is also member of the HiPEAC network of excellence (http://www.hipeac.net/). His research currently focuses on Networks-on-Chip, Distributed Virtual Environments and Crowd simulations. Dr. Orduna served as a member of the Program Committee in different conferences and workshops (ICPP, Europar, VR, ICPADS, etc.) as well as a reviewer for scholarly journals like Parallel Computing, IEEE TPDS, JNCA, and JASC. He has published papers about his research in a number of international journals and conferences.

Torsten Reiners is a postdoctoral researcher at the University of Hamburg, Germany, and University Associate with the Curtin University of Technology in Perth, Australia. His research and teaching experiences are in the areas of operations research (meta-heuristics/simulations models for container terminals), fleet logistics, information systems and several topics in eLearning and software development. His PhD-thesis "Simulation and OR with SmartFrame" demonstrated concepts for didactical models.

Besides scientific publications, he conducts research in semantic networks to improve cross-border communication, (e)learning and machine translation. Another interest is about (virtual) worlds and their interconnectivity/ exchange without barriers. This research includes the development of adaptive systems, automatic processing, analysis, and evaluation of documents, innovative platforms in combination with emerging technologies like mobile devices. Torsten Reiners is co-founder of the Second Life Island University of Hamburg and Students@work, an initiative to promote education in Web 3D as well as the value of students' work.

Malu Roldan is an Associate Professor at SJSU's Management Information Systems (MIS) department who has a proven track record in building high quality, multidisciplinary, community engaged partnerships for innovation. Since 2003, she has been director of several projects on mobile computing and social innovation with primary support from Hewlett Packard and the National Collegiate Inventors and Innovators Alliance (NCIIA). Her research focuses on the impact of emerging technologies on education and other social ventures. She has published articles on the use of mobile computing and social media technologies by community-based organizations, for problem-based learning, and to support distributed learning.

Vladimir O. Safonov is a professor of computer science ad head of laboratory at St. Petersburg University, Russia. Scientific interests: aspect-oriented programming, compilers, knowledge management, trustworthy computing, Java, .NET. Author of: Trustworthy Compilers, Wiley, 2010; Using aspect-oriented programming for trustworthy software development, Wiley, 2008; Introduction to Java technology, St. Petersburg, Science, 2002; total 127 papers, including 4 USA patents.

Peter Schickel is founder of Bitmanagement Software GmbH and leads the company since its foundation in 2002. Prior he was head of research at blaxxun interactive AG which was focused to the development of 3D internet software. At blaxxun he was directing the development of 3D viewer technology within 6 EC/BMBF R&D projects and built up a network of leading European Technology Companies. Focus of his work was the transfer from R&D results into commercial products, e.g. leading to winning the Digiglobe-Award for E-Commerce of Deutsche Telecom and Focus. At the German Aerospace Centre (DLR) in Munich, Germany and the Joint Research Centre of the European Commission (JRC) in Milan, Italy, he was working from 1992 to 1998 at the development of graphical systems in the areas of Virtual Reality, Remote Sensing (GIS) and GPS. He is accredited from the Deutsches Institut für Normung (DIN) for Standardisation of VRML, X3D and MPEG technologies and is active in the board of the Web3D consortium as co-vice-president. Mr. Schickel holds a degree in information science from the University of Technology Munich (TUM).

Simeon Simoff is a Professor of Information Technology and Head of the School of Computing and Mathematics, University of Western Sydney. He is also an adjunct professor at the University of Technology, Sydney (UTS). Prior to this, he was a Professor of Information Technology at the Faculty of Information Technology, UTS, where he established the e-Markets research program, running between UWS, UTS and UNSW (e-markets.org.au). He is also founding director of the Institute of Analytics Professionals of Australia and Series Editor of the ACS Publication Series "Conferences in Research and Practice in Information Technology". From 2000 to 2005 he was the associate editor (Australia) of the ASCE International Journal of Computing in Civil Engineering. He is founder and chair of the ACM SIGKDD Multimedia Data Mining conference series MDM@KDD, the Australasian Data Mining conference series AusDM, and the Visual Data Mining international conference series collocated with ECML/PKDD and ICDM events. His research interests include information-rich 3D trading environments and technologies that facilitate extraction, synthesis, and delivery of condensed information from them, including network data mining, text analytics, multimedia, and visual data mining. He received his PhD in Computer Science from Moscow Power Engineering Institute.

Yesha Sivan is a senior lecturer at the Department of Software Engineering at the Shenkar College of Engineering and Design. He is also the founder of Metaverse Labs (MVL) - a leading think tank focusing on connecting virtual and real worlds. Dr. Sivan professional experience includes developing and deploying innovative solutions for corporate, hi-tech, government, and defense environments (see for example: the Harvard 9-Keys for Knowledge Infrastructure). He published numerous papers in the areas of Strategy and IT, knowledge, 3D3C virtual worlds, and standards. Dr. Sivan received his doctorate from Harvard University. His avatar is Dera Kit, and his blog is http://www.dryesha.com. He has taught EMBA, MBA, engineering and design in the areas of strategic value of IT, the emergence of virtual worlds, and software development in virtual worlds.

Eugene H. Spafford is a professor of Computer Sciences at Purdue University, and is the founder and Executive Director of the Center for Education and Research in Information Assurance and Security (CERIAS). His research and education over three decades has contributed to many of the technologies used in modern computing system protection. Spaf's current research interests are in information security, cybercrime, software engineering, professional ethics, and security policy. Dr. Spafford is a Fellow of the ACM, AAAS, IEEE, ISC2, is a Distinguished Fellow of the ISSA, and has received many other awards for service, scholarship, and education.

Krzysztof Walczak holds a PhD in Computer Science (Database Modelling of Virtual Reality, Gdansk 2001) and is an assistant professor in the Department of Information Technology at the Poznan University of Economics in Poland. His research interests focus on virtual reality, 3D Internet applications, multimedia systems, distance learning and databases. He was acting as a technical coordinator in numerous research and industrial projects in these domains. He is the author of one book and the author or co-author of over 70 research papers and several US and European patents in these domains. He is a member of the ACM, the Web3D Consortium and the Board of Directors of VSMM – Virtual Systems and Multimedia society.

Sascha Wriedt is a postgraduate researcher, associated to the University of Hamburg. Besides his field of industrial engineering with business studies his research experiences are in the area of logistics and virtual environments. Graduating with his thesis about simulating processes of supply chain management in virtual worlds he started deeper researches in the areas of education in virtual environments, interconnectivity between virtual worlds, collaborative approaches and new developments in virtual worlds. Sascha Wriedt is also co-founder of Students@work, a student initiative to include virtual environments into the educational process of the University of Hamburg.

Adam Wójtowicz holds a M.Sc. degree in Computer Science from the Poznan University of Technology and is a research assistant in the Department of Information Technology at the Poznan University of Economics in Poland. His research interests include VR modeling, VR security and multimedia systems. Currently he is working on his PhD dissertation titled Selective Semantic Modeling Method SSM for Building Secure Multiaccess Virtual Environments. He has participated in a number of software development research projects which include VR modeling, interactive television, virtual museums, service-oriented architectures and others.

Index

Symbols

3D3C Identity 20, 21, 23, 28, 29, 30, 31, 32, 33
3D3C worlds 20
3D characters 124
3D content modeling 263
3D e-government 136
3D entertainment 202
3D environment 144, 150, 153, 171
3D graphics 208, 210, 214, 215
3D immersive spaces 72, 73, 74, 78, 84, 85,
    86, 89, 94, 95, 96
3D interaction environment 140, 142
3D Interaction Space 143, 145, 146, 147
3D models 150, 152, 153, 164
3D objects 152, 170, 173, 183, 185, 191, 201,
    202
3D object security 191, 202
3D spaces 72, 73, 75, 77, 82, 83, 89
3D virtual objects 170
3D Virtual World 123, 124, 125, 135, 136, 140,
    142, 143, 144, 145, 148, 150, 152, 153,
    154, 155, 163, 167, 169, 211
3D Web 173, 202, 221, 222, 223, 224, 225,
    226, 229, 254, 259, 261
3D web applications 263, 264, 265, 266, 267,
    279, 280
3D world 20, 21, 22, 124, 186
3D world, Community, Creation and Com-
    merce (3D3C) 20, 21, 22, 23, 28, 29, 30,
    31, 32, 33, 35
360-Degree 92
360o security 72
.NET 222, 224, 225, 226, 227, 229, 230, 239,
    255, 259, 261

A

acceptable risk 67, 68
Access control lists (ACL) 193
Active Server Pages (ASP) 224, 229, 230, 232,
    234, 243, 247, 249, 255, 261
adult grid 27
alteroids 146, 147, 155, 158, 162, 164, 166
AMELI 154
Annual Loss Expectancy (ALE) 65
APML (Affective Presentation Markup Lan-
    guage) 266, 281
ARCO (Augmented Representation of Cultural
    Objects) 273, 274, 276, 277, 278, 279,
    282
artificial intelligence 140
artificial society 123, 124, 132
Aspect.NET 221, 222, 223, 226, 227, 228, 229,
    230, 232, 237, 240, 244, 247, 250, 251,
    255, 257, 259, 261, 262
aspect-oriented programming (AOP) 221, 222,
    223, 224, 225, 226, 227, 228, 229, 230,
    232, 235, 237, 239, 243, 244, 247, 250,
    257, 259, 261
Attribute-Based Access Control (ABAC) 286,
    296
augmented reality 20, 34, 170
Automatic Radiation Environment Control
    System (ASKRO) 50, 51
autonomous agents 142, 145, 146, 150, 153,
    166
avatar 2, 8, 20, 21, 23, 24, 27, 28, 32, 60, 61,
    64, 75, 77, 81, 82, 85, 86, 87, 89, 92, 93,
    98, 99, 101, 102, 103, 105, 106, 107,
    108, 109, 120, 142, 143, 144, 145, 146,